Educational Innovation in Economics and Business IX

Educational Innovation in Economics and Business

Volume 9

The titles published in this series are listed at the end of this volume.

THE ROSPIGLIOSI BUREAU

asher's books- please feel free to borrow
but can you let me know ?
And, if you need these shelves
- tell me

Educational Innovation in Economics and Business IX

Breaking Boundaries for Global Learning

Edited by

Richard G. Milter
*Ohio University,
Athens, OH, U.S.A.*

Valerie S. Perotti
*Rochester Institute of Technology,
Rochester, NY, U.S.A.*

and

Mien S.R. Segers
*Maastricht University,
The Netherlands*

 Springer

A C.I.P. Catalogue record for this book is available from the Library of Congress.

ISBN-10 1-4020-3170-X (HB) Springer Dordrecht, Berlin, Heidelberg, New York
ISBN-10 1-4020-3171-8 (e-book) Springer Dordrecht, Berlin, Heidelberg, New York
ISBN-13 978-1-4020-3170-0 (HB) Springer Dordrecht, Berlin, Heidelberg, New York
ISBN-13 978-1-4020-3171-7 (e-book) Springer Dordrecht, Berlin, Heidelberg, New York

Published by Springer,
P.O. Box 17, 3300 AA Dordrecht, The Netherlands.

Printed on acid-free paper

Dedication

Contents

Dedication   v

Foreword   xi

Preface   xiii

Acknowledgments   xv

Contributing Authors   xvii

Part 1: INTRODUCTION   1

Breaking Boundaries for Global Learning   3
    RICHARD G. MILTER

Part 2: TEAMS AND COLLABORATIVE LEARNING   11

Creating Conditions for Collaborative Learning   13
    DIRK TEMPELAAR

Michaelsen's Model of Team-Based Learning Applied in Undergraduate
    Kinesiology Classes   33
    HARRY J. MEEUWSEN & GEORGE A. KING

Cross-Cultural Virtual Teamwork: Implications from the Multicultural
    E-classroom   49
    KEN MORSE

Collaborative Learning Applied in the Orientation Process of
Undergraduate Students 75
MYRTA RODRÍGUEZ

Part 3: TRANSITIONING FROM ACADEMIC SETTINGS TO THE
WORKPLACE 91

Online Learning: Learner's Liberation? 93
TESSA OWENS

Learning to Work: Easing the Transition 117
CATHRINE LE MAISTRE & ANTHONY PARÉ

Breaking the Boundaries between Academic Degrees and Lifelong
Learning 137
THOMAS J.P. THIJSSEN & FONS T.J. VERNOOIJ

An Innovation in Access: Developing the Generic Skills of Business
Students through a Virtual Corporate Experience 157
JENNIFER RADBOURNE

Part 4: ROLE OF INFORMATION TECHNOLOGY IN THE
LEARNING PROCES 179

Can "Learning by Teaching" Contribute to E-learning? 181
RAFFI DUYMEDJIAN

A Collaborative Tool for Argumentation-based Learning: Examining
Face-to-Face and Computer-based Approaches in a UK
Secondary School 195
LIA LITOSSELITI, LAURIE HIRSCH, JEANNE CORNILLON &
MASOUD SAEEDI

Adapting a Face-to-Face Training Program to a Distance Delivery
Model: a Case Study of a Professional Training Program 221
MENNO VAN DOORN & RICHARD G. MILTER

An Innovative Approach to Addressing Heterogeneity of Large
Classes: Results from Teaching Business Statistics 237
MARC HUMBERT

Using Information Technology in Teamwork during Collaborative
    Extra-Class Activities   249
    SILVIA SÁNCHEZ VIZCARRA

Part 5: PROGRAM-LEVEL INNOVATION STRATEGY   275

Contextual Learning in Higher Education   277
    CLAUS NYGAARD & IB ANDERSEN

A Multi-Step Process for Assessing Student Outcomes in the
    Business Curriculum   295
    WENDY L. PIRIE, MICHAEL K. MCCUDDY & MARY Y. CHRIST

Student Characteristics and Academic Success   317
    LUKE B. CONNELLY

Making Space for Twenty-first Century Management Learning   341
    CLIVE HOLTHAM & MARTIN RICH

The Value of Multidisciplinary Integration: Evidence from Two
    Engineering Courses   363
    WILLEM VAN WOERDEN[†] & WALING BANDSMA

A Survey of Distance Education Programs   383
    MORGAN M. SHEPHERD, BEN MARTZ, JEFF FERGUSON
    & GARY KLEIN

Index   399

Foreword

The Boundary Busters

Global learning requires boundary-less knowledge sharing and collaborative learning. This volume of papers shows how to create boundary-breaking behaviour in the areas of teams and collaborative learning, integrating working and learning in the workplace, the added value of IT in the learning process and innovative educational processes. The key message is: erase the boundaries that separate work and learning. Reinvent work, re-imagine learning.

Breaking boundaries down requires the making of radical changes and transformations. However in many cases those boundaries continue to exist in the minds of people responsible for leading those changes. Enter the 'boundary busters'- people with a boundary-breaking mentality. Are you ready to live in a world without boundaries? The present volume, based on research, analyses, and examination of good practices, proves that 'boundary busting' is part of the 'daily routine' of the authors representing the EDiNEB Network. Join them before they pay you an unexpected visit and break your boundaries.

Frank Lekanne Deprez, September 2004

Frank Lekanne Deprez is part-time associate professor "Knowledge Organizations and Knowledge Management" at the Universities of Professional Education Zuyd, Heerlen, The Netherlands, lecturer Human Resources Management at Nyenrode University, Breukelen, The Netherlands and is director of ZeroSpace Advies, Amstelveen, The Netherlands. He advises national and international organizations on human resources management, operational and strategic knowledge management, knowledge innovation, knowledge economy and ZeroSpace organizations. His passion is helping organizations target and apply knowledge when and where it is really needed.

His research interests include (strategic) human resources management, knowledge management, knowledge innovation, knowledge economy and implementing the ZeroSpace mindset in organizations. Frank Lekanne Deprez is co-author of Value-Based Knowledge Management (1998) and The Knowledge Dividend (2000) and Zero Space. Moving Beyond Organizational Limits (2002).

Preface

The chapters in this book were drawn from conference papers presented at the EDiNEB IX Annual Conference held in Guadalajara, Mexico in mid June of 2002. Our sessions were held on the ultra-modern campus of the Tec de Monterrey (ITESM) with its fountains, pervasive network availability, outstanding catering services, and very comfortable meeting rooms. The major theme of the conference was "Breaking Boundaries for Global Learning" and the papers that were presented targeted the future of learning on a global stage.

Our hosting institution, ITESM, provided the ultimate in graciosity as we experienced a wonderful mixture of new learnings about educational innovations and the rich history of the Mexican culture. Serving as liaison and site coordinator for the conference at the Tec was Miguel Zaldivar. Professor Zaldivar is an active participant in EDiNEB events and also serves on the editorial board for this book series. We thank Miguel and his colleagues for their leadership in providing a wonderful conference venue that contributed to a very successful conference experience.

Following the conference a double-blind peer review process was used to evaluate the best papers submitted for review by the presenting authors. The list of reviewers and editors is listed on the EDiNEB website. The selection decisions were made by the book editors in consideration of their own reviews and the feedback from the reviewers. Once the best papers were selected, a thorough and systematic review and enhancement process was undertaken with those authors willing to subject their papers to that process. It is only after this comprehensive approach that we are able to provide the chapters in this book for your enlightenment.

Like previous volumes in the "Educational Innovation in Economics and Business" series, this one is genuinely international in terms of its coverage. With contributions from nine different countries and three continents, it reflects a global interest in, and commitment to, innovation in business education with a view to enhancing the learning experience of both undergraduates and postgraduates. It should prove of value to anyone engaged directly in business education, defined broadly to embrace management, finance, marketing, economics, informational studies and ethics, or who has responsibility for fostering the professional development of business educators. The contributions have been selected with the objective of encouraging and inspiring others as well as illustrating developments in the sphere of business education.

Finally a few words about the EDiNEB Network. At the December 1993 EDiNEB Conference (Maastricht, the Netherlands) the EDiNEB Network was founded to serve as a continual basis for exchanging experiences and knowledge about educational innovation in economics and business. Among the activities of this Network are workshops, providing expertise about innovations, publications (Series on Educational Innovation in Economics and Business, published by Kluwer Academic Publishers), international conferences, and other forms of exchange. Network members have served both education and industry in the development of innovative practices around the globe. Information about the EDiNEB Network can be found at www.edineb.net.

Acknowledgments

The editors of this book first wish to thank the authors for their tenacity in working with us to insure the book meets with highest quality requirements of the EDiNEB Network and Kluwer Academic Publishers. We also thank Wim Gijselaers, President of the EDiNEB Foundation, and Ellen Nelissen, EDiNEB Network Coordinator, and Tamara Welschot, publishing editor of the series for Kluwer Academic Publishers for their steadfast support. We next wish to express our most sincere gratitude to Olga Duranova and Jennifer Hackenberg at Ohio University for their work in the organization and final review of the chapter editing process. We wish to give special note of thanks to Olga and her zeal for excellence in pushing us to greater limits of clarity and higher quality. Finally, we express our gratitude to Henny Dankers at Maastricht University for her unyielding assistance in the final templating stages of the book manuscript.

We end these acknowledgements on a rather sad note. Before the publication of this book, one of the contributing authors, and an active member of the EDiNEB Network, was released ever too quickly from this world. The editors join with the entire EDiNEB community in expressing our sadness regarding the passing of Willem van Woerden. Our thoughts and prayers remain with his family, friends, and associates as they attempt to recover from their loss. We were all supported and encouraged by his presence; may we continue to push the innovation boundaries that were so important to Willem.

Contributing Authors

Ib Andersen

CBS Learning Lab, Copenhagen Business School, Grundtvigsvej 37, 1864 Frederiksberg C, Denmark. IA.LL@cbs.dk

Ib Andersen is Managing Director of CBS Learning Lab and he is also Associate Professor in organisation theory, leadership and social science methodology at CBS. Ib Andersen is interested in higher education pedagogy in general and has a special interest in the pedagogy of management education. His research focus is on educational learning processes and the design of effective learning environments. Over the last 10 years he has been involved as an internal consultant in the development of most of CBS' study programs. In the same period he has trained several members of the faculty staff of CBS.

Waling Bandsma

School of Business, Public Administration & Technology, University of Twente, P.O. Box 217, 7500 AE Enschede, The Netherlands. w.bandsma@bbt.utwente.nl

Waling Bandsma is an Assistant Professor at the Department of Technology & Organization, School of Business, Public Administration & Technology, University of Twente. His activities cover course development and lecturing in areas such as Production Management, Organizational Theory, Management of Technology and Innovation, as well as the supervision of graduation assignments in these fields.

He has special interest in the use of interactive, video or computer based simulation games to hone students' skills in the analysis of business organizations, and in multidisciplinary graduation assignments.

Formerly he taught physics, chemistry, and environmental technology, and was as a consultant in quality management for hydraulic engineering materials, and in environmental management.

Luke B. Connelly

Queensland University of Technology, Herston, Australia. l.connelly@uq.edu.au

Luke Connelly was appointed Associate Professor of Health Economics and Associate Director of the Centre for National Research on Disability and Rehabilitation Medicine (CONROD) in May 2003. His main research interest is in health economics and includes interests in insurance, provider and consumer behaviour in health care markets, and the impact of health policies. He also has an interest in the economics of education. The main focus of his current research is injury, disability, rehabilitation and the systems that have been put in place to improve health and economic outcomes following injury. Luke's previous experience includes full-time academic posts positions in the Brisbane Graduate School of Business as well as the Schools of Public Health and Economics and Finance at QUT. He has more than 10 years' experience teaching economics and health economics at graduate and undergraduate levels and was one of the architects of The University of Queensland new Master of Health Economics program. His most recent peer-reviewed publications include articles in *Health Economics, European Journal of Health Economics, Journal of Health Care Finance, Applied Economics Letters* and *Controlled Clinical Trials*. He is also the author of a book (with Doessel) entitled *Medicare and General Practice: An Economic Analysis*.

Jeanne Cornillon

School of Management, Royal Holloway, University of London, UK. jeanne.cornillon@rhul.ac.uk

Jeanne Cornillon, Laurie Hirsch and Masoud Saeedi have been involved in the research design, implementation and management of the SCALE research project, based at the School of Management, Royal Holloway, University of London. The project received funding by the European Commission, and focused on an internet-based intelligent tool to support collaborative argumentation-based learning in secondary schools (http://www.euroscale.net/).

Jeanne Cornillon has been involved in the application of linguistic techniques to text decomposition and text summarisation. Her interests include formal linguistics, text decomposition, argumentation, and human-computer interaction.

Mary Y. Christ

College of Business Administration, Valparaiso University, 217 Urschel Hall, Valparaiso, Indiana 46383-6493, USA. Mary.Christ@valpo.edu

Mary Y. Christ is an Assistant Professor of Accounting at Valparaiso University in Valparaiso, IN, USA. She received a Ph.D. in Accounting from the University of Texas at Austin as well as an M.S. degree in Accounting from the University of Wisconsin-Madison and a B.B.A. in Management Science and Management Systems from the University of Iowa. A CPA, she previously worked for Arthur Young & Co. Dr. Christ has taught at the University of Wisconsin-Madison, the University of Texas at Austin, Penn State University, Bryant College, and Texas A&M University-Corpus Christi. In her current position at Valparaiso University, she primarily teaches financial and managerial accounting and auditing at the undergraduate and graduate levels and is actively involved in assessment activities at both the College and University level. Dr. Christ's research interests include behavioral and cognitive aspects of accounting and audit decision making, expertise in decision making, and issues in business education, curriculum design, assessment, and pedagogical approaches. She has published in *The Accounting Review*, *Managerial Finance*, *Advances in Accounting Education*, and the *EDiNEB* book series. She has presented at numerous conferences and seminars including those of the American Accounting Association, the Institute of Management Accountants, Institute for Operations Research and the Management Sciences, Decision Sciences Institute, EDiNEB, the National Society of Experiential Education, and AACSB International.

Menno van Doorn

Research Institute for Analysis of New Technology (ViNT), Sogeti Netherlands B.V., Postbus 263, 110 AG Diemen, The Netherlands. menno.van.doorn@sogeti.nl

Menno van Doorn is leading the Research Institute ViNT of Sogeti. His interest lies in the IT-business dichotomy, technology decision making and the use of new technologies. This year he published a book and several articles on IT-governance. His new research focus is the development of future scenario's for the IT-industry. As a director of the Sogeti Academy Menno introduced problem based learning and E-learning concepts. Before that, Menno was working for seven years as a business consultant with expertise in business intelligence and knowledge management.

Raffi Duymedjian
Grenoble   Ecole   de   Management,   Grenoble,   France.
duymedjian@grenoble-em.com
Raffi Duymedjian is Associate Professor at the Grenoble Graduate School of Business. He holds a First Doctoral Degree in Industrial Engineering at the Ecole Nationale Supérieure de Génie Industriel (Grenoble) and a Master degree in Management from the Grenoble Graduate School of Business. His research and teaching concentrate on the use of communication and information systems in organizations, with a focus on the process of managing Knowledge and creating collaborative structures. He is currently exploring ways by which the concept of bricolage can be used to enrich the analysis of the incremental innovation process. He also has interest in learning technologies, i.e. multimedia and web for improving learning processes, as well as innovative teaching methods.

Jeffery M. Ferguson
University of Colorado at Colorado Springs, P.O. Box 7150, Colorado Springs, CO 80933-7150, USA. jferguso@uccs.edu
Jeffery M. Ferguson is a Professor of Service Management and Marketing at the University of Colorado at Colorado Springs. He received a B.S. in Physics from Denison University, an MBA from the University of Montana, and a Ph.D. in Business with an emphasis in Marketing from Arizona State University. Jeff's teaching interests include service management, service marketing, and marketing research. His research interests include: service quality, work place spirituality, and service management. He has published in *Journal of Organizational Change Management, The Journal of Marketing Theory and Practice, Marketing Management, Industrial Marketing Management, Health marketing Quarterly,* and *Information Strategy.* He does consulting in the areas of marketing research, and strategic planning.

Laurie Hirsch
School of Management, Royal Holloway, University of London, UK.
laurence.hirsch@rhul.ac.uk
Laurie Hirsch, Jeanne Cornillon, and Masoud Saeedi have been involved in the research design, implementation and management of the SCALE research project, based at the School of Management, Royal Holloway, University of London. The project received funding by the European Commission, and focused on an internet-based intelligent tool to support collaborative argumentation-based learning in secondary schools (http://www.euroscale.net/).

Laurence Hirsch has been involved in the development of software to facilitate debate among secondary school students and to provide feedback on their arguments. He has been investigating possible applications of evolutionary programmed techniques to the problem of text classification and has developed a rule based genetically programmed system for this purpose.

Clive Holtham
Cass Business School, City of London, London, United Kingdom. c.w.holtham@city.ac.uk

After taking a Masters degree in management, Clive Holtham trained as an accountant and was Young Accountant of the Year in 1976. Following six years as a Director of Finance and IT, he moved to the Business School in 1988. His research is into the strategic exploitation of information systems, knowledge management and management learning. He has managed a number of large applied research projects including a major research project for the Institute of Directors, examining the IT needs of executives and as research director of the European Union's 1.6m euro study PRISM (Measurement and Reporting of Intangibles). Clive Holtham has been one of the leading architects of the "electronic boardroom", involving the use of information technology by executives in meetings. He has been an adviser to the European Parliament on educational multimedia, and was named as one of the UK's top 3 "e-tutors of the year" by the Times Higher Education Supplement in summer 2001. As part of the conceptualisation of the new building for the business school, he has extensively researched the nature of space for knowledge work, as well as the nature of the change management process related to space. He was appointed as the inaugural Director of the Cass Business School Learning Laboratory in 2002. In 2003 he was awarded a UK National Teaching Fellowship as one of the 20 leading university teachers in the UK. He is author of a large number of publications, and lectures, broadcasts and consults in the UK and internationally. He was a founding member of the Worshipful Company of Information Technologists, the City of London's 100th livery company.

Marc Humbert
Grenoble Ecole de Management, Europole, 12, rue Pierre Sémard, BP 127 Grenoble Cedex 01 - France. marc.humbert@grenoble-em.com.

Marc Humbert is a Senior Professor of Statistics and Information Systems at GEM (Grenoble Ecole de Management), France. He is interested in all relationships between information technology, management and education. His current research focuses on blended-learning for management education (effectiveness, teaching and learning styles, improvement of online activities). He received his Ph.D. degree in computer science from INPG in 1984 and joined GEM faculty at that time. From 1993 to 2000, he served as Associate Dean for faculty at GEM and since 2001 he is Associate Dean for e-learning and Pedagogical Innovation.

George A. King

Human Performance Laboratory, University of Texas, El Paso, TX 79902, USA

George A. King is an Assistant Professor and the Director of the Human Performance Laboratory at the University of Texas at El Paso. He earned a B.S. and M.S. degree from Colorado State University and his Ph.D. from The University of Tennessee. Much of his research has focused on assessing the validity and reliability of various instrumentation including body composition and metabolic measurement systems, and pedometer and accelerometer type motion sensors. George A. King's research areas of interest include the relationship of hormones to body composition and cardiovascular disease risk, hormonal responses to physical activity, and the energy cost of daily, occupational, and leisure-time physical activity. Since the year 2001, George A. King has been extensively involved in developing, adapting, and implementing course designs to facilitate student responsibility and student ownership for their own learning.

Gary Klein

University of Colorado at Colorado Springs, P.O. Box 7150, Colorado Springs, CO 80933-7150, USA. gklein@uccs.edu

Gary Klein is the Couger Professor of Information Systems at the University of Colorado in Colorado Springs. He obtained his Ph.D. in Management Science from Purdue University. Before that time, he served with the company now known as Accenture in Kansas City and was director of the Information Systems Department for a regional financial institution. His research interests include project management, system development, technology transfer, and mathematical modeling with over 100 academic publications in these areas. He teaches programming, analysis and design, statistics, management science, and knowledge management courses. In addition to being an active participant in international conferences, he has made professional presentations on Decision Support Systems in the US and Japan where he once served as a guest professor to Kwansei Gakuin University. He is an active member of the Institute of Electrical and Electronic Engineers, the Association for Computing Machinery, the Society of Competitive Intelligence Professionals, the Decision Science Institute, and the Project Management Institute.

Cathrine Le Maistre

Faculty of Education, McGill University, 3700 McTavish Street, Montreal, QC, Canada, H3A 1Y2. kate.le.maistre@mcgill.ca

Cathrine Le Maistre is an Associate Professor and Associate Dean, Academic Affairs in the Faculty of Education, McGill University. She has a Ph.D. in Educational Psychology, with a focus on expert performance in Instructional Design, and has continued her interest in the development of expertise. Most recently, her work has focused on University to work transitions, especially among teachers, and she is currently working with a team of doctoral students who are researching in the area of teacher induction and support.

Lia Litosseliti

Department of Language and Communication Science, City University, Northampton Square, London EC1V OHB, U.K. l.litosseliti@city.ac.uk

Lia Litosseliti (BA Athens, MA Lancaster, PhD Lancaster) is Lecturer in Linguistics at City University, London. Her teaching involves focusing on different areas of linguistics (theoretical and socially oriented) and working with a large cohort of postgraduate students. Her research interests range from critical linguistics, discourse analysis, and language and gender, to education and research methodologies. She has published in the areas of argumentation, discourse and gender identities, language in the media, and research methods, and has presented widely in international conferences on these topics. She is the author of '*Using Focus Groups in Research*' (2003, Continuum), a book which takes a step-by-step look at focus group methodology, and is relevant to researchers across academic disciplines as well as organisations. She is the author of *Gender, Language and Discourse* (an introduction and resource book, forthcoming), and co-editor/ co-author of *Discourse Analysis and Gender Identity* (2002, Benjamins), a collection exploring new theorisations of gender and discourse in a variety of contexts.

Ben Martz

University of Colorado at Colorado Springs, P.O. Box 7150, Colorado Springs, CO 80933-7150, USA. wmartz@uccs.edu

Ben Martz is an Associate Professor of Information Systems at the University of Colorado at Colorado Springs. Ben Martz's teaching interests include e-business, software development, groupware and team-based problem solving. He received his B.B.A in Marketing from the College of William and Mary; his M.S. in Management Information Systems (MIS) and his Ph.D. in Business, with an emphasis in MIS, from the University of Arizona. Ben Martz was one of the founding members, as well as President and COO, of Ventana Corporation – a technology, spin-off firm from the

University of Arizona - incorporated to commercialize the groupware software product GroupSystems. In 1994, GroupSystems won PC Magazine's Editor's Choice award for best Electronic Meeting System software. Ben Martz has published his groupware research in *MIS Quarterly*, *Decision Support Systems,* and the *Journal of Management Information Systems* and his student learning environment research in the *Decision Sciences Journal of Innovative Education, Journal of Cooperative Education* and *Journal of Computer Information Systems*.

Michael K. McCuddy
College of Business Administration, Valparaiso University, 217 Urschel Hall, Valparaiso, Indiana 46383-6493, USA. Mike.McCuddy@valpo.edu
Michael McCuddy holds The Louis S. and Mary L. Morgal Chair of Christian Business Ethics and is a Full Professor of Management at Valparaiso University in the United States of America. He is interested in issues associated with innovative education as well as various aspects of personal and business ethics. His current research focuses on the teaching of ethics, the issues and implications associated with teaching-centered versus learning-centered models of education, managerial and leadership skill development, linkages between freedom and ethics in a global context, and the role of stewardship in personal and professional ethics. He has written numerous instructional supplements and cases for management and organizational behavior textbooks. He has also authored or co-authored a wide range of papers, articles, and book chapters that address a variety of educational issues and ethical topics. He received his Ph.D. degree (1977) from Purdue University in the United States. Currently, he teaches courses in ethics, business and society, management and organizational behavior, high performance organizations, and human resource development. He also serves on the editorial board of Education Innovation in Economics and Business (EDiNEB).

Harry J. Meeuwsen
Chair Department of Kinesiology, University of Texas at El Paso, El Paso, TX 79902, USA. meeuwsen@utep.edu
Harry Meeuwsen is a Full Professor of Kinesiology at UTEP. His interest is in various aspects of effective teamwork and team-based learning strategies. His current research focuses on individual roles in effective teams and their impact on team cohesion and performance levels. In addition, he is working on effectively integrating e-portfolios in the undergraduate Kinesiology curriculum. He received his Ph.D. degree (1987) in physical education from Louisiana State University in Baton Rouge, Lousiana, USA.

Richard G. Milter
Ohio University, Ohio, Athens, USA. milter@ohio.edu
Richard G. Milter (Ph.D., University at Albany, SUNY) is Associate Professor of Management at Ohio University. His teaching experience includes positions at Boston College, the University at Albany (SUNY), Loyola University of Chicago, and Janus Pannonius University (Pecs, Hungary).

His personal management experience includes positions in the construction, retail, education, housing, and consulting industries. He is one of the original designers of the MBA Without Boundaries degree program, Global Competitiveness Program, Global Learning Community, Ohio University Without Boundaries, and the Ohio University Institute for Applied and Professional Ethics. He is a recipient of the Ohio University College of Business Faculty/Staff Contribution Award for "outstanding service to the college and university."

He has consulted or served as a training facilitator or organization effectiveness specialist for dozens of corporations and government agencies. He has directed executive development seminars across the U.S. and Malaysia. His research and publications have paralleled his consulting activity in the areas of executive judgment, group decision-making processes, management information systems, negotiation strategies, managerial ethics, leadership, and innovative learning platforms.

He serves as chairman of the executive board of EDiNEB, an international network of innovative educators based in Maastricht, the Netherlands. He has delivered executive seminars in decision making, innovation, leadership, business policy, and strategic management in the US, Malaysia, Sweden, Mexico, and Hungary. He has presented workshops to educators on action-learning strategies across the U.S., Sweden, Hungary, the Netherlands, Mexico, Russia, Japan, and Malaysia.

Ken Morse
Department of Marketing and International Management, Waikato Management School, Private Bag 3105, Hamilton, New Zealand. kmorse@mngt.waikato.ac.nz
Ken Morse is Senior Lecturer in International Management at the Waikato Management School. After 18 years of public sector employment as a translator of Russian and Chinese Mandarin, he began his academic career as an instructor in economics before completing a doctoral programme in International Studies. In his three previous academic positions prior to coming to New Zealand, he developed a research interest in innovative teaching techniques and practices, which he has applied to both his teaching a research responsibilities. He is currently involved in

developing cross-cultural teaching techniques in the expanding multicultural undergraduate and graduate teaching environments at the University of Waikato. His research publications have contributed extensively to understanding online learning and teaching in the multicultural environment.

Claus Nygaard

CBS Learning Lab, Copenhagen Business School, Grundtvigsvej 37, 1864 Frederiksberg C, Denmark. cn.ll@cbs.dk

Claus Nygaard, Ph.D., holds two positions at Copenhagen Business School. He is Associate Professor in Economic Sociology at the Department of Organisation and Industrial Sociology and Senior Advisor at CBS Learning Lab. He has been employed as a researcher and teacher at Copenhagen Business School since January 1995, and he holds a Ph.D. in Business Economics for his dissertation "The Affect of Embeddedness on Strategic Action" (1999). He is editor and main author of a popular text book on strategizing (first issue 2000, second issue 2001) which has also been published in Swedish (2002). At CBS Learning Lab he works on the themes of quality development of the educations at CBS, and strategic analysis of the Danish and the international Higher Education-sector. He has a special interest in strategic development of management education. He has developed several courses at CBS, and has designed education programmes at other higher education institutions and companies in Denmark and Norway.

Tessa Owens

Management & Business Centre, Liverpool Hope University College, Hope Park, Liverpool, UK. L16 9JD. owenst@hope.ac.uk

Tessa Owens is a Senior Lecturer in Management & Business at Liverpool Hope University College. She also holds the post of Learning & Teaching Fellow for the Deanery of International Business Information Technology and Enterprise.

Her background is in the financial services sector within the UK, specifically within banking and insurance, where she held posts in lending, systems analysis, management development and administration management. She joined higher education in 1999 to pursue her love of teaching and research.

Her research interests include assessment and appraisal, personal development, e-learning, problem based learning, human resource development and learning through work.

Anthony Paré

Faculty of Education, McGill University, 3700 McTavish Street, Montreal, QC, Canada, H3A 1Y2. anthony.pare@mcgill.ca

Anthony Paré is an Associate Professor and Chair of the Department of Integrated Studies in Education at McGill University in Montreal, Canada. His interests include academic and workplace writing, literacy education, genre studies, and nonformal/situated learning. His most recent research, conducted with colleague Cathrine Le Maistre, focuses on the transition from higher education to professional practice in the fields of education, social work, physiotherapy, and occupational therapy. He is co-author of Worlds apart: Acting and writing in academic and workplace contexts (Erlbaum, 1999) and co-editor of Transitions: Writing in academic and workplace settings (Hampton Press, 2000).

Valerie Perotti

Faculty of the Department of Management, Marketing and International Business, The College of Business, Rochester Institute of Technology, Loewenthal Building #12, Rochester, New York, 14623, USA vsperotti@cob.rit.edu

Valerie Perotti is currently Distinguished Lecturer in the College of Business at Rochester Institute of Technology. She is also Professor Emeritus of the Ohio University College of Business. In addition, she is serving as a "Subject Matter Expert" for the Ohio Learning Network's action learning project and maintaining a small private consulting practice serving business, industry and educational institutions.

Valerie Perotti is currently teaching and researching in organizational behavior as it relates to globalization and technology. Her primary career-long interest, however, has been in the human dynamics of teaching and learning. In that regard, her experience has come both from the implementation of a college wide, integrated project-based curriculum at the undergraduate level at Ohio University and from participation in the design of a ground-breaking MBA Without Boundaries--to her knowledge the first fully integrated, problem-based, action learning, online MBA in the US.

Valerie Perotti has been involved as a participant, contributor and now Associate editor with the EDINEB network for the past 10 years. If asked, she would say that it is the academic community where she has felt truly "at home."

Valerie Perotti's Ph.D. is in Organizational Communication. Over a 35 year career in undergraduate and graduate higher education she had held a wide array of positions ranging from Instructor to Grant Writer to Dean in academic areas from Business Communication to International Business. Notably, she was the founding Director of the Center for International

Business and Development at Ohio University and Director of Undergraduate Curriculum for the College of Business. She retired as a full professor in 2001.

Wendy L. Pirie

College of Business Administration, Valparaiso University, 217 Urschel Hall, Valparaiso, Indiana 46383-6493, USA. wendy.pirie@valpo.edu
Wendy L. Pirie, CA, Ph.D., is an Associate Professor of Finance at Valparaiso University, Valparaiso, IN. She received her PhD from Queen's University at Kingston and her MBAs from the Universities of Toronto and Calgary. She is currently teaching a variety of finance courses but she has also taught accounting, business law, international taxation, management, marketing, policy and strategy, and statistics. Her research interests include microstructure issues in finance; stewardship and finance. However, over the years, an interest in teaching issues has developed based on experiences with her students and her own three children. Currently, her research interests also include issues in business education, curriculum design, assessment, and pedagogical approaches.

Jennifer Radbourne

Queensland University of Technology, Queensland, Brisbane, Australia. j.radbourne@qut.edu.au
Associate Professor Jennifer Radbourne is Director of the Queensland University of Technology Faculty of Business Hong Kong Program. Prior to this Jennifer was Assistant Dean from 1998 to 2003 in the Faculty of Business, responsible for the teaching and learning issues in the Faculty including course development and course evaluation. She also held the positions of Director of Graduate Studies and Chair of the Faculty Education Committee. Jennifer has taught in the university for over 20 years and has particular expertise in flexible delivery, intensive mode of teaching, and in assessment review, policy and practice. She has researched and written on assessment, plagiarism, case method as a teaching tool, graduate capabilities, and the development of innovative teaching strategies to support the learning of international students. Her Accountability Model for assessment has been published on the web. In 2002 her teaching and learning project on curriculum integration was highly commended by ASCILITE (Australian Society for Computers in Learning in Tertiary Education) for Best Web Project in a Learning Management System, and in 2003 nominated as a finalist in the Australian Awards for University Teaching.

Martin Rich
Cass Business School, City of London, London, United Kingdom.
m.g.rich@city.ac.uk
Martin Rich initially worked in the information systems sector as a consultant and project manager, before joining Cass Business School as a lecturer. During his career at Cass he has taken responsibility for a series of innovative applications of technology to management learning, all of them underpinned by a thorough research foundation. For the 2003-2004 academic year, he is one of City University's teaching and learning fellows, and as such is pursuing particular interests, in the scholarship of teaching and learning, as applied to management education.

Myrta Rodríguez
Faculty of Industrial Engineering, Department of undergraduate programs, ITESM Campus Mazatlán, Carr. Mazatlán-Higueras km.3, Mazatlán, Sinaloa, México. myrta.rodriguez@itesm.mx
Myrta Rodríguez is a Founding Director of the Department of Industrial and Systems Engineering (IIS) at ITESM Campus Mazatlán, México. She is interested in research on the new educational model implementation at ITESM System, which is based on active learning and collaborative work. Over the past 7 years, she was one of the persons responsible for the implementation and further development of the educational model at ITESM Campus Mazatlán. Her work involves the redesign of undergraduate courses in order to change the student learning process, introducing designed activities on syllabus, based on collaborative work and problem based learning. She received her Master degree (1995) in Science in Systems and Quality. Currently she holds the positions of Director of the undergraduate Program of Industrial and Systems Engineering, and chair of the Department of Industrial Engineering at ITESM Campus Mazatlán.

Masoud Saeedi
School of Management, Royal Holloway, University of London, UK.
m.saeedi@rhul.ac.uk
Masoud Saeedi, Laurie Hirsch, and Jeanne Cornillon have been involved in the research design, implementation and management of the SCALE research project, based at the School of Management, Royal Holloway, University of London. The project received funding by the European Commission, and focused on an internet-based intelligent tool to support collaborative argumentation-based learning in secondary schools (http://www.euroscale.net/).

Masoud Saeedi has been involved in the management and co-ordination of the SCALE project. His research interests include Knowledge

Management and Transformation, Artificial Intelligence and Evolutionary Programming, Management Information Systems, Decision Support Systems, Computer Mediated Communications and Internet/ Search Engines.

Silvia Sánchez Vizcarra
ITESM, Sinaloa, Mazatlán, Mexico. ssanchez@campus.maz.itesm.mx
Silvia Sánchez Vizcarra received her Master degree (1998) in Administration of Information Technology from Monterrey Institute of Technology and Higher Education (ITESM) in Mazatlán México. She was involved in the coordination of Educational Technology at the Mazatlán Campus, and was instructor of the didactic Technique of Method of Cases by the ITESM and North Caroline University. She was one of the persons responsible for the implementation of the educational model at ITESM, training professors in the technological area, and the administration of the technological platforms used (Learning Space and Blackboard) in the educational model at ITESM. Since 1992 she has been Professor in the area of computer systems in diverse universities in Mexico at level degree and masters degree, as well as instructor in diverse seminaries and conferences. Her current research focuses on the use of the technologies of information in education.

Mien Segers
Department of Educational Sciences, University Leiden, P.O. Box 9555, 2300 RB Leiden, The Netherlands. segers@fsw.leidenuniv.nl
Department of Educational Development and Research, Faculty of Economics and Business Administration, University Maastricht, P.O. Box 616, 6200 MD Maastricht, The Netherlands. m.segers@educ.unimaas.nl
Mien Segers is Professor of Educational Sciences at the department of Educational Sciences of the University Leiden (The Netherlands) and at the department of Educational Development and Research of the University Maastricht (The Netherlands). Her major research interest are the evaluation and optimisation of student learning in learner-centred learning environments and the qualities of new modes of assessment within these environments. The research projects take place in school as well as organizational settings. She has been the coordinator of the Special Interest Group Assessment and Evaluation of the European Association of Research on Learning and Instruction (EARLI) and is currently appointed as the coordinator of the Special Interest Group Higher Education of EARLI.

Morgan M. Shepherd
University of Colorado at Colorado Springs, P.O. Box 7150, Colorado Springs, CO 80933-7150, USA. msheper@uccs.edu

Morgan Shepherd is an Associate Professor of Information Systems at the University of Colorado at Colorado Springs. His research focuses on improving the performance of distributed groups. His teaching interests are in telecommunications, decision support for virtual teams, and e-commerce. Morgan helped develop the distance MBA program at the University of Colorado, and teaches several sections each year. He received his B.S. in Mechanical Engineering from the University of Virginia and his Ph.D. in MIS from the University of Arizona. He worked for ten years in industry prior to returning for his Ph.D., spending most of that time with IBM as a staff level network engineer. His work has been published in the Journal of Management Information Systems, DSIJE, Informatica and several national and international conference proceedings.

Dirk Tempelaar
Faculty of Economics and Business Administration, Department of Quantitative Economics, University Maastricht, PO. Box 616, 6200 MD Maastricht, The Netherlands. D.Tempelaar@ke.unimaas.nl

Dirk Tempelaar is Lecturer Quantitative Methods at University Maastricht, The Netherlands. He is interested in various aspects of learning in the domains of statistics, mathematics, and applied computer science: problem-based learning, assessment and its role in the learning process, e-learning and the design of learning environments that allow a heterogeneous inflow of students, compensating deficiencies in prior education. His current research focuses on the development and implementation of flexible e-learning tools suited for both regular and remedial learning, and diagnostic assessment. Over the past 20 years, he was one of the persons responsible for the implementation of problem-based learning in the economics and international business programs at this university. He is member of the founding board of EDiNEB, an international network of innovative educators.

J.P.Thomas Thijssen EMIM
Hamilton International, Epe, The Netherlands. hamint@wxs.nl

Thomas Thijssen is the CEO of the VIA NOVA ACADEMY for personal entrepreneurship founded in 2004 and Managing Director of Hamilton International since 1989. A company focused on supporting Business and Governments in process of innovation, learning and entrepreneurship. EMIM stands for Executive Master in Information Management, a Master degree from the University of Amsterdam. Thomas

Thijssen also holds a degree in Marketing. He is currently completing his PhD study at the University of Amsterdam on Co-creating Value through Learning by Sharing. He teaches at several universities and schools for higher education and is a research fellow at the PrimaVera Research Group at the University of Amsterdam and is a member and reviewer of ED*i*NEB.

The first 25 years of his career Thomas Thijssen fulfilled all relevant positions in the international hospitality industry, working in Australia, England, United States and the Netherlands. For Holiday Inns he was a Food & Beverage Manager and General Manager. In the Netherlands Thijssen was Commercial Director on group level for Postiljon Hotels (currently Mercure).

Since 1998 as Managing Director of Hamilton International, Thomas Thijssen worked in the fields of international tourism & hospitality, the health sector and in the field of education.

Fons T. J. Vernooij

Faculty of Economics and Business (FEWEB), Department of Accounting, Free University, De Boelelaan 1105, 1081 HV Amsterdam, The Netherlands. fvernooij@feweb.vu.nl or mail@fons-vernooij.nl

Fons Vernooij is Assistant Professor in Accounting at the Free University in The Netherlands. He is specialized in educational development, especially in paradigms of systematic approaches to problem solving. His research started with the development of computer assisted instruction and the educational requirements of using the difference between human and computer interactions. His current activities are focused on rich learning environments, based on interactive management games.

Fons Vernooij has been in education for nearly thirty years. He started as a teacher in secondary education and after five years he switched to vocational education, where he remained for seven years. His first concern was not economics, but the teaching of economics and the quality of learning material. For that reason he went to a company that developed computer assisted instruction. Computer interactions require insight in the way students think and therefore he wrote a dissertation about the way students solve accounting problems.

He received his Ph.D. degree in 1993 from the Erasmus University in Rotterdam and worked at the department of teacher education at the University of Amsterdam until March 2002. At this moment he is involved in a project of the Dutch Digital University aimed at supporting management games with modules of artificial intelligence.

Willem M. van Woerden[†]
School of Business, Public Administration & Technology, University of Twente, P.O. Box 217, 7500 AE Enschede, The Netherlands. w.m.vanwoerden@utwente.nl

Willem van Woerden was a Senior Educational Consultant of the School of Business, Public Administration & Technology. His consultancy was especially focussed on instructional methods accomodated to business education, like the case method, the project method of teaching and simulation & gaming. Both on the case method and the project method he edited instructional books for teachers. In 1991 he received his Ph.D.- degree on a case study of the project method in a civil engineering programme. Besides, he promoted integrating courses in business administration & technology: The Integration Case (1st year), the Management of Technology Course (3rd year) and the Multidisciplinary Design Course (4th year). For years, he was Advisor of the World Association of Case Research & Application (WACRA), a worldwide network of teachers, educational consultants and researchers in the field of business education and related disciplines.

PART 1

INTRODUCTION

Chapter 1

BREAKING BOUNDARIES FOR GLOBAL LEARNING

Richard G. Milter
Ohio University, Athens, Ohio, U.S.A.

1. LEARNING ON A GLOBAL STAGE

Global events in the past few years have clearly changed the way people communicate, work, travel, live, trust, and learn. We have witnessed those changes in the world's economy, public policy, and the operational mechanisms within thousands of corporations. Leadership and vision are among today's requisite skills for defining the future of business organizations. Knowledge, skills, and an ability to sustain values are critical concerns for learning organizations. Developing a competence for international collaboration and global competitiveness has become a mainstay for both small and large companies. As organizations deal with the winds of global change, learning programs for leadership in the new economy need to reinforce key values and prepare learners for dynamic change. Incorporating appropriate technology, content, and learning methods has become more critical than ever before.

To sustain competitiveness in the global marketplace of the knowledge age, workers require more sophisticated education and learning programs. Educational institutions increasingly view themselves as competing in the global marketplace. Technology and information access have leveled the education landscape. For-profit corporations now compete with large universities and corporate learning centers in the education and human resource development arena. Learners are released from single-source educational providers as they access knowledge via channels unbounded by

R.G.Milter et al. (eds.), Educational Innovation in Economics and Business IX, 3–10.
©2004 Springer. Printed in the Netherlands.

time and space. The chapters in this book address evolving issues on boundaries that need to be broken to develop the future of global learning.

2.   KEY BOUNDARY AREAS

Teams have become an integral element of organizational life. Although individual efforts are still valued, a majority of critical strategic decisions and innovative developments are the products of teamwork. But working in teams is more than merely placing groups of individuals together and providing them with a task. Skills in leadership and followership must be developed and refined in order to take full advantage of team value. Educational institutions are taking significant strides to develop and enhance learning activities targeting team skills. Evidence suggests that teaming enhances learning and learning satisfaction (Johnson, Johnson, & Smith, 1991). Collaborative learning is in itself a teamwork process that has also become a standard feature in many educational programs (Beckman, 1990; Bosworth, 1994). Of course as many organizations pride themselves in placing emphasis on learning, the ability to develop skills in learning with others is another area of importance for educators.

Learning must continue throughout people's careers. But moving from the structured routines and systematic processes of academic settings into the robust and dynamic business environments is an important juncture. Instructors in higher education institutions would do well to anticipate this issue as "traditional" students under their tutelage will soon be challenged to make this important transition. But even for "non-traditional" students who have stepped back into academic endeavors after spending some time in the workforce, the transition both into and out of the educational processes is challenging. Such challenges should be aided by the learning support structures within educational institutions.

The importance of lifelong learning and the drive for learning organizations are energized by the support of information technology (IT). It is obvious that many more forms of learning models are available today than ever before. A comprehensive review of studies that have examined how technology affects learning is reported by Nancy Millichap (2000). It is evident that younger students entering institutions of higher education have grown up with rapid advances in modern technology. For them there is little accommodation necessary as they respond to the technology requirements of their classes. Although many instructors have a large learning curve regarding the use of IT in the classroom, this tends not to be the case with students. And yet, in order for learning to be enhanced by information technology, instructors must find ways to appropriately integrate IT with the learning processes and course structures. Technology benefits should always be sought as educators attempt to enhance their learning protocols and work toward future innovations.

Much of the learning activity in higher education institutions takes place in a classroom. The course is typically used as a vehicle for learning. Instructors are typically provided with great latitude within the confines of their individual courses, as long as they are meeting some baseline standards. Yet, many of the most innovative changes in education are found at the program level. Leaders at educational institutions are charged with keeping their units as viable providers of learning. So keeping things as they are might seem a good tact for these leaders. The problem is that education has grown into a highly competitive industry. As with other competitive industries, organizations that offer innovative programs will often gain a competitive edge. The innovations necessary to advance learning are not necessarily tied to traditional educational institutions. And yet, more traditional institutions have rich histories that can be drawn upon in their efforts to innovate.

In order to break boundaries for global learning, therefore, it is imperative that we seek for ways to 1) improve our use of teams and collaborative learning, 2) offer assistance to learners as they transition from academic settings to the workplace, 3) make appropriate use of the role of technology in the learning process, and 4) seek out ways to develop program-level innovation strategy. These areas make up the four remaining parts of this book. Each part includes chapters that provide insights for educators as they seek to expand their own thinking in the area.

3. TEAMS AND COLLABORATIVE LEARNING

The next section of this book "Teams and Collaborative Learning" includes the chapters that explore and analyze the different aspects of the collaborative learning approach and the ways to enhance its effectiveness.

The first chapter "Creating Conditions for Collaborative Learning" by Dirk Tempelaar of Maastricht University, the Netherlands, investigates the conditions that should lead to a successful team performance. The author considers such factors as group processes, student, and tutor characteristics in creating a new predictive model.

The following chapter "Michaelsen's Model of Team-Based Learning Applied in Undergraduate Kinesiology Classes" by Harry J. Meeuwsen and George A. King of the University of Texas at El Paso, USA, describes the application of the team-based learning strategy developed by Michaelsen et al. in two Kinesiology classes at the University of Texas. The chapter pays special attention to the application of the so-called Readiness Assessment Test, suggested by Michaelsen et al. and analyzes its impact on learning outcomes.

The next chapter "Cross-cultural Virtual Teamwork: Some Implications from the Multicultural E-classroom" by Ken Morse of Waikato Management School, New Zealand, evaluates the results of conducting a virtual teamwork simulation in the e-classroom and its implications for e-learning institutions, firms, and other constituents.

The final chapter in this section "Collaborative Learning Applied in the Orientation Process of Undergraduate Students" by Myrta Rodríguez from the ITESM Campus Mazatlán, Mexico, focuses on the development of collaborative skills during the students' initial adaptation period and on forming a positive attitude toward a new teaching method right from the start of the academic process.

4.   TRANSITIONING FROM ACADEMIC SETTINGS TO THE WORKPLACE

The subsequent section of this book "Transitioning from Academic Settings to the Workplace" contains the chapters dedicated to the importance of preparing students for a smooth transition from the academic environment to the practical world and the need to develop the skills that would assist them in this process.

The initial chapter in this section "On-line Learning: Learners' Liberation?" by Tessa Owens of the Liverpool Hope University College, UK, reviews the outcomes of a new work-based teaching module conducted via the Virtual Learning Environment and its role in developing the skills required for future lifelong learning. The chapter provides the evaluation of the new learning experience from the point of view of students, their tutors, and employers.

The next chapter "Learning to Work: Easing the Transition" by Cathrine Le Maistre and Anthony Paré of McGill University, Montreal, Canada, reviews school-to-work transitions in a variety of disciplines and provides better understanding of the transition processes and the ways to prepare students for entering the "communities of practice."

The following chapter "Breaking the Boundaries between Academic Degrees and Lifelong Learning" by Thomas J.P. Thijssen of the Hamilton International and the University of Amsterdam and Fons T.J. Vernooij of the Free University of Amsterdam, the Netherlands, provides an insight into the value chains of the learners, educational institutions, and employers, and their roles in supporting lifelong learning. The authors encourage the educators to reevaluate their program design so as to avoid the conflict of interests and meet the requirements of all the parties involved.

The final chapter in this section "An Innovation in Access: Developing the Generic Skills of Business Students through a Virtual Corporate Experience" by Jennifer Radbourne of Queensland University of Technology, Brisbane, Australia, concludes the discussion of the transition to the "real world" by highlighting the importance of assessing and developing the generic skills that are often underestimated by traditional academic curricula. The author examines the principles of work-based learning, multi-media case method, and online teaching, and their contribution to the development of generic skills, such as time management, communication, leadership, and so forth.

5.   ROLE OF INFORMATION TECHNOLOGY IN THE LEARNING PROCESS

The following section of this book "Role of Information Technology in the Learning Process" provides some insights into the application of information technology in both in-class and extra-class activities, its role in enhancing the learning environment and facilitating the learning process.

The opening chapter "Can 'Learning by Teaching' Contribute to E-learning?" by Raffi Duymedjian of Grenoble Ecole de Management, France, examines the concept of 'Learning by Teaching' and suggests the conditions under which both students and teachers can benefit from such an experience. The author discusses the situations when non-professional teachers are required to transfer their knowledge to others, and analyzes the relationship between 'Learning by Teaching' method and e-learning.

The next chapter "A Collaborative Tool for Argumentation-based Learning: Evidence from Classroom Studies in a UK Secondary School" by Lia Litosseliti, Laurie Hirsch, Jeanne Cornillon, and Masoud Saeedi of Royal Holloway University of London, UK, presents the results of the study on the role of information technology in general, and the Internet in particular, in the acquisition of debating skills. The authors draw a comparison between the impact of face-to-face and Internet tools on learning the above skills, as well as on their quality and diversity.

The following chapter "Adapting a Face-to-Face certificate Program to a Distance Delivery Model: A Case Study of a Professional Training Program" by Menno van Doorn from the Institute for Analysis of New Technology, Sogeti, the Netherlands, and Richard G. Milter of Ohio University, Athens, Ohio, USA, presents a case study of a technology-based distance program between the two institutions. The authors describe the evolution of the collaborative professional training program over time and provide a comparison between the outcomes of the traditional face-to-face and distance models.

The next chapter "An Innovative Approach to Addressing Heterogeneity of Large Classes: Results from Teaching Business Statistics" by Marc Humbert of Grenoble Ecole de Management, France, explores the results of the experiment with a two-phase organization of the Business Statistics course. The author presents the outcomes of an innovative clustering approach that meets the requirements of students with diverse backgrounds and levels of motivation. The final chapter "Using Information Technology in Teamwork during Collaborative Extra-Class Activities" by Silvia Sánchez Vizcarra from ITESM Campus Mazatlán, Mexico, looks specifically at the use of information technology in extra-class team activities, the role of professors in promoting IT applications, and the impact of IT tools on enhancing learning environments and learning outcomes. The chapter is based of the results of a survey conducted among the undergraduate Business Majors at ITESM Campus Mazatlán, Mexico.

6.   PROGRAM-LEVEL INNOVATION STRATEGY

The final section of this book "Program-Level Innovation Strategy" includes chapters that deal with different aspects of the educational process that pertain to curriculum and program design, educational settings, and general student characteristics.

The initial chapter "Contextual Learning in Higher Education: Curriculum Development with Focus on Student Learning" by Claus Nygaard and Ib Andersen of the Copenhagen Business School, Denmark, describes the role of the Higher Educational institutions and the shift from decontextual to contextual learning as a theoretical framework for innovative curriculum development. The authors highlight the importance of developing high-order thinking skills and identify the new role of students, professors, study board, and other constituents in the contextual learning environment.

The following chapter "A Multi-Step Process for Assessing Student Outcomes in the Business Curriculum" by Wendy L. Pirie, Michael K. McCuddy, and Mary Y. Christ of Valparaiso University, Valparaiso, Indiana, USA, provides the guidelines for establishing an effective multi-step assessment process that should be incorporated into the overall curriculum design and reflect the mission and goals of a particular educational program with an idea of continuous learning in mind.

The next chapter "Student Characteristics and Academic Success: An Econometric Study of the Performance of 'Equity Groups'" by Luke B. Connelly of the University of Queensland, Australia, is dedicated to the analysis of the equity issues in Higher Education. Based on the analysis of statistical data, the author examines the role of student characteristics as predictors of their academic performance and draws attention to the relative success of students in equity groups versus general student population.

The following chapter "Making Space for Twenty-First Century Management Learning" by Clive Holtham and Martin Rich of Cass Business School, London, UK, extends the discussion of the importance of the learning environment to the analysis of the physical space and its impact on learning outcomes. The authors provide a detailed description of the requirements to the modern physical university facilities and review several innovative models, such as school, medieval craft studio, museum/art gallery, and club.

The next chapter "The Value of Multidisciplinary Integration: Evidence from Two Engineering Courses" by (the late) Willem van Woerden and Waling Bandsma of the University of Twente, the Netherlands, addresses the issue of integration of knowledge, concepts, and skills, and explores the academic settings and other conditions that can foster such integration. The study is based on the comparison of two interdisciplinary engineering courses, Management of Technology and Multidisciplinary Design, which employ different didactic set-ups.

The final chapter of the section "A Survey of Distance Education Programs" by Morgan M. Shepherd, Ben Martz, Jeff Ferguson, and Gary Klein of University of Colorado at Colorado Springs, USA, provides an assessment of distance education programs offered by different educational institutions throughout the USA. The survey conducted by the authors contains a rich set of data on different aspects of distance education, including motivation for undertaking distance education, program design, assessment of outcomes, application of technology, and sources of funding.

REFERENCES

Beckman, M. 1190. Collaborative Learning: Preparation for the Workplace and Democracy. *College Teaching, 38* (4), 128-133.

Bosworth, K. 1994. Developing Collaborative Skills in College Students. In K. Bosworth & S. Hamilton (Eds.), *Collaborative Learning 59: Underlying Processes and Effective Techniques. New Directions for Teaching and Learning* (pp. 25-31). San Francisco: Jossey-Bass.

Johnson, D. W., Johnson, R. T., & Smith, K. A. 1991. *Cooperative Learning: Increasing College Faculty Instructional Productivity.* ASHE-FRIC Higher Education Report No.4. Washington, D.C.: School of Education and Human Development, George Washington University.

Millichap, N. 2000. *How Using Technology Affects the Learning Process and Faculty Behavior.* The Technology Source, May/June 2000.

PART 2

TEAMS AND COLLABORATIVE LEARNING

Chapter 2

CREATING CONDITIONS FOR COLLABORATIVE LEARNING

Dirk Tempelaar[1]
University of Maastricht, Faculty of Economics and Business Administration, the Netherlands

1. INTRODUCTION

Research has shed light on different perspectives that are relevant to making collaborative learning successful (Slavin, 1996). Based on that research, we are able to develop quantitative models that explain the success of a collaborative learning group in terms of underlying motivational, cognitive, and interactional processes (Dolmans, Wolfhagen, & Van der Vleuten, (1998). Having measured the extent to which students in a problem-based learning group motivate each other, form a cohesive group, participate actively, or in contrast, sponge or withdraw, these models contribute to our understanding of why some groups are productive, and others are not.

Models of this kind are, however, of limited practical use: they are useful for explaining *ex post* why specific groups have less than average productivity, but cannot explain *ex ante* what conditions (except for choices of instructional technology) are needed to increase the perspectives of success in collaborative learning groups. In order to develop a model with predictive power, this study investigated group processes in a problem-based learning environment in relation to the types of group interaction taking place (based on Bales' Interaction Process Analysis, IPA) and personal

[1] The author is grateful to Sybrand Schim van der Loeff for great help in the revision of this contribution.

R.G. Milter et al. (eds.), Educational Innovation in Economics and Business IX, 13–32.
©2004 *Springer. Printed in the Netherlands.*

characteristics of students and tutors. The aim of the research is to develop a model that explains the success of collaborative learning groups, via motivational, cognitive, and interactional processes, by variables that are relatively stable and that can (in principle) be measured long before the collaborative group starts, such as personality traits and preferred learning styles. Such models are effective not only in building understanding of why collaborative learning groups fail but also, perhaps, of how to intervene to prevent failure.

The University of Maastricht uses a problem-based learning approach. In such a program, students learn collaboratively, in groups of 12 to 14 students, coached by a tutor. A tutor will coach several groups, maybe up to six during one specific "block." Being in charge of several groups, one experience is inevitable: some groups do a perfect job, while others fail dramatically. In many cases, it is difficult to predict which group will belong to what category; for example, there is no guarantee that bright students mix together into a supreme collaborative group. If prior knowledge is not a good predictor, which other variable will do better? Or in other words: if you were free to compose your own tutorial group of 14 students out of the 900 freshmen available, how would you pick them?

According to the recent review study by Slavin (1996), no choice will guarantee success. There is little evidence that "pure" cooperative methods such as problem-based learning, which depend solely on interaction to produce higher achievement, will do so. Necessary conditions for the instructional effectiveness of cooperative learning models are group-based goals such as the sum of individual learning performances (Slavin, 1996). In such conditions, the students who learn most are the students who give other students explanations. Students who prefer cooperative learning, learn more than those who prefer competition.

Two other reviews on collaborative learning in small groups are Bosworth and Hamilton (1994) and MacGregor et al. (2000). These studies contain, in their own words, "insights from successful practitioners"-- insights that, without exception, refer to instructional settings. Most research in collaborative, small group learning can be characterized as process/output (P/O) models: differences in learning outcomes (output) are explained by differences in group interaction (process). But the link to the students' characteristics on which the group composition can be based (the inputs) is lacking. Dolmans et al. (1998) is an example of one such study.

One of the few I/P/O studies is Houldsworth and Mathews (2000). Their group composition is based on gender and entry qualifications, so as to make groups as heterogeneous as possible. The group process is described in terms of "process loss" factors like free riding, withdrawing, social loafing, and so forth, and of "process gain" factors like cohesiveness, group characteristics (as perceived by the members), and norms and standards within the group. Personality traits of students are measured, but not explicitly used in the analysis. Six different groups are composed, one of which appears to perform poorly, another to perform quite well. The statistical analysis focuses on the differences between these two groups in terms of group characteristics.

The Houldsworth and Mathews (2000) study is based on Driskill, Hogan, & Salas, (1987), in which an Input/Process/Output model is sketched with three different types of inputs: individual-level factors such as member skills, knowledge, and personalities; group-level factors such as group size, group structure, group norms, and cohesiveness; and environmental-level factors such as nature of task, and reward structure. The process is formed by the group interaction process, with intermediate variables being process gain and process loss. Output is the group performance. On the basis of this I/P/O-structure, the authors derive several hypotheses regarding the relation between personality and group performance, leaving however the test of these hypotheses to further research.

Another example of an I/P/O study is given by Oetzel (2001). In this model, inputs are chosen like student and group characteristics, the process is measured by participation, cooperation and respect, whilst two sets of output variables are distinguished: task effectiveness, measured in terms of performance and decision quality, and relational effectiveness, specified as cohesion and satisfaction. Individual data were aggregated to group data. While task efficiency variables cannot be explained by the process, some relational variables, such as satisfaction and withholding, can.

Studies on the optimal composition of learning groups are limited. Most research in collaborative learning is of P/O nature. Those do not allow for conclusions on optimal group composition. In addition, most studies focus on group data, whereas the requirement of optimizing group composition cannot be fulfilled without analyzing models based upon individual data.

2. MATERIALS: THE INPUT, THE PROCESS, AND THE OUTPUT OBSERVATIONS

In this study, all input variables are assumed to be student related; for example, no data on tutor characteristics are included. From a modeling point of view, this implies that tutor characteristics and instructional settings are assumed to be constant over all tutorial groups.

Input variables are taken from two questionnaires that were administered as part of project-work of students in the first two blocks (both in the first semester). Process and output variables are derived from an extended block evaluation that was administered in the last week of each block, and from student performance in the final exams. In total 860 students participated in the final exam; however, not all students and not all tutors completed all questionnaires and evaluations. As a consequence, many student records contain missing data for some variables, and had to be excluded in the modeling procedure described in Section 4. The two main models described in Subsection 4.4 were estimated on data of 550 and 390 students, respectively. The next subsections contain a description of the several input, process, and output variables.

2.1   The Inputs

The input variables are derived from two questionnaires that were administered in different blocks: the Inventory of Learning Styles or ILS, administered in the very first block of the program, and the Goldberg's 100 Big-Five Factor Markers (Goldberg., 2004), referred to hereafter as *Big5*, administered in the second block of the study.

The learning styles theory developed by Vermunt (1996, 1998) emphasizes individual differences in the use of learning strategies in higher education. In contrast to other research in this area, Vermunt starts from a broad and integrative definition of individual differences in learning. Based on that definition, the self-report instrument Inventory of Learning Styles (ILS) was constructed, covering four learning components: see Table 1.

Table 1. Vermunt's ILS Domains, Scales, and Subscales

Domain AI: Processing strategies
  Scale 1: Deep processing, consisting of:
    Subscale 1a: Relating and structuring, and
    Subscale 1b: Critical processing;
  Scale 2: Stepwise processing, consisting of:
    Subscale 2a: Memorizing and rehearsing, and
    Subscale 2b: Analyzing;
  Scale 3: Concrete processing.

Domain AII: Regulation strategies
  Scale 4: Self-regulation, consisting of:
    Subscale 4a: Self-regulation of learning processes and results, and
    Subscale 4b: Self-regulation of learning content;
  Scale 5: External regulation, consisting of:
    Subscale 5a: External regulation of learning processes, and
    Subscale 5b: External regulation of learning results;
  Scale 6: Lack of regulation.

Domain BI: Learning orientations
    Scale 7: Personally interested;
    Scale 8: Certificate directed;
    Scale 9: Self-test directed;
    Scale 10: Vocation directed, and
    Scale 11: Ambivalent.

Domain BII: Mental models of learning
    Scale 12: Construction of knowledge;
    Scale 13: Intake of knowledge;
    Scale 14: Use of knowledge;
    Scale 15: Stimulating education, and
    Scale 16: Cooperation.

In Vermunt's theoretical model, mental models of learning and learning orientations are underlying factors that influence the regulation and cognitive processing strategies. In the context of our research on collaborative learning in a problem-based program, students' mental models of learning were thought to be the most relevant factors in the functioning of the tutorial group process. For that reason, we focused on the 40 items of Domain BII. Table 2 specifies that Domain in some further detail, and adds some advice students typically receive in case the ILS is used as a feedback instrument on study habits.

Table 2. Vermunt's ILS Domain BII

Domain BII: Mental models of learning

Scale 12: Construction of knowledge: Learning viewed as constructing one's own knowledge and insights. Most learning activities are seen as tasks of students. High score: this is a fruitful perspective. Low score: it is attractive to gradually adapt your ideas about the division of tasks in education. Especially in your graduate study, the faculty will assume a rather independent position of its students.

Scale 13: Intake of knowledge: Learning viewed as taking knowledge provided by education through memorizing and reproducing; other learning activities are tasks of tutors and lecturers. Low score: please do not forget the factual knowledge. High score: do not expect too much from tutors, writers of blockbooks and lecturers. Studying is nicer if you place yourself in a somewhat more independent position.

Scale 14: Use of knowledge: Learning viewed as acquiring knowledge that can be used by means of concretizing and applying. These activities are seen as tasks of both students and tutors and lecturers. High score: attractive property, but: you cannot do without the more theoretical parts of the courses. Low score: you may be missing an important vehicle in learning: the relation between new knowledge and reality.

Scale 15: Stimulating education: Learning activities are viewed as tasks of students, but tutors and lecturers and textbook authors should continuously stimulate students to use these activities. High score: stimulus is important and attractive, but: be careful not to become too dependent on it.

Scale 16: Cooperation: Attaching a lot of value to learning in cooperation with fellow students and sharing the tasks of learning with them. High score: if cooperation is important, try to arrange regular contact with other students.

As a second area of individual differences relevant to collaborative learning, the Big5 model developed by Digman (1990) was adopted. The Big5 model comprises five trait dimensions that conceptualize general individual differences in the affective and cognitive domains: see Table 3.

Table 3. Big5 Personality Traits

Big5 Personality Traits	
I	Extraversion
II	Agreeableness
III	Conscientiousness
IV	Emotional Stability (or reverse: Neuroticism)
V	Intellect (or Openness to Experience)

For the purpose of easy comparison to other studies, we chose to use the traits identified in the Big5 as the instrument to measure these traits. Each trait corresponds with ten items.

2.2   The Process

In all blocks, several aspects of the course are evaluated, amongst others the functioning of the tutorial group, and the tutor. In their third block (first half of second semester), students of the first-year programs, Economics and International Business (about 850 in total), received an extended block evaluation, assessing both output characteristics and several process aspects.

Table 4 contains one section of this extended block evaluation: the items dealing with the tutorial group process.

Table 4. Section of Block Evaluation on Tutorial Group Process

Tutorial group evaluation

All statements are expressed in a 1-5 Likert scale ranging from Totally disagree (1) to Totally agree (5)

1. The tutorial group used systematic working procedures (for example, the Seven-jump) to discuss the tasks.
2. I found the meetings of the tutorial group stimulating.
3. The tutorial group made clear appointments for further study of the subject matter.
4. I am not satisfied about the manner in which students kept their appointments.
5. I found it a pleasure to work in this tutorial group.
6. The meetings of the tutorial group turned out to be productive.
7. I consider the tutorial group meetings as an impediment to my ongoing study.
8. To a large extent I've studied independently of the learning issues generated in this tutorial group.
9. In this group, there is a lot of involvement (students participate actively).
10. In this group, there is a lot of cohesion (students know and help each other, are friendly).
11. In this group, it is not done to study more seriously than the others do.
12. In this group, members are careful about what they say.
13. In this group, members are rather straight.
14. This group is task oriented (a strong focus on completing planned activities, staying on the subject matter).
15. In this group, I felt a lot of competition.
16. In this group, students feel responsible for the group performance.
17. In this group, I felt a lot of friction (students do not get along, are unfriendly).
18. In this group I felt stimulated by other students in my study.
19. In this group, I felt that students withheld sometimes information.
20. In this group, most students show solidarity and interest in each other, give help, support and reward.
21. In this group, most students give information, repeat, clarify and confirm, give opinions and suggestions.
22. In this group, most students ask for information, repetition and confirmation, ask for opinions and suggestions.
23. In this group, most students are critical to each other, defend or assert self.

The last four items are derived from Bales' Interaction Process Analysis (IPA) (Bales, 1950, 1966). In fact, those four questions refer to the four main types of interaction distinguished in IPA: social-emotional positive, task giving, task asking, and social-emotional negative (in that same order, items 20-23). In a regular IPA, students are scored by an observer while participating in a group process, whereby the scoring is one level deeper: each main type of interaction is subdivided into three different categories (see Table 5).

Table 5. Bales' IPA Scoring Grid: 4 Types and 12 Categories of Group Interaction

SE+, Soc Emot Plus: Social-emotional area, positive

    Shows solidarity, raises other's status, gives help, reward

    Shows tension release, jokes, laughs, shows satisfaction

    Agrees, shows passive acceptance, understands, concurs, complies

TG, Task Giving: Task area, giving

    Gives suggestions, direction, implying autonomy for other

    Gives opinion, evaluation, analysis, expresses feeling, wish

Gives orientation, information, repeats, clarifies, confirms

TA, Task Asking: Task area, asking

    Asks for orientation, information, repetition, confirmation

    Asks for opinion, evaluation, analysis, expression of feeling

Asks for suggestion, direction, possible ways of action

SE-, Soc Emot Min: Social-emotional area, negative

    Disagrees, shows passive rejection, formality, withholds help

    Shows tension, asks for help, withdraws out of field

Shows antagonism, deflates other's status, defends or asserts self

So, four major adaptations compared to traditional IPA have been applied: self-scores instead of observer scores; scores are given on aggregate categories that typify interaction; scores are of Likert 1-5 type, and no counts of specific formats of interaction; the group process is measured, not the contributions of individual students.

Bales' IPA scoring grid observations provided one of the process variables on tutorial group level: interaction in the tutorial group. Four other tutorial group indicators are composed by combining information on other items of the evaluation questionnaire: the use of Systematic procedures; Cohesion in the tutorial group; and Conflict in the tutorial group.

A second group of process variables refers students' views on the functioning of the tutor. Four different aspects of tutor functioning are assessed: The tutor's awareness of problem-based learning principles, the tutor's disciplinary knowledge, the tutor's involvement and a grade for overall tutor functioning (these aspects are covered by 13 items, in the Tutor section of the questionnaire, not included in Table 4). The choice of constructs for describing both the tutorial group process and the functioning of the tutor is based both on evaluation principles in use in the UM, and on research based on these evaluations, such as Dolmans et al. (1998). The choice on the grouping of different items into one subscale is partially based on theoretical considerations, partially on the correlation structure of individual item responses in this study. For example, from this correlation structure it is apparent that the feeling of competition, although theoretically an independent construct, is strongly related to the feeling of conflict and friction. The response on the involvement item correlates strongly with satisfaction and feeling stimulated; for that reason, this item was incorporated as one of the items measuring output, as discussed in the next subsection.

2.3   The Output

The outcome of the learning process is the third component of the model describing students' learning. An obvious choice for an indicator measuring this aspect is the grade students receive on the final exam. Another seemingly obvious choice is students' participation in tutorial sessions, expressed as the number of sessions for which each student receives a mark "satisfactory participation." In addition to these indicators, the quality of the learning within the tutorial groups as perceived by the student was regarded as a further dimension of the output of the learning process. The regular block evaluation questionnaire contains several questions related to the output of the tutorial group that were hypothesized to group in two indicators. The first indicator is the productivity of group meetings, the second indicator measures the extent to which group sessions motivate and stimulate individual learning.

2.4   The Experimental Conditions

In order to study the impact of group composition with more homogeneous groups than an observational study allows for, the group composition was manipulated. Criteria on which the experimental set-up was based are: gender, value that the student attaches to cooperation, and cooperation skills scored by a tutor of the preceding block. Examples of experimental groups are: groups composed of students valuing cooperation above average (positive condition), groups valuing cooperation below average (negative condition) and groups having an average score on the value of cooperation (neutral condition). Also all female groups (positive condition), all male groups (negative condition), and mixed groups (neutral condition) were composed, where the qualifications "positive" and "negative" are based on earlier experiences with homogeneously composed groups. Of a total of 57 tutorial groups, 14 were in the positive condition, 10 in the negative, and 33 in the neutral condition.

3.   METHOD

Theoretical constructs like the Big5 dimensions are regarded as latent traits: they cannot be measured directly, but only indirectly through indicators. On the basis of these indicators (items), we construct latent traits by applying factor analysis. Traits remain latent in the sense that we will never be able to determine them exactly: we know them up to an error. Factor analysis allows for the identification of factors, that are traits including these errors, and provides an impression of the size of these errors (in terms of its variance-covariance structure) (Bollen, 2002).

The first modeling step was to develop factor models, or measurement models, for mental models of learning and personality traits. Given the large size of the model, we applied a technique called item-parceling (Bandalos, 2002) to reduce the number of indicators per factor. Item-parceling implies the grouping of items into three or four parcels (subscales), and taking the aggregated score of the items in each parcel as the new indicator variable (assumed to be measurable). So ten items for each factor, as is the case for Big5, are reduced to three parcel-scores per factor, whereby parcels contain three of four items. Parcels were selected on both the similarity of item wordings and on descriptive item characteristics. In this research, a confirmatory factor analysis for the several measurement models (of inputs, of process variables, of outputs) is the first step in the model analysis, meaning that we set out to statistically test an a priori hypothesized factor structure that draws on knowledge of the theoretical structure of the variables. An exploratory factor analysis was undertaken whereby an improvement of the factor structure was investigated. To prevent "capitalization on chance" or, in other words, running the risk of allowing for a complex factor structure that fits quite well in the specific sample but not in others, a so-called split-sample approach was applied. The sample was split into independent sub-samples (in our case: female versus male students, and Dutch versus German students), and model improvement steps were only adopted if they appeared to be statistically significant in every sub-sample. A detailed presentation of the modeling approach is beyond the scope of this contribution; we refer to Byrne (1998) for an extensive discussion. A full description of the procedure applied can be obtained from the author, on request.

Having derived a latent factor structure for each of the measurement models of inputs, process variables and outputs, the next modeling step was to estimate relationships between those constructs. Since all factors are latent, it is on methodological grounds incorrect to apply regression analysis on these factors. Doing so would implicitly assume that factors corresponding to inputs, the Big5 factors and the ILS factors contain no errors, while the dependent factors, corresponding to process and output variables, may contain an error. The correct approach to modeling the factor relations is to account for errors in all variables. The statistical method that takes into account both the existence and the size of errors in latent factors is called structural equation modeling, or SEM. Once again we will refer to Byrne (1998) for a detailed description of this modeling approach.

A drawback of latent variable modeling is the requirement that it poses on data availability in relation to model size. Since the Big5 and ILS questionnaires were administered in different tutorial sessions, a rather large group of students completed only one questionnaire, but not both. As a consequence we could not estimate the comprehensive model using both sets of inputs. Instead we will estimate two separate models, one in which the dimensions of the ILS Mental Models of Learning play the role of inputs, and one in which the dimensions of the Big5 Personality Traits act as inputs.

The very last step in our modeling tour refers to incorporating group effects in our models based on individual data. Ideally, one would like to contrast groups in different experimental conditions, for example, to detect systematic differences in the functioning of all female groups, all male groups, and mixed groups. However, for finding statistically significant effects on the basis of the SEM methodology, a much larger number of groups than available in the several experimental conditions is needed. Aggregating several different experimental conditions into three categories, indicated as positive, neutral, and negative, did however allow for conclusions. This final part of the analysis was performed by testing on invariant latent mean structure (Byrne, 1998).

4.   RESULTS

4.1   The Input Factor Models

As a first step, we determine the measurement models of the two alternative sets of inputs: the ILS Mental models of learning and the Big5 Personality factors. Both input models consist of five factors. The factors of the ILS input model are given as Scale 12-16 in Table 2, the factors of the Big5 input model are given in Table 3. The data fits both hypothesized factors quite well: factor loadings, factor correlations and model fit are consistent with outcomes described in the literature. In the model improvement step for both input models one cross-loading is suggested that is not at odds with other research. Since these two cross-loadings were

robust over independent samples, they were incorporated in the final
measurement model.

4.2   The Process Factor Model

Most process and output indicators were based on the several items in the
tutorial group section of the block evaluation. Some related items were
aggregated in parcels of three to four items; some other items were taken as
indicators themselves. The criterion used for deciding on whether to
aggregate items or not was the practical rule to have at least three indicators
per factor in the hypothesized factor model, and the presence of strongly
related items that are natural candidates for the parceling process.

For the tutorial process, two different latent variables are developed: the
variable "Group Process," measuring several aspects of the group process as
such, and the variable "Tutor Functioning," measuring different aspects of
the functioning of the tutor. The latent "Tutorial Group Process" construct
has four different parceled indicators, as described in Table 6; all items are
from Block evaluation (see Table 4). The latent Tutor Functioning construct
has three different parcels and one grade as indicators: tutor's awareness of
PBL principles, tutor's disciplinary knowledge, tutor's involvement, and the
grade for the tutor's overall functioning. The items are taken from the "Tutor
Section" of the block evaluation. The choice of parcels is immediate, since it
corresponds to the design structure of the block evaluation with regard to
subscales and scales.

Table 6. Items, Parcels, and Factors for the Process Model

Items	Parcel or Indicator	Factor
Items 20 – 23	Interaction	
Items 1, 3, 4, 8	Systematic procedures	Tutorial group
Items 10, 11, 16	Cohesion	process
Items 12, 13, 15, 17, 19	Conflict	
4 items	Awareness of PBL principles	
4 items	Disciplinary knowledge	Tutor
4 items	Involvement	functioning
grade	Overall functioning	

The hypothesized process factor model fits the data very well. The model
improvement search strongly indicates that the inclusion of one cross-
loading would further improve model fit: the loading of Tutor Functioning
on the indicator the use of systematic procedures in the group. Although not
hypothesized, this cross-loading does not come as a surprise: groups can

only operate in a systematic way if the tutor supports, or even motivates, group members to do so. So the cross-loading was included in the model. After inclusion, the correlation of the errors of latent variables Group Process and Tutor Functioning appeared to be non-significant, implying that outside their common indicator, the two factors are unrelated. So in the final process model this error correlation was constrained to be zero.

4.3   The Output Factor Model

The development of an output factor model appeared to be less straightforward than the development of the other models. The first try was to develop a factor model with one single latent output construct: "Outcome," see Table 7, and three indicator parcels: measures on the productivity of group meetings and the satisfaction experienced by participating in groups, measures on the extent in which group sessions motivate and stimulate individual learning, and the participation in group session and the grade on the final exam, being the most explicit output variables.

Table 7. Items, Parcels, and Factors for the Output Model. First Pass

Items	Parcel or Indicator	Factor
Items 5, 6, 9	Productivity	
Items 2, 7, 18	Motivating individual learning	Outcome
Final grade, Participation	Performance	

This factor model was not supported by the data: the relation between the two tutorial group indicators and the two student performance indicators was too weak to defend the inclusion of all four as indicators of one common output factor. This is perhaps not that surprising, considering the requirement that students have to participate in most of the tutorial sessions in order to pass the block. This makes this variable a characteristic of the educational system rather than a personal characteristic of the student. For these reasons, it was decided to develop an alternative output measurement model (see Table 8).

In this model, the variable "Students' Participation" was dropped, and separate factors for tutorial group and student outputs were created. For the student output factor, only one observation was available: the grade achieved in the final exam. Since one cannot estimate latent factors on the basis of only one indicator, the error variance of the indicator was set to zero, equalizing the factor "Student Performance" to the observed grade in the exam. For the second factor, "Group Performance," we adapted the hypothesized measurement model described in section two by splitting up the hypothesized parcel "productivity of group meetings" back to its constituent items. The second hypothesized indicator, the parcel measuring the extent to which group sessions motivate and stimulate individual learning, was maintained, implying five different indicators for the "Group Performance" variable.

Table 8. Items, Parcels, and Factors for the Output Model. Second Pass

Items	Parcel or Indicator	Factor
Item 5	Satisfaction	
Item 6	Productivity	Group
Item 9	Involvement	performance
Items 2, 7, 18	Motivating individual learning	
Final grade	Performance	Student performance

The estimation of this two-factor output model led to satisfactory results. Once again, the model improvement search did not result in any substantial increased fit, so the final model is a pure factor model without cross-loadings and with both factors constrained to be uncorrelated.

4.4 The Relations Between Input, Process, and Output

The development of the several partial models as described in the preceding subsections is best regarded as the preparatory step to the development of a full structural model integrating the measurement models of the inputs, process, and outputs. Or in fact, two structural models, since alternative input sets result in two different I/P/O models, depicted in Figures 1 and 2 in their final state.

The hypothesized final model is very general in structure: for both models, the several input factors are assumed to have a positive impact on both process factors and output factors, and both process factors are assumed to have a positive impact on the two output factors. Since the process factors refer primarily to the tutorial group process, their impact on group outputs is expected to be much stronger than that on students' outputs. But instead of starting from this most general case, the development of the structural models was organized in the opposite way: starting from the most restrictive case in which no input has any impact on the process, and the process has no impact on the output. From that point on, in sequential steps of model improvement, relations were added that, from a statistical point of view, demonstrate substantial model fit increase and render significant regression coefficients, and from a learning theory point of view do not contradict the hypothesized character of the relationships.

In the ILS-based I/P/O model, two input factors have a significant impact on process factors: Construction of knowledge, explaining Tutor Functioning, and Cooperation, explaining Tutorial Group Process. The parameter estimates included in Figure 1 are so-called completely standardized estimates: achieved after standardizing all latent variables. The estimates can thus be interpreted as correlations between the latent factors. The output factor, Student Performance, cannot be explained by this model. Group Performance can, however, be explained by both process factors, Tutor Functioning and, quite strongly, Tutorial Group Process. In addition to these relations, the model improvement procedure suggests a strong relation between the two process factors. The procedure is however uninformative as to the direction of that relation: improvement in quality of model fit is comparable. Since tutor behavior was regarded as more stable, and less context-dependent than the tutorial group process, the direction of the relation was chosen as indicated in Figure 1: Tutor Functioning explains Tutorial Group Process.

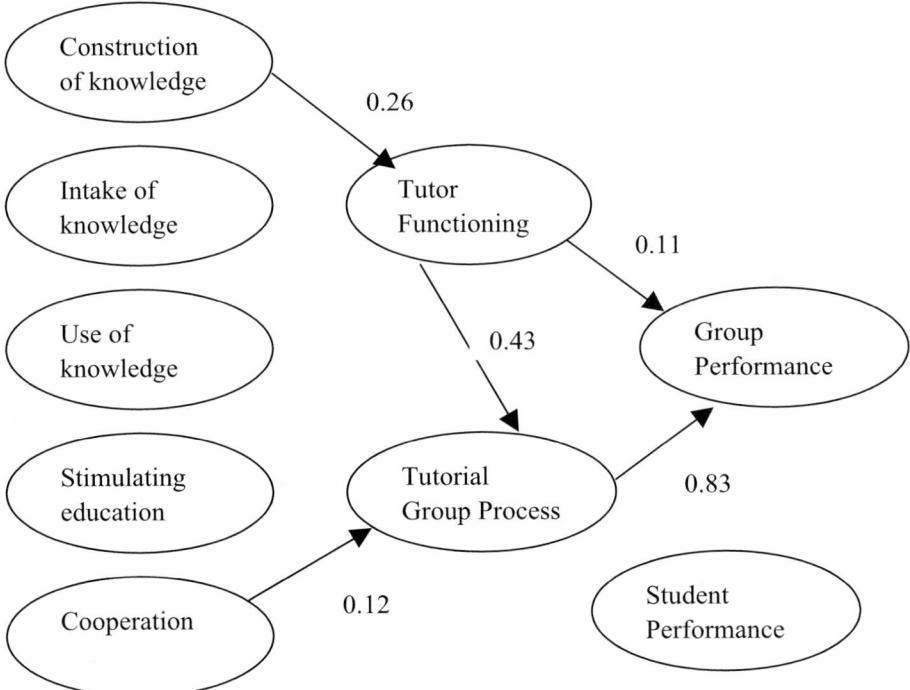

Figure 1. I/P/O Model with ILS Mental Models of Learning as Inputs; Completely Standardized Parameter Estimates

Although all five relationships are statistically significant, their practical significance differ widely. In Table 9 the multiple correlations of process and output factors according to both the structural equations and the reduced form are described. Multiple correlations can be interpreted as explained variation; for that reason, they are expressed as percentages.

Table 9. Squared Multiple Correlations, or Explained Variation, Expressed as Percentage of Process and Output Factors, in Structural Equations and Reduced Form, of ILS I/P/O Model

	Tutor Functioning	Tutorial Group Process	Group Performance	Student Performance
Structural equation	7%	21%	79%	-
Reduced form	7%	4%	4%	-

Table 9 indicates that the impact of the ILS input factors is modest whereas Group Performance is quite well explained by the process factors. So the P/O part of the model does a much better job than the I/P part.

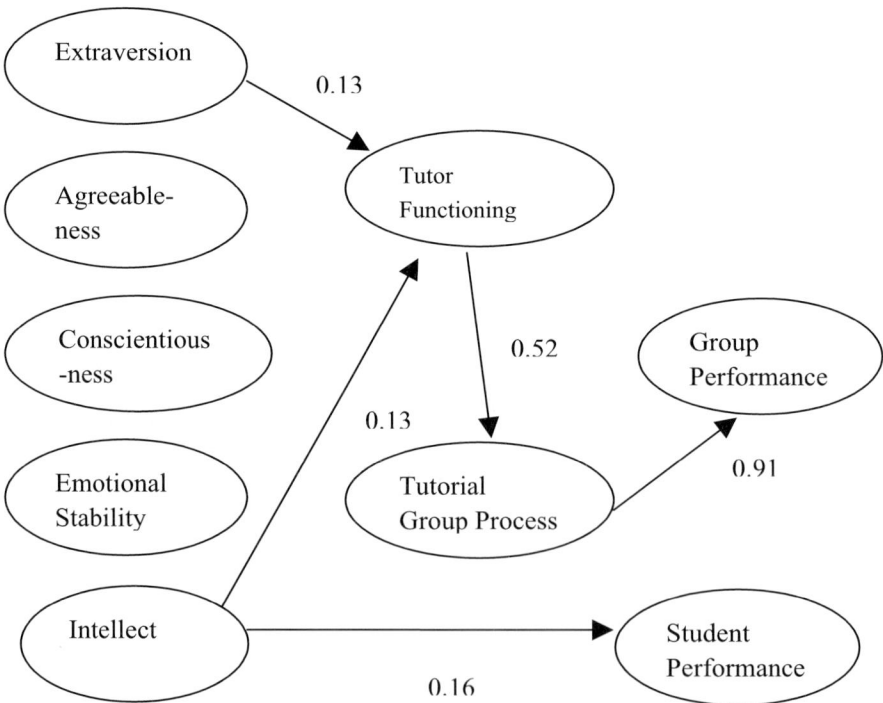

Figure 2. I/P/O Model with Big5 Personality Factors as Inputs; Completely Standardized Parameter Estimates

In the Big5-based I/P/O model depicted in Figure 2, most of the process-output relations are identical although the samples were different. Group Performance is strongly dependent on Tutorial Group Process, and Tutorial Group Process on Tutor Functioning. Two input factors explain Tutor Functioning: Extraversion and Intellect. And, surprisingly, Intellect has a direct effect on Student Performance. (In general, one expects a trait as Intellect or Openness to Experience as a good predictor to learning outcomes. However, in this study all inputs are derived from self-assessment instruments, and it is not obvious at all that students' self-assessed intellect is a good predictor of learning performances.)

As in the ILS-based model: relationships are statistically significant, but are of a moderate size, as indicated by the multiple correlations in Table 10.

Table 10. Squared Multiple Correlations, or Explained Variation, Expressed as Percentage of Process and Output Factors, in Structural Equations and Reduced Form, of Big5 I/P/O Model

	Tutor Functioning	Tutorial Group Process	Group Performance	Student Performance
Structural equation	5%	27%	82%	3%
Reduced form	5%	1%	1%	3%

Again the conclusion is that the P/O part of the model is adequate, but the explanatory power of input factors to process and output factors is less than modest.

4.5 Different Experimental Groups

The analysis in the preceding subsections was based on student data only, without taking into account the composition of different tutorial groups. As described in Section 2, a limited number of tutorial groups were homogenized with regard to value assigned to cooperation in learning (scale cooperation in ILS), cooperative attitude in previous block (tutor impression), and gender. Since study of these specific experimental conditions require much more data than available, several groups were regrouped in groups with positive, neutral, and negative conditions. These three groups were confronted to find differences in means of the latent factors (testing on invariant latent mean structure).

In both models, the clearest divergence in invariance of latent means was for the Student Performance factor. In the positive conditions group, the average grade in the final exam is 6.2 (on a 0-10 scale), whereas the average grade in the negative conditions group is 5.8. This difference is not only statistically significant, but also very crucial. In the Dutch grading system the grade 6 is the lowest grade to pass an exam; grades lower than 6 imply a failure. In the Big5-based model, no significant differences exist in the means of input factors. In the ILS-based models, such differences do exist, but these are implied by the fact that the ILS-scale Cooperation has been used as one of the instruments of designing experimental groups, and all ILS-scales are positively correlated.

5.   DISCUSSION

The analysis discussed in Subsection 4.4 leads to two conclusions. One is strong, but not new: the quality of learning in tutorial groups is dependent upon the process variables like the functioning of the tutor and type of interaction in tutorial groups. These "P/O" outcomes are well described in literature, for example, Dolmans et al. (1998). The second conclusion is new, but much weaker: input variables of the type of student characteristics can help explain the difference in process and output variables.

To give two examples based on the ILS model: students that view learning as a construction process, do value the proper functioning of the tutor more than other students. In contrast, students who regard cooperation as the best vehicle to learn, attach most value to proper functioning of tutorial groups. In the Big5-based study, a similar outcome refers to extravert students.

These outcomes suggest that the best way to organize education in a problem-based system, is to take these differences between students into account when composing tutorial groups. Students with similar dispositions could be matched, and other conditions (like tutor characteristics) could be tuned in. Gains in learning outcomes are probably modest, but compared with the tradition of most problem-based learning systems, in which students are randomly assigned to tutorial groups, there is nothing to lose.

The character of this study is partial: many more other factors than personality traits and mental models of learning determine learning processes and their outcomes. For that reason, explained variation in terms of several percents, instead of several dozens of percents, does not surprise. Developing "intake instruments" to cover a more substantial domain of student characteristics will certainly increase the impact of systematic group composition beyond random assignment above several percents.

Interpretation of the analysis described in Subsection 4.5 is not straightforward. The significant difference in the Student Performance factor cannot be explained by our model: Student Performance appears to be independent of the tutorial process. In addition to that argument: process factors do not demonstrate invariant means, so one expects that other causes unrelated to the tutorial process have an impact. A speculation on one of these causes is that female students are overrepresented in the experimental groups under the positive condition since all female groups were defined to be part of the positive condition, and all male groups to be part of the negative condition. Since female students are better students than male students (at least in the undergraduate study), this model outcome can be an artifact of the experimental design: it is not that female students make up better functioning groups, but they prepare better for their exams. Much more research on the combined effect of student characteristics and group composition on student learning is needed to arrive at firm conclusions; however, it requires more data (students and groups) than usually available in problem-based educational systems.

REFERENCES

Bales, R. F. (1950). *Interaction process analysis: A method for the study of small groups. Cambridge*, Mass.: Addison-Wesley.

Bales, R. F. (1966). The equilibrium problem in small groups. In A. P. Hare, E. F. Borgatta, & R. F. Bales (Eds.), *Small groups, studies in social interaction.* New York: Alfred A. Knopf.

Bandalos, D. L. (2002) The effects of item parcelling on goodness-of-fit and parameter bias in structural equation modeling. *Structural Equation Modeling*, 9 (1), 78-102.

Bollen, K. A. (2002). Latent variables in psychology and the social sciences. *Annual Review of Psychology*, *53*, 605-634.

Bosworth, K., & Hamilton, S. J. (1994). *Collaborative learning: underlying processes and effective techniques.* San Francisco: Jossey-Bass.

Byrne, B. M. (1998). *Structural equation modeling with LISREL, PRELIS, and SIMPLIS: basic concepts, applications, and programming.* Mahwah: Erlbaum.

Digman, J. M. (1990). Personality structure: Emergence of the five-factor model. *Annual Review of Psychology*, *41*, 417-440.

Dolmans, D. H. J. M., Wolfhagen, I. H. A. P., & Vleuten, C. P. M. van der (1998). Motivational and cognitive processes influencing tutorial groups. *Academic Medicine, 73* (10, Supplement), S22-S24.

Driskill, J. E., Hogan, R., & Salas, E. (1987). Personality and group performance. In C. Hendrick (Ed.), *Group processes and intergroup relations.* Newbury Park, Sage.

Goldberg, L. R. (2004*) International personality item pool.* Retrieved 4/14/2004 from http://ipip.ori.org/ipip/.

Houldsworth, C., & Mathews, B. P. (2000). Group composition, performance and educational attainment. *Education + Training, 42* (1), 40-53.

MacGregor, J., Cooper, J. L., Smith, K. A., & Robinson, P. (2000). *Strategies for energizing large classes.* San Francisco: Jossey-Bass.

Oetzel, J. G. (2001). Self-construals, communication processes, and group outcomes in homogeneous and heterogeneous groups. *Small Group Research*, *32* (1), 19-54.

Slavin, R. E. (1996). Research on cooperative learning and achievement: What we know, what we need to know. *Contemporary Educational Psychology*, *21*, 43-69.

Vermunt, J. D. (1996). Metacognitive, cognitive and affective aspects of learning styles and strategies: A phenomenographic analysis. *Higher Education, 31*, 25-50.

Vermunt, J. D. (1998). The regulation of constructivist learning processes. *British Journal of Educational Psychology, 68*, 149-171.

Chapter 3

MICHAELSEN'S MODEL OF TEAM-BASED LEARNING APPLIED IN UNDERGRADUATE KINESIOLOGY CLASSES

Harry J. Meeuwsen & George A. King
The University of Texas at El Paso, USA

1.   INTRODUCTION

In the recent past, many publications have documented the effectiveness of cooperative and collaborative learning activities in the classroom. Numerous books are available to help instructors with the implementation of cooperative learning. For example, Millis and Cottell (1998) give an excellent overview of the research data and the rationale for adopting cooperative and collaborative learning in the classroom. However, the manner in which cooperative and collaborative learning is implemented may impact its effectiveness. When group work focused on collaborative and cooperative learning is applied poorly, outcome-oriented, motivated students often perform most of the work. This typically results in the "under-achievers" relying on the motivated students to complete the assignments, and the motivated students complaining about other group members not contributing their share. In addition, group dynamics do not develop, appreciation of diversity and effectiveness of teamwork is absent, and ultimately, the results are poor team performance and low levels of learning.

Despite these consequences of poorly applied cooperative learning, the traditional lecture format may even be less effective. Michaelsen, Black, and Fink *(*1996), among others, have characterized the traditional lecture format as mostly a one-directional teaching strategy in which the students are passive receivers and the instructor is the active "sage on the stage."

R.G.Milter et al. (eds.), Educational Innovation in Economics and Business IX, 33–48.
©2004 *Springer. Printed in the Netherlands.*

Students are expected to process the information presented by the instructor on their own and often do not receive feedback about their performance other than scores on exams. The students are often disengaged and minimally prepared for class.

Larry Michaelsen and colleagues (e.g., Michaelsen, 1999; Michaelsen & Black, 1994; Michaelsen, Black, & Fink, 1996; Michaelsen, Knight, & Fink, 2003) have also extensively promoted the use of cooperative learning in the classroom. However, their cooperative learning strategy is quite different from the conventional approaches. Michaelsen (1999) has argued that using small teams of three to four students and rotating members among teams, as recommended in most cooperative and collaborative texts and papers, lead to less effective cooperative learning when compared to situations in which teams remain intact for the entire semester and consist of six to eight members rather than three or four. His arguments stem from data concerning group dynamics development first presented by Tuckman (1965) and subsequently modified by Tuckman and Jensen (1977), and from the fact that six to eight individuals bring more resources to the group than three or four. Tuckman argued that high-performing groups develop along a predictable sequence of five stages including a "Forming" stage, a "Storming" stage, a "Norming" stage, a "Performing" stage, and an "Adjourning" stage.

1.1   Stages of Group Development

During the "Forming" stage, the members of the group get acquainted with each other. They deal with issues related to belonging, trust, and acceptance. The members are polite and formal, they search for similarity, and they avoid conflict and disagreement. Resistance to assigned tasks, rebellion against leadership, one-upmanship, and conflict and confusion about team members' roles and places in the group characterize the "Storming" stage (Tuckman, 1965). Once the group members work through the storming stage, they move into the third stage when the team begins to come together; Tuckman (1965) called this the "Norming" stage. Norms of acceptable behavior are established, a group identity emerges, conflicts are reduced, team cohesiveness develops, knowledge of individual strengths and weaknesses leads to balance and acceptance, and opinions are more clearly expressed and communicated by group members. Individuals become more involved in the functioning of the team.

The "Norming" stage is a prerequisite to the "Performing" stage. In this stage, team behavior becomes the norm as the group matures. The team becomes a self-organizing, highly functional organism that is able to effectively deal with issues and challenges. The team is able to quickly define and solve difficult challenges and problems resulting in high productivity, competence, and pride. Conflicts are dealt with constructively and trust and intimacy develop between the members. Finally, there is the "Adjourning" stage when the teamwork is done and the team dissolves. This stage can bring feelings of separation, satisfaction, and transformation. Some team members may show signs of grieving for the loss and withdraw, expressing anxiety about what is next. In this stage, members need to focus on how they may be able to apply what they have learned from the team experience to their personal life.

Michaelsen (1999) argued that a group of individuals needs to go through these stages of team development before the true benefits of cooperative and collaborative learning and teamwork can be obtained. He professes that students should remain in permanent teams throughout an entire semester. The benefits of such an arrangement compared to the use of incidental groups are clear: The students get to know each other much better, and trust, communication, leadership, accountability, and responsibility develop. They come to accept each other as individuals with strengths and weaknesses, and they come to understand how each student can best contribute to the team effort. They start to appreciate the benefit of diversity within the team and are more likely to experience the stages of team development. They learn how a highly performing team functions and they may be able to help future groups achieve such performance levels. In addition, the individual students develop a sense of accountability and responsibility towards the team and the other team members. Finally, they also tend to enjoy the class more. All this takes time to develop, and using incidental groups that change from class session to class session prevents the development of such dynamics.

Based upon strong arguments made by Michaelsen (1999), we decided to apply their team-based learning strategy to two different Kinesiology courses during two consecutive semesters. One was a sophomore-level Motor Learning and Control class, while the other was a senior-level Exercise Physiology class. In both classes we had previously attempted cooperative learning activities. More often than not, we received complaints about fellow students not contributing their share to the projects, thus resulting in frustration and anger among some group members. Another reason to adopt this method was the claim that it would result in greater student accountability and responsibility for preparation outside of the classroom. Many of the students at our university commute, maintain full-time employment, and/or have significant family responsibilities. Upwards of 50 percent of the students are the first in their family to attend a university. These are factors that lead to poor preparation and often poor performance in our classes. In addition, these courses were selected because they are required for all students majoring in Kinesiology. Students often perceive these courses as difficult and demanding, creating anxiety about their potential for success. We expected that being part of an established team might help reduce students' concerns and anxiety.

The goals of adopting the team-based learning strategy were focused on: 1) increasing student preparation for class sessions, and promoting student responsibility and accountability for their own learning; 2) creating a more intense, higher level learning experience in the classroom; 3) developing and improving thinking skills; 4) increasing immediate feedback concerning student performance; and 5) teaching students about teamwork, cooperation, and social responsibility.

2.   METHODS

2.1   Implementation of Team-Based Learning

At the beginning of the Fall 2001 and Spring 2002 semesters, we restructured the two Kinesiology courses to incorporate all elements of the team-based learning strategy as proposed by Michaelsen (1999). Previously we had used mostly lecture and one or two out-of-class group assignments per semester that students presented as a group to the whole class. We randomly assigned students enrolled in four classes to teams of six to eight individuals (N =169), and those teams remained intact for the entire semester. The strategy also included forward-looking "Readiness Assessment Tests" (RAT) procedures and in-class group assignments.

2.2   Readiness Assessment Tests

To ensure student preparation preceding class, we adopted Michaelsen and Black's (1994) concept of the forward-looking Readiness Assessment Test (RAT). In their syllabus, students were informed about the materials they needed to study for each RAT. Without additional lecture or elaboration by the instructor, students completed the RAT at the start of a content module (a module incorporated two-three class sessions). The RAT served as an evaluation of a student's readiness to engage in additional application, analysis, synthesis, and evaluation assignments (Bloom, 1956).

The RATs consisted of 5-10 questions, depending on the class. The questions mostly involved knowledge, comprehension, and application items (Bloom, 1956). Ten RATs were given during each semester. The students first completed the RAT as an individual and then completed the same RAT again as a team during prescribed time intervals. Following completion, the individual and team answer sheets were given to another team for grading, after which the instructor discussed the questions and answers. Each question on the RAT was designed to address an important concept and acted as a springboard for further elaboration of that concept, if needed. As such, the RATs also functioned as a valuable classroom assessment tool for the instructor. A simple show of hands allowed the instructor to determine whether students did or did not understand a concept. Following correction and elaboration on misunderstood concepts, the students had the opportunity to write a "team appeal," if they disagreed with anything related to the questions on the RAT. Every appeal had to be well reasoned and show their capacity to evaluate the question and synthesize a coherent, logical answer.

2.3   In-Class Assignments

When the RAT was given to the students, that class session was dedicated to content coverage. The subsequent class session was then used to present students with in-class problems and assignments that they then solved as a team. Michaelsen et al. (1997) describe three essential characteristics of effective team assignments. First, give the same problem to all teams; second, require them to make a specific choice or have them create a specific product; third, have all teams report their findings simultaneously. The intent of these guidelines is to create intra- and inter-team give-and-take discussions. These principles were applied, and after reporting results of their assignments, teams received immediate feedback about their product from each other and the instructor using a rubric of standards. The in-class assignments were designed to encourage analysis, synthesis, and evaluation (Bloom, 1956).

The assignments are a key component to enhancing individual and team-based learning. Michaelsen, Fink, and Knight (1997) suggested that the following questions be considered when developing assignments. First, do they promote a high level of individual accountability for team members? Second, do they bring members into close physical proximity? Third, do they motivate a great deal of discussion among team members? Fourth, do they ensure that members receive immediate, unambiguous, and meaningful feedback in direct comparison with the performance of the other teams? Fifth, do they provide explicit rewards for team performance?

We implemented poster presentations in the Motor Learning and Control course, because Michaelsen, Fink, and Knight's (1997) recommendations for designing effective assignments are all represented quite well in a poster presentation. Students were asked to develop a model in which they portrayed the relationships between several different concepts. For their first poster presentation, they were to show the relationships between motor abilities, measurement, performance, and predictions of future performance success in motor skills. We will not go into the details of the process here, but during one class session all teams hung the posters they prepared on the classroom wall. The students then examined each other's posters and critiqued them using a rubric of standards in order to provide the authors with immediate feedback. At the end of this class session, the students completed 1-Minute Papers (a classroom assessment technique to be described later) to provide the instructor with feedback about these teamwork assignments.

2.4   Team Performance Survey

A survey related to teamwork was given at the beginning of all classes and again at the end of every semester. The survey incorporated the following factors: 1) Individual aspects of teamwork; 2) Working as a team member; 3) Use of team assignments by teachers; 4) Team assignment effectiveness; 5) Grading; 6) Success in the class; and 7) Social aspects of teams. Students scored each statement on a scale from 1-"strongly disagree" to 10-"strongly agree" with 1-point intervals.

2.5   Focus Group Evaluation

The students were also asked about their experiences with team-based learning during the focus group evaluation at the end of each semester. The instructors composed open-ended questions specific to the team-based learning strategy in order to receive specific feedback from the students. An instructor not affiliated with the department conducted the evaluation. Students first completed the evaluation on their own. They then answered the same questions again in their teams followed by a discussion of the questions by the entire class. The instructor conducting the evaluation wrote the answers of the class on the board and included them in the final report. This instructor also gathered all written responses, which were typed for the final report. Finally, this instructor debriefed the evaluation with the instructors who never saw the original responses.

3. RESULTS

3.1 The RAT

We analyzed the students' performance on the RATs for the Fall-2001 and Spring-2002 classes. We found a main effect for Classes: $F(1,106) = 5.685$, $p = 0.019$, with a mean score for Fall 2001 = 68.635 and a mean score for Spring 2002 = 71.464 (on a 100-point scale). This small increase in the average score may have been due to more effective use of the strategy by the instructors.

There was also a main effect for Mode (team versus individual score): $F(1,106) = 513.593$, $p < 0.001$, with the scores on the individual RAT = 60.33, and the team RAT = 79.97. That the scores were so low on the individual RATs can be explained by the fact that no discussion or lecture preceded the students taking these quizzes individually. A discussion within each team during the team RAT raised the score by nearly 20 points, supporting the effectiveness of team discussions when students come to class prepared.

3.1.1 Focus group evaluation results of the RATs

At the end of the semester, a trained outside person with no connection to the students conducted a focus group evaluation. The following were some of the positive comments made by the students:

"(The RATs) made me read before class. I took it more seriously."

"Each person had to learn, not just memorize the information."

"The team test and the feedback were most important to our members."

"As a group we view different angles and approaches to the questions, and the repetition sinks in."

"Other people's ideas helped one to understand the material individually."

There were also some negative comments:

"Would like lecture before RATs."

"Tricky questions."

3.2   In-Class Assignments

3.2.1   Focus group evaluation results of the poster assignments

Students expressed numerous valuable comments concerning the poster presentations. To follow are two examples of such comments.

"...(the poster assignment) allowed me to really go over the material, get a firm understanding of the relationships between learning, memory, and forgetting and skill performance, and just, in general, be more prepared. Beforehand, just the process of trying to think of potential questions the other teams might ask, also drove the material home for me."

"…(the poster assignment) allowed me to comprehend how memory works because I was able to see how the other groups thought of it. This time around everyone's posters were very different so I was able to see the process from different points of view."

Other students commented, "Eight minds are more effective than one; The sharing of ideas and the discussions lead to better understanding; It taught us how to cooperate with the team; It took seven different people's ideas and had to compromise to form a united decision."

3.2.2   One-Minute Papers about the poster assignments

The 1-Minute Paper is a classroom assessment tool that asks students to write what they learned from the preceding assignment in a few minutes. We analyzed the 1-Minute Paper contents provided by the students directly following completion of the poster presentations. The comments were organized in three categories: a "Learning" category, a "Content" category, and an "Other" category. The Learning category included statements that reflected insights about global learning strategies. Examples of statements included in the Learning category were: "Being able to answer the questions not only involves knowledge from the book but also being able to logically reason out the answers," and "The entire process enabled anyone who took advantage of the situation to further their knowledge on the subject, learn from their peers, and find out whether or not they fully understood the material."

The Content category included statements directly related to content items from the textbook and other sources. Examples of statements included in the Content category were: "I now can basically describe more on how to define ability (and its link) to measurement and future assessments," and "I learned that bandwidth of errors should stay constant through practice."

The Other category included statements not related to learning and content insights. Examples of statements included in the Other category were: "This process was very stressful," "While we were doing the model, the assignment wasn't clear," and "Lucky 7 has a very creative team."

The first poster was completed in the 3rd week of the semester after only 6 hours of teamwork. The second poster was done in the 7th week after 18 hours of working together. The last poster assignment was performed during the 11th week of the semester after approximately 30 hours of working as a team in class, and the data indicate that it took our students until the latter third of the semester to reflect more strongly on their learning of content (see Figure 1).

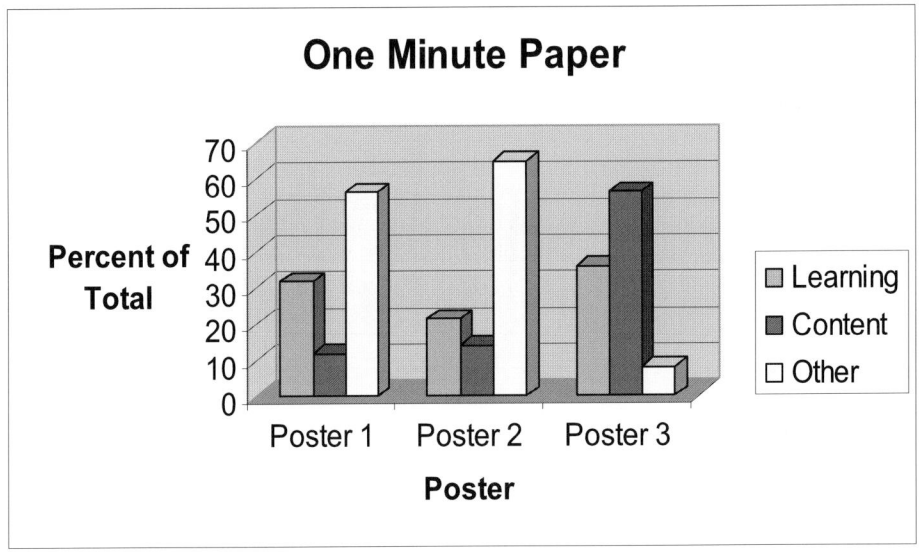

Figure 1. Poster presentation assignments were given three times during one semester

Watson, Michaelsen, and Sharp (1991) indicated that it took participants in their study more than 24 hours of face-to-face interaction for group decision making and successful performance to develop. Similarly, Watson, Kumar, and Michaelsen (1993) found that it took diverse teams more than 20 to 30 hours of working together to learn to problem solve effectively. The students in these earlier studies were not guided in their group development processes. Similarly, we did not explicitly help the teams reach Tuckman's (1965) performance stages. However, we found out that teams do need assistance in this process and will address this issue later in the chapter.

3.3   Team Performance Survey

A copy of the complete survey is included in Appendix A. An analysis of the survey results indicated that there were no differences between the two courses, suggesting that the perceptions of teamwork were similar between sophomores and seniors regardless of the topic of the class. We applied the Greenhouse-Geisser correction, because the sphericity assumption was not met, and found a Pre-post x Question interaction, $F (11.5,1286.4) = 5.122, p < 0.0001$. Further analysis of the interaction indicated that students changed their scores on a number of survey items over the course of one semester. These items are shown in Figure 2.

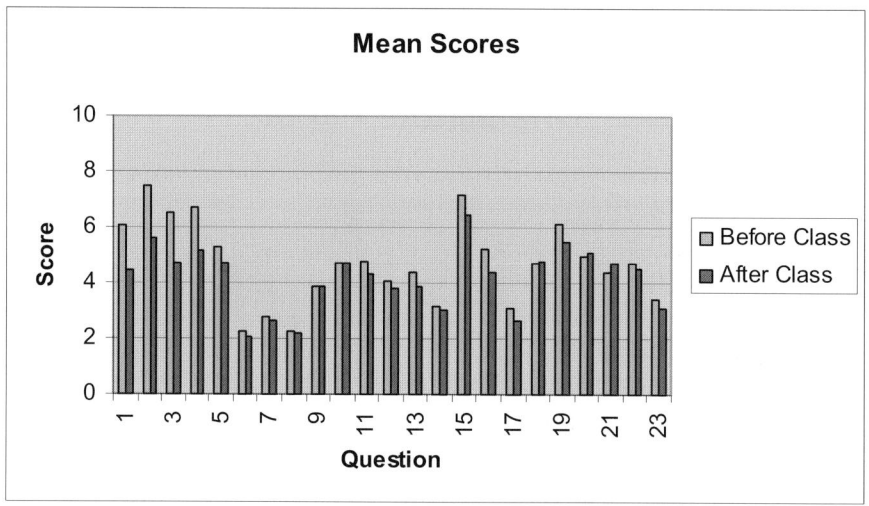

Figure 2. Responses on Questions 1, 2, 3, 4, 5, 11, 13, 15, 16, and 19 changed significantly from beginning to end of the semester, reflecting an improved perception of teamwork by the students

The responses to Questions 1, 2, 3, 4, 5, 11, 13, 15, 16, and 19 improved significantly. These items were worded negatively and students changed their responses to more "strongly disagree." This reflected a positive change in their perception of teamwork. There were no other items that differed significantly before and after class.

3.4   Focus Group Evaluation Results

Examples of positive comments about team-based learning expressed by the students during the focus group evaluation were: "Sharing knowledge with teammates; Explain information to each other; Help get teammates prepared; Didn't want to let teammates down; More ways than one to look at something; Helped clarify and synthesize information; Collective knowledge is greater than individual; Teammates helped my grades; Accountability towards my teammates." These comments suggest that the students appreciated and acknowledged the intended benefits of the team-based learning strategy.

4. CONCLUSIONS

The team-based learning strategy had a positive impact on our students and the learning atmosphere in our classes. Analyses of the students' RAT performance, their comments about in-class assignments, the team-based learning survey, and focus group evaluations indicated that students:

- studied the assigned course material before coming to class;
- were able to discuss concepts from the text without a preceding lecture;
- scored higher on combined team RATs than individual ones (with regular exceptions);
- were able to develop coherent reasons for an appeal of RAT questions;
- really liked being in a team for the entire semester;
- learned how to perform as a team and were proud of their accomplishments on the poster assignments;
- realized the benefits of diversity within and among their teams;
- learned how to carry on a team discussion and come to consensus or an agreeable solution;
- practiced and showed higher-level thinking and reasoning skills; and
- made new friends and enjoyed themselves in class.

These were meaningful changes compared to effects of lecturing and the incidental use of cooperative learning in previous classes. Team-based learning places a great deal of responsibility on the students for their own preparation and learning. Making the students accountable for their own preparation to others allowed the instructors to engage them in more challenging assignments during the class sessions.

4.1 Conditions for Effective Implementation of Team-Based Learning

Weber (2002) argued that instructors must first articulate a clear personal philosophy on learning and teaching. Accordingly, they should then choose a teaching strategy that fits their personal philosophy rather than gather a "bag of tricks," none of which may truly fit their personal learning and teaching philosophy. The instructor must also shift the focus from teaching to student learning. Learning requires active engagement of the students; therefore, instructors should dedicate substantial time to the development of effective assignments rather than one-directional lectures. Lectures, particularly in the form of a mini-lecture, should serve to eliminate confusion concerning a concept rather than being used as the sole vehicle to introduce and present concepts.

Implementing team-based learning also necessitates a change in classroom culture that requires changes in attitudes and behaviors of both the instructor and the students. It requires that instructors learn facilitation, coaching, conflict mediation, and assignment development skills. It also requires that instructors adopt a new system of checks and balances to judge students' performances. For example, to ensure that students understand what the performance expectations are, an instructor should develop relevant performance rubrics and explain these to the students. The rubric should then be used to evaluate and give feedback on how to improve student performance. Providing students with frequent feedback that can be used to enhance their individual and team performance, is essential.

The instructor must explain clearly at the beginning of the semester why he or she is using a particular teaching strategy. The instructor should also ensure that the structure and organization of the class are fully understood by the students, as well as the reasons why it is being done this way. This requires that the instructors share their teaching and learning philosophy. Communicating the reasons and principles behind this still unorthodox approach to teaching and learning is essential, because most students continue to experience the traditional lecture format in the majority of their courses, and therefore, may resist this "radical" departure.

4.2   Recent Modifications

Since the EDiNEB conference in 2002, we have made several changes to further improve team-based learning. First, the Motor Learning and Control course has been changed to a theme-based course with seven thematic units. Second, the instructor now posts clarifications and study questions for each unit on the course Web site. Third, students are allowed to use their handwritten notes when taking the RAT. This has improved their performance and decreased the demand for lectures preceding the RAT. Fourth, students are assigned to permanent teams based on the results of a background survey, gender, and their GPA, to ensure the greatest possible diversity within the teams. Fifth, during the first week of the semester, they develop a Full Value Commitment (FVC) that spells out the rules of behavior for the semester. They also develop a list of consequences should a team member fail to follow the FVC. The FVC functions to clarify teamwork behavior expectations. Twice during the semester the students evaluate each other's teamwork behavior and assign points toward the final grade of each team member after they take the final exam. Sixth, for all in-class assignments the students are given a performance rubric based on David Perkins' (1986, 1987) critical thinking questions. These questions relate to the purpose, organization, application, explanation, and evaluation of a concept. The instructor models this strategy for every concept, and students are required to address each of the components on their assignments. Preliminary analyses indicate that the students have received these changes favorably.

It is clear that despite the use of the FVC, some groups need more guidance to achieve the performing stage of group development. While a substantial number of groups did develop into performing teams, several struggled, as evidenced by the teamwork behavior scores they assigned to each other at the end of the semester. We believe that requiring students to develop an "active" portfolio -- a dynamic vehicle of learning rather than a static depository -- in which they place all documents for the course, their personal notes, their personal reflections concerning the development of their learning and teamwork, personal and group goals, and the results of several explicit team building activities, may further improve this component of the class.

APPENDIX A

Team Performance Survey

Please rate the following items on the scale from **1 (strongly disagree)** to **10 (strongly agree)**. Circle only one number.

1. Performing assignments in small groups always results in one or a few persons doing all the work
   (strongly disagree) 1 2 3 4 5 6 7 8 9 10 (strongly agree)
2. There is always one person who tries to get away with doing as little as possible.
3. There is always a person who abuses the trust of the others by bringing up excuses why he/she could not complete the assigned work on time and with quality.
4. When you have to complete team assignments outside of class, it is a hassle to organize meetings.
5. There is usually one person who doesn't show up during the agreed upon meeting times outside of class when we're to work on assignments.

6. Team assignments outside of class rarely help the team members learn more about the topic.

7. Team assignments don't make students work harder for the class.

8. Team assignments often result in frustration and anger in some team members.

9. Receiving the same grade for a team assignment is a fair way of grading all team members.

10. When performing team assignments in class, students mostly socialize instead of working on the task.

11. Most team assignments in class are ineffective, because the teacher doesn't explain them well.

12. Most team assignments in class are ineffective, because the teacher doesn't give the groups enough time to work on the assignments.

13. Most team assignments in class are ineffective, because the teacher often doesn't give the students immediate feedback about their performance/opinions.

14. Working in small groups leads to the teacher covering less material than if he/she would just lecture and explain the content of the textbook.

15. Team projects enable less motivated or less capable students to go along for a "free ride" and get a good grade on the backs of the hardworking students.

16. Teachers use team assignments so they themselves don't have to prepare for class.

17. Teachers using team assignments do so because they themselves don't really understand the topic well.

18. Teachers use team assignments so they don't have to do much work in class.

19. Teachers who use team assignments are poorly organized and prepared for class.

20. The products of other groups in a class are typically not shared with everybody else.

21. The opinions that arise as a result of teamwork are often not presented to the rest of the class, and in-depth discussion is prevented.

22. Team assignments are mostly boring and irrelevant to the topic to be learned.

23. Teamwork helped me network and make new friends.

24. I communicated with my team members via e-mail.

25. Completing the Ticket To Class on WebCT helped me learn difficult concepts better.

26. Working in a team became more enjoyable as the semester progressed.

27. Working with my team on assignments in class helped me learn and understand difficult concepts better than I could have on my own.

28. Working in a team helped me improve my grades.

29. I can apply what I learned in this class to my future profession.

30. My grade reflects how well we worked together as a team during the semester.

31. The poor grades I received were due to other team members not contributing to the team effort.

32. The grade I received did not reflect my effort and my contribution to the team performance.

33. My team members helped me get motivated and work hard on projects.

34. That I received a good grade was more due to the efforts of the other team members than my own efforts.

35. The grades I received were accurate and are a fair reflection of how well I personally understood the material.

36. As the semester progressed, we became more and more effective as a team when performing the assignments.

37. My team members helped me perform well in the class.

38. My success in the course was a result of being part of the team.

REFERENCES

Bloom, B. S. (Ed.). (1956). *Taxonomy of educational objectives: The classification of educational goals: Handbook I, cognitive domain.* New York, Toronto: Longmans, Green.

Michaelsen, L. K. (1999). Myths and methods in successful small group work. *National Teaching and Learning Forum, 8* (6), 1-4.

Michaelsen, L. K., & Black, R. L. (1994). Building learning teams: The key to harnessing the power of small groups in higher education. In Collaborative learning: *A sourcebook for higher education (Vol. 2).* National Center for Teaching, Learning, and Assessment: State College, PA.

Michaelsen, L. K., Black, R. L., & Fink, L. D. (1996). What every faculty member needs to know about learning groups. In L. Richlin (Ed.), *To improve the Academy: Resources for faculty, instructional and organizational development* (pp. 373-397). New Forums Press: Stillwater, OK.

Michaelsen, L. K., Fink, L. D., & Knight, A. B. (1997). Designing effective group activities: Lessons for classroom teaching and faculty development. In D. DeZure (Ed.), *To improve the Academy: Resources for faculty, instructional and organizational development* (pp. 373-397). New Forums Press: Stillwater, OK.

Michaelsen, L. K., Knight , A. B., & Fink, L. D. (2003). *Team-based learning: A transformative use of small groups.* Westport, CT: Praeger Publishers.

Millis, B. J., & Cottell, P. G. (1998). *Cooperative learning for Higher Education faculty. American Council on Education,* Phoenix, AZ: The Oryx Press.

Perkins, D. (1986). *Knowledge as design.* Hilldale, NJ: Erlbaum.

Perkins, D. (1987). Knowledge as design: Teaching thinking through content. In Baron, J. B., & Sternberg, R. J. (Eds.), *Teaching thinking skills: Theory and practice.* New York, NY: W.H. Freeman and Company.

Tuckman, B. W. (1965). Developmental sequence in small groups. *Psychological Bulletin, 63,* 384-399.

Tuckman, B. W., & Jensen, M. C. (1977). Stages of Small-Group Development Revisited. *Group and Organization Studies, 2,* 419-427.

Watson, W. E., Kumar, & Michaelsen L. K. (1993). Impact of cultural diversity on group process and group performance over time. *Academic Management Journal, 36,* 590-602.

Watson, W. E., Michaelsen, L. K., & Sharp, W. (1991). Member competence, group interaction and group decision-making: A longitudinal study. *Journal of Applied Psychology, 76,* 801-809.

Weber, R. (2002, June). *Small group teaching and learning in humanity classes: A place for the humanities in business education*. Paper presented at the annual international conference of the EDiNEB network, Guadalajara, Mexico.

Chapter 4

CROSS-CULTURAL VIRTUAL TEAMWORK: IMPLICATIONS FROM THE MULTICULTURAL E-CLASSROOM

Ken Morse
Waikato Management School, Hamilton, New Zealand

1.   INTRODUCTION

Knowledge, skills, and sustainable values are critical concerns for learning organizations. The quality of information available and the speed at which information can be gathered and disseminated has increased dramatically. Commensurately, the environment of management has also changed. "Downsizing" and "rightsizing" have resulted in flatter organizations with fewer levels of information flow and decision making; the complexity of management problems and the importance of knowledge management as a competitive advantage have increased. The increased complexity of problems and the importance of effective knowledge management have resulted in an increase in the role of teamwork within organizations (Donnellon, 1996). The implementation of Information and Communication Technology (ICT) has changed the availability of information, the flexibility of dealing with information and knowledge, modes of solving professional problems, and communication within and between organizations. Proliferation of cross-border communication nodes and advances in the speed and convenience of international transportation have coincided with the rapid growth of international trade in the past several decades (Hill, 2000). Responding to the global diffusion of communication technology imposes major pressures on firms and employees

R.G.Milter et al. (eds.), Educational Innovation in Economics and Business IX, 49–74.
©2004 *Springer. Printed in the Netherlands.*

– pressures that are exacerbated by the wide range of cultures within which 21st century learning organizations must participate.

As the international environment increasingly turns to electronic communication technologies, experience in manipulating such technologies is in itself a critical experiential learning objective for the 21st century (Hill, 2000). Some of these changes have been reflected in the curriculum as business education has responded in a number of ways, with increasing group work and teambuilding exercises as integral components of course requirements (Jacobs, 2000). Business education has also responded to these changes by adopting/adapting the new communications technologies to the traditional classroom delivery method and by pursuing the concept of e-learning. As a result, because international "best practice" increasingly demands improved communications skills, improved teamworking experience, greater interpersonal skills, and electronic communication abilities of executives/employees, students as well as faculty are attempting to work cooperatively over communication media and computer networks. But both the development of communication technology and the development of e-learning techniques have been driven by a small number of dominant, primarily English-speaking, economies with their inherent cultural context (Gupta, 2000). Increasingly, however, both learning organizations and individual e-learning participants emanate from cultures other than those of the dominant economies – a shift which has major implications for learning organizations, e-learners, and e-delivered education providers.

To that end, using the foundation developed in a previous publication (Morse, 2001), this chapter reports on the implications of conducting a virtual teamwork simulation in the e-classroom. After a very brief review of relevant literature, the simulation is described, which provides the foundation for discussion of the differential impact of the virtual environment on e-learners from a contrasting set of cultural backgrounds, drawing some implications for both firms and e-learning institutions in anticipation of future development of teamwork in the virtual environment.

2.   THEORETICAL BACKGROUND

As a background to the discussion of this exercise, a brief review of the concept and constraints of teamwork may be helpful. A team is *"...a group of people who interact through interdependent tasks guided by a common purpose"* (Lipnack & Stamps, 1997, p. 6). Key characteristics of effective teams include: complementary skills that together are equal to the assigned task; established goals and individual and collective accountability for achieving these goals; an agreed approach to getting the necessary work done (Katzenbach & Smith, 1993), but the driving factor of effective teamwork is "the common purpose," which is an externally determined outcome facilitated by an internally determined (and negotiated) agreement (Benson-Amer & Hsieh, 1997). A large body of supporting literature has developed that elaborates these concepts (Heywood, 1998; Mankin, Cohen, & Bikson, 1996; Shapiro & Varian, 1999; Townsend, De Marie, & Hendrichson, 1998).

2.1 Building Blocks of Effective Teamwork

This brief review highlights two key relationships in the teamwork/teambuilding literature that are important to the development of effectively functioning teams. Firstly, the team goal or expected outcome must be clearly defined. The identification of clear incentives for successful completion helps to ensure that the goal is achieved, and that the integration of the participants occurs. These are the essential aspects of the "project" itself – the technical and corporate characteristics that must be developed to achieve the goal initially established for the team/project, which is the first hurdle in developing an effective team.

But to achieve the objective, no matter how precisely formulated, it is necessary to develop a concept of cooperation and interaction among the participants. A team is formed from individuals who bring differing skills, experiences, and motivations to the group. To be effective, the group must develop a sense of community for sharing their skills, experiences, and motivations, often referred to as the development of "teamwork" (Mankin et al., 1996). This development is necessarily a function of the characteristics of the individuals who make up the team, leading to the development of an internal team dynamic, which is the result of the socialization process whereby these individuals gradually discern and/or develop their role within the team. These are the essential "people" aspects of teambuilding.

2.2 Virtual Teamwork

As with any team, a virtual team is a group of discrete individuals assigned to achieve a common goal or purpose. However, a virtual team employs electronic communication to enhance mobility and the speed of information sharing by operating both asynchronously and without collocation (Lipnack & Stamps, 1997). Recent literature relative to virtual communication cites a large pool of difficulties that face participants in the virtual environment. Although a relatively new management tool, there already exists a rich literature identifying both development of virtual teamwork capabilities (Benson-Amer & Hsieh, 1997; Shapiro & Varian, 1999; Townsend et al., 1998) and the accompanying difficulties (Duarte & Snyder, 1999; Heywood, 1998) in imposing this additional skill requirement on participants. A growing body of literature suggests that computer mediated communication lacks the non-verbal cues of face-to-face communication, thus increasing the necessity for explicit rather than inferential communication (Harasim, 1990; Hiltz, 1994; Shedletsky & Aitken, 2001; Turoff, Hiltz, Bahgat, & Rana, 1993;). Likewise, that literature suggests that not only is the virtual communication mode different, the speed at which non-verbal cues are transmitted is also different, leading to further communication difficulties in the virtual environment (Althaus, 1997; Hiltz & Wellman, 1997). This comprises the "virtual environment" aspect associated with virtual teamwork.

While each of these aspects requires their own dynamics that result in team performance, it is clear that the "project" aspects are dependant on the "people" aspects of team performance. The effectiveness of teams is dependant on the ability of the constituted team to overcome these hurdles to develop a bond between "project" and "people." Because the virtual environment differs dramatically from the traditional face-to-face physical environment, an additional hurdle faces the team, that of the changed nature of the environment in which the virtual team operates.

2.3   Cross-Cultural Issues?

A wide range of evidence clearly shows that cultures differ, behaviors differ, and responses to technology differ by ethnicity (see Morse, 2003 for a detailed literature review). These intercultural differences impose additional interpersonal communications requirements on the successful implementation of teamwork activities, which thus influence the effectiveness of teams. These differences are exacerbated in the virtual environment, as many of the expected cultural communication tools are eliminated, due to the nature of "virtual" communication. The lack of face-to-face visual cues, the nuances of the spoken word, and body language are cases in point (Morse, 2003).

Morse (2001) presented an analysis of multi-cultural e-learning, in which participants were discriminated by English language ability (EPL/ESL). However, this artificial distinction was less than satisfactory in directly linking language to culture, and thus behavior to language. As a result, an alternative conception of culture has been developed to distinguish student seminar participants for a further evaluation. Ethnic group (cultural) differences are reflected in learning styles that are based on the modal behaviors of societal learned values (Parhizgar, 1998). These are influenced by both communication behavior (Gundykunst, 1997; Gundykunst & Ting-Toomey, 1988; Korac-Kakabadse, Kouzmin, Korac-Kakabadse, & Savery, 2001) and education systems (Entwistle, 1991; Makepeace, 1996; Maxwell, Adam, Pooran, & Scott, 2000). Participant culture – their learned rules of behavior in a group setting – are therefore important to the development of learning interaction and learning achievement.

Communication has been identified as a key linkage between underlying culture as identified above and overt individual behavior in a group environment (Schneider & Barsoux, 2003). This linkage has been differentiated along a continuum between low-context and high-context cultures (Hall & Hall, 1990). On one end of the continuum, in a low-context culture, low levels of programmed (mutually understood) information provide context, therefore communication requires a large amount of explicit information to convey meaning (Korac-Kakabadse et al., 2001) as "in low-context communication, the listener knows very little and must be told practically everything" (Hall & Hall, 1990, p. 11). Practically speaking, these communications have been associated with "contract cultures" that operate on the basis of the unambiguous written word (Hall & Hall, 1990; Korac-Kakabadse et al., 2001). On the other end of that continuum is a high-context culture in which high levels of programmed (mutually understood) information provide context, which requires a greater cumulative effort to program (conceptualize) and to interpret in order to convey meaning (Korac-Kakabadse et al., 2001); "In high-context communication, the listener is already "contextualized" and so does not need to be given much background information" (Hall & Hall, 1990, p. 11). Likewise, practically speaking, these communications have been associated with "relationship cultures" which operate on the basis of personal networks, relationships, and respect (Hall & Hall, 1990; Korac-Kakabadse et al., 2001). This distinction is similar to Glenn's "associative/abstractive" construct (Bhagat, Kedia, Crawford, & Kaplan, 1990; Glenn, 1981), Servaes' "direct/indirect" continuum (Osland, 1990; Servaes, 1989), or Hofstede's "individualism/collectivism" dimension (Gundykunst & Ting-Toomey, 1988; Hofstede, 1980; Hofstede, 1991;).

The foregoing clearly develops a linkage between culture (ethnicity), learning behavior, and communication modes. Low-context individuals, acculturated toward environmentally related learning variables anticipate that their role in learning is to attain some minimum level of competence (Hall & Hall, 1990) which to some extent sees these individuals competing on an individual basis against a standard that may grow or change rapidly over time, and perhaps to a lesser degree, with their peers as well. On the other hand, high-context individuals are acculturated to adjust their level of effort to a predetermined performance outcome, and therefore look inwardly at self-behavior to achieve a socially acceptable level of excellence, taking the externally determined standard as a given. Thus, their perception is to change or develop the individual to meet the predetermined standard as opposed to pressing the boundary of knowledge, and therefore indirectly influencing development of some higher learning standard (Goodfellow, Lea, Francisco, & Mason, 2001).

Current research indicates that communication provides a linkage between underlying cultural assumptions and behavior patterns (Schneider & Barsoux, 2003). Similarly, behavior patterns have been grouped into clusters of similarity, based on the fundamental artifacts of those cultural assumptions (Ronen & Shenkar, 1985), which have been correlated with the context of communication patterns (Hall & Hall, 1990). Figure 1 illustrates the alternative extremes of these communications patterns, based on the previously identified high/low-context dichotomy.

			China
New Zealand		Fiji	Japan
Australia		Samoa	Korea
England	Germany	Sri Lanka	Vietnam
Canada	Denmark	India	Thailand
USA	France	Pakistan	Malaysia
LOW CONTEXT		HIGH CONTEXT	
(Explicit)		(Implicit)	

Figure 1. Communication (culture) context (Adapted from: Schneider & Barsoux, 2003; Morse, 2003; Hall & Hall 1990; Ronen & Shenkar, 1985.)

This framework has been adopted, and applied to qualitative data collected from a cross-cultural virtual teamwork simulation. That context and the conceptual application are discussed next.

3. A CROSS-CULTURAL TEAMWORK SIMULATION

Over the course of the past three years, a term length simulation has been used to approximate the communication and learning organization environment in which modern trans-national firms operate (Morse, 2002). This exercise incorporated the characteristics of the virtual environment that would be expected to exist for the foreseeable future (Editors, 1999), and to represent the capabilities today's students would be expected to offer in the employment market. The academic learning objectives of the simulation included the desire to encourage participants to draw on past academic learning in an integrative environment, to experience through exposure the unexpected difficulties of communication in the virtual environment, as well as the opportunity to benefit from sharing their past experience from non-virtual teamwork. Additionally, the behavioral learning objectives expected participants to reflect on their virtual teamwork experience, to compare this experience with their own past experience in the non-virtual environment, and to develop their virtual environment behavior patterns in a systematic and controlled academic environment. These objectives are in keeping with the expected growth of virtual management requirements in the participant's future workplace.

3.1   The Simulation

This simulation was conducted in seven sequential phases over a 13-week period as indicated in Figure 2. In this simulation, participants were expected to experience the disorientation and uneasiness of the cross-border organizational and communications issues to be expected in this environment.

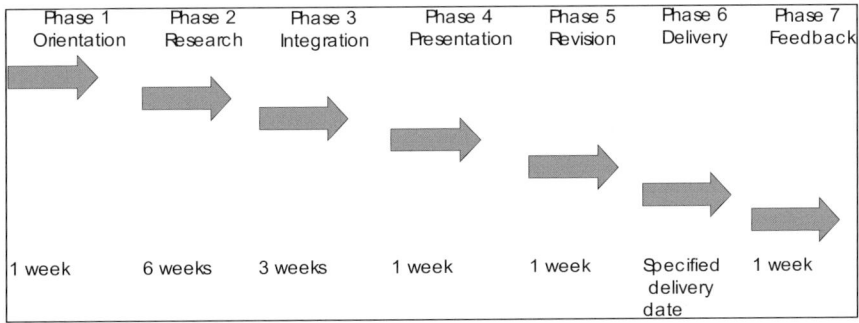

Figure 2. Simulation phases (Morse, 2002)

Technical capabilities for each individual team included asynchronous email (deposit and wait), a live chat facility (synchronous interactive communication), as well as a synchronous editing capability (allowing multiple simultaneous access to an open document). Videoconference capabilities were provided for presentation delivery, and electronic document handling was developed for written report delivery. Such capabilities were deemed the minimum necessary, given the restriction of no face-to-face communication.

In the operation of this simulation, teams were formed, and assigned an identical major international feasibility study to complete. As detailed in Appendix A, each study required detailed investigation to determine the potentially most profitable offshore location for a new production (manufacturing) facility, given a series of explicit limitations. Upon completion, an oral presentation (delivered by videoconference) and a formal written feasibility report (submitted electronically) were the expected "deliverables." The resulting virtual teams were composed of three to five members who were only allowed to communicate via electronic means.

3.1.1   The research question

In a trial iteration of the simulation, a series of identified issues indicated differential performance among participants. Evaluation of the cause of such differential performance suggested that at least some of the differential performance could be associated with cultural differences, broadly defined, while other causes might be directly linked to prior educational preparation and learning, which is also strongly culturally based. Thus, data collection and analysis were undertaken to discover whether a link could be identified between participant culture and their associated educational preparation on the one hand and participants' perception of their contribution to the viability of the virtual team during the course of an extended virtual team simulation on the other hand.

3.1.2   The research method

As indicated in the literature, culture is an inherently qualitative characteristic, limiting the appropriateness of sophisticated statistical techniques. Thus, qualitative analysis of cultural variables leading to differential participant performance was undertaken to attempt to show tentative links between culture and performance in the virtual environment. To this end, an open-ended qualitative data collection instrument was used, and evaluated using content analysis and a qualitative analysis software program, as described below.

3.1.3   Data collection

Participants in the simulation provided background information relative to their skills, past experience, and cultural background, as indicated in Appendix B. The information was used to assign participants to different teams using the following criteria for establishment of each team: a broad range of employment experience, a broad range of past teamwork experience, a range of cultural backgrounds, and where relevant, a range of academic preparation as well. These four criteria were expected to duplicate, to the extent possible, the criteria firms would be expected to use in establishing work teams – that is, each team member would have differing background and would bring differing competitive advantages to the team.

At the conclusion of the simulation exercise, students were asked to comment at length on their experience. They were given an instrument containing six open-ended questions for the collection of qualitative data (Appendix C). The participants were given an additional four demographic questions to allow categorization of qualitative responses. Seventy-four participants as members of 27 virtual teams provided qualitative data regarding their virtual teamwork experience. All had been participants in at least one face-to-face team or group project prior to this simulation exercise. This data pool provided the basis for analysis.

From the foregoing literature review, current research indicates that communication provides a linkage between underlying cultural assumptions and behavior patterns (Schneider & Barsoux, 2003) coupled with the essential nature of communication in the virtual environment (Shapiro & Varian, 1999; Benson-Amer & Hsieh, 1997). Therefore participants were grouped according to their demographically identified communication context (see Figure 1). The participants in the simulation are widely multicultural. Demographic data were used to assign participants to communication context groups in line with the literature review (Hall & Hall 1990; Ronen & Shenkar, 1985; Schneider & Barsoux, 2003). Conveniently, a clear distinction emerged between high-context participants on the one hand and low-context participant groups on the other.

Using the low-context/high-context cultural distinction identified in the literature review (Hall & Hall, 1990; Ronen & Shenkar, 1985; Schneider & Barsoux, 2003), the demographic characteristics of the participants were used to distinguish qualitative feedback as collected in the data collection instrument. Cumulatively, the participants consisted of 56 percent low-context and 44 percent high-context participants, as indicated in Table 1. Low-context participants represented Australia, Chile, Denmark, France, Germany, New Zealand, the United Kingdom, and the United States – the largest representative group of which were New Zealanders (41 percent of the total). High-context participants represented China (Mainland, Taiwan, and other overseas Chinese), India, Malaysia, Sri Lanka, and Vietnam, the largest representative group of which was Chinese (39 percent of the total).

Table 1. Simulation Participants

Low Context	n=	%	High Context	n=	%
Australia	1	1.4%	India	3	4.1%
Chile	1	1.4%	Malaysia	2	2.7%
Denmark	1	1.4%	P R China	19	25.7%
France	4	5.4%	Sri Lanka	2	2.7%
Germany	2	2.7%	Taiwan	6	8.1%
New Zealand	30	40.5%	Viet Nam	1	1.4%
United Kingdom	1	1.4%			
United States	1	1.4%			

Thus, the group of participants was broadly multicultural in nature, allowing some cross-cultural inferences to be drawn.

3.1.4   Data analysis

Using content analysis, the qualitative data received in response to the open-ended questions was evaluated for major themes, or issues, which were thought to impact on their ability to function within this virtual teamwork simulation. Content analysis is "a systematic, objective, quantitative analysis of message characteristics, ... especially useful for examination of human interactions" (Neuendorf, 2002, p. 1). This analytical method facilitates identification of similarities in communication messages, and identification of underlying behavior patterns to ascertain links between communication and behavior to be used for theory building.

Content analysis is a laborious process, but major improvements in computer software in the past few years facilitate content analysis of qualitative data. For this data analysis, collected data were coded separately by two graduate assistants, then analyzed using the NUD*IST (NVivo) software program – a qualitative analysis program designed to assist in the development of links within qualitative data (Richards, 2000). To facilitate content analysis, data are collected, coded, and entered into a database. Internal algorithms then allow the development of summary data, links, and models of the data that can then be reported in a number of forms (Richards, 2000).

4.   OBSERVATIONS

Though specific statistical measures do not result from the qualitative analysis presented above, a series of observations have been made on the basis of frequency of recurrence, which is linked to participant background as provided by the demographic data. Based on the qualitative data provided by the simulation participants, some precautionary observations must be made. The vast majority of participants (63 of 74, or 85 percent) were reticent regarding the use of a virtual team simulation at the beginning, but after completion reflected that, in their opinion, it was an excellent learning tool. This correlates well with much of the literature relative to use of simulation for learning purposes (Anderson & Lawton, 1992; Larreche, 1987). Further, to varying levels, both cultural groups perceived the simulation to be a more valuable learning device as a result of the "real life" application used as a simulation foundation – an observation which conforms to previous research (Atsumi, Misumi, Smith, Peter, Peterson, Tayeb, Kipnis, Minami, Yamaguchi, & Tanzer, 1989; Fowler, 1994). At the same time, however, they collectively suggested that the virtual team exercise was more difficult than a similar physical team exercise. With these general precautions as a foundation, cross-cultural observations can be made in the areas of technology, technology skills and language, cultural accommodation and the virtual environment. The following observations report those recurring themes in the qualitative data.

4.1   Technology

A majority (17 of 21, or 81 percent) of participant teams cumulatively identified a series of technology issues that impacted on their performance in the virtual team simulation. These included hardware and software interconnectivity issues, Internet security issues, and reliability issues. It became apparent upon reviewing the qualitative responses of participants that both hardware and software are significant issues across the board. While a large number of participants used student computers in student labs connected to a local intranet, and thus were assured identical equipment, many of those same participants became disenchanted with technology once they tried to connect to the intranet from outside the computer labs. Using computers with older generation operating systems, dated microprocessors, and low speed modems led to a wide range of difficulties: inability to connect and low data transfer rates (especially frustrating in a graphics intensive Internet environment).

Following from the above, another key issue for participants arose because both hardware and software incompatibilities restricted participation. Choices of software which were platform dependant (i.e., minimum Windows 98 O/S or better) precluded participants with older installed software from participation, unless they upgraded their software, a solution which also potentially meant hardware upgrade as well – at a significant personal cost to the participant. Of course, the alternative was to simply go to the student computer labs, but this travel effectively negated some of the "real world" benefit of the simulation.

In the same vein, a number of students suggested that the textual language of specific software programs was a detriment to their early participation in the virtual team simulation. One student from Japan was unable to obtain a program that would allow him to participate in the simulation with his personal laptop computer, which was loaded with the Japanese language version of Windows 98. Thus, he had to choose to translate materials from English to Japanese and back to English and vice versa, or to simply use the computer labs, again negating some of the benefits of the simulation. Likewise, several Chinese students found it difficult to use their own Chinese language operating systems with the intranet-based simulation. As with their Japanese counterpart, they had to choose between acting as translator and using computer labs, with the same deleterious effects.

Another key irritant for participants was the issue of interconnectivity – the ability to actually access the required intranet and software, assuming there were no difficulties as identified above. Increasing concerns regarding intranet security have led to the installation of not only intrusive anti-virus software, but also Internet security tools that include firewalls and security screens. Participants found these devices detrimental to their ability to participate in the virtual team environment, as they reported no personal technical abilities to deal with these interconnectivity issues. The solution, to use student computer labs, again effectively negated some of the "real world" benefit of the simulation.

Finally, a minor, but continuing irritant developed due to the less than full reliability of the communication pathway – both intranet and Internet (Butler & Sellbom, 2002). Because the intranet was mounted on a single server, with an offline backup system, any unanticipated interruption would result in any number of negative outcomes (lost data, unplanned disconnect, software freeze, etc.). While no single incidence was a great trauma, recurring unplanned interruptions detracted from the reliability of the virtual team environment, leading to behavior modification and participant dissatisfaction.

Thus, technology itself is a hurdle that must be overcome for the effective operation of cross-cultural virtual teams. But the technology itself is only a part of the problem, as skills in the use of that technology also present a hurdle to cross-cultural virtual teamwork.

4.2   Technology Skills and Language

The demographic data from the participant teams indicate a very wide range of incoming ICT skills. While all the low-context participants were familiar with computer operations, and most were proficient in e-mail and chat room participation, information searches, data retrieval, and post-retrieval compilation, many of the high-context participants lacked some or all of these basic skills. Thus, reflective of the current international business environment (Hill, 2000), participant levels of ICT skills in a cross-cultural virtual team environment are an obvious difference, and a problem.

Another key difference between these two cultural groups was the ability to simply enter data into a data retrieval system – specifically, typing skills. While the low-context participants thought nothing of the requirement to participate in an asynchronous discussion or a chat room while sitting at a keyboard, most (85 percent) of the high-context participants regretted their poor typing skills. This was especially true of those participants from a culture which uses an ideographic language, such as Japanese, Chinese, Thai, or Hindi. These participants found their typing skills woefully inadequate at the beginning of the simulation, and many suggested that, though they had improved during the simulation, they still lacked confidence in their keyboarding skills. This difficulty is in part attributable not only to technology skills, but language skills as well.

Of greater significance in this context was the high-context participants' impression of the "live chat" sessions. This brought to the fore yet another cross-cultural difference which has a significant impact on virtual teamwork – that of language itself. Though all participants had obtained an IELTS score of six or higher as a precondition for university enrolment, for all (100 percent) of those participants for whom English was a second (or third) language, the ability to keep up with a live online chat was reported to be poor. A general comment from the high-context participant group as a whole suggested that they failed to participate (or appeared to fail to participate) in online chat sessions simply because they could not keep up with the discussions. The insertion of tangential material (similar to a normal conversation) would break their train of thought, and by the time they had decided what to say, the conversation had moved on to the second or third topic. Coupled with the lower level of physical data entry skills, most of these participants reported that they simply gave up after a short period of time and read the material posted in the chat room, but did not participate (Rosen & Van de Wiel, 1995). Given that a key element of successful teamwork is the ability to develop an agreed approach to goal achievement, these participants felt as though they were simply left behind, told what to do, and then ignored. Of all the negative feedback from this exercise, this was the most negative.

At the same time, one of the key positive impacts of this virtual team simulation, as reported by the high-context participants, was their impression of the improvement achieved in ICT skills during the simulation. Many reported developing new skills (information search, data manipulation, data analysis, report compilation), as well as improving existing skills – though by far the most noticeable improvement for these participants was in their English language typing skills.

The forgoing indicates that not only is technology itself a hurdle that must be overcome for the effective operation of cross-cultural virtual teams but also that the wide ranging differences in cross-national ICT technical skills also presents a hurdle. Yet another difficulty for cross-cultural virtual teamwork participants stems from the cross-cultural environment.

4.3   Cultural Accommodation

Cultural diversity raises a number of issues that can only be briefly mentioned here. As described in the literature review, culture determines both learning philosophy and communication context (Hall & Hall, 1990; Korac-Kakabadse et al., 2001; Parhizgar, 1998; Rosen & Van de Wiel, 1995). An earlier presentation (Morse 2001) briefly described a series of cross-cultural issues worth noting. The following expands that theme.

Perhaps the most obvious difficulty citied by participants was that of language, a problem that has been raised in the literature (Brogden & Williams, 1995). Intuitively for anyone who has studied a foreign language, the requirement to communicate in a second language rather than one's primary language is problematic. As a result of this condition, several irritants relative to language and linguistic communication were noted by the high-context participants. As mentioned earlier, typing ability presented a difficulty, and the speed at which English language communication takes place can inhibit the comprehensibility of the communication to the non-native speaker. A further identified culturally based communication difficulty is the use of slang, jargon, and idioms that are culturally based (or perhaps simply personal experience based). The continuous use of these culturally based devices led to rising frustration as a number of high-context participants bemoaned the fact that they knew what the words meant, but they simply misunderstood the English grammar and context, thus misunderstanding the point of a virtual conversation.

Not unexpectedly, this led to a backlash on the part of the low-context participants for whom the cultural nuances of the English language were less of a problem. Many saw this communication difficulty as a drawback to the virtual teamwork effort, as they were required to spend more time on explanation, and be clearer in their English language usage, as well as make an effort to reduce the cultural nuances of their communication. To these low-context participants, this meant slower and less effective information sharing, which detracted from their quest for a completed effort. From an academic standpoint, several participants were concerned that they would be penalized as a result of this slowdown – penalties in the form of reduced compensation (lower grades) due to the need to "carry" their cross-cultural counterparts.

But beyond language, cultural differences lead to differing group behavior (Rosen & Van de Wiel, 1995), which significantly affects the development of a virtual team. All low-context participants perceived that high-context team members were reticent, aloof, and passive while participating in this simulation. Thus, they would devote extra effort to give precise instructions, explanations, and guidance to their high-context counterparts, in an effort to draw them further into the virtual team environment. On the other hand, all high-context participants perceived their counterparts as driving, individualistic, and overbearing in their quest for the final objective – compensation through a quality product. Thus, their reaction was reticence, withdrawal, and, in the virtual environment, a resort to "lurking" behavior. As a result, a large majority (79 percent) of the low-context team members perceived their cross-cultural counterparts as "free riders," an interpretation consistent with such behavior in their own cultural context.

A wide range of other minor issues, some peculiar to the specific simulation, or to the specific team, were cited as well. However, the above gives a clear indication that cultural accommodation is yet another hurdle to the effective completion of the cross-cultural virtual team assignment.

5.   CONCLUSIONS

In keeping with recent literature relative to virtual communication that cites a large pool of difficulties that face participants in the virtual environment, the observations of this group of participants by and large replicated and confirmed a wide range of difficulties in adjusting to work in the virtual environment (Harasim, 1990; Hiltz, 1994; Shedletsky & Aitken, 2001; Turoff et al., 1993). These concerns were reiterated by all participants, who found the experience somewhat frustrating, especially when compared to past experiences with face-to-face small team exercises (Althaus, 1997; Hiltz et al., 1993). However, perhaps the perception of the relative priority of those difficulties differs by cultural group. In line with Falk and Carlson (1990) many of the participants – both low-context and high-context - see the virtual environment as a culturally neutral arena, and do not readily perceive cultural differences except through written language usage. In keeping with the literature (Harasim, 1990; Hiltz, 1994; Turoff et al., 1993), all participants recognized a series of benefits associated with the virtual environment. Flexibility in terms of time and location of participation was seen as a very positive benefit of virtual teamwork. Likewise, speed of communication was seen as a positive factor, from the instantaneous feedback of the live chat room to the speed of delivery of e-mail attachments, to the simultaneous editing of team documents/presentations. Also, many of the low-context participants (24 of 41, or 58 percent), and all of the high-context participants suggested the positive benefit of the off-line editing capability of the virtual environment. Unlike a face-to-face team meeting, participants can stop and gather their thoughts while the team meeting continues. For the high-context participants, this additional benefit, to some extent, compensated for the language and cultural difficulties mentioned previously.

However, as might be expected, the high-context participants found this environment significantly more difficult than their low-context counterparts, perhaps because of their relative timidity in the use and interpretation of the English language. Most disconcerting was the lack of visual cues, which meant that these participants needed to obtain meaning from the written word, a skill that few admitted to having developed prior to this simulation. As befits their lack of technical and/or language skills, high-context participants generally agreed that any form of live or synchronous communication experience was simply too fast for them to follow. A majority (17 of 33, or 52 percent) suggested that this would also be true in a non-virtual environment, though all suggested that in that environment at least they thought they could make their presence felt. However, in the virtual environment, because there was no physical presence, these participants expressed a great deal of concern for their lack of inclusion in the group decision making, even when such group decision making was an assigned task.

Having all had prior experience in small group face-to-face exercises before this simulation, both groups of participants suggested that their participation in the virtual team environment felt less organized, and therefore, was a more stressful experience than the equivalent face-to-face team project. There was less ability to influence the behavior of team participants, less commitment to a fixed schedule, and less direct communication in the virtual team environment. Thus, their participation, though generally positive, was to some extent less than ideal – similar to the reported virtual team experience of firms (Duarte & Snyder, 1999).

The above observations indicate that beyond the requirements of successful virtual team experience, there are three additional hurdles that must be overcome for successful goal achievement in the multicultural virtual team environment. First and foremost is the need for reliable technology (the combination of hardware and software) to create the necessary "virtual space" within which the team may operate. While a wide range of literature in a number of disciplines indicate that there is growing confidence in the technological ability to support virtual teamwork (Butler & Sellbom, 2002), and the evidence from this simulation reinforces that literature, there are clear indications that in a cross-border environment, there are significant technological differences – differences which are exacerbated simply by a plethora of hardware and software, all with differing characteristics. Participants indicate that, cross-culturally, this is a significant hurdle for virtual teamwork.

Second and following from the above, individual participants must have minimum technology related skills to function successfully in the created "virtual space." Lack of these skills ensures that participant efforts are diverted into skills development, rather than goal completion. These two, technology compatibility/reliability and technology skills, are likely to be simply an irritant within a single culture or nation. However, operating trans-nationally, these differences are exacerbated by all the same issues which cloud other trans-national cooperation, such as multiple government regulations and regulatory agencies, language differences, and group behavioral differences (as illustrated in this simulation). One needs only to look at the problems of integration in Europe for a current example.

Third,, specific to the cross-cultural virtual team, is the need for cultural accommodation. As evidenced by the experience of these participant teams, the greater the diversity of the virtual team, the higher the likelihood of difficulties in developing participants' sense of community and teamwork. Each issue presents additional hurdles to the virtual team participant, and consequently added difficulties in reaching a successful virtual team outcome.

As a final note, the virtual environment differs from the face-to-face environment – a difference that significantly disadvantages those from alternative culture groups. A growing body of research literature indicates that cultural behavior patterns are unintentionally superimposed on individual participation in the virtual environment, including lurker behavior in a chat room, alternate persona due to the anonymity of electronic communications, and so forth (Althaus, 1997; Goodfellow et al, 2001; Maxwell et al., 2000).

Using the feedback provided by the participants in this virtual teamwork simulation, there appear to be six conditions to achieving effective cross-cultural virtual teamwork: 1) be able to connect to the virtual environment; 2) be able to operate the equipment/software; 3) be able to communicate across cultures; 4) be able to communicate in the virtual environment; 5) be able to internally agree on processes, procedures, and work norms; and 6) strive for clearly defined, achievable objectives or goals. These six conditions indicate much greater difficulty in reaching successful outcomes for virtual cross-cultural teams than for their mono-cultural counterparts. To some extent, with the exception of cultural accommodation, the technology hurdle (Butler & Sellbom, 2002) and the ICT skills hurdle (Woolnough, Guo, Leike, De Alemeida, Ryu, Wang, & Young, 1997) exist in the non-cross cultural environment. However, these differences are highlighted more clearly by those from high-context cultures, indicating the latter four hurdles are significantly more important for cross-cultural participants than for mono-cultural participants.

The observations above indicate a significant potential for further research in this area. Admittedly there is great difficulty in attributing outcomes to behavior in the physical or face-to-face environment, a difficulty highlighted by the continuing effort to refine behavioral and cultural characteristics in a wide range of disciplines external to business and economics. Such attribution is the more difficult in the newer virtual environment – an area in which little work has been done. Likewise, although there is an emerging body of literature relative to the virtual environment, similar research relative to links between culture, behavior, communication activity, and virtual multicultural performance lags significantly. These all appear to be potentially fruitful areas for research as the virtual environment becomes more important to both firms and e-teaching institutions.

5.1   Implications for Firms

For firms, the implications of the technology hurdle are great. To ensure interoperability across hardware configurations, operating systems, and software requires more than a dedicated firm intranet. It also requires the ability to accommodate alternative hardware, operating systems, and software in a compatible communication environment. This implies costs – in terms of physical expenditures, but also in terms of labor resources, in the form of technical support. This invokes yet another cross-cultural concern – intercultural communication in the staff support/service sector.

The differing level of ICT skills across individuals is also problematic for firms, and creates another potential great expense. As indicated by this sample group, widely varying skill levels can lead to frustration and dissatisfaction across a wide range of cultural backgrounds. While this can be solved through training, that training in itself may be costly, especially if it exacerbates the time required for task completion. Taken in conjunction with the technology hurdle, addressing both technology and skills issues may portend significant improvement in the functioning of cross-cultural virtual teams, but at some significant cost to the firm.

Finally, the requirement for cultural accommodation is another major area of concern for firms, especially in light of research which increasingly indicates that firms do not deal well with this issue in the face-to-face environment (Fontaine, 1997). While awareness and understanding play a considerable role in accommodation early on, reduction of irritants between cross-cultural participants portends long-term integration of team members into a composite firm culture – one which requires careful management development and cultivation. Again, this can only be measured in terms of the additional cost to firms, not only in monetary terms, but also in the addition of time to develop such corporate culture. This will be one of the key success factors of truly trans-national learning organizations.

5.2 Implications for E-teaching Institutions

For e-teaching institutions, the technology hurdle implications are just as significant. Though teaching institutions have clearly addressed, to a greater or lesser extent, the issues of hardware, interconnectivity, and software through development of campus computer labs, faculty, school, and university intranets and, in some cases, the dissemination of individual student computers, these institutions have done less well in servicing the off-campus customer – student or faculty. Issues identified above clearly indicate that for e-teaching institutions there are still significant technology issues to be solved, with the same potential cost implications as those for firms.

The differing level of ICT skills across cultural groups is likewise problematic for e-teaching institutions, and another potential great expense. This is all the more pressing an issue as e-teaching becomes not a national, but a worldwide phenomena. Burgeoning education markets portend rapid potential expansion across national boundaries. Yet, much of this effort can be subverted by simple issues of hardware/software incompatibility. As with firms, the potential solution is costly, in both monetary and temporal terms.

Finally, the requirement for cultural accommodation is another major area of concern for e-teaching institutions. While many campuses encourage international student participation, they do so with the expectation that the international student will adjust to the dominant cultural environment. This may not be the most appropriate solution for those institutions wishing to take advantage of the aforementioned burgeoning education markets.

Knowledge, skills, and sustainable values are critical concerns for learning organizations. This research has suggested six hurdles to be overcome to address these concerns in an increasingly multicultural virtual team environment. For firms to efficiently use knowledge resources in an increasingly international economy, awareness of and response to the needs of individual knowledge holders increasingly means accommodation to alternative cultural background. This need will continue to drive a similar need in the e-teaching/e-learning community as it comes to grips with the shift to knowledge resources management. As the global village shrinks, a rapidly rising cultural awareness will set the boundaries for learning organizations – a limitation which can be reduced by redressing the issue of cultural differences in the technology of learning, which should become an integral component of the internal culture of the learning organization.

APPENDIX A: VIRTUAL TERM PROJECT TASK

Introduction

The firm has hired you, a recent University graduate, to work in their international projects group. You were selected because you bring a unique combination of research and analytical skills, and some international management background. The international projects group engages in a wide range of consultancy activities, from feasibility studies to prime contractor management. Most of its work is concentrated in the Asia/Pacific region, as this is the geographical area in which the firm has its greatest expertise and experience.

Background

Among its other activities, the firm has recently been approached by a large multinational enterprise to produce a feasibility study for them. The client firm wishes to build a production facility in the Asian region that will produce handheld palmtop organisers. The client firm has provided the following background information.

The Product

The client firm's palmtop organiser is a hand-held diary that eliminates the need to carry a paper diary. It is small, lightweight, and uses relatively little power. It has a wide range of technical features that make it highly desirable. Although there are a number of similar devices currently entering the market, the client firm believes that its current range of capabilities, coupled with their ability to rapidly adjust the technology to meet market improvements over the relevant period, make their product ideally suited to the growth phase of this product's life cycle.

Demand

After looking at projections for the international demand for palmtop organisers for the next decade, the client firm projects large potential sales, and an annual growth rate of in excess of 20% per year for the next five years, decreasing to a growth rate of 10% per year for the following ten years, as the product becomes more widely distributed, and the technology ages. The demand is expected to be especially high in Asia due to the discriminating, technologically sophisticated consumers, as well as the generally rising consumer income in the rapidly expanding Asian economies.

Production

The firm currently produces in plants located in both North America and the United Kingdom, from which it may initially service potential Asian markets. Each of these plants, while technologically sophisticated, are nearing production capacity, and are only capable of sustaining anticipated Asian demand for 1-2 years at most – about the time it would take to build and staff a new plant. The client firm can currently produce this product in three models (low, standard and premium) for an average cost of NZ$300, NZ$400 and NZ$600 respectively. However, they believe that, when it is fully operational, a state-of-the-art production facility can produce a palmtop organiser for an average price of NZ$150 (lower end) to NZ$300 (upper end), approximately one-half of current cost capability.

For two years, the client firm had been conducting its own internal research, and had thought that expansion into Asian production could provide improved profit margins. However, potential production in Japan, Korea, Taiwan, Hong Kong and Singapore appears to be too expensive to realise any significant profit. Thus, the firm is convinced that any expansion must be located in one of the other countries of Asia.

The client firm currently has a negligible share of the Asian market, but would like to capture 5% of the potential Asian palmtop organiser market within 5 years of opening an Asian production facility, although a smaller market share early in the production process would be acceptable. The client firm expects to devote its existing North American and European palmtop organiser production capacity to satisfy expected increases in demand in those markets, and therefore wishes to satisfy this new Asian demand from its new Asian production facility.

Finance

The client firm has been historically successful with products similar to this, and has managed to establish a very good international credit rating. The client firm suggests it may finance a production facility in the NZ$200 million range, should that be necessary, though a smaller financial burden would be preferred. The client firm would also prefer to recover its fixed costs over a ten year period as well, such that the facility would be fully depreciated by the end of its expected 10 year lifetime. The client firm expects that, at some time within this ten year period, it may have to shift production from palmtop organisers to another product with a similar technology using similar resources. Thus, flexibility in plant operation and utilisation is preferred.

Your Task

You will be teamed with a small group of your contemporaries in the consultancy firm. Using the expertise for which the firm hired you, complete a feasibility study which answers the question: "If the client firm chooses to build a new palmtop organiser production facility in the Asian region, where (specific geographic location) would you suggest as the optimum location for maximum profitability, and why?"

Deliverables:
1. Prepare a <u>summary presentation</u> (7-8 minutes) of the key analytical components of your feasibility study for delivery to your group manager and other senior staff within the consultancy firm (**due -date**);
2. Prepare a <u>detailed written report</u> supporting your recommendation for delivery to your group manager (**due - date**).

APPENDIX B: TEAM ASSIGNMENT DATA WORKSHEET

Student Information Survey: Please provide the following information to assist in creating tutorial groups with complementary skills and experiences. This material will only be used for that purpose, and will be returned to you at the first tutorial session.

1. **Name**: _____
    Preferred to be called? _____

2. **Nationality:**
    New Zealand citizen or permanent resident?   Yes   No
    If not, what is your country of citizenship? _____
    How long have you lived in New Zealand? _____

3. **Language Skills:**
    What is your native (primary) language? _____
    Do you speak/read/write other languages?   No   Yes
    If yes, which ones (in order of fluency, from best to poorer)?
    _____
    _____

4. **Work Experience:**
    If you have been employed full time in a firm in your home country, please briefly describe your full time work experience: _____
    _____

    If you have been employed part time in a firm in your home country, please briefly describe your full time work experience: _____
    _____

    If you have been employed full time or part time in a firm outside your home country, please briefly describe your work experience: _____
    _____
    _____

5. **Travel Experience:**
    Have you lived for an extended period (more than 30 days consecutively) in a country (or countries) other than your home country?   No   Yes
    If yes, which country (or countries), and how long did you live there?

_____
_____

Have you visited (less than 30 days consecutively) a country (or countries) other than your home country?   No   Yes

If yes, which country (or countries), and how long did you visit there?

_____
_____

6. **Team working Experience:**

In this term project, you will work in a small group with three or four students. Have you worked in a small group for an entire term before?   Yes   No

If yes, for which course? Please briefly describe your experience with this term length small group exercise? _____
_____

Have you previously worked in a small group with students from a country other than your

own?   Yes   No

If yes, which country or countries were these student(s) from?

_____
_____

Please briefly describe your experience with this small group?

_____
_____

7. **Academic Programme:**

In which academic programme are you enrolled (indicate from the following)?

Waikato Management School: BMS   MP   PGDiploma   Other

(Specify) _____

Non-Waikato Management School: Major_____

Department/School/Faculty_____

0346.311 International Business Environment is a course pre-requisite. What other international courses (business, language, social sciences) have you completed, if any?

_____
_____

What do you expect to gain by taking this course (or, Why are you taking this course?)

_____
_____

APPENDIX C: DATA COLLECTION INSTRUMENT

1. Completing this project "on-line" was "different" from completing a group project in a physical or "face-to-face" environment. What did you find to be the major differences between this "on-line" group work and "face-to-face" group work?

2. Describe your experience with the communications program "Class Forum & Net-Meeting."

a. What did you find to be "positive" with this tool?
b. What did you find to be "negative" (or frustrating) with this tool?
c. What difficulties did you encounter in learning to effectively use this computer based productivity enhancement tool, other than the computer program itself?
3.   Comparing this "virtual team experience" with other team projects you have completed, what did you learn about "on-line" group interaction?
4.   Comparing this "virtual team experience" with other team projects you have completed, what did you learn about "cross-cultural" interaction?
5.   What did you learn about "international management" by completing this term project?
6.   What "frustrations" did you experience in the process of completing this term project?

Demographics:

a. What is your age?
b. What is your nationality?
c. What is your native (birth) communication language?
d. In what country did you complete your primary/secondary education?

REFERENCES

Althaus, S. (1997). Computer-mediated communication in the university classroom: An experiment with online discussions. *Communication Education, 46* (3), 158-174.

Anderson, P., & Lawton, L. (1992). A survey of methods used for evaluating student performance on business simulations. *Simulation & Gaming, 23* (4), 490-498.

Atsumi, T., Misumi, J., Smith, P., Peter, B., Peterson, M. F., Tayeb, M, Kipnis, D., Minami, H., Yamaguchi, S., & Tanzer, N. (1989). Groups, leadership and social influence. In J. P. Forgas & J. M. Innes (Eds.), *Recent advances in social psychology: An International Perspective* (pp. 369-428). Amsterdam, The Netherlands: North-Holland.

Benson-Amer, R., & Hsieh, T. (1997). Teamwork across time and space. *The McKinsey Quarterly, 4*, (Sept 22), 18-27.

Bhagat, R. S., Kedia, B. L., Crawford, S. E., & Kaplan, M. R. (1990). Cross-cultural issues in organizational psychology: emergent trends and directions for research in the 1990's. In C. L. Cooper & T. Robertson (Eds.), *International Review of Industrial and Organizational Psychology: Volume 5* (pp. 59-99). New York, NY: Wiley.

Brogden, J., & Williams, C. (1995). Using advanced communications and multimedia applications to provide real life benefits to remote rural area: BARBARA. *Computers in Human Services, 12* (1-2), 141-150.

Butler, D., & Sellbom, M. (2002). Barriers to adopting technology for teaching and learning. *Educause Quarterly, 25* (2), 22-28.

Donnellon, A. (1996). *Team Talk: The power of language in team dynamics.* Boston, MA: Harvard Business School Press.

Duarte, D., & Snyder, N. (1999). *Mastering Virtual Teams.* San Francisco, CA: Jossey Bass Publishers.

Editors. (1999). The net imperative: business and the Internet. *The Economist, 351* (8125) Jun 26-Jul 2, 6-44.

Entwistle, N. (1991). *The Impact of Teaching on Learning Outcomes in Higher Education: A Literature Review.* Washington, D. C.: U. S. Gov't Printing Office.

Falk, D., & Carlson, H. (1990). Interactive technology impacts on increasing cultural awareness in education for the human services. *Computers in Human Services, 7* (3-4), 265-276.

Fontaine, G. (1997). Skills for successful international assignments to, from, and within Asia and the Pacific: implications for preparation, support and training. *Management Decision, 35* (8), 631-43.

Fowler, S. (1994). Two decades of using simulation games for cross-cultural training. *Simulation & Gaming, 25* (4), 464-476, 536-554.

Glenn, E. (1981). *Man and Mankind.* Norwood, NJ: Ablex Publishing.

Goodfellow, R., Lea, M., Francisco, G., & Mason, R. (2001). Opportunity and e-quality: Intercultural and linguistic issues in global online learning, *Distance Education, 22* (1), 65-84.

Gundykunst, W. B. (1997). Cultural Variability in Communication: An Introduction, *Communication Research, 24* (4), 327-348.

Gundykunst, W. B., & Ting-Toomey, S. (1988). *Culture and Interpersonal Communication.* Newbury Park, CA: Sage, 1988.

Gupta, I. (2000). *Information Systems: Success in the 21st Century.* Upper Saddle River, NJ: Prentice Hall International, Inc.

Hall, E., & Hall, M. (1990). *Understanding Cultural Differences.* New York, NY: Intercultural Press.

Harasim, L. (Ed.). (1990). *Online Education: Perspectives on a new environment.* New York: Praeger Publishers.

Heywood, M. (1998). *Managing Virtual Teams: Practical techniques for high-technology project management.* Boston, MA: ARTECH House.

Hill, C. W. (2000*). International Business.* Boston, MA: Irwin/McGraw Hill.

Hiltz, S. R. (1994). *The Virtual Classroom: Learning without limits via computer networks.* 2nd ed. Norwood, NJ: Ablex Publishing Company.

Hiltz, S. R., & Wellman, B. (1997). Asynchronous Learning Networks as Virtual Classrooms. *Communications of the ACM, 40* (9), 44-49.

Hofstede, G. (1991). *Cultures and Organizations: Software of the Mind.* Maidenhead, U.K.: McGraw-Hill.

Hofstede, G. (1980). *Culture's Consequence: International Differences in Work-related Values.* Newbury Park, CA: Sage.

Jacobs, N. (2000). Issues concerning incorporation of virtual team skills into the curriculum. *Seventh Educational Innovations in Economics and Business (EDINEB) Conference.* Newport Beach, CA., 21 July.

Katzenbach, J., & Smith, D. (1993). The discipline of teams. *Harvard Business Review,* (Mar/Apr), pp. 111-120.

Korac-Kakabadse, N., Kouzmin, A., Korac-Kakabadse, A., & Savery, L. (2001). Low- and High-Context Communication Patterns: Towards mapping cross-cultural encounters. *Cross Cultural Management – An International Journal, 8* (2), 3-24.

Larreche, J. C. (1987). On simulation in business education and research, *Journal of Business Research, 15*, December.

Lipnack, J., & Stamps, J. (1997). *Virtual Teams: Reaching Across Space, Time and Organizations with Technology.* New York, NY: John Wiley & Sons.

Makepeace, E. (1996). Overseas students – Challenges of institutional adjustment. *OECD Report on the Internationalization of Education.* Standing Conference on Educational Development (SCED) Paper 56.

Mankin, D., Cohen, S., & Bikson, T. (1996). *Teams and Technology*. Boston, MA: Harvard Business School Press.

Maxwell, G., Adam, M., Pooran, J., & Scott, B. (2000). Cultural diversity in learning: developing effective learning for South East Asian hospitality management students. *Cross Cultural Management – An International Journal, 7* (3), 3-12.

Morse, K. O. (2003). Does one size fit all? Exploring asynchronous learning in a multicultural environment. *Journal of Asynchronous Learning Networks, 7* (1), Feb, 37-55. [Available: http://www.aln.org/publications/jaln/index.asp]

Morse, K. O. (2002). International management virtual teamwork: A simulation. *Developments in Business Simulation and Experiential Learning, 29* (1), 121-127. Reprinted in the Bernie Keys Library, 3rd ed., Hugh M. Cannon (ed). [Available: http://www.ABSEL.org].

Morse, K. O. (2001). International management: Early experience in multicultural virtual team interaction. Presentation at *8th Annual Educational Innovations in Economics & Business Conference*. Nice, France, 22 June.

Neuendorf, K. (2002). *The Content Analysis Guidebook*. Thousand Oaks, CA: Sage Publications.

Osland, G. E. (1990). Doing business in China: A framework for cross-cultural understanding, *Marketing Intelligence and Planning, 8* (4), 4-14.

Parhizgar, K. D. (1998). International cross-cultural collaborative teaching and training theories (ICCCTTT), *Journal of Teaching in International Business, 9* (3), 21-41.

Richards, L. (2000). Using NVivo in Qualitative Research. Doncaster, Victoria, Australia: QSR International Pty. Ltd.

Ronen, S., & Shenkar, O. (1985). Clustering countries on attitudinal dimensions: A review and synthesis. *Academy of Management Review, 10* (3), 435-54.

Rosen, L., & Van de Wiel, M. (1995). Computer anxiety: A cross-cultural comparison of university students in ten countries. *Computers in Human Behavior, 11* (1), 45-64.

Schneider, S., & Barsoux, J. (2003). *Managing Across Cultures* 2nd ed. Harlow, Essex, England: Pearson Education Ltd.

Servaes, J. (1989). Cultural identity and modes of communication. In J. A. Anderson (Ed.), *Communication Yearbook 12*. Newbury Park, CA: Sage, 383-416.

Shapiro, C., & Varian, H. (1999). *Information Rules: A strategic guide to the network economy*. Boston, MA: Harvard Business School Press.

Shedletsky, L., & Aitken, J. (2001). The paradoxes of online academic work, *Communication Education, 50* (3), 206-217.

Townsend, A., De Marie, A., & Hendrichson, A. (1998). Virtual teams: Technology and the workplace of the future. *The Academy of Management Executive, 12* (3), 17-29.

Turoff, M., Hiltz, S. R., Bahgat, A., & Rana, A. (1993). Distributed group support systems. *MIS Quarterly*. December, pp. 399-417.

Woolnough, B., Guo, Y., Leike, M. S., De Alemeida, M., Ryu, T., Wang, Z., & Young, D. (1997). Factors affecting student choice of career in science and engineering: Parallel studies in Australia, China, England, Japan and Portugal. *Research in Science and Technological Education, 15* (1), 105-121.

Chapter 5

COLLABORATIVE LEARNING APPLIED IN THE ORIENTATION PROCESS OF UNDERGRADUATE STUDENTS

Myrta Rodríguez
ITESM Campus Mazatlán, Mexico

1.   INTRODUCTION

Universities are institutions in continuous transformation. They are involved in the process where the teaching-learning model has been changing, from a model centered on teaching to a model centered on learning and integrating teaching of knowledge, skills, attitudes, and values. Although students starting this academic level have different backgrounds and learning models, they must participate in the new community, in many cases by actively working together instead of "consuming" education as an individual. Some will adapt fast to the new environment, some may not. Could the university help them to jump barriers and support a better adaptation process?

The study presented in this chapter is part of a project embedded in the transformation process in Tecnológico de Monterrey (ITESM), an educational system in Mexico with 33 campuses in different cities. Since 1995 this University is working on changing the educational model from a model centered on teaching to a model centered on learning. One of the tools in this process is collaborative learning. Collaborative learning is implemented to help the students to integrate efficiently, in a confident setting, developing academic skills to full capacity. It is expected that the collaborative learning process, when implemented in an effective way, will help the students to set the basis for adaptation in the following years of their

R.G.Milter et al. (eds.), Educational Innovation in Economics and Business IX, 75–89.
©2004 *Springer. Printed in the Netherlands.*

study, a generation of students that will integrate real high quality teams that will solve the challenges of their courses, with a solid support for the various projects in each discipline. Beside the courses with collaborative learning processes as described in this chapter, there are courses working with problem-based learning, project-based learning, and case methodology.

Because students might be inexperienced with collaborative learning settings, Fogarty and Bellanca (1992) suggest that the inroad in the collaborative learning model must be incremented, starting with simple and specific teamwork activities designed for class work. Afterwards, these activities can gradually increase in complexity and the level of students' involvement. Additionally, resistance to change might occur. The initial perception of a student involved in a learning model, which is an educational model where he or she is expected to participate actively to create learning, is naturally based on the previous experiences that a student may identify as school life. When a student has participated in educational processes based on teaching, referring to the situation where a student is a listener and the professor is the transmitter of knowledge, resistance to a new academic learning environment might occur. According to Hertz-Lazarowitz, Kirkus, & Miller, (1992), students are often reluctant to ask for help from their peers, because this is a kind of dependency, perceived as a negative characteristic. Furthermore, in the new learning environment, the students have to leave the "areas of comfort" and work actively as well as collaboratively to acquire significant knowledge and skills.

Because resistance to change might happen, one of the goals of the research project was to monitor the students' appreciation of the collaborative learning process after experiencing it for the first time at our institution. The results of the study, measuring the students' change in their perception of collaborative learning, are presented in this chapter.

2. THEORETICAL FRAMEWORK

2.1 Changing the Learning Model

Universities recognized the importance of changing the educational model from the traditional teacher-centered model to the student-centered model. Some barriers made this change difficult (Christensen, Garvin, & Sweet, 1991), with students addicted to the passive teaching model with a teacher at front of the room (Akerson, Medina, & Wang, 2002; Caprio, McIntosh, & Koritz, 1989; Felder, Stice, & Rugarcia, 2000).

For teachers as well as for the students, change implies a significant challenge. To some of them, the active approach is "unknown" and "dangerous," because they can see more work coming but probably can't see more rewards. As Christensen et al. (1991) explain:

> Many instructors are uncomfortable with the loss of control implied by active learning, and find the lack of predictability unsettling. Students accustomed to lectures often have a similar reaction. But their concerns have different roots. Active learning requires high levels of personal involvement, and such involvement is lacking in most students' educational backgrounds. Many fear that they will fail in the new environment or, worse yet, will expose their true selves. This creates enormous self-doubt and vulnerability; without a supportive learning climate, cultivated and led by the instructor, resistance is inevitable (Cornerstones and Building Blocks section, para. 5).

In order to decrease the resistance to the student-centered learning model with a focus on active learning, the collaborative learning model was implemented gradually taking into account the students' development as well as their different backgrounds. Collaborative learning was used as a didactic strategy for the students' adaptation to this new teaching and learning model.

2.2 Collaborative Learning

Collaborative learning as a teaching tool is strongly based on the Social Interdependence theory (Lewin, 1935) and has been studied and promoted for the last 30 years by David and Roger Johnson (Johnson, Johnson, & Smith, 1998). Basically, the technique considers teamwork in small groups with specific and planned activities that include five basic elements:

- Positive interdependence. Students working together build the group success. Students perceive that they need the others to reach the goals.
- Individual responsibility. Individuals are responsible for their own learning, as well as the teammates' learning. Everyone must do his or her job.
- Face-to-face interaction. Students must promote participation as well as encourage the classmates' job.
- Interpersonal skills. The team needs to communicate effectively and to solve conflicts if necessary.
- Group processing. Teams must discuss how they do the job, make reflections about the "good" and "bad" procedures, in order to improve.

We differentiate between three different types of teams (Johnson, Johnson, & Smith, 1998).

1. Base teams. Students stay all the course in the same base team, working a few minutes at the beginning of each class, reflecting on the last class they attended, sharing classroom experiences, and giving each other support and respect. Base team activities include two basic elements: face-to-face interaction and interpersonal skills.

2. Formal teams. Teams are formed to work in a group during the class or to make the homework. Students are requested to reach some specific objectives by working together, usually during one class or more time. Students could be moved in different formal groups for different activities. Formal team activities are designed including the five elements in an intentional form.

3. Informal teams. These teams are used when the main activity in class is lecture. The professor stops from time to time and asks the students to solve a problem, or answer a question, sharing ideas and working with one or two classmates during a few minutes. Informal team activities are designed including the elements of face-to-face interaction and interpersonal skills.

As most students are not familiar with working collaboratively in teams, students need to develop team skills. To facilitate this process, the level of difficulty in assignments evolves from simple to complex, allowing time for the group to grow in strength as a team.

According to a classification designed by Johnson and Johnson (1997), the skills included in collaborative learning go through four growing stages. Forming skills correspond to basic and simple elements, for example, "Staying in a group." Functioning skills are more complex as are abilities to perform within the group, for example, "Sharing ideas and opinions." Formulating skills correspond to formal methods that process materials, such as "Summaries complete lessons orally." Finally, Fermenting skills stimulate cognitive conflict and reasoning, for example, "Criticizing ideas without criticizing the person."

When it is intended to learn collaboratively in a group, it is important to explore first of all whether the members of the group are familiar with this work style, what their experiences and expectations are. If the group does not have a reference, or has had bad experiences, this might lead to resistance to collaborative learning.

The Johnson and Johnson's model is part of the framework for the instructional model used at ITESM (see Table 1).

Table 1. Collaborative Activities Performed during the Different Weeks of the Course

Growing Stage	Activities to perform (skills)	Week
Forming	Stay with the group	1-4
	Take turns	
	Listen and look at speaker	
	No "Put-Downs"	
Functioning	Share ideas and opinions	5-7
	Offer to explain or clarify	
	Ask for facts and reasoning	
	Encourage everyone to participate	
	Express support and acceptance	8-10
	Paraphrase other's contribution	
	Describe feelings when appropriate	
Formulating	Summarize out loud completely	11-13
	Check understanding by demanding vocalization	
Fermenting	Criticize ideas without criticizing people	14-17
	Test reliability by checking the group's work	

3. RESEARCH METHOD

3.1 Introduction

The educational model presented in this chapter addresses the issue of Collaborative learning as a tool to support high school students in their adaptation to a new academic level in undergraduate studies. The research presented focuses on the students' appreciation of the collaborative learning model as a teaching and learning model and the change in their appreciation after experiencing this model. It is an exploratory study where the evaluation instrument has not been previously tested. The study was applied in Mexico, at the Tecnológico de Monterrey (ITESM), Mazatlán Campus.

3.2 Research Question

Could collaborative learning, developed in an explicit form, conceptually as well as in procedure, help high school students to adapt to a new academic level in undergraduate studies? Does this process change their perceptions about a model centered on learning?

3.3   Procedure

The project began in August 2001, with the designing of an introductory class that was given to all of the freshmen students enrolling in the undergraduate level. Four programs were involved: Industrial Engineering, Information Systems Engineering, Business Administration, and the Liberal Arts program where a student completes credits and later selects his program.

The introductory class was originally designed as an informative session. It was modified to facilitate students' integration, including the objective of developing collaborative learning skills and trust. The objective was twofold:

1. To facilitate student integration in their new academic encounter, offering, through the use of collaborative learning, the liberty and confidence of belonging to a group.
2. To explain what collaborative learning is, with the intention that students accept the Institutional educational model and develop the abilities required for the academic results to be outstanding.

For each undergraduate major, the same model was followed in the four different programs. Professors followed the same collaborative learning design, working together through the implementation process.

The model of the course included the different types of teams presented before (base, formal, and informal) and used all of them in the four different study programs (Business Administration, Industrial Engineering, System Information, and Liberal Arts).

Base groups consisted of three members, people that did not know each other but at least had a minimum characteristic in common, which was checked by asking them about their preferences. They worked throughout the semester with the intention of giving students the time to interact and share ideas regarding the content as well as personal aspects. These groups had the function of creating trust and support towards their classmates in the team.

Formal and informal teams participated in activities oriented to reach the academics goals, referring to activities with cognitive objectives about the topics included in the syllabus, but also, activities to develop the collaborative skills from formation up to fermentation (see Table 1).

Each class had the same structure. First, at the beginning of each session, the students went to their base groups. They shared experiences from the last class they participated in and reflected on some personal questions suggested by the professor. Next, the professor presented the topic of the class as well as the collaborative skill to be used. Afterwards, the students worked together in formal teams. At the end of the session, the formal teams processed their work – collaborative process and product- reflecting on the areas of improvement and success. When the class was mostly lecture-based, the professor worked with informal teams.

Professors of all four groups met before and after each session to exchange experiences and to complete their registration forms. All of them worked with collaborative learning and also explained each part of the technique to their students, in an explicit and planned form. They acted under the premise that once the student understood the nature of this work style, the student would take full advantage of its benefits, accept it as an efficient way of learning and would develop the skills involved.

It is important to mention that the four groups in this study belonged to different disciplines, but all the courses were similar in content. In the first half of the course, all groups worked according to the same instructional design. This part was mainly related to the programs and processes that the students would encounter along their career. In the second part of the course the design of the activities was shared, but for each group the content was oriented towards the discipline the student was going to study (the undergraduate program). Along the course all the activities aimed to develop collaborative skills, all groups following the same procedure.

The course started with simple activities and the students were gradually challenged. The students engaged in well-structured activities aiming for group integration, as a preparation for later, more complicated, activities.

In order to support the process, a folder was handed to each team. As their first group activity, after forming base teams, they had to find a name for their team and decorate their folder. This was the first activity aimed at bringing the group together by finding its common personality. It intended to help the students to feel comfortable in the group.

The folder was gradually "constructed" by the teams. They included all their comments reflecting on cognitive topics as well as collaborative aspects (Table 2). Together with the observations by a student-observer (Table 3) and by the professor (Table 4), this formed the "Team profile."

Table 2. Example of Questions for Reflection to be Answered in the Registration Forms as Used by each Base Group during Each Session
(The questions could vary depending on the activity)

Example of Question	Objective
What kind of music you like? Which is your best memory from childhood?	Provide personal support to members. Questions about personal items to introduce teammates and develop confidence.
Could the team write five principals items from this lesson? Would the team clarify the doubt from the others? Did your partner make a good homework?	Discuss what was learned. Check for doubts. Check progress.
Our group is really good at… Next time we will be better if… My teammates really helped the group when they…	Processing. Check the process make like team, ensuring every group member receives positive feedback.

Table 3. Examples of a Registration Form used by the Teacher after the Class

	Observations and Comments
Strategy	
Resources	
Evaluation	
Time distribution	
Motivation/ participation	
Abilities	
Others	

Table 4. Example of a Collaborative Skills Registration Form, Indicating the Frequency of Skills Demonstrated by Each Student as Observed by a Student-Observer

Student name	Share ideas and opinions	Offer to explain or clarify	Encourage everyone to participate
Ana	///	/	
Arturo		////	////
Omar	//		/

3.4   Research Method

The collaborative learning process was monitored in a variety of ways, by interviewing students, analyzing the registration forms (Tables 3, 4, and 5) and by administering a student evaluation questionnaire. In this chapter, we will focus on the results of the student evaluation questionnaire as the analysis of the other data is still in a premature phase.

In order to measure students' change in appreciation of the collaborative learning process, the student evaluation questionnaire was administered twice. The student evaluation questionnaire was first administered in the orientation course at ITESM, before the students had contact with the class or classmates. The questionnaire was administered a second time at the end of the course, one day before the final session.

3.5   Sample

The evaluation instrument (questionnaire) was administered to 70 students at the first session and to 68 students at the last session. Table 5 presents the number of students in each group.

Table 5. Number of Students Participating in Each Group

Introduction to Industrial Engineering (IIS)	28 students
Introduction to Systems Engineering (ISI)	11 students
Introduction to Business (LAE)	23 students
Introduction to Liberal Arts (TC)	8 students

3.6   Instruments

The student evaluation questionnaire consisted of five general questions to measure some parameters related to the collaborative learning process. The first question intended to measure the extent to which students had prior experiences with collaborative learning. The second question intended to measure a general appreciation of teamwork. At the first administration, it refers to the prior experiences of the students. At the second administration, the answers to this question reflect the students' experiences with collaborative learning in this course. Questions 3 and 4 refer to the effects of collaborative learning on the level of knowledge and skills. Question 5 is parallel to the second question, asking for a general appreciation. Table 6 presents the questions.

Table 6. Questionnaire Applied to the Study Groups (pre-test and post-test)

QUESTION	OPTIONAL ANSWER				
Have you ever participated in teamwork for assignments? (For example, homework, projects, presentations)			Yes	No	I am not sure
What has been your experience in teamwork for assignments?	Excellent	Very good	Satisfactory	Bad	Terrible
Do you consider teamwork helps you to have a better learning of your courses?	Definitely yes	Yes, in general	A bit	I don't think so	Definitely no
Do you think teamwork helps to develop individual abilities?	Definitely yes	Yes, in general	A bit	I don't think so	Definitely no
In your courses, would you like to work collaboratively, in teams?	Definitely yes	Yes, in general	A bit	I don't think so	Definitely no

4.   RESEARCH STUDY

4.1   Method of Analysis

The data of the questionnaire were analyzed with MINITAB software for comparative testing. Each of the 5 questions had optional answers. The rating scale was recoded to a numerical scale, from 1 to 5, with 1 representing the most desirable answer and 5 the least desirable answer. Answers were registered according to the questionnaire results.

To control for differences in perceptions between the four groups at the beginning of the class, an ANOVA was performed. The results indicated that there were no significant statistical differences. This means we can affirm that the groups were comparable with respect to their perceptions of collaborative learning.

To measure changes in the students' perceptions after the experiences with collaborative leaning in the course under study, paired t-test were used on the total sample level. Additionally, we conducted a breakdown analysis on the level of the programs.

4.2   Results

In this section, the results of the student evaluation questionnaire are presented on two levels. First, the data concerning the change in perceptions for the total sample of students are presented. Second, the results of the breakdown analysis on the level of the programs are described.

4.2.1   Students' perceptions on the sample level

The results in Table 7 show a significant increase in the students' appreciation of collaborative learning after their experiences in the course under study.

Table 7. Students' Perceptions Before and After Experiencing Collaborative Learning in the Course

Process	Questions	Before	After	Difference	t	P value	Result
Study Groups	2	2.0882	1.8088	0.2794	2.92	0.005	Significant
	3	2.0588	1.5735	0.4853	5.25	0.000	Significant
	4	1.7353	1.4118	0.324	3.19	0.002	Significant
	5	1.7761	1.4627	0.3134	3.91	0.000	Significant

With respect to the first question of the study, the data indicated that all students of the sample have prior experiences with working in teams on assignments.

Table 8 shows the percentages of the students' answers for each option before and after experiencing collaborative learning in this course.

Table 8. Percentages of "Before-after" Answers for Each Question (from 2 to 5). Results of the Student Choices

Ques-tion	Choice 1		Choice 2		Choice 3		Choice 4		Choice 5	
	Before	After	Before	After	Before	After	Before	After	Before	After
Q2	11.42	39.7	67.14	41.17	21.42	17.64	0	1.47	0	0
Q3	18.57	50.00	60.00	42.64	18.57	7.35	2.85	0	0	0
Q4	44.28	63.23	38.57	32.35	15.71	4.41	1.42	0	0	0
Q5	34.78	55.88	53.62	41.17	11.59	2.94	0	0	0	0

When asking, "What has been your experience when working in teams for assignments?" - the percentage of students answering "Excellent" increased from 11.42 to 39.7 percent. For almost all other options, the percentage of students decreased. This result indicates that the general perception of collaborative learning has improved.

For the question "Do you consider teamwork helps you to have a better learning of your courses?" - the percentage of students answering

"Definitely yes" increased from 18.57 to 50 percent. The results indicate that students changed their perception that collaborative learning does indeed help them to improve learning in their courses.

For the question, "Do you think teamwork helps you to develop individual abilities?" - the percentage of students answering "Definitely yes" increased from 44.28 to 63.23 percent. For the second option, "Yes, in general" - there was a similar pattern. The results can be considered as favorable.

The results for the last question of the questionnaire "In your courses, would you like to work collaboratively, in teams?" showed a similar pattern as the previous questions. The percentage of students answering "Definitely yes" increased from 34.78 to 55.88 percent. For the other options, the changes were smaller.

In general, we can conclude that the results indicate that the students' perceptions changed in a positive way. This means they appreciate collaborative learning more after experiencing it in this course.

4.2.2   Students' perceptions on the program level

The group results on the level of the program are shown in Table 9.

IIS	Introduction to Industrial Engineering group
ISI	Introduction to Systems Engineering group
LAE	Introduction to Business group
TC	Introduction to Liberal Arts group
M (std) Pre	Average result in pre-test application
M (std) Post	Average result in post-test application
t	t-pared result (for pre-test and post-test comparison)
P	P-value

Table 9. Group Results for Significant Perception Change on Questions 2-5 at 95% Reliability

	IIS M(std) Pre	IIS M(std) Post	IIS t	IIS P	ISI M(std) Pre	ISI M(std) Post	ISI t	ISI P	LAE M(std) Pre	LAE M(std) Post	LAE t	LAE P	TC M(std) Pre	TC M(std) Post	TC t	TC P
Q2	1.964	1.643	1.97	.059	2.0	1.90	0.10	0.36	2.304	1.87	3.15	.005	2.0	2.143	-0.55	0.604
Q3	1.893	1.536	2.59	0.015	2.2	1.500	3.28	0.010	2.174	1.565	3.73	0.001	2.143	1.857	0.79	0.457
Q4	1.750	1.286	3.86	0.001	1.5	1.6	-0.43	0.678	1.696	1.435	1.37	0.186	2.143	1.571	1.19	0.28
Q5	1.786	1.357	3.58	0.001	1.90	1.70	0.80	0.443	1.783	1.435	2.58	0.017	1.50	1.667	-1.0	0.363

For the second question, "What has been your experience in teamwork for doing assignments?" - the results indicate that only for the Business students (LAE) there was a significant change in perceptions. The other groups apparently had no significant change.

Regarding the third question, "Do you consider teamwork helps you to have a better learning of your courses?" - it can be concluded that the groups that showed a significant improvement were the "Industrial Engineers" (IIS), the "Business students" (LAE) and the "Information Systems Engineers" (ISI). For the "Liberal Arts" group (TC), there was no significant change.

For the forth question, "Do you think teamwork helps you to develop individual abilities?" - the only group that showed a significant improvement was the "Industrial Engineers" (IIS).

With respect to the fifth question, "In your courses, would you like to work collaboratively, in teams?" - the groups that presented improvement in their perception were the "Industrial Engineers" (IIS) and the "Business students" (LAE).

The Liberal Arts students did not seem to have changed perceptions concerning collaborative learning. Although this group followed the same process like others, probably one aspect can offer an explanation for the results. For the Liberal Arts program, the group consisted of students studying various disciplines. This implies that they did not belong to the same academic program and therefore were probably less familiar with each other. The impact of the factor "familiarity between team members" on collaborative learning is important to investigate in future stages of the project.

5.   CONCLUSIONS

The results of the student evaluation questionnaire have been satisfactory to the research project group. The objectives of this project are considered partially reached, as there were many areas that can be improved and will be included in the following stage of the project, that is, with new enrolled students for the Fall-2002 generation.

Regarding the objective "improving the appreciation of the students towards the ITESM educational model," the data are promising. The students demonstrated a significant change in their appreciation of collaborative learning, as part of the ITESM model.

However, on the level of the four programs participating in this study, the results indicate that the Industrial Engineering group and Business Administration group showed the most significant changes in appreciation.

Further research is necessary to unravel the reasons for these differences on the program level.

The students' development of collaborative skills has become a topic of concern for the ITESM Campus Mazatlán. The application of the instructional design as described in this chapter intends to support new enrolled students to develop a sound base for collaborative learning in the following years of their study. We hope to contribute to a generation of students that will learn in and from high quality teams, dealing collaboratively with the challenges the courses and the various projects in each discipline offer. The institute will implement collaborative learning in all its courses. The students' development of collaborative skills will be at the heart of the entire curriculum and will be monitored, not only per semester, but gradually during the curriculum.

On the basis of follow-up research, administering the student evaluation questionnaire to future cohorts of students, and the analyses of the registration forms as additional quantitative data, we hope to be able to improve the instructional design of the collaborative learning process for freshmen as described in this chapter.

REFERENCES

Akerson, V. L., Medina, V., & Wang, N. (2002). A collaborative effort to improve university engineering instruction. *School Science and Mathematics*. Bowling Green, Dec 2002.

Caprio, M. W., McIntosh, W., & Koritz, H. (1989). Science education for the non-major: The problems. *Journal of College Science Teaching, 18*, 424-425.

Christensen, R., Garvin, D., Sweet, A. (1991). *Education for Judgment*. Boston. Harvard Business School. Retrieved on May 06, 2004, from http://www.hbsaai.org/case_method.htm

Felder, R. M., Stice, J. E., & Rugarcia, A. (2000). The future of engineering education: Making reform happen. *Chemical Engineering Education, 34 (3)*, 208-215.

Fogarty, R., & Bellanca, J. (1992). The new school "lecture": Cooperative interactions that engage student thinking. In: Davidson and Worsham (Eds.), *Enhancing Thinking Through Cooperative Learning*. NY: Teachers College Press.

Hertz-Lazarowitz, R., Kirkus, V., & Miller, N. (1992). An overview of the theoretical anatomy of cooperation in the classroom. In: Hertz-Lazarowitz (Ed.), *Interaction in cooperative Groups: The theoretical anatomy of group learning*. NY: Cambridge University Press.

Johnson, D. W., & Johnson, F. (1997). *Joining together: Group theory and group skills*. Boston : Allyn & Bacon.

Johnson, D. W., Johnson, R. & Smith, K. (1998). *Active Learning: Cooperation in the college classroom*. Edina, MN: Interaction Book Company.

Lewin, K. (1935). *A Dynamic Theory of Personality*. New Cork: McGraw Hill.

PART 3

TRANSITIONING FROM ACADEMIC SETTINGS TO THE WORKPLACE

Chapter 6

ONLINE LEARNING: LEARNER'S LIBERATION?

Tessa Owens[1]
Liverpool Hope University College, UK

1.   INTRODUCTION

This research tracks the experiences of a group of third-year undergraduates in one of their final modules prior to graduation. The module, entitled "Work-Based Learning," required students to conduct a project in a business organization, in which they were expected to apply academic theory to real problems encountered by their organizations.

This module moved students away from the traditional university mode of learning and teaching characterized by theory-bound lectures and seminars. Students set their own questions, on which they would be assessed, in negotiation with the employer and academic tutor, and were expected to address these questions in methodical ways, applying the theory learned in previous modules to a real business problem.

There was one other notable difference to the students' typical experiences. They had, until this point, been traditionally taught in classrooms and lecture theatres. Due to the nature of this module, students were at their work placements on different days, and experience suggested that it was difficult to keep in touch with them on a regular basis. Previous students had also reported a certain degree of isolation when completing this module.

[1] My grateful thanks to Bill Norton, Honorary Research Associate in Learning and Teaching for his help in the data analysis for this chapter.

R.G.Milter et al. (eds.), Educational Innovation in Economics and Business IX, 93–115.
©2004 *Springer. Printed in the Netherlands.*

This module, therefore, was conducted using *Learnwise*, the university's new virtual learning environment (VLE). It was anticipated that this VLE would provide the medium for students to stay in contact with one another and provide a forum in which they could discuss their individual business problems and become involved in the co-construction of knowledge.

The innovation of work-based learning as a learning and teaching method was also believed to have potential impact on the students as learners. Recent educational debate has built upon the concept of "deep and surface" learning introduced by Marton and Säljö (1976), and the tutor wanted to examine what impact this module may have on the students' approaches to learning (Tait, Entwistle, & McCune, 1998). There was a desire to discover whether exposure to real problems altered the ways students learned. If this was the case, there could be an impact upon these students as learners in the future. This research was also intended to consider the wider implications for learning in general, of moving from a highly theoretical base, to more "blended" problem-solving approaches, and to assess what potential role VLEs may have in facilitating this.

Evaluations of this ground-breaking module and of the student learning would appear to be incomplete if limited to the tutor and academic theory. Therefore, employers were asked to contribute their views of this method of student learning and to comment on their requirements of graduates as employees; and students were asked to comment on their experiences, and evaluate their own learning in this context.

This module appeared to have the potential to "liberate" the students in a number of important ways. They were free to determine the specifics of the problems they addressed. There were no pre-set investigations or unknown examination questions. They were liberated to a large extent in terms of time and space, doing their work at times they could control. They were liberated in that they initiated the questions and determined "the curriculum" depending on their individual needs. They may be liberated in that they could begin to use each other, business leaders, and other non-traditional resources to gain answers to the problems they encountered. They may even be liberated from the naive perception of the tutor as expert, of an understanding of knowledge as concrete and applicable, and of the belief in absolute solutions that, if applied, had no further consequences.

2.   METHODOLOGY

The ASSIST questionnaire (Tait, Entwistle, & McCune, 1998) was given to the students at the start and upon completion of the 12-week module. There were 13 students studying on this module, eight of whom completed both questionnaires. In this questionnaire students describe their learning and studying preferences. It was hoped that the results of this questionnaire would illustrate the approaches to learning that these students were taking and attempt to gauge any change in their approach at the conclusion of the course. The results of this analysis are located in the Research Results section.

Semi-structured telephone interviews also took place with employers at the students' placements. Employers were aware that these students did not meet in the traditional sense and that they discussed their projects and sought support via a virtual learning environment. They were asked to appraise the students' contribution to their organizations and comment on any perceived advantages/disadvantages of the use of a VLE.

All students were required to reflect on their learning during this module as part of the final assessment. A summary of these reflections is provided, in particular concentrating on the use of the VLE as an effective learning environment, and on their own learning.

3.   THEORETICAL FRAMEWORK

The recent expansion in student numbers within Higher Education is well documented. Many writers have commented upon the heavy demands on today's students in terms of their work and family responsibilities (e.g., McInnes & McNaught, 1995, cited in Peat, 2002) to the extent that full-time attendance at university has increasingly become an unrealistic goal. "Widening Participation" has also influenced the nature of students attending universities, who are increasingly from more diverse backgrounds, with multiple demands on their time. Due to these demands on their time, students have been less able to attend their classes and access libraries and other, traditional, learning resources.

Biggs (1999) points out that not only are there more students but that these students have a different profile from the traditional "high achieving" school leaver, with a wider *range of ability* now found within classes. This is further exacerbated as increases in numbers of students have not been followed by increases in numbers of staff, and class sizes have continued to grow (Race, 1998). This expansion has revealed deficiencies in the types of learning and teaching environments used by universities (Hattie & Marsh, 1996; Rowland, 1996), and it has been anticipated that this will have a profound effect on teaching and learning for all students both in educational establishments and work organizations (Inglis, Ling, & Joosten, 1999; Ryan, Scott, Freeman, & Patel, 2000).

Information communication technology has been heralded as a potential savior in this scenario. It is possible to deliver to a mass international audience reaching more students (particularly traditionally excluded students), while simultaneously improving IT skills and potentially gaining economies of scale in terms of the numbers of academic staff employed. There are many however, who are concerned by such a development. This move towards online learning follows the trend towards online "everything," and some believe this could seriously damage the quality and outcomes of the learning experience. The graduate we produce may be less valuable because of this.

In order to ensure a quality educational product, it would therefore be appropriate to consider effective pedagogical practice. The findings in this field have been comprehensively discussed by Prosser and Trigwell (1999), and it is not the writer's intention to review this here. The essential focus originated from the work by Marton and Säljö (1976) on the conceptions of deep and surface approaches to learning and subsequent research by Biggs (1987) and Ramsden (1988).

With a deep approach to learning, the students intend to understand and seek meaning from their studies. These students relate concepts to existing experience, they are able to distinguish between new ideas and existing knowledge, and to critically evaluate and determine key themes and concepts. The surface approach is typified by an intention to complete a task, memorize information, with these students making no distinction between new ideas and existing knowledge. They treat the task as though it were externally imposed (as extrinsic). The students want to offer the impression that maximum learning has taken place, which they achieve through superficial levels of cognitive processing. Facts are learned without a meaningful framework.

Biggs (1987) identified a third approach to study, the strategic or achieving approach. Here the stress is on organizing learning specifically to obtain a high grade. With this goal, a deep learner may adopt some of the techniques of the surface learner to meet the requirements of a specific activity. Thus taking a deep approach is not a fixed and unchanging characteristic. The achieving approach is intimately linked with assessment.

In designing this module assessment, the tutor determined what was a key driver in determining the student's motivations and achievements (Brown, Bull, & Race, 1999). Ramsden (1992, p. 187) warns us that "from our students' point of view, assessment always defines the actual curriculum." If this is so, then our students will only learn what they think they will be tested on. The design of assessments must therefore be carefully considered. In Biggs' (1999) terms, assessment needs to be aligned to the curriculum. As critical discussion was one of the learning outcomes of the module, it needed to be assessed. Twenty percent of the grade available for the module was therefore given for online contributions. Students were expected to demonstrate their skills in listening and questioning, to be constructive and supportive, and to demonstrate their ability to apply the concepts under discussion.

The additional module grades were made up from an oral presentation (20 percent) in which they outlined their projects as negotiated with the employer and a final "portfolio" (60 percent) which summarized their project findings and recommendations, along with a reflection of learning. These assessments were the result of a negotiated learning contract where the student had agreed with the tutor and the work placement supervisor, exactly what they would do in their project, the expected learning outcomes, and the means of assessment. The "portfolio" therefore could be the traditional paper evidence file or, for example, video submissions or training "role plays."

In recent years considerable attention has been paid to the need for graduates to become "lifelong learners." The responsibility for preparing students so that they can continue to learn throughout their careers is frequently placed with universities. The mix of work-based learning in an online learning environment could be one of the keys in achieving a learning opportunity, which could begin to mold the "lifelong learner" who needs to be able to learn effectively in as yet unknown situations. The adoption of a deep approach in an effective learning environment, therefore, is seen to be essential if the individuals concerned are to be responsive to the demands of the future and be able to adopt the role of economic generators of the twenty-first century.

The use of virtual learning environments could potentially become a vehicle to widen participation in the university sector. Using an online delivery mode could provide an accredited route for the attainment of a relevant degree level qualification, and assist in attracting suitable people into "matched" employment and encouraging existing employees to engage with the insight which academic theory can bring. It also provides a vehicle which enhances skills in management that are needed and prepare students to meet the demands of future employment, such as problem solving and application of technology. VLEs may be able to provide a type of distance education which, Hedge suggests (1996), "...represents opportunities for continuing education that are, already, enabling notions of lifelong learning to advance beyond rhetoric and into reality" (p.7).

The modification from traditionally taught modules to the use of online learning for students separated by space and time, where each can use context specific problems as their "case study" on which to apply the academic curriculum, is a new model of business education for the future.

Such a model will allow the broadening of access, as delivery will be achieved while students continue to be active within the workplace. This will enhance the learning experience and the employability factors, as the knowledge will be directly transferable to the work environment.

Delivering the program via e-learning means that instead of the students moving to the location of the resource provider, and studying at times convenient for the institution, the program is taken to the students and they can study at times convenient to them.

It was the intention of the tutor to encourage a deep approach to learning, but students who are absent, tired, shy, de-motivated, and struggling to understand are unable to take a deep approach. It has been shown that students in these circumstances typically adopt a "strategic approach" (Biggs, 1987) to their learning – doing what is required to pass the assessments, unable or unwilling to do any more.

The students studying on this module were in their final year, indeed the final semester, of their B.A. (Hons.) degree. Their experience of learning and teaching methods employed in other modules to that point had been conventional. Students typically received a lecture (input) as part of a large group of students in lecture theatres (100-150 students), followed by a smaller group (20-30 students) seminar in which students were expected to apply the theories and concepts discussed in the earlier lecture or discovered from their subsequent reading.

The tutor's dissatisfactions with this conventional approach were that attendance at lectures and seminars was spasmodic and that student contributions during these class contact times were confined to those who attended, and a few enthusiastic and/or confident students. Students who were particularly disadvantaged, therefore, were those who were unable/ unwilling to attend; those who had a naturally quieter disposition; those with some special needs; and those who did not have English as a first language. There was also a concern that some dominant students tended to absorb the limited class time available.

The main difficulty of the existing learning and teaching approaches seemed to be that the students had too few opportunities to collaborate and jointly reflect upon the focus of their study. Lave and Wenger (1991) believe experiences take on meaning within communities of practice. Students who do not form "communities of practice" cannot therefore interpret, in a shared context, their experiences. Dewey (1966, c.1916) describes learning as a social and interpretive activity in which multiple members collaboratively construct explanations and understandings of materials, artifacts, and phenomena within their environment. If students learn through active engagement with problems along with reflections upon the association between ideas, behavior, and outcomes, then engaging the students in activities and discussing their experiences are seen to be essential in order to impact their learning.

Skeptics of online learning frequently hold traditional teaching methods up as an ideal. However, the changing nature of students and their circumstances demands a review of the learning and teaching methods employed. In traditional classes it is frequently the lecturer who does the talking; hence, as Newman, Johnson, Cochrane & Webb, (2002, p.5) discovered, "it is quite easy for face-to-face discussions to degenerate into monologues, silence is filled by the teacher." In such situations the student is passive and therefore unlikely to learn.

It was anticipated that the use of a VLE may overcome many of the problems experienced in the more traditional settings. A VLE may be able to provide the space in which "a community of practice" could collectively analyze, interpret, and reflect upon current business problems. Students were required to contribute every week, but they were given seven days in which to make their contributions to the online discussions. This allowed students to fit this into their schedules at a time that suited them.

Learnwise is a VLE currently being piloted by Liverpool Hope University College. It provides the student with many of the features found in the new generation of VLEs. In particular it has a "Forum" space in which students can join or initiate asynchronous discussions. These discussions are archived so that all students have access to all discussions whenever they take place over the course of the module.

It was intended to expose students to a wide range of experience by the use of these forums. It is appropriate that business studies students should learn about the use of additional technologies, particularly when this media is likely to be increasingly used by work organizations. Owen and Birks' (2002) report on the Eurobarometer survey that found that 81 percent of Europeans believe that the new communication technologies will change teaching methods, and that 76 percent believe that this new technology will improve the quality of education. There is an apparent belief that learning technologies will be a key focus in the development of lifelong learning.

Learnwise provided a "Frequently Asked Questions" (FAQ) section, and at the outset of the module most students' questions revolved around the use of the VLE and the sorts of contributions they should be making each week. Students were advised that they would be expected to discuss the practical dilemmas arising from their placements and the application or misapplication of concepts and theories to these problems. They were advised that they would be expected to offer practical suggestions to assist one another and through this process, it was hoped that they would learn how to manage their own problems (Schön, 1983).

The usual way to ascertain information is to ask questions. By asking appropriate questions, the participants could illustrate their various perceptions of the problem under review. Beaty, Bourner, and Frost (1993) recommend attempting to create an environment for investigation rather than rationalization. Therefore, students were given a lot of guidance in questioning in the FAQs. They were advised that questions were intended to open up each others' perceptions of their problems. Students should focus on each individual in turn as they came to the Forum with questions; so they were advised not to be diverted to other problems until some satisfactory closure had been reached. Their questions should be sensitive to the individual and not make them feel defensive. It was also stated that the questions should not be designed to illustrate the intelligence of the questioner and, conversely, that by asking questions the questioner should not fear being perceived as ignorant (Frank, 1998). Ultimately, a good question leads to possible changes in action as one is lead to challenge the assumptions of practice. Through this process of examining another's problem, it was hoped that the questioners may start to gain deeper insights into their own projects.

Students also received advice on "active listening." When listening in "real time," we are frequently using that time to prepare our next response. In an asynchronous conversation, it was hoped that the participants would have the luxury of "listening" when they had time to listen, and that this would transmit a feeling of empathy. Students were encouraged to consider such devises as paraphrasing and perception checking. As in counseling therefore, the listener, rather than give advice, attempts to encourage new ways of looking at the problem.

The very nature of work placements causes disruption to a student's "normal" timetable. Trying to co-ordinate times for the students to meet on a regular basis had frequently failed in other areas, with the result that students lost each other as a vital support mechanism, and the burden of "problem-solver" was kept firmly with the tutor. The availability of a VLE therefore allowed us to "meet" weekly and provided an opportunity for creating and sustaining collaborative, reflective learning experiences.

All learning environments need to be safe. Unless there is mutual support students will not feel confident enough to benefit from the process. The students needed to feel safe enough to make public comments and this needed to be handled sensitively. *Learnwise* was initially checked daily by the tutor, so that "immediate" responses could be made to students' comments. The culture of positive responses and support from the tutor was intended to set the "tone" of this learning environment. Where other students were replying to one of their peers, this was often incorporated into the tutor's response. This provided a holistic response and established norms of behavior when responding. Once students gained confidence using the forums, they were able to operate independently of tutor comment. Other devices such as the use of Student Profiles (where students could place photographs and describe themselves and their interests) were also used to create a relaxed atmosphere.

It was anticipated therefore that this module might provide the liberation to learn, which few of the students had previously enjoyed. They were free of the constraints of time; they could join in when they were able and motivated to do so. They were also free in an asynchronous conversation to take the conversation in new directions with what they thought was relevant, not dictated by the tutor or "significant" students. It was the tutor's intention that the students be rewarded for demonstrating a "deep approach" to learning, and that this assessment of process would allow students to grow and develop as learners.

4.   RESEARCH RESULTS

As previously stated, this is a very small sample and any statistical evidence based on the number of students involved is highly questionable. It must be remembered, however, that this was a pilot study and numbers were largely determined by the number of students registered in the module. It does provide a first step for future research, but it is clearly too early to give any solid conclusions based on the finding contained here.

Results from the analysis of eight paired questionnaires are provided in Tables 1-6 below and discussed in the following section. Please note that Student 4 left questions 42-52 blank on the second questionnaire.

Table 1. What is Learning? (Max score = 15)

Student	REPRODUCING KNOWLEDGE		PERSONAL UNDERSTANDING and DEVELOPMENT	
	Before	After	Before	After
1	12	12	14	11
2	13	14	13	15
3	13	10	14	13
4	13	12	13	12
5	11	12	13	15
6	12	12	11	11
7	13	12	15	10
8	8	15	8	7
Mean	11.88	12.38	12.63	11.75
SD	1.73	1.51	2.20	2.66

Note: Based on the conceptions of learning described by Marton and Saljo (1997). The categories can be seen as a hierarchy, although not all the steps or categories are generally agreed. The first three, to a decreasing extent, tend to relate to a surface approach and can therefore be combined to indicate a conception of learning as reproducing knowledge, while the remaining three cover a view of learning involving personal understanding and development.

Table 1 illustrates the resulting increase after the course in scores on "extrinsic interest" as a reason for entering Higher Education is statistically significant. This is usually related to a strategic approach to studying.

Student (8) has very different scores on What is learning and on Reasons for entering Higher Education from other students, which increases the standard deviations and makes the results less representative of the whole class of students.

Table 2. Reasons for Entering Higher Education (Max score = 20)

Student	INTRINSIC INTEREST		EXTRINSIC INTEREST		NO CLEAR GOALS	
	Before	After	Before	After	Before	After
1	12	10	11	13	12	12
2	15	15	12	14	3	3
3	10	12	13	13	8	5
4	14	14	16	18	7	13
5	13	12	11	11	4	3
6	12	13	13	16	7	10
7	14	13	12	13	3	3
8	8	7	8	12	11	3
Mean	12.25	12.00	12.00	13.75	6.88	6.50
SD	2.32	2.51	2.27	2.25	3.44	4.41

Note: These items are based on the reasons for taking the course described by Beaty et al. (1996). Scores can be combined to create scores on extrinsic and intrinsic interest in the course.

Table 2 shows students' reasons for entering Higher Education. Tests showed that there were no statistical differences on deep, strategic or surface approaches to studying BUT the deep approach was nearly significant. The three subscales that make up the deep approach were then reviewed, and it was found that scores on use of evidence had significantly increased by the end of the module. The other subscales were also checked but nothing else of significance was found.

As use of evidence is significant, the means and standard deviations are given below.

Table 3. Approaches to Studying (Max score = 60)

Student	DEEP APPROACH		STRATEGIC APPROACH		SURFACE APPROACH	
	Before	After	Before	After	Before	After
1	31	33	22	20	30	31
2	49	52	42	46	14	18
3	23	33	48	54	42	27
4	47		44		32	
5	45	49	42	44	17	21
6	43	53	39	48	29	47
7	49	44	48	44	22	20
8	35	40	44	43	49	37
Mean	40.25	43.43	41.13	42.71	29.38	28.71
SD	9.56	8.42	8.31	10.69	11.93	10.50

Note: Approaches to Studying derive from Marton and Säljö's (1976) ideas on approaches to learning, combined with Entwistle and Ramsden's (1983) descriptions on a strategic approach to studying. The first three sub-scales in each approach are most consistently related to each other, and can be combined with confidence. Subsequent sub-scales are more likely to vary in their relationships across different samples. Relationships thus need to be checked in the particular sample used for the study.

Table 4. Use Of Evidence Subscale

	VALID N	MEAN	SD
Use of evidence before	8	14.00	3.12
Use of evidence after	7	15.00	3.27

Table 5. Preferences for Different Types of Courses and Teaching (Max score = 20)

Student	SUPPORTING UNDERSTANDING		TRANSMITTING INFORMATION	
	Before	After	Before	After
1	11	11	16	17
2	20	20	8	7
3	6	8	20	19
4	17	19	10	17
5	16	16	14	11
6	16	16	19	20
7	14	18	12	6
8	8	13	20	16
Mean	13.50	15.13	14.88	14.13
SD	4.78	4.16	4.64	5.41

Note: Supporting understanding (related to a deep approach).
Transmitting information (related to a surface approach).

Table 6. How Well Do You Think You Are Doing?

| | SELF-RATING | |
Student	Before	After
1	4	6
2	8	9
3	8	8
4	5	5
5	6	7
6	7	7
7	7	7
8	5	4
Mean	6.25	6.63
SD	1.49	1.60

Note: Rating range from 9 (very well) to 1(rather badly).

5.   DISCUSSION

5.1   "Deep" or "Surface" Learners?

Bearing in mind previous caveats as to the size of this sample, it can be seen that there are two statistically significant results here. The results suggest that students have adapted their approaches to studying by the end of this course in their "use of evidence." This would suggest that they would now adopt a "deeper" approach than previously, reviewing evidence more carefully, attempting to draw their own conclusions, questioning things they read and hear in lectures, examining details more carefully to establish a "fit" between it and what is being said, and finally, that the student is more likely to look for the reasons behind the argument. This is encouraging and may suggest that students have adopted a "deeper" approach.

The other result of statistical significance, however, is that there was an increase after the course in scores on extrinsic interest as a reason for entering Higher Education. This is usually related to a strategic approach to studying.

Ramsden (1992) asserts that students will only learn what they think they will be tested on. The importance of assessment must not, therefore, be underestimated. There is a dilemma here however. Unless students could see a tangible reward for any required activity, they seemed unlikely to take part. The tutor's wish that these students would take a "deep" approach to their learning was, therefore, flawed in that she had to provide them with an initial inducement in order to ensure their participation. Assessment criteria for online contributions advised students that they should "…contribute fully to on-line discussions...be constructive and supportive...initiate and develop other's discussions...display knowledge and understanding of academic theory to support comments made and ...display an ability to critically analyse, evaluate and reflect" (Owens, 2002, p.3).

Students did contribute weekly to the discussions, gaining marks for "turning up." However, their next step was not so easy. All students contributed, but what mattered then were the skills they displayed in joining the on-going discussions, or the initiative they displayed in starting new discussion threads. Once they were "in," their reference to academic theories and concepts were monitored, initially to illustrate understanding and then to assess their ability to apply, analyze, evaluate, and reflect upon these theories.

All students contributed. All were supportive of one another. All students quoted academic theories and provided details of useful Web sites and journal articles for each other. The online discussion was carried out over a period of six weeks, culminating in a one-hour "discussion" assessment, where students were drawn together in a classroom to summarize their thoughts on the dialogue of the previous weeks. This could have been carried out as an "online" assessment, but in order to ensure the authenticity of the student contribution, it was decided that it would be administratively easier to physically meet. At this event some students displayed a much less-certain knowledge of the concepts they had previously discussed online, and it was the students who demonstrated an ability to do this in both virtual and real settings, who gained the highest marks. It would appear, therefore, that some students took a "strategic" approach to this assessment, that is, they wanted to give the tutor, and possibly their peers, the *impression* that they had learned something, whereas in reality they had not. The VLE was used by some students as an "information dump," in the misconception that merely bringing undigested information to the environment was sufficient. Many failed to read and summarize, in order to improve their own understanding and be able to explain their findings to their peers. As Honey (2001) discovered, learning was perceived by some as the presentation of data and not as a process of understanding and construction.

Whilst this was obviously disappointing, this form of assessment did allow the tutor to assess the students accurately and fairly. Had this form of assessment been more common, students may have been better prepared, but it was the students who had taken a "deep" approach who were rewarded, as they could display wider knowledge and understanding, greater background reading, and make connections between concepts, theories, and practice.

The module encouraged reflective practice both online and via the students' learning logs. It should therefore be a more effective learning experience for the students (and later comments found this to be the case, see

Student evaluations). As part of the developmental process, students discussed "learning" as a subject while simultaneously developing their own skills as researchers and reflective practitioners. This proved to be a particularly effective mix.

Schön (1983) suggests individuals will change their everyday practice by discussing and reframing their understanding of particular problems. Students then need an environment in which they can converse. Virtual learning environments can provide this.

6.   STUDENT EVALUATION

6.1   Liberated Learners?

Significant features identified by students were peer and tutor support, together with analysis of their own learning.

One student quoted from Sean O'Casey:

> "'All the world's a stage and most of us are desperately unrehearsed.' Has anyone felt out of depth in their work placement? ..."

Another replied:

> "I have felt unrehearsed in my placement due to the fact that my manager thinks I know all the answers to his problem, and anything I suggest is correct.... I get the impression that this is because he has absolutely no idea about marketing and thinks because I did ONE module in the subject, I am an expert. But when I produce the report for him and it does not provide him with the information he was looking for, he will probably blame me!! Although you would think that this would make you more confident, as it seems that the manager has lots of confidence in me, it has the opposite effect and I'm wondering if all the work I have been doing for him for the last three weeks is completely wrong. Although, if at the end of the placement he is impressed with the work and it does provide him with the information he needed, I will feel much more confident for my next job."

This brought a large number of empathetic responses.

Among these responses:

"Hi (x), I do understand how you feel, when you move from a learning environment to a work based one it can be scary to think that suddenly you are the one with the knowledge and expertise. While it may be right to say that you are not a marketing expert (yet!), you sound like you are a thorough person who wouldn't suggest ideas unless you had thought them through so don't underestimate your own ability. This is something I think we are all guilty of at times. If you do want to get your manager more involved in the ideas stage perhaps tackling him from the angle of his own expertise might be a way in. By this I mean not confessing your relevant inexperience in the subject of marketing, but rather suggesting that his own day to day contact with customers, gives him information that you may not be party to from the data cards…His expectations that you are the expert may be keeping him from suggesting things!"

This use of the forums to make suggestions developed to the stage where students were eventually suggesting things which they might say themselves in their work placements and then ask for comments from their peers. This enabled them to "role play" some potentially difficult situations, and they were able to get a large number of views on the best way forward.

On "Understanding Learning":

"Does anyone else feel that they have learned more about the learning process since starting the WBL module than they have in the previous 2 years? I know that is how I feel, not with regard to the knowledge, but definitely with regard to the process of learning."

"Hi (x), I totally agree with you. I think it's because in the past two years we have been "force fed" all our knowledge, however in this module we have been given much more freedom and we have to learn for ourselves. I think when you are left to do something on your own, you are usually much better at it than your think!"

Others, however, were not as convinced:

"…I think I'm more suited to being told what to do, and then getting on with it."

Most students commented upon the role of the tutor as an important facilitator in the early weeks, encouraging each student's contributions and generating possible discussion topics. As the module continued, however, the tutor took a less prominent role, leaving the students to debate the problems without the "interference" of a supposed expert. Even at this stage students felt confident to continue, with the following being typical of student understanding of the tutor's role:

> "Even though (the tutor) didn't always join in the conversation, I knew she was in there, checking regularly and would tell us if we were going wrong."

The chief role that the tutor tended to take was one of "cheerleader." The tutor was also involved in extracting more general principles and abstract concepts from the specific problems the students were discussing. The existence of live work problems provided the context in which we could strive to understand the theory. All students were working on real problems in a highly visible way, and although the students did not have the same problem, they had the same struggle, and all participants could refer to anyone else's contributions and projects to illustrate their points. Unlike traditional classroom conversations the students also had an ongoing permanent record of their discussions, so they could return to old conversations and pick up points made there. This allowed students to see their own and others' progress with a particular topic, and it also served to illustrate the process of learning.

Students' contributions were made on weekdays and weekends, and at all times of the day. However, no contribution was made after 10 PM and none before 9 AM.

No student mentioned the flexibility of this contact as a benefit. Two students stated that by having no set "class time" they found it difficult to motivate themselves to log onto *Learnwise* and contribute to the ongoing conversations. They wanted an externally imposed structure to guide their actions, which can be seen as typical of the "surface" learner. Whether this was a problem with being motivated to use the technology or motivated to learn could not, unfortunately, be established.

More enthusiastic students stated that they liked the fact that all their contributions were timed and dated. They wanted the tutor to be aware that any new idea was their idea, and therefore receive the "credit" for it. The risk of plagiary appeared to be significantly reduced because of this, which is consistent with work carried out by Ciborra & Andreu (2001). Students also could use "lockers" in which they could store personal documents, such as their learning contracts. These lockers could be made private to each student – but not to the tutor. However, the students were asked to leave their lockers "unlocked" to allow a free exchange of information. Students were willing to do this, although we did experience some technical problems with the lockers, when the contents of lockers could not be viewed, which was not resolved before the end of the module.

Students were asked to produce individually negotiated learning contracts against which they would be summatively assessed. The only requirement here was that they should also submit a reflection of their learning as part of this final submission. This was the first time they had completed a negotiated learning contract and it is fair to say that this was unpopular. Students had particular problems with establishing their learning outcomes. Although this proved to be a real challenge for the students, many subsequently commented that they found this a really useful exercise, with many stating that up until this module they had rarely bothered to read the learning outcomes which were provided in each module handbook.

Students appeared to feel "safe" in the *Learnwise* environment. They occasionally used it for other purposes, such as to discuss other modules on which they were studying, encouraging each other to apply for jobs and arranging end of semester social events. Some students, in the early weeks of the course did attempt to circumvent *Learnwise* forums by visiting the tutor in person. When this occurred, a summary of our discussion would be posted on *Learnwise* so that all students could have access to our discussion.

It is certain that students did experience a very different learning experience in this module but whether that could be described as "liberation" is open to debate. Most students mourned at one point or another the loss of comfortable structures and routines provided in traditional classes. The anxiety of getting their final grades and graduating was a significant factor, education was something to be got through, the degree was a product which was a passport to a "good" job; taking time to *really* learn was seen by many to be an exhausting additional requirement.

7. EMPLOYER EVALUATION

Employers were asked the following questions in semi-structured telephone interviews following the students' placements:
1. How do you think your students performed in their project?
2. What were the most significant things they learned?
3. Your students did not attend regular classes and received support and assistance for this module via a "virtual learning environment." Did they discuss this with you and, if so, how useful do you think it was?
4. Do you see any long-term drawbacks or advantages in the use of VLEs?
5. What do you think universities can do to better prepare their students for work placements and working in general?

Employers' comments were generally positive about the student contributions to their organizations, but the employers seemed to find it difficult to specify the most significant things that students had learned. Six suggested that practical skills were the most obvious gain, highlighting communication and team-working skills. One employer commented that by working on a "real" problem the students were able to see how chaotic most business problems were, and that they needed to consider a large number of variables before any decisions could be made. She commented that the student who had been placed at her organization had been relieved to find, from the online contributions, that all the students were struggling with their problems and no one appeared to have a "straightforward" project, which had an immediately obvious, rational, or logical solution.

All the employers were aware that the students did not attend traditional classes, although few appeared to understand what a virtual learning environment was. Comments suggested a comprehension of this as a mere e-mail exchange. All employers seemed to believe that any sort of support provided for students on a work placement was a good thing, but only two stated that their students had found this to be the case.

As there was an apparent confusion as to the nature of VLEs, it was difficult for employers to comment on their possible long-term benefits or drawbacks. The benefits of support were again mentioned, although one employer suggested that it might be a "keener" learning experience to make the student "fend for themselves." One other employer (the owner manager of an SME) also had some reservations about multiple students having "access" to information about his organization. He expressed some concern over loss of confidentiality, and suggested that the students be asked to adopt a "no naming" policy for their organizations.

Employers made few suggestions as to what additional tasks universities could perform in order to prepare students for their work placements and their future careers. There was, however, a general dissatisfaction with graduate skill levels, particularly communication skills. Employers' conceptions of communication were not common, however. The employers appeared to want very specific knowledge and skills, which may only be possible to learn in the context of their particular organization. Communication for some was the ability to deal with customers politely and promptly; for others, it was the ability to write effective responses to letters of complaint; yet for others, the ability to prepare an influential marketing presentation. Many in the academic community would question the role of universities in developing such skills. A closer relationship between universities, businesses, and the individual student/employee would seem to be essential to gain an understanding of each other's positions and to fulfill or at least "manage" expectations.

8. CONCLUSIONS

The mix of work-based learning delivered with the support of an online learning environment could make a significant contribution in the process of molding the "lifelong learner." The cyclical model of learning (Kolb, 1984) requires four kinds of abilities/undertaking, if learning is to be successful. These are concrete experience (CE), reflective observation (RO), abstract conceptualization (AC), and active experimentation (AE). By providing students with work placements they were offered new experiences (CE); they were provided with time and space in which to reflect (RO), both in online weekly conversations and via their learning logs; students were able to form, reform, and process their ideas in a safe environment and integrate their new ideas into sound, logical theories (AC); and finally, the students were able to use theories to make decisions and to problem solve and test implications in new situations (AE).

Learning does occur naturally from the accumulation of direct experience and its analysis, but this is a long-term process and it is not possible to state whether "deep" learning occurred in the module under review. The assessment methods currently employed within a modular system may even be counterproductive in achieving the stated aims. It is sufficient to say that this sort of experience appears to have the potential to deliver an effective learning environment, and that the students found these fulfilling and effective learning experiences in a supportive environment.

With the emergence of an information-rich "knowledge society," the need to produce lifelong learners has become even more of an imperative. Universities equip students with the requisite knowledge and generic skills necessary to sustain and develop the national economy (Williams & Fry, 1994), but to view universities as merely molding the worker of the future would be to underestimate the roles which they attempt to fulfill. Knowles (1990) believes that a prime purpose of universities is to develop cognitive and moral understanding for their communities. We should not, therefore, strive for "lifelong learning" with mere economic motivations. This must be continuing personal as well as professional development.

If experiences take on meaning within "communities of practice" (Lave & Wenger, 1991), then students need a community within which to operate. VLEs enable collaboration between students to take place. The advantages of the VLE and asynchronous discussions established in this study were that *all* students were given more time to reflect upon contributions and develop their thoughts before responding. This process provides an opportunity for establishing relevant and authentic examples of the abstract concepts discussed. This provides students with the opportunity not only to contribute to the learning of the group, but to develop a sense of their own learning progress, which is not available in traditional classroom settings. Students also have a permanent record of all their discussions to refer to at any time. The use of a VLE brought contributions from all students on a regular basis, a rare event in traditional classrooms.

There are advantages for the tutor in that there is greater opportunity to establish whether the points made have actually been understood. Large student numbers and a lack of time in traditional classrooms mean that this is not always possible there. The pace of learning in VLE can be dictated by the learner. *Learnwise* also provides a "search" facility in the fora allowing both staff and students to search conversations for particular words or phrases. This enables relatively speedy summaries to be made of who said what and when - a distinct advantage over real time classrooms.

There is, however, a lack of traditional "non-verbal" feedback, which alerts the experienced tutor to a problem with understanding, such as frowning and lack of eye contact. Students may all be contributing, but without being able to hear their tone of voice and see how they have struggled with the point they have just made, may mean that the tutor fails to intervene. Clarifying understanding also takes longer and poor written expression can further obfuscate meaning.

To compare these environments is somewhat unrealistic, however. Considering the over-populated and under resourced nature of most Higher Education institutions, we need to search for a "best fit" rather than an ideal. In any learning environment today, few, but the very privileged, will have the luxury of time and space to discuss academic concepts with competent "others." Virtual learning environments will only be effective if the student participates, and there is a mix of aligned and appropriate assessment that could allow this to occur. Enthusiastic students will participate whatever environment they find themselves in. It is the growing masses of diverse students who need the support, which traditional learning and teaching environments are not currently delivering. This support could be provided by online learning.

Alexander and Boud (2001) suggest that online learning is a tool or support for learning that *will take place elsewhere,* and this view is supported here. The VLE can provide a good support for all students, regardless of time, personality, ability, and language skills. The learning which occurs does not "happen" while they are online, but at some later point when they reflect on the process. Again, the necessity of appropriate and aligned assessment is essential here, and reflection must, therefore, be part of the teaching, learning, and assessment process.

The results of the ASSIST questionnaire and other noted behaviors suggest that many students continued to behave strategically on this module, whilst there is some evidence that other behaviors may have changed, and the students may have adopted "deeper" preferences elsewhere. Biggs and Moore (1993) are firmly of the view that approaches to learning can be modified by the teaching and learning context, and are themselves learned. They contrast approaches to learning (modifiable) with learning styles (fixed and part of personality characteristics and traits). Biggs (1999) agrees that students do have a predilection for one type of approach or another, but that these predilections may or may not be realized in practice depending on the teaching context.

This research illustrates that there may be a case for the use of VLEs in Higher Education. The technology can offer a wider range of learning resources, and students have the opportunity to learn at their own pace, being able to discuss their experiences in context with academic theories and concepts. In this particular study, however, no reliable conclusions can be drawn. For the final-year students who participated in this module, the changes in learning and teaching methods, learning environments, and assessments were probably too little too late. They had, by this point in their academic careers, learned norms of behavior, which had successfully got them to the threshold of a degree, and any reluctance to adopt a different approach may have been caused by their survival instincts to get to the finishing line.

It is the writer's intention to continue research in this area. It is anticipated that students who are properly inducted in the use of virtual learning environments from the start of their degrees, and are appropriately rewarded for adopting "deep" approaches, could thrive here. In order to assess this additional research, larger samples over longer periods of time are required. Further analysis should also be considered with a content analysis instrument to scrutinize the quality of online contributions.

REFERENCES

Alexander, S., & Boud, D. (2001). Learners still learn from experience when online_in Stephenson, J. *Teaching and Learning Online Pedagogies for New Technologies.* London: Kogan Page.

Beaty, L., Bourner, T., & Frost, P. (1993). Action Learning: Reflection on becoming a set member. *Management Education and Development,* 24: 350-367.

Biggs, J. & Moore, P. J. (1993). *The process of learning.* Sydney: Prentice Hall of Australia.

Biggs, J. (1987). *Student approaches to learning and studying.* Hawthorn, Victoria: Australian Council for Educational Research.

Biggs, J. (1999). *Teaching for quality learning at university.* SRHE and Open University Press.

Brown, S., Bull, J., & Race, P. (1999). *Computer assisted assessment in Higher Education.* London: Kogan Page.

Ciborra, C. U., & Andreu, R. (2001). Sharing knowledge across boundaries. *Journal of Information Technology,* 16 (2), 73-81.

Dewey, J. (1966). *Democracy and education.* New York: Free Press.

Entwistle, N., & Ramsden, P. (1983). *Understanding student learning.* London: Croom Helm.

Frank, H. (1998). Another review of the Revans Centre seminar. *Link up with Action Learning,* 1 (4): 21-22.

Hattie, J., & Marsh, H. W. (1996). The relationship between research and teaching: a meta analysis. *Review of Educational Research, 66,* 507-42.

Hedge, N. (1996). Introduction. In *Going the distance: Teaching, learning, and researching in distance education* (pp. 7-10). Sheffield: USDE publication.

Honey, P. (2001) E-learning: a performance appraisal and some suggestions for improvement, in: The Learning Organization, Vol8:5: pp.200-202

Inglis, A., Ling, P., & Joosten, V. (1999). *Delivering digitally: Managing the transition to knowledge media.* London: Kogan-Page.

Knowles, M. (1990). *The adult learner: A neglected species*, 4th ed. Houston: Gulf Publishing Company.

Kolb, D.A. (1984) Experiencial Learning: Experience as the Source of Learning and Development, Englewood Cliffs, NJ:Prentice Hall

Lave, J., & Wenger, E. (1991). *Situated learning: Legitimate peripheral participation.* Cambridge: Cambridge University Press.

Marton, F., & Säljö, R. (1976). On qualitative differences in learning –I: Outcome and process. *British Journal of Educational Psychology, 46,* 4-11.

McInnes, J., & McNaught, C. (1995). In M. Peat. (2002). *To lure and catch the imagination of first year biology students: reflections on a virtual learning environment.* Retrieved from http://www.ltss.bris.ac.uk.

Newman, D. R, Johnson, C., Cochrane, C., & Webb, B. (2002). *An experiment in group learning technology: evaluating critical thinking in face-to-face and computer –supported seminars.* Retrieved from http://www.qub.ac.uk/mgt/papers/ccvsem/contents.html.

Owen, M., & Birks, E. (2002). *Why virtual learning environments?* Retrieved from http://xiram.doe.d5.ub.es/IVETTE/Why.htm.

Owens, T. (2002). *Work based learning module handbook.* Management and Business Centre, Liverpool Hope University College.

Prosser, M., & Trigwell, K. (1999). *Understanding learning and teaching: The experience in Higher Education.* Society for Research into Higher Education. Buckingham: Open University Press.

Race, P. (1998). Helping students to learn from resources. In S. Brown, & B. Smith (Eds.), *Resource based learning.* Staff and Educational Development Series. London: Kogan Page.

Ramsden, P. (1988). *Improving learning: New perspectives.* London: Kogan-Page.

Ramsden, P (1992). *Learning to teach in Higher Education.* London: Routledge.

Ryan, S., Scott, B., Freeman, H., & Patel, D. (2000). *The Virtual University: The Internet and resource-based learning.* London: Kogan Page.

Rowland, S. (1996). Relationships between teaching and research. *Teaching in Higher Education, 1* (1), 7-20.

Schön, D. (1983). *The reflective practitioner: How professionals think in action.* London: Basic Books.

Tait, H., Entwistle, N., & McCune, V. (1998). ASSIST: a reconceptualization of the approaches to studying inventory. In C. Rust (Ed.), *Improving student learning: improving students as learners.* Oxford: The Oxford Centre for Staff and Learning Development.

Williams, G., & Fry, H. (1994). *Longer term prospects for British Higher Education.* London: Committee of Vice Chancellors and Principals.

Chapter 7

LEARNING TO WORK: EASING THE TRANSITION[1]

Cathrine Le Maistre & Anthony Paré
Department of Integrated Studies in Education, Faculty of Education, McGill University, Montreal, Canada[2]

1.   INTRODUCTION

The final years of education and the first years of working life mark a critical period in the passage to professional expertise. The transition from university to workplace is a huge step in many professions, especially in those where school or university preparation has been largely theoretical, because the world of school and the world of work are radically different contexts. Processes of scaffolding the transition between the contexts differ by profession and by workplace: some rely on a final year of field education with close supervision and ties to school-based programs (e.g., internships and practica); others offer students periods of relatively unsupervised, work-like conditions (e.g., work-study programs); still others assume (explicitly or implicitly) that periods of apprenticeship within the workplace after graduation will ease the newcomer into professional practice. In all cases, the individual is transformed from student to practitioner with some degree and type of assistance from veteran practitioners. The mentorship process is

---

[1] Some of the findings in this chapter were previously reported in the Second International Conference on Work and Learning, in Calgary, AB, Canada, July 2001 with the title: 'Learning through limited peripheral participation: On-the-job mentoring of new workers.'
[2] The research reported in this chapter is supported by funding from the Social Sciences and Humanities Research Council, whose help is gratefully acknowledged.

R.G.Milter et al. (eds.), Educational Innovation in Economics and Business IX, 117–136.
©2004 *Springer. Printed in the Netherlands.*

necessarily and highly situation-specific, with each discipline and each workplace developing distinctive enculturation practices. Many studies (e.g., Huling-Austin, 1990) have shown that mentoring helps neophytes cross the threshold into working life and helps decrease the high rates of attrition among newcomers to the professions we are studying. The research reported in this chapter seeks to compare the school-to-work transitions in a variety of professional disciplines and workplaces. The dual objectives of our research are to understand better the range of processes involved in the transition, and to situate these processes on a firm theoretical base so as to assist the disciplines in improving their practices.

We believe that much of the professional workplace literature in the disciplines under study is un-, under-, or ill-theorized. Un-theorized accounts of the school-to-work transition offer tips, guidelines, evaluation procedures, narratives of success and failure, and other practical advice for those interested in the implementation and management of transition processes. Under-theorized accounts portray knowledge, activity, and learning as unproblematic and essentially unchanged across contexts, so that learners need not adjust their expectations, attitudes, or behaviors as they move from school to work. Ill-theorized accounts are based on a transmission model of learning, in which knowledge passes from the full expert to the empty novice. Although this model has been widely discredited in the literature on school learning, it persists in the professional and workplace education literature.

This chapter presents findings from the second year of a four-year longitudinal study of the school-to-work transition in four professions traditionally called "helping professions," where university preparation includes experience in the environment typical of the workplace where the graduate will be employed. Even then, first year practitioners report great differences from their earlier experiences as students on a practicum. This multi-site, multi-year, team research project is investigating the final year of professional education and the first years of professional practice in the fields of education, social work, occupational therapy, and physiotherapy. All these professions are characterized by a long tradition of close, individual supervision during field education, a commitment to the deliberate enculturation of students, and the organized or informal mentoring of newcomers. In particular, the study seeks to understand the nature and process of the mentoring relationships that sustain and develop newcomers to professional life. The varying disciplinary perspectives offered through a comparative analysis of practice in each profession demonstrate similarities and differences across professions, indicate some of the key problems and possibilities faced by people as they make the passage from school to work, and offer models of practice suitable for other enterprises.

2. THEORETICAL FRAMEWORK

The research reported in this chapter emerges from contemporary theories of activity, cognition, and learning which emphasize the cultural nature of knowledge and knowledge making. These cultural-historical (or sociocultural) perspectives (e.g., Cole, 1995, 1996; Wertsch, 1991) take us a long way from behaviorist or cognitive views of learning. Knowledge is viewed as being shifting, dynamic, local, and relative, rather than fixed, universal, and generalizable; cognition is seen as a social, collective, and distributed activity, rather than as a mental process inside the heads of individuals; learning is seen as the gradually increasing ability to participate in socially-situated, collaborative practices, rather than as the accumulation of discrete skills and context-free knowledge. The implication of this perspective is a shift in the research viewpoint: the focus is on collective activity in disciplines, organizations, institutions, and other "communities of practice" (Lave, 1991), rather than on the individual as the unit of attention and analysis in educational research. The unit of analysis that emerges from this perspective might be called, to use Lave's term, "persons-engaged-in-activity," and learning can be considered as the process of gradually improving engagement or participation in particular activities. With this in mind, the focus of our study has been "persons-learning-to-engage-in-activity."

Perhaps the most elaborated cultural-historical approach is offered by activity theory, a perspective that began in the work of L. S. Vygotsky (e.g., 1978) and his colleagues (e.g., Leont'ev, 1981), and has been developed more recently by a variety of theorists, such as Cole, Engeström, or Wertsch. A central assumption of activity theory and related perspectives is that

> ...humans have access to the world indirectly, or mediately, rather than directly, or immediately. This applies both with regard to how humans obtain information about the world and how they act on it – two processes that are usually viewed as being fundamentally intertwined (Wertsch, Del Rio, & Alvarez, 1995, p.21).

Within this scheme, the individual acts on and knows the environment through the intercession of mediating artifacts that range from simple tools to complex semiotic or conceptual resources. Such artifacts are cultural and historical products – that is, they are always already saturated with cognitive and social content. To act on and know the world is to act and know *with* others.

When the research focus switches from the individual to "individual(s)-acting-with-mediational-means" (Wertsch, 1991, p.12), certain phenomena become clear:

People appear to think in conjunction or partnership with others and with the help of culturally provided tools and implements. Cognitions, it would seem, are not content-free tools that are brought to bear on this or that problem; rather, they emerge in a situation tackled by teams of people and the tools available to them (Salomon, 1993a, p. xiii).

Engeström's activity theory perspective (e.g., Cole & Engeström, 1993) has encouraged us to consider how newcomers develop a subject position within activity systems, how they learn to participate in the divisions of labor that characterize those systems; how they come to understand and internalize the community's rules, and how they manage to master the mediational means – the signs and tools – that both define and drive the community's activities. Some of the research sites we are visiting (such as hospitals) represent complex and overlapping activity systems, where physiotherapy or social work newcomers, for example, must learn not only to participate in the activity of their own professional communities, but must also learn how to perform what Wenger (1998) calls "boundary practices" (p. 114), which are tasks or encounters at the overlap between disciplines or communities.

As we observe these communities of practice in our research sites, we have observed many examples of situated learning. In comparison with the structured curriculum of the university classroom, we have seen and appreciated the complex, serendipitous, and largely tacit curriculum of learning that takes place when learners participate in workplace activity. Indeed, we have extended the idea of situated learning to something we have come to call "situated evaluation"— that is, the methods and measures used by veteran practitioners to track growth in a newcomer's ability to take part in professional practice.

Supervisors must monitor and regulate a tension as they guide the newcomer's developmental trajectory. They must determine if the newcomer's grasp of accepted practice is sufficient to allow them the space to act independently, or at least semi-autonomously, and then they must scaffold or support that practice so that neither the newcomer nor his or her patient, client, or student is threatened. Supervisors in each of the professions have told us that they appreciate students who "know their limits," and who ask questions when that limit has been reached, but they equally value students who attempt to develop beyond their limits by taking on new and challenging tasks. This balance between caution and confidence is at the heart of situated teaching and learning, and we have been deeply impressed by the supervisors who manage this balancing act effectively. They must be watchful of much that is subtle and not easily measured: tone of voice, eye contact, facial expressions, levels of certainty and doubt, physical and emotional presence, a sense of authority and confidence, all the delicate signs of progress toward professional practice.

Jean Lave and her colleagues (Chaiklin & Lave, 1993; Hanks, 1991; Lave, 1991, 1996; Lave & Wenger, 1991; Wenger, 1998) and Barbara Rogoff (1990, 1991, 1995) have helped us describe the gradual transformation of neophyte into expert. This movement occurs through what Rogoff calls "guided participation," and what Lave and Wenger (1991) call "legitimate peripheral participation." In each case, the movement might be described as centripetal: the learner is drawn from initial, hesitant performance toward proficiency under the guidance of more experienced individuals (parents, teachers, mentors, old-timers).

Lave and Wenger's (1991) notion of "legitimate peripheral participation," the term they use to describe that developmental progression, matches our own understanding of the measured and deliberate process that veteran community members use to draw newcomers into professional practice. It is in these communities of practice that newcomers can engage in practice which is legitimate (that is, of worth to the functioning of the organization, rather than contrived), peripheral (failure to accomplish the task does not damage the organization, can be redone by the newcomer or can be remedied by experienced practitioners), and participatory (the newcomer is engaged in tasks of increasing complexity, rather than being an observer). By engaging newcomers in authentic but not critical or central tasks, by gradually increasing both the difficulty of the work and the autonomy of the learners, and by the subtle application of just-in-time teaching and assessment, old-timers create a centripetal force that pulls these newcomers toward capable participation in the community's activity.

The essence of that skill appears to be the careful creation of a sequence of "zones of proximal development," which Vygotsky (1978) defines as the "distance between the actual developmental level…and the level of potential development" (p. 86). We have come to see this zone as an intellectual space, where students expand their thinking and problem-solving; a social space, where students learn to engage in the relationships and interactions characteristic of their communities; an activity space, where students experiment with tools and procedures; and a physical space, where students have - quite literally - the room to stand alone as practitioners. This last notion of "zone" has been most intriguing to us: supervisors have described to us, and we have observed, their gradual physical movement away from the novice. One physiotherapy old-timer referred to this as "hovering"; another, working in a hospital, described how he monitored the student from the next cubicle, so that neither the student or patient sensed his presence, and yet he was only one curtain away; expert teachers will gradually diminish their physical presence, leading to that moment all student teachers dread: being left alone in the classroom; social work supervisors will move from a seat beside the student during client interviews to their office across the hall.

Much of the data we have collected illustrates that developmental process, and highlights the extraordinary skill of old-timers, whose "situated teaching" allows students to be transformed into practitioners during field education, and newcomers to be absorbed into their professional life.

3.   METHODOLOGY

The methodological goal of this research project has been to create a multiple-perspective, multi-disciplinary, longitudinal, thick description of the transition from school to work. Data collection for all four disciplines has been the same. In the first year of the research, pairs of researchers at each of twenty field education sites (five hospitals, clinics, group homes, schools, or offices in each discipline under study) made initial observations and independently made field-notes based on their observations. Once initial visits were completed, the researchers compared their field-notes and journals. Pairs of researchers visited students in their field placement settings during the last practicum of their programs and conducted semi-structured interviews with the students and their supervisors. To encourage candid responses, students and supervisors were interviewed separately. Interviews were based on a prepared list of questions, but allowed enough flexibility for unanticipated issues to emerge and be explored. Students were asked if they would be willing to engage in follow-up interviews in their first year of practice, the second year of our study.

In the second year, we interviewed the new practitioners who were still in the vicinity, as well as their supervisors or mentors. Because some of the new practitioners had moved away, we also interviewed more students in their final year of university, as well as their supervisors. In addition, we held a series of focus group discussions with students and practitioners from the four disciplines in a variety of combinations: newcomers in the same discipline; supervisory practitioners in the same discipline; newcomers and practitioners from the same discipline; newcomers across disciplines; supervisory practitioners across disciplines; newcomers and practitioners from across disciplines. All the interviews and focus groups were audiotaped, transcribed verbatim, and the transcripts and field-notes were analyzed for emerging themes and patterns. The third year of the study included interviews with second-year practitioners, as well as a few interviews to fill in gaps caused by practitioners who had moved away. The total number of interviews over three years is given in Table 1.

Table 1. Number of Respondents Interviewed over Three Years

	Students	Neophytes	Supervisors
Education	8	4	12
Social work	11	5	9
Physiotherapy	13	4	12
Occupational therapy	10	5	10

We began to analyze the wealth of transcribed data from a number of standpoints and to disseminate our findings. So far, our findings have allowed us to describe in some detail students in the final months of their training, and also their supervisors, who play the double role of mentor and evaluator. We have also investigated the first months of professional practice, where the expert student becomes the neophyte professional, with or without formal mentoring or supervision. At the end of the fourth year, when we have analyzed the data that tracks the same beginning professionals from the last year of training to the second year of practice, we anticipate being able to report changes in their behavior and attitudes as well as their performance. We also anticipate that we will be able to add to the theory base as well as recommending changes in practice to the stakeholders in preparing and employing young professionals.

Because of the multi-disciplinary nature of our group, our team meetings began to reveal the range of differences and similarities among the four communities of practice we are studying, even before we began to collect data. We identified differences in the terminology used in each profession (student teaching, rotation, field placement, practicum, or *"stage"*; cooperating teacher, supervisor, associate). We identified important commonalities in the general plan of all four baccalaureate programs (such as the attempt to integrate theory and practice by having several practical placements distributed throughout the programs), the close involvement and commitment of field supervisors in the training process, and the general format of the field placements. We noticed the presence of organized supervision and evaluation of beginning professionals in some fields (such as social work) and none in others (such as teaching).

A number of key units of analysis have been employed. First, the broad activity of each field education setting has been captured in detail, using categories drawn from activity theory: the subjects, the objects/outcomes, the mediational means, the structure and make up of the community, the ways in which it divides or shares the physical and cognitive labors, and the rules by which it operates. Second, particular attention has been paid to participant involvement with mediational means, with a specific focus on language, which Vygotsky calls "the master tool." Third, close observation has been made of the learning activity that occurs in and through field-education mentorship dyads. From this analysis, the verbal protocols have allowed us to validate the theoretical constructs that formed the basis of our research, as well as to identify some recommendations for practice. The rest of the chapter will focus on four of the most salient issues that may be extrapolated to a variety of practices from our analysis of the first two years of data.

4.   FINDINGS AND IMPLICATIONS

The quotations are identified by the abbreviation for the profession (Education: ED; Social Work: SW; Occupational Therapy: OT; and Physiotherapy: PT) and by the speaker, whether student (stu), neophyte (neo), or supervisor (sup).

4.1   The Need for Time

One of the first findings to emerge from our analysis was the fact that the transition from university to work is not a spontaneous event. As they begin their professional experience in the practicum, or on the first days on the job, newcomers are beginning their enculturation into their profession. They are learning a language that transcends the technical terminology they have learned in university courses, and making links between the theory and daily practice. They are learning to make the transition from student to professional by working with professionals. This is a difficult process for some students, who do not make the link between theory and practice until they have been in the field for several years (Le Maistre, Boudreau, & Paré, 2001).

In all four professions, the first days of the practicum are spent on orientation to the site. This usually involves being provided with a workspace, keys, handbooks; reading files, records, documents; meeting other colleagues in the team; learning laws, policies and procedures; shadowing and observing the supervisor. Newcomers are learning the physical surroundings and "house rules." To orient them, old-timers frequently show newcomers around or send them on errands:

> "[My supervisor] brings me around. She brings me to the nurses. Like, things that I might not even be dealing with right now, just to say, 'well, this is where the nurses' station is,' or, 'go and speak to Carl or go and speak to Mara and go and speak to Carolyn'" (SW stu).

Students describe their experience during this time as: "...getting the feel..." (SW stu).

"The first days I observed more than I'd intervene. And then I'd be more comfortable intervening afterwards" (OT stu).

A supervisor described this as:

"...Shadowing.... Sending the student to areas I know are active. Following, asking social workers if the student can go with them to a meeting, an interview, if they can sit in on a variety of lectures" (SW sup).

In post-Industrial Revolution Britain, this was known as "sitting by Nellie": that is, sitting beside and closely observing the work of a more experienced colleague:

"I think it's important that a student can sit in with a supervisor while the supervisor is doing the interview and be able to observe" (SW sup).

But by doing this, beginners also learn what Fineman (1993) calls "The emotional architecture of organizational culture" (p. 21). A newcomer to a school discovers that he or she should sit in a certain area of the staff lounge. The physiotherapy newcomer learns where in the hospital's multidisciplinary group to stand when viewing x-rays. The new social worker finds out that he or she should not enter a patient's room during medical rounds. The novice occupational therapist discovers how to hold an infant. All beginners learn appropriate language and even clothing:

"It's amazing how many [students] are not appropriately attired. . . . You're going into families, you're going into people's homes. And if you're dressed in a way that says, 'this is me, I'm a professional, here I am,' rather than 'I'm just popping by on my way to the beach' [laughs], or whatever, it gives the self more presence" (SW sup).

Even more important, the newcomer must absorb cultural knowledge—the ethics and mores of the institution in which the profession is being practiced, or the placement is occurring. This may involve developing pride in the profession:

"...social workers have a bad name...there's a lot of PR work that has to be done for social workers" (SW stu).

"proud to be ..." (OT stu).

It certainly involves a developing sense of membership. We asked new professionals when they felt a sense of belonging to the profession. Answers varied, depending on the individual:

"I felt like an OT in last 2 [practica]. I'm in a field I want to work in" (OT stu).

"When you open that door and say, 'This is my class'" (ED neo).

"The first time as a student teacher I gave an assignment to students and it came back with Mr [Name] on it, I thought Woooaaaoow!" (ED neo).

"I think back and it was always in me when I was young" (ED neo).

We believe that the language, teamwork, and pride are best developed in the workplace because they are developed in the context of the "communities of practice" in which they are most relevant. Every school is different from every other school; a private physiotherapy clinic is different from practice in a hospital; a social worker's role is different in a group home than in a foster home program. Although many university professors who teach students theoretical knowledge have experience in the field, workplace culture—especially the ethos particular to each individual workplace—is beyond their knowledge. The student or beginning professional is in survival mode, and getting through the week—or even the day—is a challenge. It is clear to us that the employer must acknowledge that learning-to-belong is a slow process and that time must be built in to the newcomer's schedule to accommodate it.

4.2   The Need to Scaffold

Each of the professions we are examining places great importance on the practicum and the learning that takes place there under the tutelage of the supervisor. The supervisor may deliver direct instruction, but they always perform a supportive role as the newcomers are moving in from the periphery to the center of the action. Initially, the supervisor provides considerable support and is sensitive to the needs of the student, recognizing, in the words of some supervisors:

"It takes courage to be a student" (SW sup).

"…you don't want to give them something horrific that they will feel overwhelmed" (SW sup).

"…they are getting so much all at once" (SW sup).

Actual participation in this phase of the practicum is minimal, and the beginner is truly on the periphery. Because of the quantity of new information, students may not perceive this as being a gradual process:

"I got integrated right away. Really fast. We have to because this is a really short placement" (OT stu).

Some supervisors acknowledge that even if they provide the most careful nurturing, asking:

"Are you comfortable with doing this? Because, if not, why put student in situation of failure?…" (PT sup).

there comes a moment when:

"…whether they are ready or not ready, they have to do it" (SW sup).

The increase in participation involves the assignment of legitimate tasks, initially with the support and close mentorship of the supervisor. Withdrawal of the scaffolding, whether gradual or not, is an essential part of the learning process, and represents an increase in the student's participation in the activity of the practicum site. The process of enculturation obviously involves learning the skills of the profession so that by the end, the student is:

"an 'Entry-level therapist'" (OT sup).

"comfortable as a working professional in the school" (ED sup).

This corresponds to an increase in the complexity and responsibility for all aspects of client care for occupational therapy and physical therapy, or more classes taught during the day for a student teacher, or writing assessments and developing intervention plans for a social worker. But the process is much more complex and subtle than learning practical skills, and is a component of the enculturation described in the previous section. It is matched by a growing independence in the newcomer, encouraged by good supervisors:

"I promote autonomy. I specifically ask for students who are more autonomous because we don't have a lot of structure here" (PT sup).

This is recognized by the students:

"By third year you should be a lot more independent …the supervisors sort of back off …you know your material" (PT stu).

Knowing the material is one component that makes it possible for the student's participation to be more central, or less peripheral, to the activity of the organization. Allowing the student to be more autonomous—"Backing off"—may be difficult for the supervisor since it involves a release of agency, although it appears that the supervisors in our study were experienced enough in the supervision process to be able to judge when to do this quite quickly and confidently:

> "I'm not in the classroom all the time because that defeats the purpose of the exercise…I'm there as much as needed but no more than necessary" (ED sup).

But the beginner is still a beginner, with mixed emotions and oscillating feelings of confidence and insecurity. She may:

> "… feel like an OT when I'm confident," (OT stu)

or realize that:

> "…this is like a transition for me. I feel ready and then sometimes I am kind of anxious about it" (OT stu).

But a PT student told us that:

> "Learning occurs steadily—always learning, picking up little things—but it also jumps and plateaus" (PT stu).

In the words of a beginning teacher:

> "Part of becoming a professional is figuring out what the rules are—the politics of the school. It's similar to when you walk into the school as student for the first time. My staff were very welcoming, but the kids have to see that you know the building, the little details. [You learn it] day by day. No book will tell you" (ED neo).

Membership in the profession has begun. Students are learning the register appropriate to their profession, ways to collaborate with other professionals, and the tacit cultural knowledge they will need in their careers. They need less scaffolding than on their first days on the job, and they have moved in from the periphery closer to the center. However, they are still insecure, and still in need of mentoring from an experienced practitioner, although they may be reticent in expressing it.

4.3   The Need to be Proactive

Beginning professionals are vulnerable and insecure for a variety of reasons, such as their youth; their lack of knowledge of the profession and of the rules of the particular site where they are working; their lack of tenure and consequent sense of constantly being evaluated. Beginning teachers are often given inconvenient schedules and the "worst" classes and their recollections are especially poignant:

"My first year was teaching first grade in an inner city school where a large percentage of the students was either learning disabled or came from 'bad'/dysfunctional families. Very few services were offered for the teachers or students" (ED neo).

"My main problem was adjusting to the amount and scope of work involved. Paperwork and other housekeeping detract from time needed for planning, marking, etc. Also, fatigue is greater than expected" (ED neo).

"I feel overwhelmed by and poorly prepared for the negative behaviors of students in my classroom as well as the planning required on a daily, weekly and monthly basis" (ED neo).

In an earlier study (Le Maistre, Boudreau, & Paré, 2001), it appeared clear that the onus was on the beginning teachers to ask for help, even though this was at a time when they were feeling vulnerable and unlikely to want to expose their lack of knowledge, and when, occasionally, requests for help were refused. It was a relieved student teacher who reported:

"My cooperating teacher found me" (ED stu).

Supervision and mentoring are time-consuming and demanding, and supervisors need to develop strategies for fitting the extra responsibilities into their day. It is common practice in social work, physical therapy, and occupational therapy for a supervisor to use the review of student-written charts or records—which the supervisor must co-sign—as a chance to go over the day's events with the student. But it is easy for old-timers to ignore a newcomer who appears to be surviving if the newcomer does not ask for help. All the supervisors we interviewed reported the benefits of working with newcomers:

"I enjoy [supervising] because it causes me to rethink and refresh" (SW sup).

"[Students] make you think about ethics, morals, education, knowing more" (ED sup).

"[Supervision] brings you back to . . . the beginning. Sometimes when you have been around a long time you get so caught up in all the bureaucracy of things and all the things that weigh you down. . . . [A] student that's coming in [is] always very eager to help and to change things and to make things better for the clients; it's nice to go back to that and say 'that's why I started'" (SW sup).

Since the mentoring role is beneficial to both protegé and mentor, it seems important to us for organizations to build mentoring into its professional development activities, as well as for universities to encourage students to be proactive in asking for help.

4.4   The Need to Avoid Conflicting Roles

The mentoring literature is replete with references to mentoring as a strategy for mid-career growth: worthwhile, although needing a time commitment from both the mentor and the employer (see, e.g., Reiman & Thies-Sprinthall, 1998). Less evident in the literature are descriptions of the situations we have observed of conflict between the roles of supervisors as mentors and supervisors as evaluators. The experienced practitioner who is supervising a new practitioner acts as mentor—someone who supports, nurturers, or acts as an advocate or intermediary—for the newcomer, and newcomers in all the professions we are studying include formal or informal mentoring. In social work, physical therapy, and occupational therapy, the same person also acts as an evaluator of the probationer. At the pre-service stage in all four professions, including teaching, the student in a field experience is mentored and evaluated by the same person. The double role of ally and evaluator can cause tension when the time comes for evaluation:

"Having a failing student is draining on everyone" (PT sup).

" ...every suggestion that my partner and I made—because there were both of us at the time—he would have nothing to do with it. And I put a failing mark" (ED sup).

"I feel offended when they don't take criticism. A good student teacher will accept feedback and not be so defensive. I don't want to have to walk on eggshells" (ED sup).

"They should be willing to learn. It's hard to take criticism, but that's the way we learn" (ED sup).

It should be noted that we found some newcomers who engaged in rigorous self-reflection and evaluated themselves more harshly than their supervisors would have done.

"It [the experience of a tough class] taught me to look at what I'm doing and critique myself. Because some people could say, 'oh that lesson didn't go very well. But maybe it was just the group.' But you have to look at yourself and what you're doing and say, 'well actually, maybe it was me. Maybe it was the way I was teaching them'" (ED stu).

We also found that most newcomers welcomed and expected feedback on performance, and are explicit on their expectations:

"...positive and negative feedback, choosing words carefully and being sensitive" (ED stu).

"Provide feedback that is specific and constructive" (ED stu) (original emphasis).

"...less time in this setting for supervision ...[it's] so busy here that sometimes I don't get feedback right away" (OT stu).

Sometimes the supervisors described feedback and evaluation that clearly involved a nurturing role:

"You have to teach them how to prioritize" (SW sup).

"What are they going to do to decompress?" (SW sup).

A supervising teacher described a powerful learning episode in a class led by a student teacher:

"...and there was a moment when they were together. And I told everybody I knew, 'I saw a teacher born today.' She didn't realize...I said, 'Did you realize that moment?...that moment, you just—you have what it takes. You have what it takes'" (ED sup).

Key in this quotation is the fact that the student teacher did not realize the impact of what she had done until it was pointed out to her by the experienced observer, and that this knowledge was an empowering event for her. It is clear that supervisors need to make explicit the strengths as well as the weaknesses of the newcomer.

We have observed that good supervisors manage the conflict between nurturing and criticizing by gradually withdrawing themselves from the supervisory role as they take on the evaluative role. The level of supervision decreases as the student's involvement becomes more central, yet there is still supervision, even though it may be occurring at a physical distance:

> "I basically used to tell my students, 'you're going to do it by yourself. I'm going to be right here. I often times look like I'm not around, but I am. I'm listening through the curtain while you interview. I'm listening to your history. I'll be peeking around here to watch you do this technique'" (PT sup).

Gauging the proper distance from which to observe is a highly skilled ability; too close, and the newcomer becomes uncomfortable, too far, and serious physical, psychological, or social damage can occur. Once the newcomer has mastered basic competencies, however, observational distance is granted so that newcomers can gain their own and others' confidence:

> "I absolutely hated it when a supervisor would stare….Your patient has zero confidence in you now because there is someone staring over your shoulder" (PT sup).

> "Because when I'm with my supervisor and with, let's say, the psychiatrist, then I'm not the person that the patient really talks to, right?" (OT stu).

> "The supervisor does more listening behind the curtain" (PT stu).

We believe that the learning opportunities provided by the gradual physical withdrawal of the supervisor are often not recognized by newcomers, at least initially. Although we saw evidence that some students realized that possibilities for growth must be grasped and exploited:

> "[My supervisor] gives me the opportunity to take the lead. Sometimes she backs off, she leaves me some space. But…it's not really obvious. So I really have to take, like savor the opportunity and think fast and take the floor if I can" (OT stu),

in general, perhaps because formal schooling has made them passive rather than proactive learners, or perhaps because they are anticipating an evaluation, most students are hesitant to be controversial, or even assertive.

In the four professions we are studying, the university grants a degree, based on success in both the theoretical courses and in the practica, which gives the graduate access to accreditation into the profession, usually after a probationary period. The supervisor plays the major role in evaluating the student's performance on the practicum. One social work supervisor summarized the criteria for success on the practicum as:

"You shouldn't leave a placement feeling that you can't go and do a piece of work somewhere" (SW sup).

When we asked supervisors to describe a good student, it was clear that they had a well-defined mental picture. Typically, they defined good students as:

"willing" (SW sup).

"...not lazy...take initiative...believe in themselves..." (SW sup).

"Someone that asks questions and wants to learn...get information from whoever...prepared to make mistakes" (SW sup).

"Someone that asks good questions, good questions at the good moment" (SW sup).

"She's quite risky--she's going to do it even if it's nerve-wracking." (SW sup)

Supervisors can identify objectives for their evaluations, even when they are evaluating rather intangible attributes:

"I'm looking for her grasp of theory and her ability to project" (SW sup).

"...judge the progress of the student by seeing that they're more active, intervene more. I gather feedback from other team members" (OT sup).

There is a clear danger that the process of evaluation may distort newcomers' activities by inflicting on them a pressure to conform. While two supervisors told us:

"Copying or mimicking other therapists doesn't promote individual thinking and thought processes for how your assessment goes. And everyone ties their thoughts together differently as far as I'm concerned," (OT sup)

"Therapy is art and science. One way is not necessarily correct. Adaptability and being unbiased ...is probably most important thing" (PT sup),

this open-mindedness did not seem to be typical. Supervisors were more likely to be conscious of their roles as gatekeepers. One expressed her awareness of the magnitude of this responsibility:

"I don't think people realize how important it is that you are having the professional life of a person in your hands" (SW sup).

"I'm proud that there are a lot of people who have worked with me who are teaching now" (ED sup).

When the stakes are as high as entry into the profession, or successful completion of a probation, only truly self-confident students will risk "rocking the boat." Their participation at this stage is certainly legitimate, but it is still peripheral.

5.   CONCLUSION

By the end of the final practicum, most students are at a stage of being expert at the role of student, and still naïve in the role of practitioner. After a year or so of practice, they look back wistfully at the expectations they had as final year students:

"[I] thought students would be more motivated. On the [practicum], the novelty (for students having a new teacher) never wears off, so it's easier to maintain interest. When you're there all the time, you really have to be innovative and sometimes it doesn't happen…. Some kids won't respond" (ED neo) (original emphasis).

A central conclusion of the study to-date is that the expertise gained in the school-to-work transitions is "an interactive accomplishment, constructed in encounters and exchanges between people and their artifacts" (Engeström, 1992, p. 1). This view contrasts with a conception of expertise as the property of a single individual, gained through the transmission of knowledge from old-timer to newcomer, and shifts the research focus to the collaborative relationships neophytes experience during field education and initial professional practice. From this perspective, expertise is viewed as the ability to participate effectively in the collaborative, situated practices of particular groups, and learning—that is, the development toward expertise – is seen as the gradual mastery of those practices through participation and under the guidance of experienced old-timers. This assumption challenges much of the professional and workplace education literature in the disciplines under study, but we believe that it is supported in our data.

Our transcripts are replete with references to the "theoretical" knowledge that students have learned in the university, usually by a transmission model. This theory is acknowledged to be necessary, but usually compared unfavorably with what students are learning in the "real" world. Students in our study have the apparent luxury of spending extended time in a carefully controlled setting, when they are truly on the periphery of the activity. Even so, when they begin the first year of practice, they exhibit the "culture shock" described by Veenman (1984), and realize, in the words of one neophyte, that until then, they had been in a "student bubble" (SW neo), shielded by the mentor from the reality of the demands and politics of the workplace. This disjuncture between school and work must be even greater in fields where there is no monitored practicum, and should surely be on the agenda of any orientation for newcomers to such professions.

When neophytes first enter communities of practice they participate in the actions and operations that comprise collective activity with conscious and often awkward self- and task-awareness. In time, and with assistance from mentors, that participation becomes more routine and knowledge becomes more tacit: it moves from focal to subsidiary awareness (Polanyi, 1964, 1967). Our findings support these social perspectives on activity, cognition, and learning. We are building up a picture of neophyte workers at a cusp in their development. It is clear to us that the transition from student to professional is not the automatic, spontaneous process that it has been assumed to be. It needs time, support from experienced and willing colleagues, and a recognition of these needs from all the participants in the process, whether students, newcomers, universities, employers, supervisors, or mentors.

REFERENCES

Chaiklin, S., & Lave, J. (Eds.) (1993). *Understanding practice: Perspectives on activity and context*. Cambridge: Cambridge University Press.

Cole, M. (1995). Socio-cultural-historical psychology: Some general remarks and a proposal for a new kind of cultural-genetic methodology. In J. V. Wertsch, P. Del Rio, & A. Alvarez (Eds.), *Sociocultural studies of mind* (pp. 187-214). Cambridge: Cambridge University Press.

Cole, M. (1996). *Cultural psychology*. Cambridge, MA: Harvard University Press.

Cole, M., & Engeström, Y. (1993). A cultural-historical approach to distributed cognition. In G. Salomon (Ed.), *Distributed cognitions: Psychological and educational considerations*. Cambridge: Cambridge University Press.

Engeström, Y. (1992). *Interactive expertise: Studies in distributed working intelligence*. Research Bulletin 83, Helsinki: Department of Education, University of Helsinki.

Fineman, S. (1993). Organizations as emotional arenas. In S. Fineman (Ed.), *Emotion in organizations* (pp. 9-35). London: Sage Publications.

Hanks, W. F. (1991). Foreword. In J. Lave & E. Wenger (Eds.), *Situated learning: Legitimate peripheral participation* (pp. 13-24). Cambridge: Cambridge University Press.

Huling-Austin, L. (1990). Teacher induction programs and internships. In W. R. Houston (Ed.), *Handbook of research on teacher education* (pp. 535-548). New York: Macmillan.

Lave, J. (1996). Teaching, as learning, in practice. *Mind, Culture, and Activity, 3* (3), 149-164.

Lave, J. (1991). Situated learning in communities of practice. In L. B. Resnick, J. M. Levine, & S. D. Teasley (Eds.), *Perspectives on socially shared cognition* (pp. 63-82). Washington, DC: American Psychological Association.

Lave J., & Wenger, E. (1991). *Situated learning: Legitimate peripheral participation.* Cambridge: Cambridge University Press.

Le Maistre, C., Boudreau, S., & Paré, A. (2001). *Mentoring the beginning teacher: Assessing the support needed and provided.* Unpublished report to the Comité d'agrément des programmes de formation à l'enseignement, Montreal, QC.

Leont'ev, A.N. (1981). The problem of activity in psychology. In J. V. Wertsch (Ed.), *The concept of activity in Soviet psychology* (pp. 37-71). Armonk, NY: Sharpe.

Polanyi, M. (1964). *Personal knowledge: Towards a post-critical philosophy.* New York: Harper & Row.

Polanyi, M. (1967). *The tacit dimension.* New York: Anchor

Reiman, A. J., & Thies-Sprinthall, L. (1998). Mentoring and supervision for teacher development. New York: Addison-Wesley Longman.

Rogoff, B. (1990). *Apprenticeship in thinking: Cognitive development in social context.* New York: Oxford University Press.

Rogoff, B. (1991). Social interaction as apprenticeship in thinking: Guided participation in spatial planning. In L. B. Resnick, J. M. Levine, & S. D. Teasley (Eds.), *Perspectives on socially shared cognition* (pp. 349-364). Washington, DC: American Psychological Association.

Rogoff, B. (1995). Observing sociocultural activity on three planes: participatory appropriation, guided participation, and apprenticeship. In J. V. Wertsch, P. Del Rio, & A. Alvarez (Eds.), *Sociocultural studies of mind* (pp. 139-164). Cambridge: Cambridge University Press.

Salomon, G. (1993a). Editor's introduction. In G. Salomon (Ed.), *Distributed cognitions: Psychological and educational considerations* (pp. xi-xxi). Cambridge: Cambridge University Press.

Veenman, S. (1984). Perceived problems of beginning teachers. *Review of Educational Research, 54*(2), 143–178.

Vygotsky, L. S. (1978). *Mind in society: The development of higher psychological processes.* Cambridge, MA: Harvard University Press.

Wenger, E. (1998). *Communities of practice: Learning, meaning and identity.* Cambridge: Cambridge University Press.

Wertsch, J. V. (1991). *Voices of the mind: A sociocultural approach to mediated action.* Cambridge, MA: Harvard University Press.

Wertsch, J. V., Del Rio, P., & Alvarez, A. (Eds.) (1995). *Sociocultural studies of mind.* Cambridge: Cambridge University Press.

Chapter 8

BREAKING THE BOUNDARIES BETWEEN ACADEMIC DEGREES AND LIFELONG LEARNING
Designing Demand-Driven Lifelong Learning Processes for Employees

Thomas J.P. Thijssen[1] & Fons T.J. Vernooij[2]
[1]Hamilton International and University of Amsterdam, the Netherlands; [2]Free University of Amsterdam, the Netherlands

1. INTRODUCTION

There are two main reasons for people who finished their regular education to continue learning when they have found a job. One is that they want to improve their competencies, understood as a combination of knowledge, skills, and attitude (Parry, 1996; Stoof, Martens & Merrieënboer, 2001). They want as well to prepare themselves for a career. The second reason is that working situations are changing fast. New developments in information and communication technology create changes in the working situation. In order to keep up with these changes, further education is required. This may either be conceived as an improvement in acquired competencies or as an extension of certificates acquired. In both situations the question arises whether this additional learning should be supply driven or demand driven.

Supply-driven learning can be understood as learning situations where the supplier develops a course or seminar, based on its own market research, resulting in an offer to customers. As far as universities and business schools are concerned, they have material available from their bachelor, master, or Ph.D. program. For some employees this might just be what they are looking for, but for many these courses are too abstract and too little applicable in

R.G.Milter et al. (eds.), Educational Innovation in Economics and Business IX, 137–156.
©2004 *Springer. Printed in the Netherlands.*

their own working situation. Such employees have other learning goals, related to the job they have or the position they want to acquire. For these employees another approach would be more suitable: demand-driven learning. In this approach the learning goals of the learner, or maybe a group of learners, are the starting point for the design of a course. The learner is in control of the learning process.

There are many concepts used to describe the learning demands of people who finished their initial education. One is lifelong learning. The national research network for new approaches to lifelong learning describes working definitions for formal schooling, further education, and informal learning (Livingstone, 1998). In this chapter we will use the definition of lifelong learning in the sense of further education. In addition to that, we limit ourselves to work-related lifelong learning, excluding such fine courses as, for instance, violin studies and sailing. One important distinction is that we will explore lifelong learning as a demand-driven learning activity of further education whereby the learner is in control.

When this concept is used in this chapter, it is restricted to situations where employees are working on their employability. Therefore, an employer is involved in most of these cases. Employers and employees have both common interests and personal interests in describing the specific learning outcomes and in creating a learning situation. They each have their own value chain with input of effort, time, and money and output in terms of competencies for the employee that can contribute to the productivity of the company. We will use the concept of the value chain (Porter, 1985) to describe the processes of creating value through learning/teaching activities.

Once the learning goals are stated, a supplier is looked for or the employer might develop a course by his or her own personnel department. If a university or business school is approached to make an offer, then a third value chain becomes involved, that is, the value chain of the institute (Thijssen, Maes, & Vernooij, 2002). As a well-organized institute it will try to reduce its costs and look for existing material as the basis for an offer. That is where demand-driven learning can collide with supply-driven learning.

In this contribution we will explore the value chains of the learners, the companies, and the educational institutions. We introduce the home front as a separate role that involves the relatives and friends of the learner whose social lives are influenced by the time the learner invests in his or her learning. The three value chains and the role of the home front are explored in order to find the research questions that would help us address tomorrow's problems. This chapter reports on the journey towards designing demand-driven education that forces educators to rethink their role in learning processes and break through the boundaries of formal schooling. The aim is to present a fresh way of looking at design problems and inspiring educators by sharing experiences. First, we will describe the various value chains and make an inventory of conflicting interests and problems. At the end of Section 1, we will formulate the design goals. In Section 2, we will describe three value chains of the learner, the company and the educational institution. In Section 3, we will introduce a framework for designing demand-driven lifelong learning for employees. In Section 4, we will share some insights on experiments with new educational design, and in Section 5, we will list the learning points from these experiments for educational institutions. We conclude with recommendations for further exploratory research.

We will first describe the characteristics of the value chain of the learner and explore the role of the home front. Secondly, we will embark on describing the value chain of the company. By comparing these value chains, we can identify conflicts of interest and specific problems. Then we will describe the value chain of the traditional educational institution and explore how this value chain fits the needs of the other two value chains. Based on this analysis we can formulate our design goals.

2. THREE VALUE CHAINS

In this section we describe the demand-driven value chain of a lifelong learner, the role of the home front, the supply-driven value chain of the employer, and the confrontation between demand and supply. Further we describe the supply-driven value chain of educational institutions and conclude with a summary of conflicting interests and problems.

2.1 The Demand-Driven Value Chain of a Lifelong Learner

As mentioned before, employees have two reasons to keep on learning after finishing formal education. To build a career, employees have to develop their employability and seek learning opportunities that fit in with their capacities and aims. From this perspective, personal aims are the driving force. The second reason is the developments in society enforced by improvements in information technology. To keep up with these changes, employees have to adapt their capacities to new requirements of the environment. From this perspective, social aims are the driving force.

The two forces come together in the characteristics of the value chain of the learner:

- The individual and his or her desired competencies are the starting point.
- The personal aims of the learner require demand-driven lifelong learning.
- The learner is in control by self-regulating the learning processes.
- The learning process must fit in the constraints of time, money, and energy.
- The learning process requires flexibility to learn as, if, and when needed.
- There is a need to make the content relevant for both the individual and the work context.
- The social aims of the learner offer opportunities for co-ordination of learning outcomes with other employees.
- To explore the value chain of the learner in more detail, an analysis can be made of the phases of the value chain of demand-driven lifelong learning.

1. *Performing self-assessment*
   1.1. Identify talents in relation to self, career, and work.
   1.2. Identify desired career steps and the learning requirements.
   1.3. Identify required adjustments to the changing working conditions.
   1.4. What do I want to learn? (Affective)
   1.5. What do I need to learn? (Cognitive)
   1.6. What do I choose to learn? (Conative)
   1.7. How much can I afford in terms of time, effort, and money?
2. *Designing a personal development plan*
   2.1. Which competencies do I choose to improve?
   2.2. What do I hope to achieve related to my current and future work at my current company?
   2.3. What do I hope to achieve from the point of view of employability?
   2.4. How much time, effort, and money am I willing and able to spend?
   2.5. How will it effect my relations at home and with friends (the home front)?
3. *Searching for learning supply*
   3.1. What is available on the job?
   3.2. What is offered by a branch organization?
   3.3. What is offered by professional organizations?
   3.4. What is available on the World Wide Web?
   3.5. What can I find in libraries (articles, books)?
   3.6. Which (short) training courses are offered by commercial and non-commercial organizations?
   3.7. What do educational institutions offer? Is that demand driven or supply driven?
4. *Matching learning needs and learning supply*
   4.1. What is the best match between learning needs and available learning supplies?

4.2. How much room is there for negotiating the gap between learning needs and learning supplies?

4.3. What will get me to my desired learning outcome best and fastest?

4.4. What inspires me most?

4.5. How much money do I want to spend?

4.6. Home much money will my employer provide for studies?

4.7. How to make a choice?

5. *Executing a learning process*

5.1. Gather knowledge and experience.

5.2. Apply and practice the knowledge.

5.3. Monitor achievements in terms of competencies gained and performances increased (job promotion).

6. *Evaluating learning achievements*

6.1. Evaluate periodically time and effort put in against results obtained.

6.2. Estimate the value learning represents.

6.3. Prepare for new future choices.

2.2   The Role of the Home Front

The impact of the home front on the learner is often ignored. Family and friends, however, can have a great influence on the aspirations, inspiration, and achievements of the learner. If a partner is supportive towards career advancement, the learner is obviously more stimulated to spend time on further education. In that case, it will be easier for the home front to carry the burden of having less time and attention from the learner. On the other hand, if the home front is not supportive, then the learner has a significant problem and will find him/herself in a time squeeze. He or she will be more interested in time-effective learning programs.

The home front can also contribute by making suggestions for lifelong learning, that is, friends may share their experiences and offer suggestions to the learner. If the learner achieves new competencies, he or she may benefit from it through better employability. The better position and income will be a benefit to the home front as well. This might be an incentive for the home front to put up with the learning activities of the learner. The role of the home front will be taken into account in the design of the framework for demand-driven lifelong learning. However, the influence of the home front will not be described as a value chain, because the role of the home front cannot be considered as a deliberate value adding process.

2.3   Supply-Driven Value Chain of the Employer

The second important value chain to be considered is the value chain of the employer (Bennebroek Gravenhorst, Boonstra, & Werkman, 2000). A clear description of this value chain makes it possible to confront the value chain of the learner (the employee) with the value chain of the employer. This results in an overview of common interests and possible conflicts (Argyris, Putman, McLain, & Smith, 1985; Argyris & Schön, 1978).

The most important characteristics of the value chain of the employer are:

- The company is focused on value creation for shareholders (in some cases stakeholders).
- It exploits the talent base of human resources amongst other resources like capital, information, and natural resources.
- The personnel department is focused on selection, training, deployment, and redeployment.
- There is a strong orientation on performance.
- The aim is quick wins through Return on Investment (Return on People).
- To explore the value chain of companies in more detail, an analysis can be made of the phases of this chain.

1. *Performing assessments*
    1.1. Identify the human talent (employees or human resources) needed for the near future to meet the organization needs.
    1.2. Assess the gap between competencies needed and current competencies available.
    1.3. Decide on hiring new talent (employees or human resources) or training current talent.
    1.4. Compare with financial resources available for training or hiring.
2. *Prioritizing learning*
    2.1. Decide on the topics that need to be addressed first.
    2.2. Decide on in-house training or outsourcing.
    2.3. Decide on budget and time.
    2.4. Select content of training/course and method of training.
    2.5. Allocate requirements to individuals.
3. *Searching for learning supply*
    3.1. What is already available in the company?
    3.2. What is offered by a branch organization?
    3.3. What is offered by professional organizations?
    3.4. What is available on the World Wide Web?
    3.5. Which (short) training courses are offered by commercial and non-commercial organizations?

3.6. What do educational institutions offer? Is that demand driven or supply driven?

4. *Convincing individuals to increase their competencies*

4.1. Communicate personally on career planning and function requirements.

4.2. Agree on content and planning of training/course.

4.3. Enroll employees in training/course.

4.4. Monitor progress of training/course.

4.5. Monitor performance on the job.

5. *Evaluating increases in competencies and performance*

5.1. Evaluate periodically the increases in competencies and performance.

5.2. Measure the contribution of training/courses to the results of the organization.

5.3. Make new plans for the next period.

2.4 The Confrontation of Two Value Chains

Confronting the two value chains described results in both common interests and conflicts of interest. Common interests exist where the employer seeks quick returns on investment by increased performance and loyalty of the employee. Especially the social aims of lifelong learning, related to adapting people to changes in working conditions, are a source of common interests. As far as personal interests are concerned, conflicts may arise between the value chains. If the career planning of the employee fits in with the company's planning, there may be some problem in timing, but both benefit from the growth in competencies of the employee. Conflicts of interest exist where the personal aims do not fit the possibilities a company can or wants to offer to a person. Then the employee must negotiate or find his or her own way to improve competencies outside the company.

2.5 Supply-Driven Value Chain of Educational Institutions

One of the phases in the value chain of both employees and employers is the search for learning supply. Some of the possible resources are traditional educational institutions, such as colleges and universities. To explore common interests and possible conflicts between this third value chain and the combined value chains of the learner and the employer (company), a thorough investigation is required into the value chain of the traditional institute (Bates, 1997). Therefore, a description of this third value chain will follow in order to explore how it fits the needs of the two other value chains. Based on this analysis we can formulate our design goals.

To be accurate, not all educational institutes are traditional. Quite a lot of them use problem-based learning (Arts, Gijselaers, & Segers, 2002) or aim at the development of competencies (Otting, Zwaal, & Eringa, 2002). Moreover, the introduction of the Internet can have a profound influence on distance education as part of lifelong learning (Itzkan, 1994; Vernooij, Thijssen, & Schermerhorn, 2001).

Just like with the employee and the employer, educational institutions have their own characteristics of the value chain. Although our research is restricted to the Netherlands, we assume the value chains of educational institutions in other countries are similar, as they work under similar conditions.

- Traditional educational institutions have difficulty in capturing the market for lifelong learning.
- They offer traditional courses with fixed curricula, certain topics at certain times over a planned period of time.
- Modules are very general and not related to the specific needs of companies and persons.
- Processes for lifelong learners are the same as processes for regular students.
- The lectures are separate from the working context.
- The institute has few benefits from the students' ability of self-regulation.
- The institution regulates everything in detail.
- Costs are very high in terms of both time and money.
- The flexibility is low as bureaucratic measures are inevitable to keep control of the whole organization.

The value adding steps an educational institution undertakes can be described as follows:

1. Identify a generic market need for a particular course.
2. Investigate whether an existing course can be offered to meet the need.
3. If not, select (top) teachers to design a course, if possible, the best teachers.
4. Decide on themes, topics and the order of topics with regard to time and space (i.e., whether the course will be given off-line and/or online).
5. Gather literature (the best content) and design each module in terms of knowledge transfer by the teacher and learning tasks by the students.
6. Execute the course by offering the best content by the best teachers.
7. Assess students' learning results through examination.
8. Award the results with a diploma or certificate (Vermunt & Verschaffel, 2000).

2.6   Conflicting Interests and Problems

The three value chains and the role of the home front are obviously different; they represent the interests of the four actors: the learner, the home front, the company, and the educational institution. Each value chain serves a different interest:

−   The *learner's* interest in terms of time, effort, and money spent in relation to benefits gained.
−   The *company's* interest in quick returns on investment and the contribution to the company's results.
−   The *educational institution's* interest in standardization as opposed to costly tailor-made courses.

Now that we have looked at the various value chains, we can formulate the design goals of demand-driven lifelong learning: design-innovative learning programs for lifelong learning, matching the interests of the learner, the home front, the company, and the educational institution. This implies process-oriented teaching (Vermunt & Verschaffel, 2000). It should also save time, effort, and money, and increase the value of the lifelong learning process for all actors involved.

3.   A FRAMEWORK FOR DESIGNING DEMAND-DRIVEN LIFELONG LEARNING PROCESSES (DDLL)

Lifelong learning must adhere to quite a lot of design criteria. In order to form a framework for designing lifelong learning processes, we identify a set of design criteria based on the value chains described in the previous section.

3.1   Design Criteria

1. *Relevance to the learner*
    a. Address the specific learning need at a specific time (competencies for increased performance).
    b. Fit in the context of actual work and career within the actual company.
    c. Fit in possible future jobs at companies or institutions (employability).
    d. Keep time, effort, and monetary expenditure as low as possible.
    e. Inspire and appeal.
    f. Fit the personal learning style and be totally flexible.

Relevance to the home front

    g. Fit in the personal circumstances of the learner (family, friends, hobbies, etc).

    h. Demonstrate potential benefits to the home front.

    i. Leave time for family activities; maintain life/work/learn/family/friends balance.

    j. Make sure that the home front enjoys the rewards of increased competencies of the learner in terms of happiness and in terms of higher income.

2. *Relevance to the company*

    a. Increase learners performance.

    b. Increase the contribution to the company's results.

    c. Immediate and long term benefits to the company.

    d. Increase company loyalty.

    e. Contribute to building the competencies for the future.

3. *Relevance to the educational institution*

    a. Open up and access the market of lifelong learning effectively and efficiently.

    b. Successful exploitation of current resources (teachers, knowledge base, infrastructure).

    c. Generate additional revenue.

    d. Provide for educational experiences for teachers that strengthen current educational programs.

4. *Serving mutual interests*

    a. Combine interests of the learner, home front, company, and educational institution.

    b. Share resources.

    c. Save time, money, and energy.

    d. Increase collective value.

In fact, there is a supply-and-demand relationship between all four actors, which needs to be aligned. An important item educational designers often forget, is the issue of the personal circumstances of the learner. We named it the *home front*. From the perspective of the learner, the home front presents a very important base for happiness and fulfillment. We are talking about family, children, and friends. They can make or break lifelong learning if they withhold their support and stimulation. On the other hand, they can be the trigger for aspirations and ambition. Therefore we introduced design criteria for the home front as well.

3.2 The DDLL Framework

Now that we have all the design criteria on our design pallet, we can start designing the DDLL Framework. Figure 1 includes all the above competing interests.

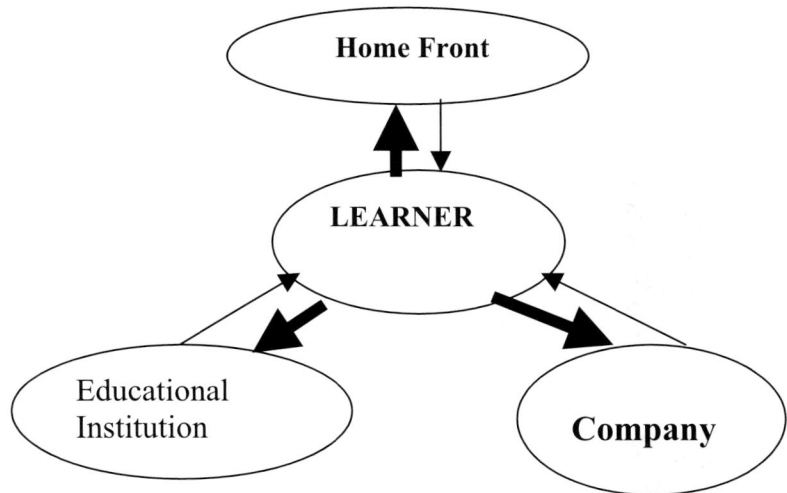

Figure 1. the DDLL Framework

Note: The thick arrow indicates the demands the learner imposes upon his or her environment. The thin arrow identifies the supply offered to the learner by the environment.

Explanation of the DDLL Framework

1. *Learner at the heart of the DDLL Framework*
   The learner wants to be in control of his (you may read as well her) own destiny and he determines personal strategies for learning and advancement. There is a trade-off between time, effort, and money spent on learning, on the one hand, and the benefits gained in each area of the framework, on the other hand. The learner plays various roles in life. Within the home front, the learner plays the role of mother, father, friend, and so forth. But in fact the learner is one and the same person. In the context of learning, we will make a distinction between the role of a person as a learner and the role of a person as a participant in the home front.

2. *Home Front on top of the DDLL Framework*
   The effort of working and learning may take away time from family, friends, children, and hobby. To achieve an acceptable balance between personal needs, private life, learning, and work, the immediate family must

see the benefits as well. Possible benefits are: a happier learner, increased performance in less time, better income, and more time to share together. It is stated that the balance between work, learning, and personal life will be a very important criterion for both the learner and his/her immediate surrounding. The home front will not hesitate to make a sacrifice, if all involved can see the short-term and long-term benefits of increased personal performance and income. But, how many companies and educational institutions are really concerned with these questions?

3. *The Company at the right side of the DDLL Framework*

The employer has a dominant role in the DDLL Framework. The employer is placed at the right side of the DDLL Framework. The company pays the monthly salary, provides for interesting work and working environment and, in return, demands a certain amount of loyalty, commitment, and a clear contribution to the company's objectives. In case the company pays for the education in terms of both time and money, it feels entitled to a specific return on investment. These returns could be: more competence and more dedication of the employee and better performance of the learner and the company as a whole.

More and more companies are committed to developing human talent. They have a clear policy on the matter allowing the learner to choose a career within the company based on very transparent information that the learner can share with the home front. No wonder large companies have started Private Label Universities, Academies, and other in-company training programs. They take the lead in the educational process and exclude the traditional educational institutions from playing a dominant role in lifelong learning.

4. *Educational Institutions at the left side of the DDLL Framework*

If traditional educational institutions play any role in the LL-process at all, they are at best placed on the left side of the model. The learner and the company do not usually regard traditional institutions as sufficiently relevant and flexible to generate specific and immediate value to them. This position is partly due to financial constraints and habits grown out of the traditional view on education. Courses are usually standardized and not tailor-made for the individual learner or company. It is, however, possible to improve this position drastically, if the educational institution is willing to individualize the courses offered, if it decides to support the DDLL process of the learner in a flexible way. That means delivering education to the learner just in time and with relevant knowledge and support from the learners' and company's point of view. This has an important consequence for the educational institution. The institution must learn that the DDLL market is a completely different market, with different needs, preferences, and prices. It requires customer intimacy (Treacy & Wiersema, 1995) with both learners and companies, and it requires operational excellence 24 hours a day, seven days a week. Educational institutions must see it as an attractive opportunity to expand their territory from the ages of 18-25 to 25 and over. Further education is not restricted by age; in fact, lifelong learners may be of all age groups.

Lifelong learning represents a huge, but very difficult market. Education must be immediately relevant to the learner and to the company. Both are clients with very specific and individualized needs and preferences. Education must be tailor made, context specific, and available just in time.

Educational institutions in the Netherlands, such as (see also Section 4): The Johan Cruyff University, the Center of Post Initial Education, and the Network University, prove that it can be accomplished in a flexible way. Four main requirements are:

1. Individualized education addressing learner needs.
2. Assessment of the competencies a learner has developed.
3. Access to knowledge and support as, if, and when needed, and
4. Distinct value from offering the best assessors, coaches, teachers, and granular content.

(By "granular content" we mean small learning units, which require only a couple of hours of learning or less, so they can be scheduled as, if, and when needed.)

If we take the three value chains of the introduction section and the role of the home front, and we focus on the learner, we can place the roles of the home front, the company, and the educational institution in a new perspective. In a DDLL process the learner is in control. This means that the learner's value chain is leading. We will repeat the main steps in the learner's value chain and place the roles of the home front, the company, and the educational institutions in a supporting function. In the design of the DDLL framework, a system of co-creation, communication, and collaboration emerges to create learning values in harmony.

3.3 A System of Co-creation, Communication, and Collaboration

In Table 1 we align the phases of the value chain of the learner and the support functions of the home front, the company, and the educational institution with the learning process.

Table 1. Relationships Between Value Chains

Roles	Exploration	Orientation	Negotiation	Decision	Consumption	Completion	Exploration
Learner	Assess	Plan	Search	Match	Learn	Achieve	Next Steps
Home Front (Family, Friends)	Stimulate (Support or Object)	Negotiate	Advise	Accept or Deny	Grin and Bear	Enjoy Rewards	Objects Stimulates Supports
Company	Personal Attention	Opportunities Resources	Recommend	Transparancy Payment	Resources Stimulate OJT	Enjoy Rewards Promote	Personal Attetntion to Career
Line Manager Mentor Trainer	Line Manager	Mentor	Mentor	Line/ Mentor	Line/Mentor Trainer	Line	Line
Educational Institutions	Provide Information	Add Knowledge and Objectivity	Match Competencies and Opportunities	Provide for Tailor made Supply of Learning Granules	Access to Best Teachers and Content as, if, and when Needed	Competence Profiles and Performance Appraisals	Build Network, Come back and Manage Relationship
Assessor Coach Teacher Animator		Assessor	Coach	Coach	Teachers, Coach	Assessor, Coach	Coach, Animator

3.4 Implications for Traditional Educational Institutions

What can educational institutions learn from Table 1?

- The learner and home front are at the center of attention and are leading.
- The company, as an employer of the learner, represents a potential paying customer for education and training.
- The demands of both the learner and the company for education are used as input for designing and offering courses.
- The assessor provides for objectivity in the assessment of existing competencies.
- The assessor, teacher, and coach team up to support the learner in matching his or her needs and to provide for granular supply, access, and support.
- The mentor, trainer, and line manager team up to support the learner in providing (financial) resources and on-the-job training as well as career opportunities.
- The coaches, mentor, and line managers team up to provide access to the best teachers, the best content, the best working and learning conditions available on demand by the learner, monitoring and evaluating competency profiles and performance appraisals.
- The assessor and the line manager assist the learner in his or her assessment during the learning process. Rewards are provided and celebrations involve the home front.
- An animator is required to stimulate and activate learners to explore the possibilities.
- The educational institution provides for ways to keep in contact and is available for the learner on a DDLL basis - as, if, and when needed.

3.5 Difference with the Traditional Value Chain

What is different from supply-driven and mostly traditional value chain?

- The learner is the starting point, and not the course offered by the institution.
- The home front is included and not ignored.
- The employer is a partner and not just a paying customer.
- The program is individualized by assessors, coaches, teachers, and organized by content, through mass customization (no fixed curriculum but granules).
- Access is as, if, and when needed and through any channel (contact, Web, e-mail, readers, articles, books, learning tasks in theory and practice).

The above DDLL framework can be applied to the design of demand-driven educational programs matching the interests of the learner (and the home front) with the requirements of the company. Educational institutes may be able to expand their market if they consider the requirements from both the learner and the company. In the next section several examples of learning practices are described.

4.   EXAMPLES FROM EXPERIMENTS

Now that we have described the outline of the DDLL framework, we will briefly examine some experiments at educational institutions in the Netherlands. We will look at the schooling of professional teachers at the University of Amsterdam and at the futuristic way of supporting demand-driven learning networks at the Network University in Amsterdam. But before going into the two examples, we will explore the roles of an assessor, teacher, and coach at the Johan Cruyff University, which is part of the economics department of the Hogeschool of Amsterdam.

4.1   Johan Cruyff University: The Roles of an Assessor, Coach, Teacher, and Trainer

At the Johan Cruyff University (JCU), a system of competency-based education has been developed that can be used to break the boundaries between traditional education and lifelong learning in companies (Vernooij, 2001). The JCU is developed to offer elite athletes in all kinds of sports an opportunity to combine their sport activity with a professional education in commercial economics and marketing. Special arrangements are made to support the athletes while they are in training and competition. In fact, the educational institution uses a traditional program in economics to fit in with the demands of the students. However, the way the educational content is offered can be used as a model for lifelong learning.

The curriculum of the JCU is built on blocks of courses and training sessions, related to functions of a marketer. At the start of the educational block, an *assessor* estimates the competencies that have been acquired by the student up till that moment. At the same time, the student explores the competencies required to fulfill the role of that period. The *coach* supports the student in formulating the learning goals that would form a bridge between acquired competencies and desired competencies. Then the student submits his or her learning goals and action plans to the assessor to acquire consent for the study program.

Teachers and trainers are involved to support the student in acquiring knowledge and developing skills. These teachers and trainers report to the student as well as to the assessor about the performance on exams and tasks. In this way the assessor does not have to be an economist to judge the growth in competencies in economics or business, as the teachers and trainers know about the development of knowledge. Neither does the coach have to be an economist, because besides supporting the study plan of the student, his or her job is to support the learning process and to make special arrangements if sports and study have conflicting demands.

4.2 Center of Post Initial Education: Teacher Training

A professional group for whom lifelong learning is important is the group of teachers. To support learning of this group, the University of Amsterdam created a special institution: the Center of Post Initial Education (CPE). This institute started out by offering existing courses from the regular master program to teachers in the area. Soon after that, special courses were created and offered via advertisements in regional papers and professional journals. However, both approaches failed to attract large bodies of students. Even research into the needs of teachers conducted in cooperation with teacher unions (dedicated to specific categories of students) did not result in larger numbers of participants. Teachers mentioned some courses they wanted to have, but once the required courses were offered, most of these teachers did not apply.

Still the CPE became a successful institution, when it switched its policy. The Center no longer approached individual teachers but rather their employers. Instead of offering complete courses or seminars, Center managers negotiated with school officers and teacher representatives about the needs amongst teachers at school and the way the CPE could come in to fulfill those needs. This led to courses that were less knowledge oriented and more skill oriented. Between learners, school representatives, and CPE, a common interest has accrued. Each made accommodations in its value chain in order to build a common process. Each was aware that only a cooperative strategy could develop a new approach that would benefit all.

4.3 Network University: Fully Demand Driven

The Network University is part of the University of Amsterdam and experiments in total freedom with demand-driven networked learning processes. It reversed the value chain completely and provides for online collaborative tools, suitable for networked learning. Anyone sharing an interest in the same topic can participate in Learning Snacks at an online session of not more than 90 minutes. If the appetite is aroused, Learning Lunches may be provided, covering knowledge exchange over a longer period of time. If the hunger for learning is substantial, the Network University designs a Burgundian Learning Dinner on demand. A call center where individuals are matched and supported to still their learning hunger supports the network.

The above three examples from practice describe early experiments in offering demand-driven learning programs. They provide input for understanding how the DDLL-framework may be applied in designing lifelong learning programs better.

5.   WHAT CAN BE LEARNED FROM THESE EXPERIMENTS?

From the DDLL framework and the experiments some interesting things can be learned:

- It requires a 180° paradigm shift for educational institutions to come to the alternative approach of demand-driven lifelong learning.
- It requires new design competencies.
- It requires customer intimacy with learners and companies.
- It requires operational excellence from personnel and systems 24 hours a day, seven days a week.
- It requires access and immediate response as well as distinctive support to add value to both learners and companies.
- It requires dedication to transforming both the educator and the learner.
- It requires money to pay for time and facilities.
- It requires breaking through existing boundaries.
- It requires an animator to oversee the total change process.

The most import lesson is that the experiments indicate that a 180° paradigm shift is needed from supply-driven to demand-driven education.

6.   CONCLUSIONS AND RECOMMENDATIONS

Since there are very few educational institutions providing truly demand-driven learning at this very moment, it is too early for conclusions. Demand-driven learning is clearly still in the experimental stage. It is, however, possible to make a few recommendations for further exploration. By studying the practical experiments, we learned that an additional support role is vital, the role of an animator. The innovation process is complex, and breaking through boundaries requires an individual who oversees the change processes and animates all actors to perform at the right time and with the appropriate support. The animator stimulates and guards the learning processes in the interest of the learners. The animator sees the learner and the company as clients to be served and collaborates with the staff from the educational institution to deliver knowledge and skills just in time.

It is recommended to explore more experiments, to describe and explain these experiments and interview learners and companies (mentors, trainers, and line managers) as well as assessors, coaches, and teachers. The next step will be to improve the framework and build a more elaborate design tool for a truly learner-driven lifelong learning.

REFERENCES

Argyris, C., & Schön, D. (1978). *Organizational Learning.* Reading, MA:Addison-Wesley.

Argyris, C., Putman, R., McLain, & Smith, D. (1985). *Action science. Concepts, methods, and skills for research and intervention.* San Francisco: Jossey-Bass Inc.

Arts, J. A. R., Gijselaers, W. H., & Segers, M. S. R. (2002). *Measuring Expertise Effects of Authentic Computer Supported and Problem-based Course.* Article submitted for Cognition and Instruction.

Bates, A. W. (1997). *Restructuring the university for technological change,* The University of British Columbia, Vancouver, Canada.

Bennebroek Gravenhorst, K. M., Boonstra J. J., & Werkman R. A. (2000). *Change capacity of organizations: five configurations.* University of Amsterdam, Amsterdam.

Itzkan, S. J. (1994). Assessing the future of telecomputing environments: implications for instruction and administration. *The Computing Teacher, 22* (4), 60-64.

Livingstone, D. W. (1998). *What is informal learning?* National research network for new approaches to lifelong learning, Ontario Institute for Studies in Education, University of Toronto.

Otting, H., Zwaal, W., & Eringa, K. (2002). *A constructivist approach to competence development and assessment.* Paper for the 9th EDiNEB conference, Guadalahara, Mexico.

Parry, S. B. (1996). The quest for competencies. *Training.* July, 48-56.

Porter, M. E. (1985). *Competitive Advantage; creating and sustaining superior performance.* The Free Press.

Stoof, A., Martens, R. L., & Merrieënboer, J. J. G. (2001). *What is competence? A constructivist approach as a way out of confusion.* Heerlen: Open University (in print).

Thijssen, T. J. P., Maes, R., & Vernooij, A. T. J. (2002). Learning by Sharing: a Model for Life-Long Learning. In T. A. Johannessen, A. Pedersen, & K. Petersen (Eds.), *Educational Innovation in Economics and Business VI.* Dordrecht / Boston / London: Kluwer Academic Publishers.

Treacy. M., & Wiersema, F. (1995). De discipline van marktleiders, Scriptum, Schiedam.

Vermunt, J. D., & Verschaffel, L. (2000). Process-oriented teaching. In R. J. Simons, J. van der Linden, & T. Duffy, (Eds.), *New Learning* (pp. 209-225). Dordrecht, Boston: Kluwer Academic Publishers.

Vernooij, A. T. J., Thijssen, T. J. P., & Schermerhorn, R. H. (2001). *New media and their role in education*. Paper for the 8th Annual EDiNEB International Conference in Nice, France.

Vernooij, A. T. J. (2001). Case study: *Centre of Post-initial Education*. University, Hogeschool van Amsterdam, Amsterdam.

Chapter 9

AN INNOVATION IN ACCESS: DEVELOPING THE GENERIC SKILLS OF BUSINESS STUDENTS THROUGH A VIRTUAL CORPORATE EXPERIENCE

Jennifer Radbourne
Faculty of Business, Queensland University of Technology, Brisbane, Queensland Australia

1. INTRODUCTION

Business education must provide the contemporary graduate with the capability to participate immediately in the competitive environment of change, risk, adventurous thinking, power plays, and corporate social responsibility. These graduate capabilities are expected to be the outcomes of a curriculum rigorously embedding the teaching and learning of the generic skills[1] essential in business, and of an intimate experience of the "real world."

The problem faced by the Faculty of Business (FOB) at the Queensland University of Technology in Australia following a review of the core undergraduate curriculum in 1999 – 2000, was that the curriculum lacked integration and relevance to the workplace, and that generic skills were not formally taught or assessed. In an ad hoc manner, academic staff across the FOB facilitated students' access to the professions through diverse means:

---

[1] For the purposes of this paper, the term "generic skills" is used to describe those skills such as problem-solving, teamwork, and oral communication, that are not the knowledge and technical skill of a particular discipline. When a student achieves competence in a generic skill, it becomes a generic attribute or generic capability.

R.G.Milter et al. (eds.), Educational Innovation in Economics and Business IX, 157–177.

industry and professional guest lecturers, workplace assignments, and professional practice subjects. Internships or other modes of off-campus work experience for more than 1000 new students each year were inconceivable.

The solution was provided through a teaching and learning project undertaken in 2001 and 2002. The project enabled classes of 1000 students access to a corporation through a multimedia multi-layered case study, interactive online experiences, and review of actual financial data, emails, reports, policy documents, and internal management decision-making systems. In addition, students examined the generic skills at work in the corporation and instigated a self-assessment process to prepare themselves for the graduate capabilities required to work in this corporation. The positive feedback from students, academic staff, and managers in the corporation leads to the hypothesis of this paper, that a virtual workplace created through a multimedia case can satisfy the principles of effective work-based learning.

The paper examines principles of work-based learning and assessment, generic skills acquisition, multi-media case method, and online teaching, in order to develop and implement a learning model that takes the student from neophyte to expert.

2.   TOWARDS A LEARNING MODEL

Curricular development or re-development begins with identification of the needs or gaps in the current program. Having identified the lack of integration and workplace relevance in the business core undergraduate curriculum, the following Table 1 was designed showing six influential factors relevant to skills acquisition. These factors are the generic skills required for employment, the context in which instruction occurs (real or imagined), the content being taught, the environment (classroom or corporation), the interactive learning group (students, teachers, industry experts), the level and access to infrastructure and technology, and the access to specialized skills and knowledge. An adaptation of Schön's Reflective Practitioner Model (Schön, 1983, 1987; Spiro & Jehng, 1990) is used to represent the professional as the embodiment of theory in practice. The professional is the expert in the corporation, business or industry whose "expertise lies embedded ... and can only be acquired through extended opportunities of practice in authentic settings, with appropriate coaching, mentoring, and other guidance with feedback" (Wilson & Cole, 1992, p. 73). The classroom offers a structured approach through theory and example of what happens in the workplace. The work-based learning domain is often ill-structured, representative of knowledge structures that are less defined, more conditional and problematic.

This learning process represents a bridging construct from a neophyte to the expert practitioner and entails identification of where and how they differ and then using this as the basis for designing the curriculum and assessment tasks. The variances are the very elements that need to be bridged to bring students closer to acquiring the "expert" level skills during the course of their study. Through the learning process students move from left to right along the continuum for each factor.

Table1. Factors in Work-Based Skills Acquisition (Reyes and Radbourne, 2001, developed for this project)

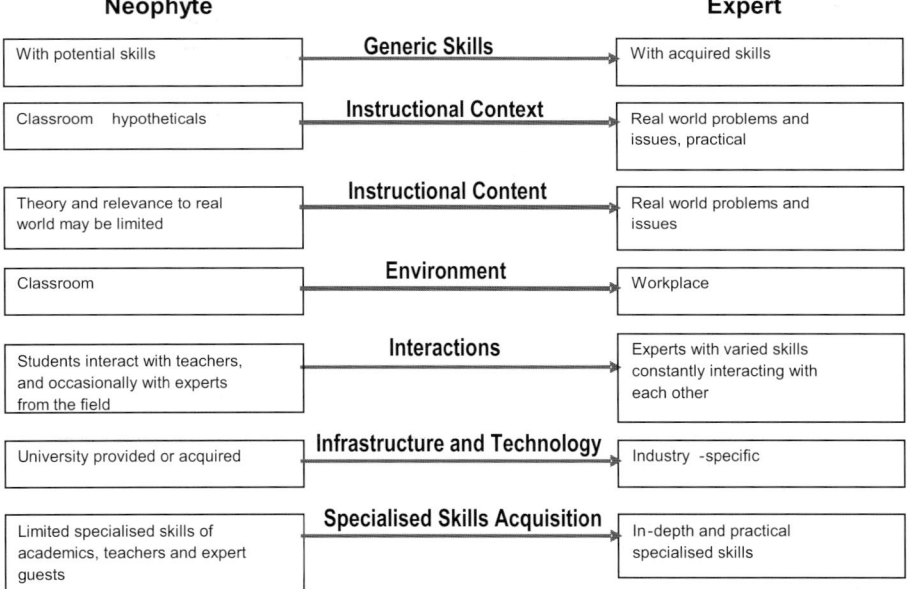

Bridging the skills between the neophyte and the expert can be seen in the following learning model developed for this project (see Figure 1). The distance between the learning experiences represents the variance in skill level, bridged by characteristic definitions of the workplace case study requirements and supported by key components for implementation. Assessment is a process of self-reflection, that of conscious participation in skills acquisition by the student. This model became the framework for the project and the development of the online case study based on supporting structures essential for successful implementation of the intended curricular change.

The learning experiences on the upper side of the bridge are not necessarily in order of participation or action. For example, students may move back and forth from reflective self-assessment as they encounter virtuality, or real world data, or increased practitioner activity. However, the deeper and richer the work-based learning becomes, the closer the student moves towards expertise.

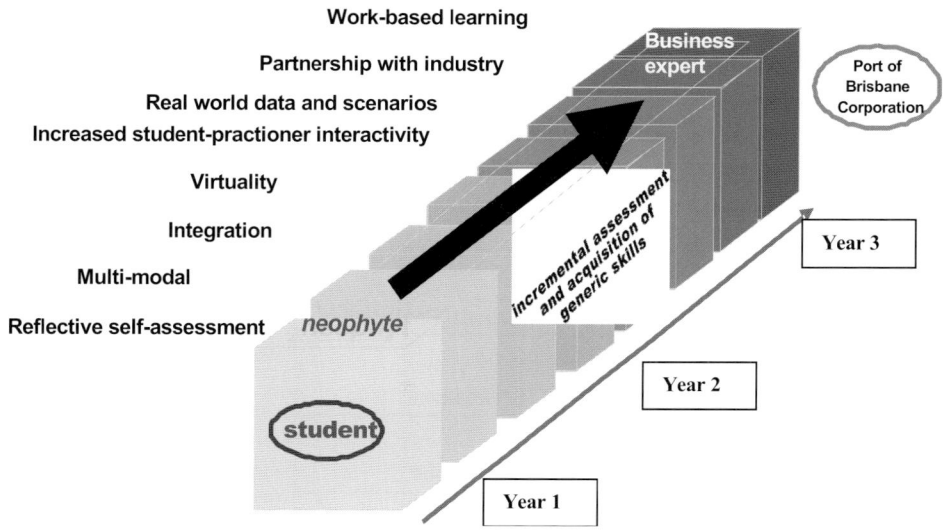

Figure 1. The Virtual Work-Based Learning Model (Reyes & Radbourne, 2001, developed for this project)

2.1   Embedding Generic Skills

From this learning model, the FOB conducted research to identify which generic skills should be taught and assessed, and which method of instruction would be most appropriate.

Masoner (1988) identified a hierarchical taxonomy of generic skills that can be achieved in case study method. This method facilitates the development of higher-order processes, such as general and specific problem-solving skills, each of which are underpinned by a range of cognitive (e.g., reasoning, thinking, creativity, oral communication, problem identification, social application, integration, and decision-making) and affective (e.g., group cooperation, self-confidence) abilities. Several decades of anecdotal and empirical evidence in the area of case study teaching, particularly in the area of business education, reveal the ability of case study to foster generic attributes of this nature. Masoner's research showed that the development of a chain of changes in generic attributes is likely to require longer than one semester. Such developments in generic attributes may only occur in an academic program, and not a single subject. A program effect should also occur when the same generic skill is developed in more than one course or discipline (Masoner, 1988). This encouraged the FOB to consider one workplace case study across the eight core subjects of the curriculum, which would have specific application and assessment for each subject and selected generic and business specific skills.

Previous research undertaken within the FOB with the objective of developing a generic skill taxonomy for business students, provided results generally consistent with published research, documenting generic skills and attributes for business graduates in the Australian context (BHERT, 1991; DETYA, 2000; Hearn, Close, Smith, & Southey, 1992; Flinders University, 1998; Karpin, 1995; McCowan & Richardson, 1998; Mayer, 1992). Factor analysis was used on this data (McCowan & Richardson, 1998), together with an analysis of current curriculum content and learning objectives from each subject, and QUT's standard set of generic skills to be acquired by all students. The list of generic business skills presented in Table 2 were selected as relevant for this project.

Table 2. Generic Skills

Leadership / Management	Interpersonal / Communicating	Individual and Corporate Social Responsibility	Adventurous Decision-Making	Technical/ Professional/Cognitive
• visioning and innovation	• interpersonal	• commitment to social justice	• risk-taking	• knowledge, skills abilities to deal with professional tasks
• leadership and influence	• teamwork	• capacity to appreciate diverse cultural backgrounds	• decision-making	• life-long learning skills
• creativity and change	• listening and responding	• community involvement	• planning and organizing	• computing
• coordinating	• oral communication	• career/life management	• standards and ethics	• problem-solving
• managing conflict	• written communication	• ability to identify personal competencies		• cognitive and research skills
• being positive and resilient	• working independently			• ability to conceptualize
• time management	• understanding organizational communication			

2.2 Work-based Learning through a Multimedia Case

The purpose of the case study method was to create a virtual workplace of a local corporation, which would provide authentic assessment tasks through direct contact with managers in the workplace. Thus "given authentic performance opportunities and appropriate coaching and reflection, surface level imitation proceeds to a kind of problem solving based on deeper understanding of the situation" (Wilson & Cole, 1992, p. 74).

The corporation selected for the case study was the Port of Brisbane Corporation (PBC). An established link between the PBC and FOB already existed. In addition this corporation met other criteria as it embraced activity in all the business disciplines represented in the eight Faculty core subjects, had a well developed and long strategic plan, had much information in the public domain, was local and accessible, and expressed a willingness to be part of the project.

Christensen and Hansen (1987) state that the case study method is supportive of a culture that places high value on review and innovation. This project was built on review and required innovation. Through the development of case study material, academic staff had to become involved in continuing contact with the world of practice and a case that was "live" and in ongoing renewal. Innovation and the need for updated case material could best be accommodated in a multimedia case.

The advantages of multimedia cases to support learning in business and economics have been well documented and tested (Haaken & Christensen, 1999; McLaughlin & Oliver, 2000). Haaken and Christensen claim that multimedia components facilitate and accelerate knowledge transfer and that a multimedia case can reach new types of potential users through the use of Internet technology for distributed delivery. It is a flexible medium without the constraints regarding time and place, and topics do not have to be learned sequentially.

A multimedia case usually has three dimensions: content, instruction, and presentation and delivery (Haaken & Christensen, 1999). The main part of the content is the case study. This may be accompanied by a theoretical framework, glossaries, links to references, learning objectives, case context, tutorials, and the issues and problems in the case or the workplace. Maximum interactivity is preferable so that students are motivated to search for more detail. Multimedia modules, that is, components with a particular instructional purpose such as a photograph, a click-and-drag exercise or live video footage, are incorporated into the instruction dimension. The presentation and delivery depend on the instructional strategies and the technology, but the text of the case is enriched by the advanced multimedia components of video, programmed animation and links to the selected corporation's own site.

The technology can be customized for the learners, their skills and their characteristics. It can be delivered in the classroom, in the workplace, in the home study, on demand whenever people have the time and motivation to learn, even in real time for a manager with a problem. Students, or those accessing the technology, can read or work on whichever aspect of the case they need for the task, leaving some or much of the content for another problem/ solution exercise.

The design of the case and the Web site resources should focus on the learning environment and learning objectives, not on the attractiveness of the interface design. While attractiveness creates interest, the design should be in response to the learner's emotional, situational, and knowledge-related characteristics, such as access to the technology, familiarity with the technology and information retrieval process and attitudes to the acquisition of knowledge and the learning process in total (Haaken & Christensen, 1999). The design must also be appropriate for the IT infrastructure. The case is realized through the virtual workplace as the learning environment. It is heavily dependent on technical support. These were the principles used to design the Web-based technology for this project. The goal was to use technology to take students to another learning environment, where their teacher was no longer the main source of information and learning. The following figure shows how Net-based communication moves beyond the traditional classroom learning environment, forming the means of interaction between teachers and students, among students, and also between students and the corporation case study.

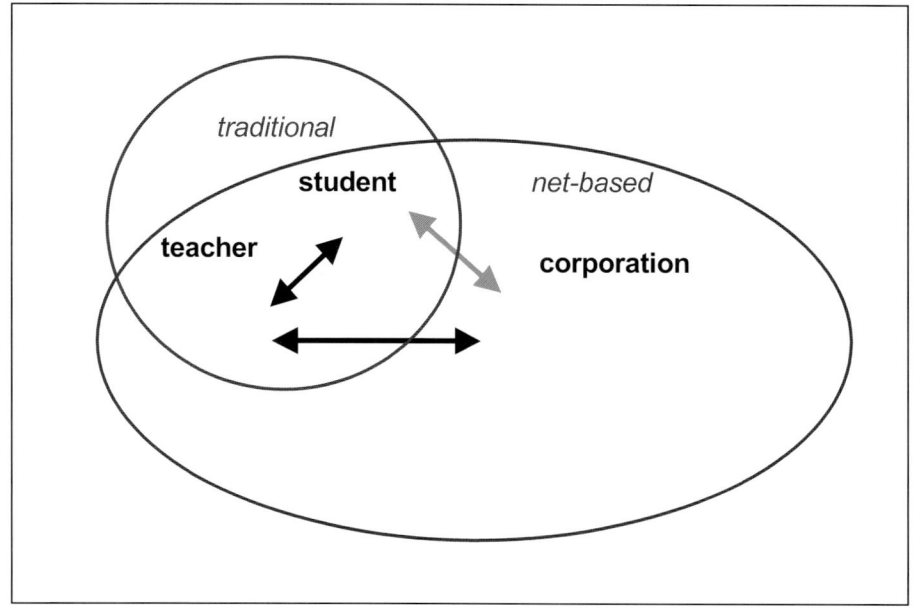

Figure 2. Interaction Model

If the technology, the instructional design and the live workplace are available, then a comprehensive virtual corporation can become a genuine work-based learning environment. The following table shows the criteria for success in using a multimedia case for work-based learning.

Table 3. Criteria for Multimedia Case as Work-based Learning (Radbourne, 2001, developed for this project)

1. Technology to support the instructional design and delivery
2. Well defined learning objectives and learning needs
3. Students with the motivation and capacity to learn in this mode
4. Teachers with the motivation and capacity to teach in this mode
5. Understanding by teachers that learning occurs in flexible times, places and sequences
6. Three well structured and designed dimensions of the case (content, instruction and presentation)
7. Willingness of a corporation to reveal data and expose itself to analysis
8. Inclusion of generic capabilities for employment in the virtual workplace
9. Authentic assessment tasks and feedback
10. Continuous monitoring and evaluation

These criteria formed a point of reference in selecting the corporation, in planning academic staff development and peer support, in selecting the Web-based delivery system, and in design of the multi-media and multi-layered case study.

3.   THE FACULTY OF BUSINESS PROJECT

The facilitation of integrating the core undergraduate business curriculum and embedding the teaching and learning of generic skills required project planning, funding, and direction. The FOB was successful in an application for central university funding which provided resources to employ a case study writer, an instructional designer, visiting international "critical friends," and time release for the academic staff to reflect on and redesign their curriculum. The project built on existing data and teaching and learning projects in generic skills at QUT and in other universities in the Australian Technology Network (ATN) to provide a model for teaching and assessing generic skills and competencies such that students of business would be able to articulate these for satisfying employment and lifelong learning experiences. The project took the conceptualization and curriculum embedding into a third stage, that of modeling and self-assessment.

3.1   Project Objectives

The objectives of the project encompassed objectives for the curriculum, for student learning, for staff development, and for the tools used in measuring and communicating competence in generic skills acquisition.

3.1.1   Curriculum

- To develop an integrated approach to embedding and assessing generic and identified business specific skills and competencies across each of the eight FOB core subjects (e.g., dual-assessment strategies).

3.1.2   Student learning

- To expose students to an Australian case study that embodies activity in all the disciplines of the eight FOB core subjects.
- To develop a method of self-assessment that encourages students to reflect on learning experiences designed to develop their generic skills and competencies.

- To help students to learn how to communicate the development of their generic skills and competencies to potential employers, and

3.1.3   Staff development

- To engage academic staff, through consultation and training workshops, to achieve effectiveness in the teaching and learning, and assessment of generic skills and competencies.

3.1.4   Documentation

- To establish methods of recording (such as an online portfolio) that enable students to document their personal experiences in the development of generic skills and competencies.

The following figure shows the developmental stages of the project from curriculum embedding through teaching and assessing the generic skills, to modeling and evaluation. Academic staff development was viewed as ongoing in every phase of the project. This figure became the basis of the project plan and timeline over two years.

The project involved curriculum redevelopment in each of the eight core subjects for the undergraduate business degree. Because of the foundational position of these subjects in the curriculum, together with the number and seniority of academic staff associated with teaching them, it was proposed that development of these subjects would have a profound effect on the whole business degree and the FOB. The redevelopment acknowledges that these eight subjects are designed to provide students with a core of knowledge and competencies required in the business profession in general, whilst at the same time providing a foundation for each of the major streams of study: accountancy, economics, marketing, management, international business, and business law.

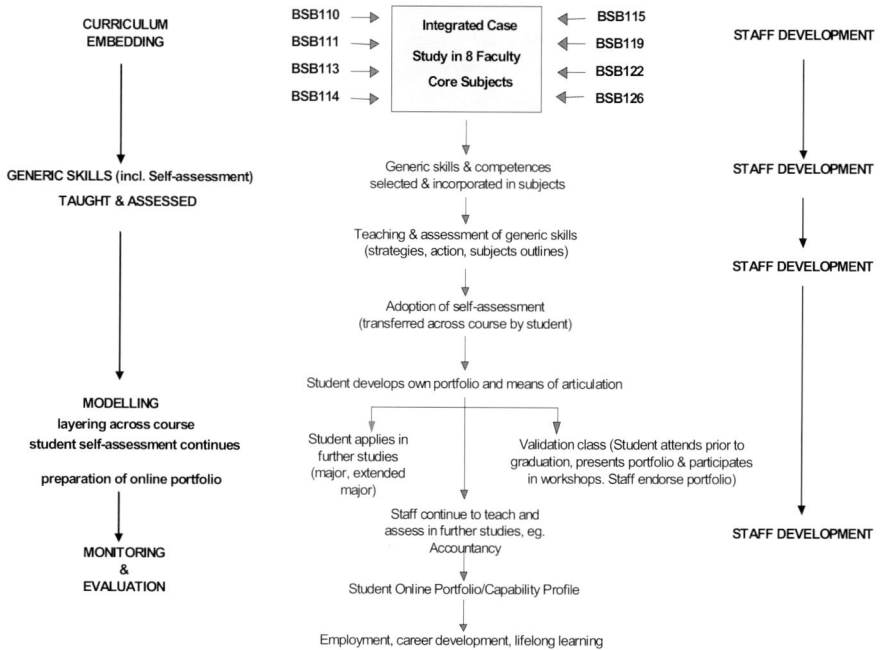

Figure 3. Project Development Model

The project team decided that it was best able to achieve enhanced integration of the eight core subjects and enhanced focus on the development of generic skills by multiple use of the single case study across all eight subjects. In each subject there is a dual assessment strategy. One part relates directly to the development of knowledge and skill in the major stream of study, the other part relates to the development of generic competency and a core of knowledge needed for business in general. For each subject, students complete assessment tasks that are derived from the one case study. Each time, therefore, they see the case from a different business perspective.

The selection or allocation process for linking generic skills to particular subjects involved an integrative team approach to curriculum review built around peer support and shared reflection. It was designed to respect the academics' integrity, independence, and need for flexibility. Extensive discussion and peer mentoring ensured a methodology for incorporation of these generic skills into learning objectives, teaching strategies, and assessment items. This component of the project fulfilled academic staff development in their own generic skills of collaboration, innovation, creativity, commitment, reflection, and academic independence and integrity. Thus staff development occurred in the curriculum development stage, generic skills allocation stage, and finally as they transferred their skills throughout the degree.

The final stage of the project involved self-assessment by students of their competence in the generic skills, and the documentation and articulation of this competence for employers. The proposed methods for documentation were the student's recording of self-assessment in class, a validation class prior to graduation where staff endorse a portfolio presentation, and entering data on each student's online Capability Profile set up by the university. This documentation could then be articulated to employers and become a tool for ongoing personal and professional development.

The project therefore became a viable means of teaching and assessing generic skills that would encourage an enduring faculty-wide change. The force driving the change was the significant need for business students to graduate with a portfolio of generic and business skills and competencies, and with the self-assessment ability to apply these to lifelong learning.

3.2   Instructional Content

Table 4 shows how all of the generic skills were included across the eight core subjects. Some skills were taught and assessed in more than one subject, but importantly, they were taught and assessed through the motivation of "real world" performance capabilities. Problem solving, decision-making, communication and research skills are introduced in the conversations and instructions of managers. Students see how these are applied in work through their tasks and through the story of the corporation on the Web site. Authenticity motivates deeper learning and provides clarity for learning objectives and assessment tasks. Formative and summative assessment form a natural continuum for the student intent on participation in personal and corporate learning strategies. In formative assessment tasks the student receives feedback to develop learning and generic skills. In summative assessment tasks the student is tested on content and skill competence. Students reflect on feedback as they move towards competence.

Table 4. Matrix of Generic Skills across the Curriculum

General skill groups / Core subjects	Leadership/ Management	Interpersonal/ Communi-cation	Individual & Corporate Social Responsibility	Adventurous Decision-Making	Technical/ Professional / Cognitive
BSB110 Accounting	Time management	Written communi-cation*		Planning and organization	KSAs for Professional tasks Problem solving Cognitive and research*
BSB111 Business Law & Ethics		Teamwork	Commitment to social justice Strengths and weaknesses (self-assessment)	Standards and ethics Decision-making Risk-taking	Cognitive and research* Problem solving Lifelong learning*
BSB113 Economics		Written communi-cation* Working independently Listening and responding		Decision-making	Ability to conceptualize Problem solving Cognitive and research*
BSB114 Government, Business & Society	Leadership and influence	Understanding organizations Written communi-cation*	Community involvement	Planning & organizing	Cognitive and research (critical thinking)*
BSB115 Management, People & Organization	Creativity & change Visioning and innovation Managing conflict	Understanding organizations		Decision-making	Cognitive and research* Ability to conceptu-alize*
BSB119 International & Electronic Business	Visioning and innovation	Listening and responding Oral communi-cation* Written communi-cation* Teamwork	Multicultural appreciation*	Risk-taking	Computing Problem solving Cognitive and research (critical thinking)*

General skill groups \ Core subjects	Leadership/ Management	Interpersonal/ Communi- cation	Individual & Corporate Social Responsibility	Adventurous Decision- Making	Technical/ Professional / Cognitive
BSB122 Business Information Analysis & Communi- cation	Time management	Oral communi- cation* Written communi- cation* Listening and responding		Planning & organization	Cognitive and research (critical thinking)* Problem solving Computing
BSB126 Marketing	Creativity and change	Teamwork Interpersonal communi- cation Listening and responding Oral communi- cation*	Multicultural appreciation*	Risk-taking	Ability to conceptu- alize* Cognitive and research*
*A component of Information Literacy skills					

3.3   Concept, Design, and Development of the Web Site

Based on the learning model and evidence in the literature, the online mode of delivery was selected as the primary vehicle of access to the case study. Each subject had its own online teaching and learning (OLT) site. These sites housed a sub-case for teaching content and generic skills. All sites were linked to a common Web site where the main case was outlined. The mixed mode delivery of the case was used in the lecture, or tutorial, or classroom activity depending on the instruction designed for each subject.

Four key components were incorporated into the conceptual design of the Web site. These corresponded to the essential and supporting structural elements of the learning model and embodied the principles derived from literature and the project objectives.

Table 5. Design Components and Principles of the Web Site

Components	Principles
Project information	• Students understand their involvement and participation as recipients of the program – emphasizing the relevance to their success as business practitioners. • Staff understands their role as facilitators of the learning processes involved in the using the case study approach. • Cross-discipline involvement of staff across eight core Faculty subjects • Process of staff development. • Curriculum re-development at the subject level – redefining subject objectives to integrate specific generic skills. • Matrix to ensure that a comprehensive and thorough integration of the generic skills is incorporated into the teaching process across all eight core Faculty subjects.
Port of Brisbane Case study	• Implementation of the case study method as a platform or springboard to develop subject-specific sub-cases – the multi-layering process. • Provide a real global and corporate business "virtual environment" for the students. • Provide real local and SME (small and medium enterprise) business "virtual environment" for the students through PBC's subsidiaries and partnerships. • Exposure to a broad base of business programs, processes and policies, reports and financial data, communication systems as well as issues involving decision-making interactions. • Accessibility of the corporation by thousands of students. • Industry and business become co-educators with QUT.
Subject Sub-cases	• Application of the multi-layering process from the main case study and within subject-specific sub-cases. • Application through tutorial exercises, assignments, lectures or any other instructional activity. • Instructional strategies designed to integrate specific generic skills as outlined in each of the subject's objectives. • Virtual and actual engagement and interaction with management and staff providing real workplace perspectives and internal management decision-making systems. • Instruction and learning become relevant to real workplace or corporate experience. • Accessibility to real data and live scenarios by thousands of students. • Allows interactivity – depending on the instructional design of each sub-case.
Assessment Center	• Student self-reflection and monitoring. • Building of student profile. • Project evaluation and development-re-development cycle – student survey (also includes staff survey and expert's critique). • Incremental assessment over three stages during student life cycle: post-activity/instruction (sub-case) assessments, post-subject assessments, post-core subjects assessment.

The **Home and Overview** page of the Web site is the main entry point for the Web site and provides direct access to the main case study. It is where the students are provided with information on generic skills and their integration into the curriculum as built and based on empirical and theoretical foundations already mentioned. More importantly, students are provided with the rationale behind their participation in the project and the impact the project will have on their future as employees.

The **Port of Brisbane Corporation Case Study** is a story of the evolution of what was once a government entity to what is now a corporate player. Though the beginnings of the case are historical, the case describes the complex challenges that have been evolutional in its development: leadership, government ownership, organizational change, geographical relocation of the head office from the city center to the river mouth, environmental concerns, strategic alliances with the airport corporation, and the contemporary reporting regulations. True to the realism of the case, the content changes dynamically as the Corporation. The case study is supported by the links to the Port of Brisbane Corporation Web site, each of the case studies of the core subjects, an Assessment Center, and other supporting links.

The **core subject case studies** are presentations of problem scenarios and a resource for data manipulation derived from actual Port of Brisbane Corporation human resources, data, and documentation. As such, each facet of the subject case study is a true and non-hypothetical presentation of problems and often complex scenarios in a corporate environment. The complexities and issues are difficult to filter and therefore provide a platform for inter-relational and cross-linking across the eight core subjects. The Web site incorporates specific generic skills in the subject cases. These are itemized as:

- Accounting
  "Accounting Practice Set: Port of Brisbane Corporation – Brisbane Multimodal Terminal" case study delivers to the student a set of financial data and a task being given by the finance manager of the Corporation. The task involves interpretation of accounting data designed to apply the skills of accountancy, time management, problem-solving, and conceptual skills.
- Business Law and Ethics "Accountability, Economy, and Efficiency – A Case Study in the Development of Triple Bottom Line Reporting" explores the practice of corporate ethics and social responsibility. It culminates in a discussion forum, engaging students in current contentious issues and develops their commitment to social justice, standards and ethics, cognitive and research skills.

- Economics

  "Brisbane Multimodal Terminal: A Case of Off-Docking Corporate Loss" looks at the economic fixed and variable costs in a docking system. Students utilize their research, planning, and conceptual skills in devising economic strategies for the operations of the Corporation.

- Government, Business, and Society "Port of Brisbane Corporation's Participation In Funding the Construction of the New Motorway" (Case 1) and "Indigenous Stakeholders" (Case 2) are cases about the inter-relationships between the government, the Corporation, and society. The ensuing discussion explores the complex issues related to the infrastructural developments introduced by the Corporation and how it impacts on the community of people surrounding it. Students are exposed to the generic skills of leadership and influence, understanding organizations, written communication, cognitive and research skills.

- International and Electronic Business "Business in an Emerging Market" looks at the international direction that the Corporation has undertaken, specifically in Vietnam. Appreciation of multicultural diversity and individual viewpoints, being able to gather information to assist in communication, and working together as part of a group are skills that accompany the understanding of concepts and theories in international business.

- Business Information Analysis and Communication "Concepts of Competition" (Case 1) and "Ownership of the Workforce" (Case 2) look at the factors affecting competition and customer service delivery issues at the Corporation. The discussion entails critical analysis of the issues and providing strategies that may be potential solutions to the problem being presented. Students utilize time management, oral communication, written communication, listening and responding, planning and organization, cognitive and research, problem solving, and computing skills.

- Marketing

  "What's So Special About the Port of Brisbane?" is a case that presents the problem of geographical, demographic, social, and political impacts on the operations involving new corporate venture decisions. The case compels the students to engage in research, think creatively, explore the issues, and arrive at a strongly supported rationale for the decision.

The link to the **Assessment Center** on the Web site allows access to the Student Capability Profile, and evaluation tools and surveys. The Student Capability Profile is a self-assessment tool that assists students in self-monitoring their generic skills acquisition invoking self-reflection and resulting in identification and qualification of their business skills and attributes acquired throughout the course of their study. The constancy in change requires formative and summative evaluation of the project in order to determine the direction of its development, and so it is crucial that the Web site reflects any such development. Online staff and student surveys, and evaluation relevant to each subject are available in the center and conducted over the course of the study.

Supporting links allow access to a variety of relevant resources and Web sites to assist students as they go through each case study, and access to university services and Web site support elements. These links are subject-specific case study support links, QUT Web site, housekeeping links (Web Administrator, copyright, and disclaimer), and download links for plug-ins.

3.4   Monitoring and Evaluation

Ongoing monitoring and evaluation of the project occurred through student focus groups, surveys with students and academic staff, and through the experience of two international "critical friends."

Surveys conducted with students and staff reveal that 66 percent of students thought generic skills were "very important" or "extremely important" to employers, 81 percent of students were either satisfied or very satisfied that they were taught and acquired particular generic skills in particular subjects. When asked to rank statements about how generic skills are best learned, the first ranked statement was "Lecturers/tutors teaching and assessing specific skills in the classroom" and the second ranked was, "The Lecturers/tutors modeling best practice in generic skills for students to follow."

The questions relating to the Port of Brisbane Corporation case study had a very positive response, with 84 percent of students nominating the benefit as "the real world data made assessment items more interesting," 77 percent nominating "the case study teaching method developed my problem solving, creative thinking, communication and other generic skills," 75 percent nominating "I learned about a local corporation and aspects of its business," and 70 percent "the links to and from the Port of Brisbane Corporation case study and the OLT site for this unit were helpful."

While these results are reassuring for the methodology undertaken, reliable measurement cannot be taken until these students graduate, and their virtual workplace experience and generic skills acquisition are measured by employment data.

In the two years of the project most of the objectives were achieved. Survey data sought ranking of the success of these objectives. The generic skills have been embedded into the eight core subjects. The case study of The Port of Brisbane Corporation integrated these subjects. Academic staff development involved workshops with experts in teaching and assessment of generic skills and in case method. This has exposed a weakness in the area of generic skills. Many academic staff are intent on assessing content and information, and are under prepared to teach and assess the process of applying knowledge. A common process for teaching generic skills was developed in 2002, and further guidelines for assessing generic skills have been included in all subjects, for teachers and students. Nevertheless, students have a new awareness and understanding of the generic skills and competencies required for employment, and have begun a process of self-assessment and development that will progress through their degree. And finally, the partnership with the Port of Brisbane Corporation provided students and academic staff with access to a "real world" case, such that a rich learning model was achieved.

4.   CONCLUSION

This paper proposed a hypothesis that a virtual workplace created through a multimedia case could satisfy the principles of effective work-based learning. Because the project relied heavily on an authentic case and direct contact with a real corporation, and because the case was represented at many levels, thorough diverse disciplines and diverse media methods, the virtual workplace maintained interest and attention. The depth and breadth of the case was developed through creative use of technology, particularly in instructional design. Here lies the success of the project and the answer to the hypothesis. Innovation and visioning, two important generic skills of business students, were the foundation for solving the FOB problem in effective delivery of business education. Through the innovative use of technology, the vision of giving students a clear and integrated view of the business of a major corporation was realized. The principles of work-based learning were tested and implemented. A longitudinal study is needed to prove students have enhanced employability.

The project was implemented over two years, but is ongoing because it has stimulated research and reflection in diverse areas of student learning: generic skills, case method, workplace experience, multimedia resources, virtuality, assessment, curriculum integration, and the "teacher as learner" principle. Importantly, the project has created a reinvigoration of teaching and learning in the Faculty of Business at QUT.

REFERENCES

Christensen, C. R., & Hansen, A. (1987). *Teaching and the case method.* Boston, Massachusetts: Harvard Business School Press.

DETYA. (2000). *Employer satisfaction with graduate skills: Research Report 1999.* Evaluations and Investigations Program, Higher Education Division. Canberra: DETYA.

Flinders University. (1998). *Employer Survey.* South Australia: Flinders University.

Haaken, S., & Christensen, G. (1999.) Interactive case studies – Enablers for innovative learning. In *Educational innovation in economics and business VI.* (2002). Dordrecht: Kluwer Academic Publishers.

Hearn, G., Close, A., Smith, B., & Southey, G. (1992). *Developing generic professional competencies in Australia: Towards a framework for professional development.* Brisbane: QUT.

Karpin, D. (1995). *Enterprising nation: Renewing Australia's managers to meet the challenges of the Asia-Pacific century: A guide to the report of the industry task force on leadership and management skills.* Canberra: Australian Government Publishing Service.

Masoner, M. (1988). *An audit of the case study method.* New York: Praeger.

McCowan, C., & Richardson, A. (1998). *Employer/graduate perceptions of the skills and abilities of recent business graduates.* QUT Careers and Employment. Brisbane: QUT.

McLaughlin, C., & Oliver, R. (2000). Designing learning environments for cultural inclusivity: A case study of indigenous online learning at tertiary level. *Australian Journal of Educational Technology. 16* (1), 58-72.

Schön, D. (1987.) *Educating the reflective practitioner: Toward a new design for teaching and learning in the professions.* San Francisco: Jossey-Bass.

Schön, D. (1983). *The reflective practitioner.* New York: Basic Books.

Spiro, R. J., & Jehng, J-C. (1990). Cognitive flexibility and hypertext: Theory and technology for the nonlinear and multidimensional traversal of complex subject matter. In D. Nix, & R. J. Spiro (Eds.), *Cognition, education, and multimedia: Exploring ideas in high technology* (pp. 163-205). Hillsdale, NJ: Lawrence Erblaum.

Wilson, B., & Cole, P. (1992). A critical view of elaboration theory. *Educational Technology Research.*

PART 4

ROLE OF INFORMATION TECHNOLOGY IN THE LEARNING PROCESS

Chapter 10

CAN "LEARNING BY TEACHING" CONTRIBUTE TO E-LEARNING?

Raffi Duymedjian
Grenoble Ecole de Management, France

1. INTRODUCTION

Learning is a complex process, and this complexity probably explains and justifies the diversity of learning methods and theories. Among the different ways of learning – by doing, observing, imitating, and so forth, – one is called "Learning by Teaching" (LbT).

The first way to define LbT would be based on the statement that teaching requires structure and the ability to understand the audience. It helps to clarify theoretical as well as practical ideas, which are essential when considering the increasing complexity of the world we are to understand and improve. Teaching is, therefore, a located activity, which challenges one's knowledge and thus can be seen as a learning process.

There are many circumstances in which non–teaching professionals happen to teach. In business schools when experts are called to share their experience, in firms for training purposes, in some class experiments when students coach younger pupils. This last situation has been defined and instrumented as Learning by Teaching and has been used with success, for instance in language courses (Skinner, 2002).

LbT has been designed and implemented in order to improve the student's learning process. However, we realized that in business schools students have a valuable knowledge to share, and that Learning by Teaching could also be very useful for extracting knowledge and experiences from students, and would enrich course content. This is particularly the case with

R.G.Milter et al. (eds.), Educational Innovation in Economics and Business IX, 181–194.
©2004 Springer. Printed in the Netherlands.

professionals following continuous training. For example, in a document and presentation design course, students had more than just accumulated experiences to share. They also possessed general knowledge that could have been very useful to capture during the course. Unfortunately, nothing was organized to allow this process to occur.

The purpose of this chapter is to explore the concept of Learning by Teaching and suggest under what conditions not just students, *but also teachers*, could benefit from such an experience, both in terms of learning improvement and *enhancing course content*.

First, we will start by defining what LbT actually means and what has to be learned from this new kind of learning. We will explore the many situations where non-professional teachers are asked to teach, and the benefits are only seen from the learner's point of view.

Secondly, we will analyze the compatibility between Learning by Teaching and e-learning. We will discuss the e-learning process from which we will suggest the introduction of two methodological "objects."

2.   WHAT IS LEARNING BY TEACHING (LBT)?

2.1   LbT: A Definition

Is Learning by Teaching a brand new concept? Not really, since, as Jody Daniel Skinner pointed out (Skinner, 2002), Seneca wrote 2000 years ago that "we learn by teaching." It is operational at St. John's College in Annapolis, USA, where students teach each other philosophy and physics while teachers play the role of tutors. The concept can also be found under the expression "Lernen durch Lehren," that is, "Learning through Teaching," developed by Dr. Jean-Pol Martin at the University of Eichstätt in Germany.

This way of Learning by Teaching consists, for example, in asking students to prepare lessons they will have to present to their fellow students[1]. As "teachers," they move from the passive role of receiving knowledge to a more active process. This technique seems to reach its main goal, that is, improve motivation and critical thinking[2]. Learning by Teaching systems, also called Intelligent Student Systems have been studied from the same presupposition, namely, placing learners in the role of a tutor (Nichols, 1994).

---

[1] They may also choose or create exercises, etc.
[2] It is also supposed to have an effect on students' autonomy and their ability to cooperate.

This definition of Learning by Teaching may serve as a basis, but it has some limitations that prevent us from exploiting it in management courses.

1. It was applied in very specific courses, that is, in the field of foreign language instruction and in literature.
2. Learners were at schools or in universities. It seems to have never been used in other situations, at least in its formal definition.
3. Learners were supposed to teach something they didn't know before and were compelled to learn.
4. One of the main objectives may be to motivate listless, uninterested students.
5. There is a slight difference or no difference at all in the level of knowledge of the teacher/tutor and that of the learners.

We believe that LbT would also be useful if it were applied in a more extended perspective. The content should not be restricted to language and literature but *a priori* any type of subject. The learners could already have a fairly high level of knowledge about what they are supposed to teach. And, finally, LbT could be valuable for very motivated and active students willing to share their personal knowledge. To reach that goal, we would define Learning by Teaching not just as a pedagogical method designed for improving the learning process of a student, but also a way by which a knowledgeable individual can share his or her knowledge with the teacher in order to enrich the course content.

Before going deeper into what we mean by "improvement," it is important to distinguish between Learning by Teaching and Learning by Training. We are not talking about training because training is bound by procedures, behaviors, short-term actions, whereas learning requires mixing theory and practice, a deep sense of conceptualization, emerging from the confrontation between what people do and the explanation they have to build from their actions.

2.2 What Can We Learn by Teaching?

Considering that LbT should not only be used to motivate listless students to learn, how has the pedagogical method revealed to be effective?

Learning by Teaching can be seen from different points of view, distinguishing the course preparation, the explanation work, and the collaborative process in which LbT should take place. Each of these sub-processes have been explored from the learning performance perspective. Studies about learning through explaining to oneself and to someone else show, for example, how explaining improves learning, the performance being conditioned by the complexity of the explanation (Webb, 1989). Studies about reciprocal teaching concluded in positive results as well, with respect to the fact that students who participated in reciprocal teaching performed better on text comprehension than other students (Palincsar & Brown, 1984). Preparing to teach, presenting materials, and responding to questions were other situations that could lead to improved learning (Bargh & Schul, 1980). Active cooperation between students has also a profound effect on the learning efficiency (Johnson, Johnson, & Smith, 1991).

We should now divide Learning by Teaching improvements into two categories. The first category can be defined as cognitive improvements and concerns the quality of knowledge. The second one concerns shifts in behavior. Both kinds of improvements are justified by new forms of organizations that are required by what is usually called the knowledge society, and more specifically by the new type of worker Peter Drucker calls the "knowledge worker" (Drucker, 1993). Indeed, our concern is to teach young future managers who should be able to produce, learn, and use actionable knowledge embedded in a social context, namely, the firm.

2.2.1   Cognitive improvements

Total Quality Management (TQM) and Knowledge Management (KM) are popular management concepts that have shaped productive organizations since the 80s. They both presume that organizational processes should be under control, all the more since organizations have become more and more complex and opaque. Formalizing processes via writing procedures is supposed to be, if not the best way, at least the first step for a company to understand itself and enter a continuous improvement process.

But more than just producing explicit knowledge from tacit knowledge, TQM and KM require one to understand the ins and outs of a productive action. For example, if an organization really wants to implement organizational learning, it has to go beyond a single-loop learning system like adapting to a specified target and controlling a feedback loop. It must, in addition, achieve a double-loop learning system that "results in a change in the values of theory-in-use, as well as strategies and assumptions" (Argyris & Schön, 1996, p.21). This implies the ability to explain and express judgment over one's action, which could be presented in terms of efficiency and effectiveness.

Moreover, management ideology moved from Taylor's One Best Way, based on a substantive rationality, to best practices, based on instrumental rationality. This changed the importance of theory versus practice, considering that no general theory has the right to model any kind of practice. Theories should be context-dependant, built from comparisons, while avoiding being just a collection of recipes. They also should be flexible and adaptable to a changing context without losing the rational roots that would prevent them from becoming mere fashionable trends.

Teachers are sometimes accused of being disconnected from the "real world," overgeneralizing their assertions without confronting them with everyday practice. But if we analyze the intellectual process of building course content, what we find is precisely what is required in knowledge companies.

Because the aim of teaching is explaining, it requires perpetual efforts of translating everything not only into words, but also into diagrams, pictures, and any other perceptible signs. To achieve this task, teachers have to use a great variety of tools and forms of expression to explicate their knowledge, which turns them into a kind of information architects (Wurman, 2001).

Teaching also means justifying the "truthfulness" and the relevance of its discourse by connecting general assertions with elements of fact. A course cannot exist without illustrations and examples that always challenge concepts and models. This prevents one from falling into the "one best way" trap because, since knowledge is context-dependant, it can always be questioned.

Efficiency and effectiveness of principles of action are also part of the teaching process, because usefulness is always the learners' main concern. "What is it for?" and "How does it work?" are questions that cannot be ignored, especially in business courses.

2.2.2 Behavioral improvements

Because organizations are becoming more and more complex, productive actions are almost systematically collective. The omnipresence of other people alters the communication process and, once again, being able to teach provides some of the behavioral competencies needed to work in groups. Through behavioral competencies, we would like to stress on the necessity to link the two dimensions of knowledge as it can be found in the knowledge management field where the knowledge capital approach (for example, Stewart, 1998) is distinguished from its interpretative and relational perspective (Wenger, 1998).

The first image we have of the teacher is someone who talks. But a pedagogical discourse is based on the ability to formulate ideas that are understandable by the learners. Words must be well chosen, illustrations eloquent. Adapting one's language and discourse to the audience does not just have a rhetorical purpose. Getting people to understand is the first fundamental skill.

Teaching is not just a monologue. It's a dialogical process during which learners may express their criticisms, share their experiences, and question knowledge and truths coming from their teacher. So teaching puts one in a very challenging position where nothing can be taken for granted without first being argued and/or demonstrated. This behavior is complementary to double-loop learning because decision criteria and the epistemological framework used to validate experiences and raise them as principles must be explained.

Finally, teaching could be a good way for developing one's self-confidence. The teacher is expected to provide debatable truths to discuss in a battle where he or she is always outnumbered. The status and the position the teachers own are not enough to protect them, and require them to have a reflexive attitude to their work.

2.3   When Do We Learn by Teaching?

"All the time" would be an easy answer. Each time we explain something, we implicitly structure our discourse in a pedagogical fashion. But we could also say "never" because what we learn is rather unconscious and difficult to identify.

Let us take those institutionalized situations where these intellectual and behavioral efforts occur. The master/apprentice relationship, for example, is one of the situations where the purpose is to hand down craftsmanship to future generations. The apprentice spends years with the master, observing gestures and reproducing his or her work. What the master actually learns from this teaching experience has never been analyzed.

The modern masters could be called experts. They are not devoted to a small group of apprentices, but rather to an organization, which expects them to have the answers to complex problems. In this case, the experts are not supposed to have pedagogical competencies. They are just asked to give solutions with their own technical vocabulary[3]. Here again, nothing has been done to evaluate what experts learn when teaching, probably because they have never been asked to do so.

Something interesting happens when experts or masters are called upon to contribute outside of their own spheres of action. Every time we called for professionals to contribute to a course where they could bring in their experience, they came willingly. And the reason that was given is even more surprising: it was a good way to check their knowledge and to confront it with "innocent" minds, who could have fresh ideas about their topics.

---

[3] Expert Systems are designed to duplicate expertise. But understanding what is in an expert's mind is so difficult that a profession appeared called 'cogniticians,' making experts talk and translate their knowledge into explicit rules (Hatchuel & Weil, 1992)

We could temporarily conclude that many people are in a teaching position without being professional teachers. But, in order for them to explicitly express what they have learned from this experience, they must be designated as teachers having to transfer knowledge to "institutionalized" learners.

3. IS LEARNING BY TEACHING COMPATIBLE WITH E-LEARNING?

We attempt to broaden the definition of Learning by Teaching in order to consider it also as a source of content enrichment. We also believe e-learning technologies and processes could be of great help in implementing such a process. This, however, implies the need to first clarify the learning process that shifts from the notion of a product to that of a service. We will then introduce two methodological "objects" that may guide us in implementing LbT in e-learning. Finally, we will examine the technical aspects of e-learning which could support the implementation of LbT.

3.1 Redefining the Learning Process

The dominant educational process has been criticized as being limited to the academic lecture and the interactive course where a simulacrum of questions-answers is organized to lead students where they are supposed to go (Vincent, Lahire, & Thin, 1994). To counter-balance this teacher-focused process, education which focuses on the student has been established and defines learning from the learner's perspective: from the perspective of a person who needs to acquire some knowledge, who feels the lack of some important information. But the risk of such a shift is to transform the learner into a customer expecting to have all needs fulfilled by what can be called a course. This typical product-oriented economic vision is fully coherent with course production processes that are increasingly scattered into more numerous stages. In this outline, the traditional teacher is called a "content provider," interactions being designed by interaction specialists, programmers for example, graphic aspects being reserved for graphic designers.

Actions are to be expected from learners during a course. They listen, memorize, understand, and answer questions. They also ask, assert, illustrate, and question when they disagree. But traditionally, there is a profound asymmetry between these two kinds of behaviors. Listening, understanding, and answering are expected actions, essential to the learning process, whereas asking or questioning just reveal the level of understanding without being "truly" indispensable nor systematically expected during the learning cycle. The "any questions?" does not always expect a reaction.

Figure 1 shows the standard learner-teacher relationship, where the teacher is the center of the stage, the attraction point of the action. The teacher's activity consists in transferring knowledge to learners whose reactions are used as feedback. Figure 2 describes what has globally changed with e-learning. The teacher also has a role of tutor or coach enabled by asynchronous communication technologies. Learners can interact with each other through newsgroups or chat rooms. But here again, the teacher is the main, if not the **unique, source of knowledge**, whose competences are only challenged by other academics, even if other students can be used as tutors or "spokesmen."

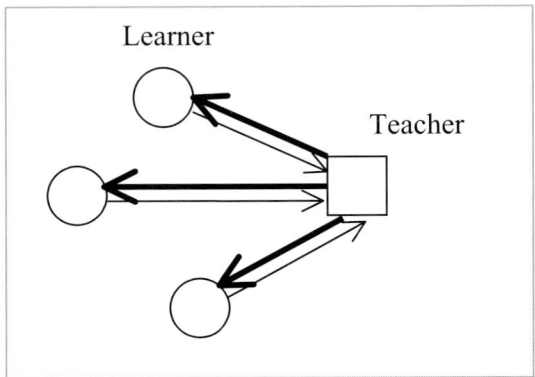

Figure 1. The standard learner-teacher relationship

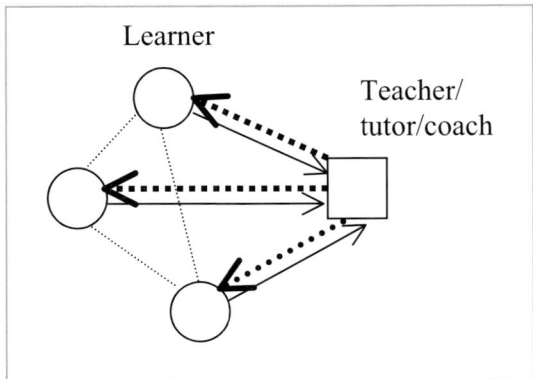

Figure 2. Learner-teacher relationship with e-learning

To see the learning-teaching process as a service requires the acceptance of the idea that the teacher puts himself or herself into a learning position, while building the course as well as conducting it. In this situation, learners are simultaneously **customers and suppliers of knowledge**. This doesn't mean complete symmetry between the learner and the teacher, because the teacher is still responsible for the success of the learning process, but responsibilities are better distributed among the different actors (see Figure 3). We can therefore now see a co-production (Eiglier & Langeard, 1991) process where both actors give and take, teach and learn.

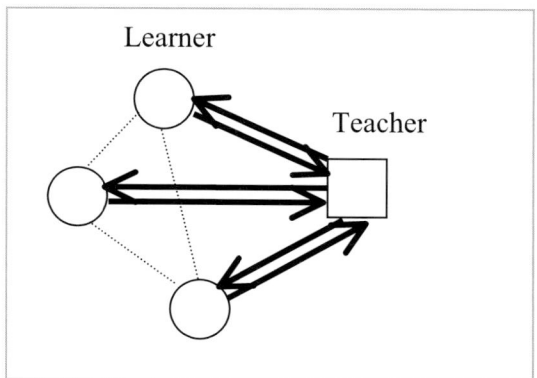

Figure 3. Learning and teaching co-production

Taking into account not only what learners but also what teachers learn requires using new methodological "objects," that is, concepts that must be used as guidelines for building and conducting courses. The teacher uses indeed the traditional methods to build courses, gathering knowledge from books and news from magazines and newspapers. In this respect, the Web has considerably modified the power of searching, cutting, and pasting multimedia symbols in digital supports. But what can be organized and applied to attract, capture, and formalize knowledge from students who attend courses in order to receive rather than to give? Below, we will explore the usefulness and the applicability of two "methodological" objects we tried to use in our courses. These ideas came from our studies and the analysis of knowledge management techniques and methods, that have also been used, but more sporadically, in the teaching ground.

3.2   Methodological Aspects

Our definition of LbT stresses the importance of seeing the pedagogical process as service-oriented, that is, as being a co-construction of knowledge emerging from the teacher-learner cooperation. But supposing that our students are depositories of valuable knowledge, does not mean they are willing to share it, or are able to do it. In this section, we propose questioning and storytelling as methodological "objects" intended for facilitating this process of knowledge extraction and knowledge sharing. Questioning may be a non-intrusive method of extracting knowledge from students without requiring them to explicitly cooperate in this process. Storytelling is more a guideline for helping them express and share their experiences.

Our first "object" is based on a better use of questions posed by the learners. Our personal teaching experience places questioning at the center of the learning process: questions teachers ask to verify what is understood, questions learners express to seek clarification or to disguise their personal opinion, questions that appear when events and facts do not match general principles (Maulini, 2000).

But often, questions are just answered. They are neither collected, nor reworked to formally enrich course contents. However, they can psychologically be considered as triggers for improving knowledge, being once again present in the concept of double-loop learning with what Argyris and Schön called "Trouble" (Argyris & Schön, 1996). They are the basis for imagination, expressing curiosity, and the awareness of one's personal knowledge limits.

We suggest using questions not just for evaluating students or assessing their level of understanding, but also to help the teacher challenge his or her knowledge. This means categorizing questions into clarification, confrontation, hypothetical situations, and other types, and integrating them into a continuous learning process. Questions could in the end become one of the most important educational resources.

Our second "object" is the use of storytelling. Storytelling is a sense-making process, which has a wide success in various fields. It has been shown to be very efficient in transferring a certain type of knowledge (Orr, 1996). It has also been studied in its ability to help create company culture and thus sustain fundamental values of a firm (Linde, 2000).

Structuring a course around stories means giving the content a living dimension where time is an essential variable. It must position actors in the context of their co-evolution. A story is also a place where general principles and values mix with the tiny details of life.

Storytelling is already considered as a teaching tool in its classical form (Rives & Cooper, 1997) as well as in other forms such as case studies, widely used in business schools. What could be experimented are confrontations of stories from which general knowledge could be produced, or the building of stories which may challenge the operationality of the concepts taught.

3.3   Technical Aspects

E-learning is based on technologies offering a very wide range of possibilities and functionalities. But what is expected for implementing Learning by Teaching, as defined in this paper, specifically requires three functions among all those technological potentialities, namely: improving the interaction process by creating low-cost virtual places; allowing the accumulation of questions-answers in forums, thus permitting a deeper reflexivity on the questioning process; and, finally, utilizing hypermedia as a basis for combining elements into virtual immersing stories full of virtual inanimate objects as well as interactive "intelligent" companions.

3.3.1   Simplified interactions

It is common to emphasize the possibilities Information Technology (IT) offers for interaction. What seems important for our purpose is the necessary cost of organizing an e-course compared to what is required for a traditional course. Before the Internet, one needed a room with tables and chairs, and the gathering of students and their teacher in one place during a specified period of time. The cost constraint only consisted in considering the learners as unique customers. The Internet considerably lowered this cost. It may now be possible to set up a course with peer-to-peer technologies or relatively cheap technological platforms allowing synchronous or asynchronous interactions, thus multiplying teaching experiences.

3.3.2   Tracking dialogues

The use of IT also gives the opportunity to track every message exchanged between the different actors. This means that dialogues, but especially questions, their context of emergence as well as the discussions they triggered, and the answers they produced can be traced, analyzed, stored, and reused. Those interactions could not only reveal the students' personal investments or the way they receive and understand what is taught. They could also open the way to new paths of exploration; information upon which one could build inferences. And the willingness of the teacher to enrich his or her course with ideas and contents coming from the students may in return strengthen their involvement in the learning process.

3.3.3   Hypermedia structuring and computer systems

Considering the computer as a theatre stage where virtual actors can interact is the idea defended by Brenda Laurel in her famous book *Computers as Theatre* (1993). We are at the infancy of storytelling structures in course design. The capacity both of integrating various media and connecting them via hyperlinks opens a new space of experiments. Using video game technologies to improve immersion into scripted worlds where learners could interact with their teacher in, for example, a team game will soon be possible. Also, computer-based systems make possible the interaction between students and a digital companion as a peer provided for help (Ramirez Uresti, 1999), or a "student" whom the real student has to teach (Leelawong, Schwartz, & Belynne, 2002).

4.   CONCLUSION

Learning by Teaching is an original method for involving students in the learning process in order to improve learning efficiency. In this way, it belongs to the shift from a teacher-orientated to a student-orientated education.

What we tried to do is broaden the definition of LbT to include an internal process in which LbT is also beneficial for the teachers in providing them with original and value-added course content. Thus, the main educational implications of this research come from the credit the teacher should give to the student's knowledge.

To achieve this goal, we proposed to modify the teacher-learner interaction into a sharing process where valuable knowledge is not the sole possession of the teacher. But having students express their experiences and general rules of understanding and actions may not be easy, particularly in the French context, where the learner-teacher interaction is supposed to be very knowledge-asymmetric. This is why working on students' questions as an indirect way of producing knowledge, but also relying on storytelling techniques for making students' knowledge explicit could be of great help.

E-learning technologies offer many possibilities for implementing this service-centered view of Learning by Teaching. Defining new kinds of flexible interactions, using questions as fundamental educational resources, and structuring content as interactive stories could allow us to design service-based interactive courses where both learners and teachers could learn from each other as well as teach one another.

However, we see one obstacle in the development of Learning by Teaching that comes from the fact that education is necessarily embedded into a global social and economical context. This is the need to adapt education to the transition from a product-oriented to a service-oriented economy. A production-based economy relies on a fundamental asymmetry, which clearly separates clients and suppliers, the latter designing products matching customer needs. A service-based economy modifies the nature of the interaction between the two parties, with customers not only giving money in exchange for goods, but also participating in their production. E-learning is clearly customer-oriented because distance learning technologies and methods expand the power of the student-as-customer to learn anytime anywhere at his/her own pace. But Learning by Teaching as we redefined it, may partially reverse the traditional knowledge transfer roles, by asking students to participate in the fundamental knowledge creation and transfer processes that are traditionally associated with the role of the teacher. In an economy where the customer is king, Learning by Teaching may be seen to be somewhat contradictory. However, we are confident that in today's societies, which give an increasing legitimacy to everyday knowledge, the teacher-learner interaction will become a powerful source of knowledge creation.

REFERENCES

Argyris, C., & Schön, D. (1996). *Organizational learning II.* Addison-Wesley.

Bargh, J. A., & Schul, Y. (1980). On the cognitive benefits of teaching. *Journal of Educational Psychology, 72,* 593-604.

Drucker, P. (1993). *Post-capitalist society.* Oxford, Butterworth Heinemann.

Eiglier, P., & Langeard, E. (1991). *Servuction.* McGraw-Hill.

Johnson, D. W., Johnson, R., & Smith, K. (1991). *Active learning: Cooperation in the college classroom.* Edina, Minnesota: Interaction Book Company.

Laurel, B. (1993). *Computers as Theatre.* Addison-Wesley.

Leelawong, K., Schwartz, D., & Belynne, K. (2002). *The Effects of Feedback in Supporting Learning by Teaching in a Teachable Agent Environment.* Fifth International Conference of the Learning Science (ICLS), University of Washington - Seattle, October 23 -26, 2002.

Linde, C. (2000). Narrative in institutions. In H. Hamilton, D. Schiffrin, & D. Tannen (Eds.), *Handbook of discourse analysis.* Oxford, UK: Blackwell.

Maulini, O. (2000). *L'institution du questionnement dans l'interaction maître-élève.* Contribution à l'étude des formes scolaires d'enseignement. Université de Genève, Faculté de psychologie des sciences de l'éducation.

Nichols, D. (1994). Issues in Designing Learning by Teaching Systems. In P. Brusilovsky, S. Dikareva, J. Greer, & V. Petrushin (Eds.), *Proceedings of the East-West International*

Conference on Computer Technologies in Education (EW-ED'94): Vol.1, 176-81. Crimea, Ukraine.

Orr, J. (1996). *Talking about machines: An ethnography of modern job*. Ithaca, NY: IRL Press.

Palincsar, A. S., & Brown, A. L. (1984). Reciprocal teaching of comprehension-fostering and comprehension-monitoring activities. *Cognition and Instruction, 1*, 117-175.

Ramirez Uresti, J. A. (1999). *Interaction with a learning companion to learn by teaching*. Hct'99 Interacting through/with Technology: Increasing the Potential for Communicating and Learning? 3rd Human Centred Technology Postgraduate Workshop

Rives, C., & Cooper, P. J. (1997). *The power of story: Teaching through storytelling*. 2nd ed. Allyn & Bacon.

Skinner, J. D. Retrieved in June 2002 from: <http://www.ldl.de/material/aufsatz/skinner.htm>

Stewart, T. (1998). *Intellectual capital - The new wealth of organisations*. London: Nicholas Brealey Publishing.

Vincent, G., Lahire, B., & Thin, D. (1994). *L'éducation prisonnière de la forme scolaire. Scolarisation et socialisation dans les sociétés industrielles*. Presse Universitaire de Lyon.

Webb, N. M. (1989). Peer interaction and learning in small groups. *International Journal of Educational Research, 13*, 21-39.

Wenger, E. (1998). *Communities of practice: Learning, meaning and identity*. Cambridge: Cambridge University Press.

Wurman, R. S. (2001). *Information anxiety 2*. Indianapolis:QUE.

Chapter 11

A COLLABORATIVE TOOL FOR ARGUMENTATION-BASED LEARNING: EXAMINING FACE-TO-FACE AND COMPUTER-BASED APPROACHES IN A UK SECONDARY SCHOOL[1]

Lia Litosseliti, Laurie Hirsch, Jeanne Cornillon & Masoud Saeedi
School of Management, Royal Holloway University of London, UK

1. INTRODUCTION AND RESEARCH QUESTIONS

This paper presents research conducted in the UK, as part of the three-year research project called "Internet-based intelligent tool to Support Collaborative Argumentation-based Learning in secondary schools (SCALE)." The project looks at how secondary school students learn how to argue or debate, and at the role software can play in facilitating and developing this process. Classroom studies have been carried out in five partner countries (UK, France, the Netherlands, Finland, Hungary), and in this paper we are focusing on those conducted in the UK, at Royal Holloway University of London.

We aimed to address the following research questions:

[1]The research reported here was carried out within the SCALE project (Internet-based intelligent tool to Support Collaborative Argumentation-based Learning in secondary schools, March 2001-February 2004) funded by the European Community under the "Information Societies Technology" (IST) Program. Information on the project can be found at: http://www.euroscale.net/

R.G.Milter et al. (eds.), Educational Innovation in Economics and Business IX, 195–219.
©2004 *Springer. Printed in the Netherlands.*

- How important is the use of Internet tools in the learning of argument?
- What are the effects of arguing with Internet tools and arguing face to face on the process and quality of argument?
- What happens in the Internet and face-to-face discussions?
- What are the attitudes of students towards the use of Internet tools for argumentation?

The design of our classroom studies has been oriented towards specific pedagogical objectives and learning goals, the UK national curriculum, and the particular school context. These theoretical and practical elements are briefly discussed in the following sections, followed by a discussion of the analysis and findings of our research.

2.   THEORETICAL FRAMEWORK

2.1   Argumentation in the UK National Curriculum

The National Curriculum in the UK determines the content of what will be taught, sets attainment targets for learning, and determines how performance will be assessed and reported (see National Curriculum online). Across the subject range, the UK Curriculum shows a strong bias towards the acquisition of factual material (e.g., students "should be taught to organize their writing in logical and coherent forms"), thus allowing limited scope for activities that practice argument and debate. In some subjects other than English - specifically mathematics, science, history, philosophy, religious education, and special educational needs - a degree of formal instruction in argument and debating skills (henceforth, ADS) is given at Key Stages 3 (ages 11-14) and 4 (ages 14-16). However, this provision is not motivated by National Curriculum requirements and is introduced on a fairly random basis by individual teachers. Furthermore, there is no provision for the teaching of ADS in Geography or Modern Languages. The marginal recommendations for developing ADS focus on reading, and to a lesser degree on listening, rather than on more interactive activities among students (such as classroom debates). For the study of *English*, the National Curriculum makes explicit reference to ADS at Key Stages 3 and 4, as regards speaking, listening, reading, and writing skills. Overall, there is limited provision in the curriculum for student group discussion and interaction. The range of purposes here include teaching the pupils how to explore, hypothesize, debate, and analyze what is being said during group discussions; and the ability to take different roles in groups, for example, roles in organizing or leading the discussion, supporting others, and enabling focused talk.

A recent initiative in the National Curriculum promotes seven important skills across all taught subjects, of which *Thinking Skills* is the most relevant to ADS. Thinking skills are sub-divided into five sections: information processing; reasoning; enquiry; creativity; and evaluation. These sections emphasize the following qualities required in ADS: giving reasons for opinions/actions; making informed judgments/decisions; hypothesizing; developing evaluation criteria; applying evaluation criteria; judging the value of information and ideas. All these feature across the Key Stages.

Finally, September 2002 saw the introduction in the National Curriculum in England of *Citizenship* for secondary school. Education in citizenship and democracy aims to develop students' understanding of their roles and responsibilities as citizens in a modern democracy. The handbooks provide for the first time a national framework for the teaching of personal, social, and health education. In the current educational and political climate in the UK, there is also a clearly articulated need for citizens to be prepared to engage with economic, social, and cultural change (including globalization and the rapid expansion of communication technologies).

Despite such recent developments, the gaps caused by an inconsistent and random approach towards developing ADS in the UK classrooms are obvious and make research projects such as the one presented here imperative. The gaps are highlighted by teachers during some of our curriculum studies in several UK schools (Backley, Saxton, & Sillince, 1999). Teachers point out weaknesses in students' ability to construct argument and debate, and problems with implementation of Information Technology (IT) resources in the classroom. As regards instruction in ADS, these findings suggest that (p. 2):

- Generally, the elements of ADS are introduced in the context of verbal debate rather than essay writing, although teachers believe that these verbal skills can be readily transferred (if students are motivated) to written work.

- As a preparation for verbal debate, emphasis is placed on the importance of (i) providing sufficient evidence to support the claims being made, and (ii) being equipped to consider and respond to counter-argument.

- These areas highlight particular weaknesses in students' ability to construct argument and debate. Teachers agree that students are generally too quick to assume that a strongly-held claim will stand up without independent justification or support; that the majority of students do not have an intuitive grasp of ADS; and that some specific instruction in this area in isolation is necessary.

Backley et al. (1999) also report that there is an assumption that responsibility for teaching in ADS lies primarily with the English teachers. English teachers currently use various resources for teaching and practicing ADS, ranging from exercises taken from English Studies textbooks, to a significant amount of self-prepared material (e.g., newspaper extracts, advertising media). Despite the difficulties facing UK schools (such as heavy exam requirements, limited funds, and lack of resources for all), teachers who participated in the above studies were keen to try an IT tool which can monitor, evaluate, and give feedback on students' argument progress (see Backley et al., 1999). Asking students to use an IT tool for argumentation independently can be problematic, but the learning of collaborative argumentation can be enhanced by the parallel use of a tool and a teacher who plays a facilitating, inquiring, and critiquing role – by not answering questions, but by reflecting inquiries back to students (Pilkington & Parker-Jones, 1996; Ravenscroft 1997; Ravenscroft & Matheson, 2000). It has been found, for example in science classes, that such a role encourages a refinement and conceptual development in students' knowledge, which can lead to more effective argumentation (see Ravenscroft & Matheson, 2000, for ideas on an educational dialectic for learning).

2.2   Computer-Based and Face-to-Face Argumentation

The results of previous work by Marttunen (1997) and Marttunen & Laurinen (2001) suggest that different learning environments are suitable for different learning aims and also can help improve skills in complementary areas. For example, face-to-face argumentation can promote discussion and improve students' ability to counter-argue (especially following irrelevant or controversial statements), whereas arguing via e-mail can improve students' skills in identifying and choosing relevant claims, grounds, and counter-arguments in argumentative texts. Moreover, the students arguing via e-mail were able to evaluate the relevance and irrelevance of different grounds for an argument, which enhances the ability to evaluate arguments.

Further, computer-based learning typically allows for sufficient time to deliberate, whereas face-to-face learning requires rapid, interaction-based skill to consider arguments (Berge, 1997). In this sense, while the former may allow for well-formulated written arguments, the latter relies considerably on the speakers' performance skills and ability to think "on their feet." For example, Marttunen and Laurinen's study (2001) of argumentative discussions among university students found that speech turns were distributed more equally when e-mail was used as a communication medium, compared to a face-to-face environment where the discussion was dominated by active students with good communication and performance skills. Contrary to face-to-face interaction, computer-based learning may hide aspects of gender, appearance, level of education and status, thus giving equal opportunities for participants to present their views (Dillenbourg, 1999). At the same time, it also hides other aspects of communication, notably non-verbal cues, body language, gestures and feelings, thus limiting self-expression to written language.

Finally, virtual forums are often seen as more difficult for students to socialize in than face-to-face environments (Anderson & Kanuka, 1997), perhaps because they often inhibit questions to other participants. It also takes more time to achieve agreement between participants electronically than face to face (Garton & Wellman, 1995; Olaniran, 1994). However, both interactive situations can stimulate the learning of argumentation and critical thinking, given that the students have to think through and collaboratively negotiate different and/or conflicting claims and points of view. If our learning aims are focused on promoting structured argumentation, as well as creativity and social relationships through argument, then computer-based and face-to-face learning are best seen as complementary.

3.   RESEARCH

In this section we describe the design of our research studies: the context of the school where participants were recruited and the pedagogical objectives and principles guiding this process; the instruments used and procedures followed; and the methods of analysis applied to the data.

3.1   Context of the Research, Objectives, and Design

We have worked with a group of 16 sixth-form students (aged 16-17) in one secondary school (Elliott school) in the London area. Elliott was founded as a comprehensive school in 1956 and is now a Foundation School (and Language College) providing for the education of boys and girls aged 11-18. The school has a good record of academic success, and an active interest in new information and communication technologies. The Sixth Form (16-18 years) in particular, includes a variety of extra activities, such as music groups, extra-curricular theatre and film visits, the Debating Society, and voluntary work in the community.

Although argumentation is not formally taught, the school offers a unique environment for argumentation, due to the commitment and effort put into the well-established sixth-form Debating Society, where students were recruited for our research project. The society was set up 25 years ago by the teacher who collaborated with us in this project, and is currently the most successful extra-curricular activity in the school, with the majority of 6th form students attending voluntarily every week. The teaching and learning of argumentation in this forum is informal and the Society allows a degree of flexibility often not afforded within a formal classroom environment. For example, the student body can decide which issues of current affairs are important or relevant enough to become topics of debate; students look after the logistic, practical side of running a debate; and they voluntarily produce pieces of writing (essays, poems etc.) following the debates.

For our project work, we organized three sessions with 16 students and their teacher, in three consecutive weeks during November 2001 (lasting one and a half hour each). The sessions took place immediately after the end of classes. The students were selected by the teacher from the group of sixth-formers participating in the Debating Society, on the basis of the following criteria: mixed-gender (half were boys and half were girls), mixed-ability in terms of argumentation, and mixed social, racial, religious, economic backgrounds, in order to have multiple and divergent viewpoints. Our **pedagogical objectives**, shared across the SCALE project, were:

1. To increase learning through the development of argumentation skills (e.g., the development of more relevant arguments, the development of multiple viewpoints and the acceptance of differing points, the development of critical thinking skills).
2. To discover when argumentation in collaborative tasks is most effective for learning, and particularly for promoting cooperation and dialogue among learners.

In addition to these pedagogical objectives, we have taken into account certain pedagogical and methodological principles, which are relevant within the setting of Elliott school: the central role of the teacher as facilitator, guide, communication manager, and the importance of teacher input for our research; the importance of facilitating constructive debate during which all students feel they can participate, express their views openly, and with minimum intervention; the significance of ensuring students' understanding of, experimentation with, and reflection on the tools for debate (before, during and after the debate); and the importance of composing the groups in ways that minimize threat and maximize interaction.

These objectives and principles have guided the development of the **teaching materials** used and the **tasks** followed by the students during our studies. The purpose of the teaching materials given to the students during our sessions was to provide a basic introduction to argumentation and debate, and consisted of:

- Introduction to the concepts (what we mean by "argument position" and "counter-argument," to "argue" and to "debate," "claims" and "evidence or grounds").
- Introduction to issues of lexical choice, connotations, and bias (with examples).
- Some key questions relating to the (debatable) issue of what makes a good argument.
- Introduction to argumentative strategies via which the relationship between evidence and claim is often established, and examples.
- Background reading on what is an argument.

In addition, students were given topic domain-related materials, in particular they were asked to read and discuss an article entitled "What Women Want: Has the feminist revolution gone too far?," published in *Prospect* magazine in 1998. The article consists of a written debate on the topic between the writers Fay Weldon and Polly Toynbee. The students were then involved in debating this key topic question (*"Have we achieved gender equality?"*) in the sessions that followed. There were various reasons for choosing this particular topic for debate. The teacher suggested the topic as appropriate and interesting for the students, and expected a rich debate, with a high degree of student involvement, yet enough "common ground." Students are uneasy about tackling topics that lie beyond their own experiences (i.e., too abstract or not involving personal knowledge), and therefore it was important to present them with a debatable topic about which they have both a degree of general knowledge and personal implication. In addition, equal opportunities have become an important part of the UK national curriculum, given the current emphasis on citizenship, democracy and social and personal development.

As we were interested in the promotion of learning (*"arguing to learn"* rather than *"learning to argue"*), our objective was that, firstly, students understood a particular domain content/ generic information about argument, and secondly, that they also understood the whole area of *debate* within that domain, and could integrate, reformulate, and evaluate such information. We thus developed specific tasks for the students. We followed a generic task sequence[2] designed for use with intelligent Internet-based collaborative learning tools, but instantiated with different content, and adapted to our educational system, computational medium and time/ space constraints (Tables 1 and 2). We have aimed to fulfill the following task requirements

---

[2] The generic task sequence used with learning tools was developed by our project partners in France (GRIC, Lyon) and in the Netherlands (Utrecht University). Details can be found in Deliverable 8 of the SCALE project, at: http://www.euroscale.net/.

(see also footnote 2 for reference): that content is discussible (different opinions and ideas are defensible), learnable (something should be learnt), negotiable (scenario allows different viewpoints); that tasks are motivating, interesting, and encourage involvement; that tasks are complex, involve multiple stages of negotiation, problem solving, decision making, and knowledge sharing (i.e., encourage argumentation); that tasks are transparent, with clear goals, where participants know what to do and what to do it for; and finally, that tasks allow reflection.

Table 1. Task Sequence Used in the UK Classroom Studies

1.	TRAINING	(reading text materials on argumentation and topic domain)
2.	PREPARATION	(looking for information and producing a list of arguments; 1st individual text writing)
3.	DEBATE	(engaging in Chat and Face-to-Face debate)
4.	REFLECTION	(collaborative reflection on debate, with written summaries)
5.	CONSOLIDATION	(2nd individual text writing)

Table 2. Details of Task Sequence Instantiation in the UK Classroom Studies.

TASK SEQUENCE (Gender Equality)

Phase	Description	Tools	Duration
Phase 1: Introduction and Training.	Students were introduced to different concepts to be treated during the task sequence, and to the topic of debate.	Written texts Chart for analyzing arguments.	30 mins for introduction; 60 mins for training.
Phase 2: Preparation.	Pre-text. Students wrote individual texts, each student presented his/her text to the group and feedback was given.	Paper and pen.	30 mins for task; 30 mins for presentation.
Phase 3: Debate.	Students were introduced to using the chat software, and to face-to-face debate. Both groups (with the chat software, and face-to-face) debated in pairs.	Chat software. Face-to-face.	10 mins for introduction; 30 mins for debate.
Phase 4: Reflection.	Reflection: students were asked to write what they liked about the debate, what they didn't like, and what they learned. Then, one student from each of the two groups presented the results to all.	Face-to-face. Paper and pen.	20 mins for reflection; 20 mins for presentation.
Phase 5: Consolidation.	Post-text. Students wrote individual argumentative texts.	Paper and pen.	Completed in students' own time.

For a full description of the phases, see Deliverables 1 and 2 of the SCALE project, at: http://www.euroscale.net/

3.2 Research Aim

In this paper, we focus on the analysis of students' individual written argumentative texts before and after debate (Phases 2 and 5) and on the students' interaction during debate (Phase 3), with particular emphasis on a comparison between debating using Internet tools and debating face to face. In line with our research questions (see Introduction to the paper), we were interested to see whether the use of Internet tools has particular effects on the process and the quality of students' arguments (the "space" for debate).

Finally, we were interested in the attitudes of students towards the use of Internet tools[3] for argumentations.

3.3 Methods of Analysis

To address the research questions outlined in Section 1 and the different issues discussed in Section 3.1, we used a combination of complementary methodologies.

Firstly, we carried out analyses of the students' productions, in both conditions (face-to-face debate and synchronous Internet debate), before and after the debate, that is, texts produced during Phases 2 and 5 (see table above). The method of analysis, which was developed by our partners in Lyon and Utrecht, is referred to as the **QED method**, aiming to measure the "quality of the space of debate" (as the acronym indicates in French)[4]. The analysis examines the differences between the student texts produced individually before and after the collaborative debates. These differences are meant to capture changes in the space of debate, that is, changes in the way a student reasons and argues about a debatable topic. A wide space of debate means that a student's texts demonstrate many relevant arguments on the topics of debate, multiple points of view, and different causes and facts. The QED method provides assessment on the following criteria (SCALE project, 2002, Deliverable 8):

- **richness**: your answer is rich when you provide a large set of arguments.
- **elaboration**: your answer is deep when you develop your arguments, with sub-arguments, examples, explanation, etc.

---

[3] In the UK, students did so via a CHAT system accessible over the Internet: www.chat-forum.com. The system was simple and reliable, it required no local installation, and allowed us to set up private chat rooms for each team and to record the text. The system has a text entry area and displays the previous chat next to the name of each team.

[4] The QED method was elaborated by M. Quignard (GRIC, Lyon), in collaboration with M. Baker (GRIC, Lyon), J. Andriessen and M. van Amelsvoort (Utrecht University). See SCALE project, Deliverable 8 at http://www.euroscale.net/.

- **balance (b)**: your answer is more objective when you are able to provide well balanced pro/against arguments. If the question is really open, there must be arguments on each side (pro and against).
- **coverage (cv)**: your answer has a wide coverage when your arguments reflect the variety of the opinions or standpoints of the different actors of the debate or covers the different topics of the question.
- **coherence (ch)**: your answer is reliable when your general point of view (or opinion) is well supported by the arguments you give.

We refer the reader to Deliverable 8 of the SCALE project (2002) for a detailed description of the QED measurement and the above factors of argumentative knowledge, and for other relevant issues[5]. For the purposes of this paper, we should point out that a QED measurement is a combination of the above factors, where balance, coverage and coherence ($QED = b \times cv \times ch$) are main factors, and the elaboration and number of arguments are secondary. This is due to an emphasis on students being able to summarize a position in relation to various and diverse points of view in a coherent manner – what can be described as argumentative knowledge. QED scores measure the above factors and also calculate other variables: number of topics, number of arguments, number of arguments pro, and number of arguments against. The QED measurement can be applied across a range of experimental conditions; for example, in the UK we focused on chat and face-to-face debate, but other project partners looked at debate with/ without chat tools and graphs.

Secondly, we carried out analyses of the students' interaction during the Debate Phase (Phase 3 above) in both computer-based and face-to-face learning environments. The debates were 30 minutes long each, and included a total of 453 speech turns (107 chat and 346 face-to-face). All computer chat debates were automatically stored by the computer, and all face-to-face debates were tape-recorded and transcribed. The interactions were analyzed using a method of analysis described as the **Rainbow method**[6], with the speech turn as the unit of analysis. *Rainbow* is a framework for analyzing pedagogically-oriented argumentative interactions between students. The functional analysis component of this method comprises seven analytical

---

[5] For example, the reliability of the QED analysis was investigated by having another analyst analyze 18.75% of texts (before and after debate, in both face-to-face and Internet conditions) randomly chosen from the original data analyzed by the first analyst.

[6] This method has been collaboratively developed by members in four of the research teams participating in the SCALE project. Details can be found in the SCALE project working paper (2002) entitled "A framework for analyzing pedagogically oriented computer-mediated debates: Rainbow," written by M. Baker and revised by M. van Amelsvoort and L. Munneke.

categories (illustrated by the colors of the rainbow). These are: *off-task/ outside activity* (any interaction not relating to the topic of debate and to the given task); *social relation* (interaction managing the students' social relations, e.g., greetings); *interaction management* (interaction which manages the interaction itself, e.g., co-ordination, contact and understanding between speakers, communication management, topic shifting, etc.); *task management* (management of the progression of the task set by the researcher, e.g., the direction the debate is going); *opinions* (opinions stated, requested, clarified, etc. with respect to the topic of debate); *argumentation* (arguments and counter-arguments directly related to a thesis); and *explore and deepen*. This last one is the most complex category of interaction, comprising three sub-categories: deepening through a (counter)argument that builds on an already expressed one; making an argumentative link between (counter)arguments, such as questioning or supporting a link; and discussing a meaning of an argument (discursive or conceptual deepening, with examples). All turns of the transcribed interactions were coded following the *Rainbow* categories and sub-categories (functional analysis) and by topic (topic analysis). Finally, we look at students' feedback (from their reflection on the debate and from questionnaires), in order to get more insight into their attitudes towards using Internet tools for argumentation.

In the following section, we discuss the results of the QED analysis of students' individual texts on the topic of debate, and the results of the Rainbow analysis of students' interaction during the Debate Phase.

4. RESULTS

4.1 QED Analysis: Results

Across the SCALE project participating countries, QED analysis results have indicated that task assignments of the type described in 3.1 have an effect on the previously described characteristics of the space of debate. However, while learning has overall taken place, in that students in the other participating countries improved their QED score from before to after discussion, the results in the UK do not show a clear or significant improvement in QED scores. Figure 1 below shows the small shifts in the variables, from the texts before discussion (01) to after discussion (02). The rating scale was from 0 to 100, in percentages. The different sub-scores in each of the variables have been added, following the formula described in 3.2, to create a QED score from 0-100. A score near the top of this scale would be very unusual, as even the best of the students who participated in our project in France scored not higher than 43. Figure 2 shows the overall score for the QED before and after the discussion[7]. We can see that there are slight differences between the pre-texts (before debate) and post-texts (after debate), in terms of the specific variables and the total mean score, but that these differences are not significant. The slight decrease from the QED01 to the QED02 score, from 6.6 to 6.3, is insignificant in a scale from 0 to 100, and the score remained low.

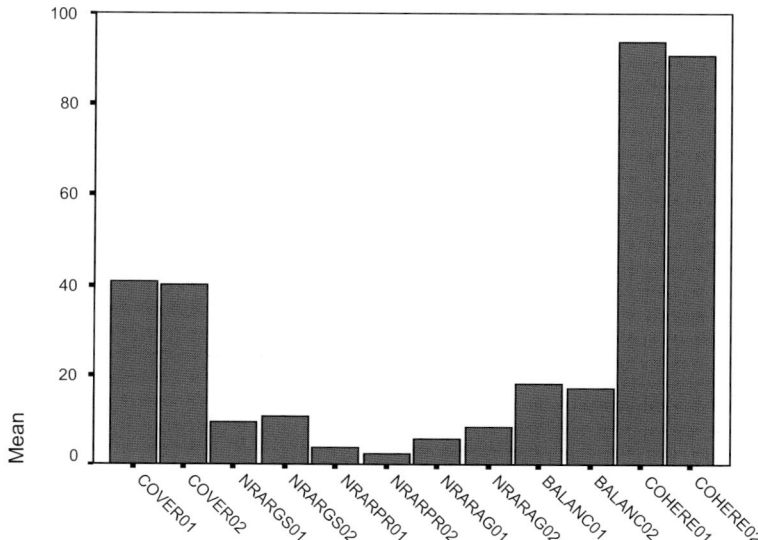

Figure1. QED mean score for individual variables, before and after discussion

(cover=coverage; nrargs=number of arguments; nrarpro=number of arguments pro; nrarag=number of arguments against; balanc=balance; cohere=coherence)

[7] The statistical processing of the QED scores obtained from the students' texts was carried out by M. van Amelsvoort (Utrecht University). See SCALE project (2002) Deliverable 8.

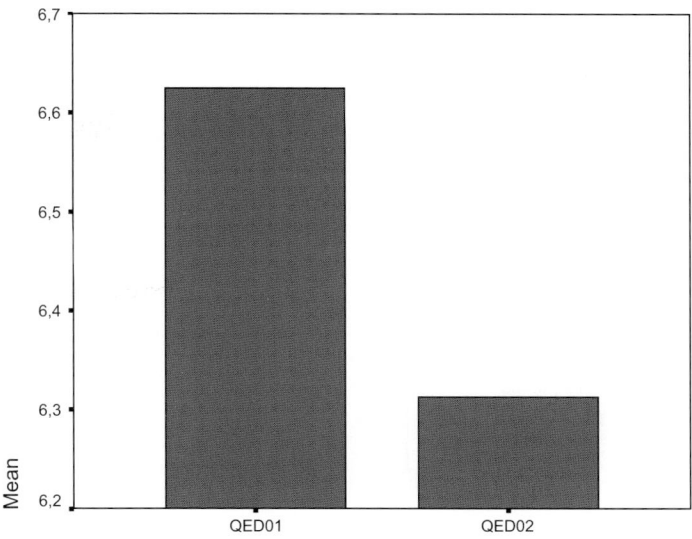

Figure 2. Total QED mean score, before and after discussion

In addition, learning, in terms of QED scores, did not vary significantly between electronic chat and face-to-face discussion. In Figure 3 we can see that students in the Chat condition improved their QED somewhat, while the opposite is the case in the face-to-face condition. But this difference between the performance of the chat and the face-to-face groups is not significant; we do not see a clear effect of the discussion on the students' QED scores (see SCALE project, 2002, Deliverable 8).

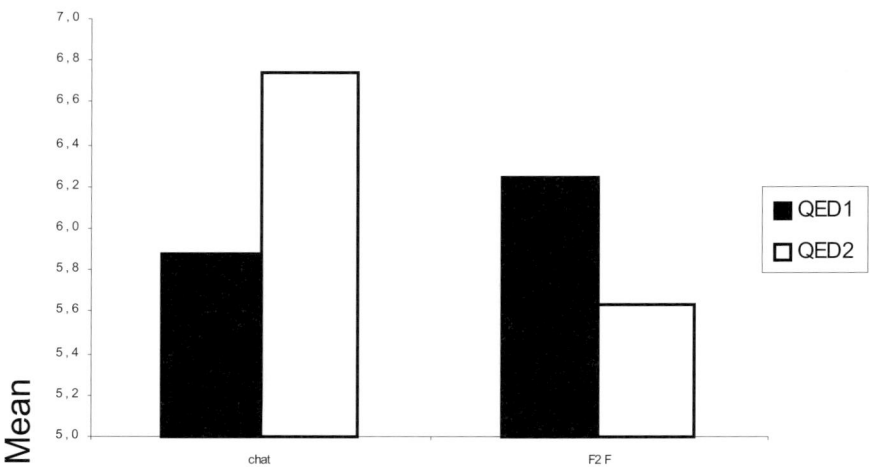

Figure 3. QED scores in different conditions (c = chat; F2F = face-to-face)

The fact that we do not see a significant improvement in the QED scores in the UK does not mean that no learning of argumentation took place during the discussions. These findings may be due to a number of reasons, for example, the low number of students participating, the uncontrolled writing procedure of the post-texts (in the sense that students wrote those in their own time; see Table 2 above, Consolidation), and the nature of the tasks themselves. For instance, one way in which the tasks may have affected the results is that in the UK we asked students to write a new second individual text (post-text, consolidation phase), while our partners in France, the Netherlands, and Finland asked students to revise their original first text. Revision is likely to be a less demanding task for the students than the writing of a new text; it also makes it easier to comparatively pinpoint changes and progression in argument. But more importantly, we think that, though useful for a basic understanding of students' claims and (counter)arguments, the QED method of analysis is not by itself appropriate for assessing co-construction and shared understanding, as an effect of collaboration. We propose that these issues, and the key question of what may have caused the learning that occurred, can be better explored through detailed qualitative analysis of the students' actual interaction during the debate phase.

Preliminary qualitative analysis of these interactions suggested that when students argue in pairs, it is difficult to assess whether and to what extent each individual's understanding of the debate and learning improves. The following is an example from one of our CHAT debates; here Kaya and Jiten [KJ] argue that gender equality has not been achieved, and Thitima and Robin [TR] argue for the opposite position. The spelling and grammar used by the students have been left unchanged.

Example 1

> [...]
> 1. [Thitima & Robin]: ok..how can u tell exactly when gender equality has been achieve?
> 2. [Kaya & Jiten]: when we are treated the same in the work place
> 3. [KJ]: when politically we have equal distribution and representation
> 4. [KJ]: when we have equal pay
> 5. [TR]: but we can never have equal distribution and representation of woman in politics
> 6. [KJ]: when paternity leave is the same as maternity leave, men will benefit as well
> 7. [KJ]: why
> 8. [TR] or the distribution to be equal, there need to be a sufficient number of woman willing to enter politics
> 9. [TR]: *needs
> 10. [KJ]: women need to feel that they can professions as easily as men
> 11. [KJ]: like in politics it is so hard for women to break through
> 12. [KJ]: they should be encouraged
> 13. [TR]: well u can say the same thing for men...
> 14. [KJ]: and it is wrong to say there aren't enough women wanting to enter politics
> 15. [KJ]: what are u basing that on
> 16. [KJ]: same for men......how
> 17. [TR]: its harder for men to enter such jobs primary school teaching
> 18. [KJ]: because of society
> 19. [TR]: because the expectations
> 20. [KJ]: not because of professional disadvantages
> 21. [KJ]: hello
> 22. [TR]: its seems like the revolution has gone too far...women seem to be taken on more masculine qualities in some cases...its jus not necessary to achieve in such way
> 23. [KJ]: some women
> 24. [KJ]: far from the majority
> 25. [KJ]: the majority are still having to fight for equal status
> 26. [TR]: men and women aren't the same
> [...]

It emerges throughout our data that an increased amount of contributions does not necessarily reflect or signify increased learning. The QED results in the case of Robin and of Kaya (participants in Example 1 above) show significant differences in the scores between their pre-texts and their post-texts. In Robin's case, there's significantly higher scoring after the debate (from 2 to 11 percent), while in Kaya's case, there's significantly lower scoring after the debate (from 14 to 2 percent), even though she is contributing more. A more detailed, qualitative analysis therefore needs to examine different types of arguments and counter-arguments, and the extent to which these are merely repetitive or descriptive (e.g., turn 26 in the above example), or more challenging and analytical (e.g., turn 8 above). The analysis also needs to consider the dynamics of the interaction. For instance, in the above example, it is possible that the many contributions by Kaya and Jiten are intimidating for Thitima and Robin, who are mainly responding (see also Section 4.3 later). And within a single pair, one student may benefit from collaborating with the other, by adding to and complementing each other's contribution, while another may suffer, if the discussion is dominated by one of them.

The preliminary analysis of the interactions also suggested that monitoring and facilitating the debates that take place over the Internet may be more complex than in face-to-face conditions. While the face-to-face debates were audible, and it was both easy and appropriate for the teacher to take part in the discussions (as an observer, and, at times, as a facilitator), this was less straightforward when debating over the Internet. In the following example from another CHAT debate, we see that when collaboration does not work very successfully, one of the student pairs takes over the monitoring/clarifying role usually played by the teacher. The result is a meta-discourse: argument about argument.

Example 2

[…]

1. [Esther & Reshad]: well we think that it has been achieved, what is you evidence for this
2. [ER]: well...
3. [Mala & Russell]: women recieve lower pay for the same job as men - its discrimination such as managment
4. [ER]: the introduction of the equal pay act surely demonstrates a radical change in the mindset of society, aligning society with a more egalitarian ideal
5. [MR]: then why is it not bein followed huh???!!!
6. [ER]: there are still some legistlative delays but society as a whole does represent gender equality!
7. [MR]: say what.........
8. [ER]: comon...
9. [ER]: COME ON!!!\
10. [ER]: you cannot use the one instance of the legal situation to represent the whole issue as most of society is not like that
11. [MR]: ok so why are women still disrespected like in engineering where it is male dominated
12. [ER]: you are jumping the subject you yourselves brought up, lets not...
13. [MR]: ???
14. [ER]: also...just because the practical means for equality has been introduced it does not mean all attitudes will change straightaway
15. [MR]: your point being
16. [ER]: do you even understand what we just said?
17. [MR]: nope
18. [ER]: what we are saying is that everything is not going to change instantly but equality has been achieved in general
19. [MR]: obviously it hasnt as otherwise we wouldnt have to be argueing this point of view
20. [ER]: the existence of a point of view does not justify it, you have your point of view...FINE...but that does not mean that you are right or that gender equality has not been achieved!!!!
21. [MR]: excuse me but equal wages have not been achieved - evidence
22. [MR]: wheres your evidence
23. [ER]: but - wouldnt you say that the majority of both men and women see each other as equals? the attitudes of the members of our society are more important than such specific hindrances
24. [MR]: but if there are inequalities then equality has not been achieved
25. [ER]: differences are not the same as inequalities
26. [MR]: end of discussion
27. [ER]: you really do not understand what we are saying, do you?
28. [ER]: you keep on making a a point and then repeating it without broadening it in anyway
29. [ER]: nice talk, godbye...
30. [MR]:   yeah and what is your point then
31. [MR]:   bye

There is considerable learning about argument in Example 2 that could not be adequately examined through quantitative analysis only. We can see evidence of students' awareness of the use of generalization in arguments (*"you cannot use the one instance of the legal situation to represent the whole issue"*); of argument progression (*"you are jumping the subject you yourselves brought up"*); of developing a point and providing evidence for it (*"the existence of a point of view does not justify it"*; and *"you keep on making a point and then repeating it without broadening it in anyway"*); and of clarifying or seeing through an argument (*"differences are not the same as inequalities"*). In addition, learning about argument also happens through students being actively involved in monitoring, clarifying, and interpreting the argument process – similarly to how a teacher would do this during a traditional face-to-face classroom debate. In the above example, we see this role played by Esther and Reshad, with varying degrees of success. The QED scores show improvement in the case of Esther (4-8 percent) and Reshad (10-20 percent), while Mala and Russell remain at 3 percent. It may well be that this role of examining argumentation at a meta level contributes to better overall learning of argument, but other aspects have to also be closely considered (e.g., degree of success, degree of understanding etc.). A combination of analyses that take into account such different aspects of collaborative argumentative learning is both necessary and productive.

4.2   Rainbow Analysis: Results

Table 3 illustrates the distribution of Rainbow analysis categories (described in 3.2) for all interactions analyzed: chat and face-to-face.

Table3. Overall Rainbow Category Distribution (chat and face-to-face)

Category	Frequency	Percent
Outside activity	7	1.5
Social relation	19	4.2
Interaction management	79	17.4
Task management	37	8.2
Opinions	65	14.3
Argumentation	100	22.1
Explore and deepen	146	32.2
Total	**453**	**100**

The low distribution of the outside activity, social relation, and task management categories, indicates that students were focused on the task and adequately prepared for the debate. There was a fair amount of interaction management throughout the debates. The majority of turns where interaction management took place fall into the communication management sub-category (such as establishing contact, understanding, attitudes), followed by many instances of interaction (who will speak or not and when), and finally few cases of dialogue structuring (e.g., topic shifting). Argumentative activities (opinions, argumentation, and explore and deepen) were common (68.6 percent of all speech turns), with the important category of exploring and deepening the debate taking a high proportion (32.2 percent). The following example illustrates one way in which students engaged in argumentative activities:

Example 3

[...]
1. Esther & Reshad   well we think that it [gender equality] has been achieved [...]
2. Mala & Russell   women receive lower pay for the same job as men
3. Esther & Reshad   the introduction of the equal pay act surely demonstrates a radical change in the mindset of society, aligning society with a more egalitarian ideal
4. Mala & Russell   then why is it not being followed huh???!!!
5. Esther & Reshad   there are still some legislative delays but society as a whole does represent gender equality!

In the analysis of this extract, turn 1 above is coded in Rainbow analysis as *Attitudes, opinions and agreement*, 2 and 3 as *Provide (counter-) arguments*, and 4 and 5 as *Explore/ deepen the question*. Overall, there were more arguments and counter-arguments than opinions, and more exploring and deepening of the arguments rather than simply expressing arguments. This is a positive result in the context of this project's pedagogical goals: aiming to broaden and deepen students' space of debate in order to help them learn argumentative knowledge (see SCALE project, 2002).

Let us now move to the results of a comparison between the chat and the face-to-face debates (Table 4):

Table 4. Comparison of Rainbow Analysis Categories in Chat and Face-to-face

Category	Chat Frequency	Chat Percent	Face-to-face Frequency	Face-to-face Percent
Outside activity	5	4.7	2	0.6
Social relation	10	9.3	9	2.6
Interaction management	24	22.4	55	15.9
Task management	6	5.6	31	9.0
Opinions	15	14.0	50	14.5
Argumentation	19	17.8	81	23.4
Explore and deepen	28	26.2	118	34.1
Total	**107**	**100**	**346**	**100**

This table shows that argumentation and the exploring and deepening of arguments took place more extensively in the face-to-face rather than in the chat debates. The combined percentage for all three argumentative categories (opinions, argumentation and exploring and deepening of arguments) in chat was 58 percent, compared to 72 percent in face-to-face debates. These results suggest that face-to-face environments may give students more opportunity to concentrate on the quality of the arguments put forward, in the sense of exploring claims and counter-arguments and deeper or hidden meanings within arguments. This seems to be in line with other findings about face-to-face environments as improving students' ability to counter-argue (Marttunen & Laurinen, 2001). Chat debates may allow for the structuring of the arguments and the opportunity to check what has been said afterwards, but these benefits may not necessarily lead to exploration and deepening of what has been said (see also 4.3 later).

As regards the often-mentioned lack of visual cues and body language in computer-based debates, this does not seem to be a barrier to students' social relation interaction in the chat debates (which was proportionally much more prominent, at 9.3 percent, than in the face-to-face debates: 2.6 percent). Perhaps students debating via chat make an effort to establish social relations in that environment, given the lack of visual contact, and thus effectively compensate for this lack. It is also likely that certain kinds of social relation talk occur in one environment more than in another; for example, most social relation talk in our face-to-face debates consisted of ironic remarks, which perhaps are more immediately effective and less likely to be misunderstood in a face-to-face context (as in the following example, turns 2, 5, and 6).

Example 4

[...]		
1.	Rachel	? (*laughter*)
2.	Jack	I'm convinced, you're convinced, yeah?
3.	Joe	[?] that it would, that, that the balance would swing back to the way it was before
4.	Rachel	well, what are you basing that on?
5.	Jack	Joe's pretty certain, that's why
[...]		
6.	Jack	it's a stalemate (*laughter*)

We can also see relatively small differences in the categories of outside activity and task management. As regards the former, the smaller amount of outside activity in face-to-face debates may be due to the teacher's presence in the classroom during those debates. Although the teacher's presence does not necessarily ensure a better debate, it is important for teaching students on-task focused argument, and it supports and complements the use of any argumentation tools in the classroom. Regarding task management (of the debate, the direction it is going to, topics to be dealt with, etc.), this may have been even more necessary in the face-to-face environment, as these particular debates were significantly longer than the chat debates and the direction of the discussion and topics raised changed often.

4.3   Students' Reflection and Feedback

During the Reflection Phase of our studies (following debate, see 3.1), students had the opportunity to jointly reflect on their debates and the argument process. This was intended to enable the students to clarify and broaden their understanding of the space of debate. They were specifically asked to brainstorm as a group, and list their comments on the argumentation that had taken place, by concentrating on *what they liked* about the debate, *what they disliked*, and *what they feel they learned*.

The group of students who debated over the Internet particularly liked the lack of interruption during the debate and having time to "gather," that is, carefully plan their arguments. They found debating over the Internet easier, because of having time to plan their strategy in pairs before the debate and because they were able to refer back to their arguments by scrolling up the screen. The group also appreciated avoiding "face-to-face confrontations," which, as they said, meant that the task was "not intimidating" and caused "no nervousness." At the same time, the group reported that "it was harder to make your point," since "you must consider phrasing" more carefully, and "because of typing," the task was "more consuming." The students told us that they learned "how to make structured arguments," how to be "clearer with their points," and "how to negotiate (i.e., plan) their arguments beforehand."

The group of students who debated face to face echoed some of these themes. They liked being allowed "more emotion in the delivery" when face to face, and a more extensive "exploration of argumentation on the chosen topic." They seemed to agree that what they disliked about face-to-face debate is that it can be "confusing," that is, "you may start to mumble or drift off the subject and forget about the original point." These students told us that they learned to be "more alert" when face to face with other debaters, as well as how to "use emotion" in their arguments.

After this phase of reflection, students were asked to complete a questionnaire about their whole experience during the debates, the responses to which further emphasized the points above. The students who engaged in computer-based argumentation found it "very useful" or "quite useful," and as something they would like to see happening in the classroom. Again they emphasized the advantages of using computers to think clearly and in a more structured way before typing an argument, and avoiding nervousness and interruption. Some disadvantages of chat debate were mentioned, which do not emerge from our actual analyses: more time-consuming, lack of emotion/ spontaneity, less change in tone and less space for expression, difficulty in showing emphasis. Among these students, more than half confirmed having learned particular debating skills during the sessions (to "clarify," "structure," "ground" their arguments, as well as "collaborating" and "thinking"), and that using the Internet improved the quality of debate.

Finally, the students who debated face to face reported a number of advantages with that environment: more "emotional, spontaneous, instinctive" debate, allows for gesture, body language and tone of voice, "forceful" and quicker delivery, fewer misunderstandings; and disadvantages: less structured/ less carefully composed, element of "prejudice," "contradiction" and "confusion," personal attack, nervousness for those less confident with public speaking. The element of prejudice or bias was associated with "revealing your identity" when debating face to face (contrary to the anonymity of the Internet). Another point made was that "on the computer you have to focus more on structure and quality rather than effectiveness." Students in this face-to-face group thought that they had learned particular debating skills during the sessions (to "deliver," "support," "structure," and balance their arguments, to be "clearer," and to "collaborate"), and that arguing face to face improved the quality of debate.

A key aspect of the students' feedback, and also emerging from our analyses, is the emphasis on structure and the organizing of arguments in computer-based debates, and on the broader, more flexible (if messy) exploration of arguments in face-to-face debates. This perceived flexibility of the face-to-face environment can be linked to the higher occurrence of argumentative categories and the deeper level of exploration found in our analysis of the face-to-face interactions. It may also explain the use of social talk in order to convey irony, which we have seen especially in the face-to-face debates. At the same time, learners appreciate the use of tools that help them clarify, structure, and negotiate their arguments beforehand. Therefore, the issue is not so much about focusing on structure and quality or on effectiveness and delivery, as one student put it, but on a combination of environments, tasks and methods, in order to focus on all these elements. In addition, the teacher's role is crucial in supporting and guiding the students towards that goal; this role will vary within each learning environment, as we saw in our analysis of the face-to-face interactions where off-task talk was limited.

5. CONCLUSIONS

To achieve our aim of promoting a collaborative and constructive exploration of a space of debate, which leads to the broadening and deepening of argumentative knowledge, our analyses and the collaborative tools developed for argumentation-based learning must take into account a variety of factors. We have looked at aspects of richness, elaboration, balance, coverage, and coherence in students' arguments, and have considered some of the dynamics of debate in more detail. We have also explored specific elements of pedagogically oriented argumentative interactions between students: off-task or outside activity, social relations, interaction management, task management, opinions, arguments and counter-arguments, and deepening and exploration of arguments. Finally, we have considered the feedback given by teachers and students, regarding their attitudes towards using (and not using) Internet tools for collaborative argumentation.

In sum, our findings following the initial analysis of students' argumentative texts (*QED* method) did not show significant differences in how students' productions developed within each of the two learning environments. The dynamics of collaborative argument are complex and an increased amount of contributions may not reflect increased learning. Detailed analysis of the students' interactions during computer-based and face-to-face debates (*Rainbow* method) indicated a deeper level of argumentation in the face-to-face environment, the development of social relationships in both environments, and the importance of the teacher's role parallel to the use of Internet tools for argumentation. Monitoring and facilitating the Internet debates was more complex than in face-to-face conditions, with students sometimes assuming that role and thus extending their learning about argument at another level. This role was, more predictably, played by the teacher during the face-to-face debates – an element that may have additionally contributed to less off-task interaction in that environment. In conclusion, in addition to their similarities, the different environments seem to require and contribute to the development of different skills, such as the ability to counter-argue and to structure one's argument. Face-to-face argumentation, in particular, seems to play a role in encouraging participants to offer counter-arguments and explore and deepen their space of debate. Such exploration and deepening involves thinking about underlying meanings and about the social-discursive aspects of interaction, as we can see with the use of irony.

Our research then points to the complexity of argumentation-based learning, and suggests that a combination of computer-based and face-to-face learning environments, in conjunction with the teacher's input and guidance, can help develop more diverse and more productive learning of argument and debating skills.

ACKNOWLEDGEMENTS

We would like to thank Patrick Frawley, teacher at Elliott school in London, and all the students who participated, for their support and enthusiasm during this phase of the SCALE project.

REFERENCES

Anderson, T., & Kanuka, H. (1997). On-line forums: New platforms for professional development and group collaboration. *Journal of Computer-mediated Communication, 3* (3).

Backley P., Saxton, M., & Sillince, J. A. A. (1999). *ADS in the curriculum: results of interviews with secondary school teachers.* Working Paper. Management School, Royal Holloway, University of London.

Berge, Z. (1997). Computer conferencing and the online classroom. *International Journal of Educational Telecommunications, 3* (1), 3-21.

Dillenbourg, P. (Ed.). (1999). *Collaborative learning. Cognitive and computational approaches.* Advances in Learning and Instruction Series. Amsterdam: Pergamon.

Garton, L., & Wellman, B. (1995). Social impacts of electronic mail in organization: a review of the research literature. In B. R. Burleson (Ed.), *Communication Yearbook 18* (pp. 434-453). London: Sage.

Marttunen, M. (1997). *Studying argumentation in higher education by electronic mail.* Report No. 127., Jyväskylä Studies in Education, Psychology and Social Research. Jyväskylä: University of Jyväskylä.

Marttunen, M., & Laurinen L. (2001). Learning of argumentation skills in networked and face-to-face environments. *Instructional Science 29* (2), 127-153.

National Curriculum online (1999). Retrieved from http://www.nc.uk.net. In addition, see http://www.qca.org.uk.

Olaniran, B. A. (1994). Group performance in computer-mediated and face-to-face communication media. *Management Communication Quarterly, 7,* 256-281.

Pilkington, R. M., & Parker-Jones, C. H. (1996). Interacting with computer based simulation: the role of dialogue. *Computers and Education, 27,* 1, 1-14.

Ravenscroft, A., & Matheson, M. P. (2000). *Evaluating and investigating learning through collaborative argumentation: an empirical study.* Dialogue and Design for New Media Research Group Technical Report DDRG-01-01, Institute of Educational Technology, Open University, UK.

Ravenscroft, A. (1997). *Learning as Knowledge Refinement: A Computer Based Approach.* PhD thesis, Computer Based Learning Unit, School of Education, University of Leeds, UK.

SCALE project. (2002). *A framework for analysing pedagogically oriented computer-mediated debates: Rainbow.* Working paper. Produced collaboratively, written by M. Baker and revised by M. van Amelsvoort and L. Munneke.

SCALE project. (2002). *European Commission, project No IST-1999-10664. First Year Deliverables. Deliverables 1 & 2*. Retrieved from http://www.euroscale.net/.

SCALE project.(2002). *European Commission, project No IST-1999-10664. First Year Deliverables. Deliverable 8*. Retrieved from http://www.euroscale.net/.

Chapter 12

ADAPTING A FACE-TO-FACE TRAINING PROGRAM TO A DISTANCE DELIVERY MODEL: A CASE STUDY OF A PROFESSIONAL TRAINING PROGRAM

Menno van Doorn[1] & Richard G. Milter[2]

[1]*Institute for Analysis of New Technology, Sogeti, the Netherlands;* [2]*Ohio University, OH, USA*

1.   INTRODUCTION

A collaborative, face-to-face training program between a US university and a Dutch IT consulting firm planned for September 2001 could have been cancelled due to the September 11th tragedy. With quick thinking, resourcefulness, extraordinary cooperation, and technical support, however, that challenge became an opportunity for building a new model of collaboration for the faculty of Ohio University and the staff of IQUIP, an information and communication technology (ICT) consulting and software testing subsidiary of CapGemini Ernst & Young company in the Netherlands. This chapter offers the experience as a unique case which may prove helpful to others exploring the movement of professional training from classroom-based to technology-based.

One week following the events of September 11, 2001, a group of 14 newly hired trainees and three training center coaches of IQUIP, were to fly from the Netherlands to Ohio to participate in a three-week training program leading to a certificate in business and technology provided by Ohio University Without Boundaries (OUWB). This was to mark the seventh such program to be delivered jointly by the faculty of Ohio University and IQUIP staff since the partnership began in June of 2000. During each of the

R.G.Milter et al. (eds.), Educational Innovation in Economics and Business IX, 221–236.

previous six programs, the trainees and coaches arrived on the Ohio University campus to participate in program after three weeks of training in the Netherlands.

Due to travel concerns following September 11, IQUIP management decided to avoid international travel for the protection of trainees and staff. Following discussions between IQUIP executives and the faculty and staff at OUWB about the value of face-to-face interaction and the key learning outcomes of the training program, the decision was made to proceed with the course and to provide the program despite the obvious limitations of time and distance. The next two days were filled with rapid-fire activity as the faculty and staff at OUWB worked to transform a face-to-face program into one that would be delivered via technological interfaces. They produced video "spotlights" to accompany content material and developed other forms of electronic information that would be provided to the trainees. Also during these days, staff at IQUIP worked diligently to prepare their venue for the electronic collaboration that would be an integral part of the program.

Without the tragic events of the 11th of September, the move toward a total distance delivery model might not have taken place. As it was, external influences led to a new learning delivery mode. A question remains though whether IQUIP (or now Sogeti, as the company is known following a merger) will choose the distance delivery model, face-to-face model, or a combination of the two approaches for its future programs.

2.   INVESTING IN E-LEARNING

This chapter reports on an experience in the development of a technology-mediated program to serve the learning needs of a specific target group. Moving from a face-to-face certificate program model to a distance delivery model is a "from-to" story that is shared on the following pages. It is primarily a story about how a Dutch company and an American university implemented an innovative e-learning concept.

Much has been written regarding both the strengths and weaknesses of this approach to learning. Littlejohn and Lofink (2001), for example, suggest that e-learning strategies at companies are bounded only by the limited imaginations of those responsible for the learning programs. They offer a list of key questions to help an organization get a handle on its "learning culture" and gauge an ability to take advantage of innovations in learning technologies. Several opportunities, threats, and pitfalls of e-learning for corporate purposes have been provided by Hambrecht (1999). In reporting on hallmark studies of corporate e-learning initiatives, both Corporate University Xchange (2002) and the American Productivity and Quality

Center (2002) provide evidence that e-learning practices will continue to impact the learning cultures in corporations. Similar challenges and forecasts regarding the impact of e-learning on the learning cultures of colleges and universities have also been introduced (Milter, 2002; Schank, 2001). With the description of experiences provided in this chapter we are setting the stage for continued exploration of better ways to develop innovative learning programs for professional workers.

The pragmatic use of e-learning is not new. But often the focus is on the technology and not on the learning goals. We believe this is an incorrect educational strategy. We made use of e-learning because we required technology to provide something that could not be provided without it. The use of technology to enable learning is clearly demonstrated in the example to follow. But we will also demonstrate how e-learning helped to deliver specific learning outcomes enabling the development of competencies by IQUIP trainees.

Specifically, this chapter provides a narrative of the transformation of a hybrid face-to-face on-campus program with some e-learning elements into an exclusive e-learning model. It also displays data from post-program interviews and surveys involving faculty members, trainees, and coaches. Finally, it offers several insights into the decision-making process by the management at IQUIP regarding the training programs.

3. DEVELOPING A PARTNERSHIP

3.1 Overview of the Company

IQUIP (now called Sogeti, as explained above) is a total supplier of information and communication technology (ICT) services. It supplies ICT services to the major government institutions and business organizations in the Netherlands. At the time when the certificate program with Ohio began, IQUIP employed 1600 people. Given the shortage of IT specialists in the Dutch market, businesses have had to put great effort into the recruitment and training of employees. This effort is required, in part, because of the gap between what businesses need and what schools deliver. This has led to a deepened professionalism of in-house training institutes of larger ICT companies and to the transformation of many of these in-house training institutes into Corporate Universities.

IQUIP had also faced this development issue. The company had made a serious attempt to transform its entire curriculum to an accredited model. As a result of several conversations between the administration and faculty of

OUWB and the board of IQUIP, the leadership at OUWB convinced IQUIP that a company university was not something they should target. It was not known, however, what the cooperation between IQUIP and OUWB precisely would yield. One thing is very clear: without these early discussions and the subsequent valued relationships, 14 professionals in Reeuwijk would never have worked together for three weeks sharing such an intense training experience in September 2001. Moreover, without the experiences gained with this program in 2000 and 2001, IQUIP would not have dared to offer the September 2001 program completely at a distance.

3.2   Why US-Based Training?

IQUIP management had strategic reasons for adopting this trainee program. As the Internet had become an enabling technology for company products and services, the role of IT support for companies had clearly changed. IQUIP professionals, therefore, needed to understand the technology from the customer's viewpoint – an enabling viewpoint. Along with this new knowledge within the ranks of its professional staff, IQUIP also needed to adapt its own structure and communicate this new competence to its clients. E-business had become an element of the organizational culture and structure of IQUIP as well as a new competency to offer to its clients. Front and back office technology support services, previously provided by separate professional divisions within IQUIP, are now provided as an integrated service.

Therefore it is not strange that a Dutch company selected the US (a country that was far ahead in using e-business at the time) to gain an educational advantage with business and technology. While some IQUIP staff resisted the idea of sending trainees away from the company at such an important time in their orientation process, the value of creating friendship bonds among trainees, coaches, and managers would be a major strategic "win" for the program. The trainee program that sent people to the US was also used as a recruitment tool, even appearing on some billboards in strategic locations along major roads in the Netherlands. To recruit and keep good professionals is of great importance in the technology consulting industry. Companies need every edge they can develop.

Along with the goal to find a program partner in the US, the IQUIP executive board also sought to find a program that was proficient with e-learning delivery systems. Even in the face-to-face collaborative program with OUWB, the use of e-learning methods was present. It was deemed appropriate that an ICT service supplier be a pioneer in the field of e-learning. IQUIP management also thought that the use of e-learning by new hires was the start of an innovation that would cascade to the rest of the employees. It was anticipated that an early push for e-learning might enable development of genuine learning communities within the professional ranks at IQUIP.

3.3 Training at a Distance

After six programs with over 160 trainees visiting the Ohio University campus, came the events of the 11th of September 2001. The air tickets for the seventh program were already purchased and both trainees and coaches were ready for departure. Even though the trainees were willing to travel, IQUIP management decided that under the circumstances, it was not advisable to leave families during those times of high travel risk. The decision to follow the proposal of Ohio University Without Boundaries to do the program completely from a distance was less difficult than the initial choice to start cooperation with Ohio University. By that time, the trust in the cooperation had grown to such strength that IQUIP management knew: if the faculty and staff at OUWB said they could deliver a virtual program, it could be done.

It is important to point out one item that was critical for success. Even when the trainees traveled to Ohio, the certificate program was completely built around an e-learning architecture. It was structured as a hybrid approach, combining the best that e-learning had to offer with activities best accomplished in a face-to-face arena. But until September of 2001, the program had always been delivered with the OUWB faculty and IQUIP coaches and trainees in the same location. Many stakeholders questioned whether the quality of the learning would decrease when the program was scheduled to run at a distance.

4. PROGRAM DESCRIPTION

4.1 Target Group

Participants of the certificate program were people newly hired at IQUIP. They were called new hires, trainees, or young professionals. These people were considered to fit well within the company culture, since every job candidate is tested thoroughly. IQUIP does not just look at candidates' potential to become good ICT specialists, but also at their social and communicative skills. More than once have cum laude graduates not been hired by IQUIP because they lacked these skills.

4.2   Original Program Structure

The Ohio program starts in the Netherlands with a three-day orientation. This is following several weeks of initial training in the IQUIP academy. This orientation is followed by a trip to Athens, Ohio where the trainees spend three weeks in the OUWB program. During the orientation, trainees are introduced to important business and technology concepts as well as a general introduction to the company.

The OUWB program, which is modeled after the award-winning MBA Without Boundaries program (see Milter, 2001), consists of three projects, each lasting for one week. In Project One trainees confront a case challenging them to propose a new business concept and develop it as a new offering that assists existing businesses in their interrelations with partners or suppliers. In Project Two the trainees are challenged to advise a simulated company, Stoney Boots, on business concepts like supply chain management (SCM), electronic data interchange (EDI), enterprise resource planning (ERP), and customer relations management (CRM). Project deliverables include briefings, reports, and presentations. In the final project, Project Three, the trainees are challenged to provide the executive board of IQUIP with a plan to develop a new service, or set of services, that IQUIP can offer to its clients. As a final deliverable for this project, a presentation is made to the executive board of IQUIP. During these three weeks trainees are also working on individual professional developmental activities such as research skills, persuasive presentations, business case making, and professional writing.

4.3   Learning Goals

As the program was designed in 2000, 28 learning outcomes were formulated. Even though the program process was modified in a spirit of continuous improvement, the learning outcomes remained the same. All learning outcomes are formulated in statements that begin with "able to." These learning outcomes span five key areas believed by IQUIP management to be important for operating in a highly demanding technology market and for proving to their clients that they were worth their hourly rates. These key areas, listed below, are deemed to prepare the trainees for this challenge.
1. Business content
2. IT content
3. Teamwork
4. Communication skills
5. Personal skills

Examples of the learning outcomes follow:

- Able to explain the strategic enabling role of IT for the business (Business content)
- Able to demonstrate an understanding of the basic systems analysis and design process (IT content)
- Able to deal with conflict resolution (Teamwork)
- Able to persuade people (Communication skills)
- Able to locate and evaluate the quality of information (Personal skills)
- Some learning outcomes are targeted in more than a single project. Other outcomes are dedicated to a single episode within a project. The projects are designed and improved with the intent that the trainees would perform on all learning outcomes by the time they complete the three-week program.

4.4   How the Distance Delivery Model Works

Although during the program in September 2001, the participants were unable to physically interact with the professors in Ohio, much of the structure of the program remained as it had been in previous interactions. The spoken and written word, videos, database, telephone, and the Internet were used to virtualize the established program.

Central to the e-learning architecture of the OUWB program has always been the Lotus Domino databases. The trainees use these databases as posting areas while working on and submitting their assignments. The faculty members post the learning exercises and relevant content material. An example of a learning exercise is a written assignment that asks the trainee to create a listing of critical success factors for companies facing tomorrow's economic situation. Initial information can be found via posted links to learning resources on the Internet. In addition to responding to nine of these individual learning exercises, the trainees collaborate with their teammates on the projects and receive feedback from coaches and faculty members via the databases. Changing the face-to-face model to a distance delivery model for the September 2001 program required dealing with the lack of direct contact between the OUWB faculty members and the trainees and coaches. Face-to-face meetings had to be replaced with technology support. Competence in using Lotus Domino for such information exchange was critical for making this virtual collaboration possible. Below is a sample of the Lotus Domino homepage used in the September 2001 program (see Figure 1).

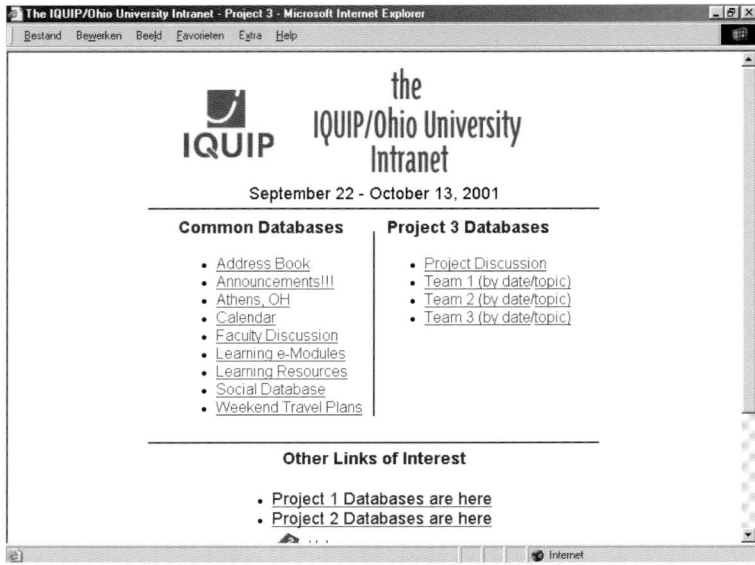

Figure 1. Lotus Domino homepage sample

In addition to the e-learning elements that were already built into the IQUIP/OUWB program prior to September 2001, new material and technology were required to support the program offered with the faculty members and participants separated by distance. The following section goes into greater detail about those additions.

4.5   Adjusted September 2001 Program

At 8:30 AM (GMT+1 in the Netherlands) Monday morning, the September 2001 program was launched. The coaches at IQUIP distributed the material and provided a "presence" as the trainees got into their project teams and began to work on the initial project. Faculty members at OUWB "met" with the IQUIP group at 1:00 PM (7:00 AM EST in Ohio), immediately following lunch in the Netherlands and breakfast in Ohio. This meeting was an opportunity for the trainees to obtain clarifications on any of the program or project items from the OUWB faculty members. Following the session with the trainees, the OUWB faculty members met with the IQUIP coaches to review the morning launch and discuss subsequent sessions. Such sessions were held throughout the three-week training program. Variations in the use of the time included sessions when faculty members could meet with individual teams. It was also an opportunity for the OUWB faculty to address the trainees directly and provide additional insights and feedback regarding their progress on the project and individual learning exercises. In addition to keeping on task, the communication sessions were also used for purposes of keeping "in touch" with the social experiences that were shared in the evenings. Trainees and coaches spent some evenings together in different social events. These dinners or other occasions were shared with the US faculty via pictures posted on the databases. Some good-natured ribbing was sometimes made of such experiences as the coaches, trainees, and faculty greeted each other the next day.

These "face-to-face" interaction sessions were made possible using a video connection via the Internet and a speakerphone call. Although both video and audio could have been accessed via the Internet, the quality of the audio was thought to be too poor and inconsistent, to meet reliable standards. The classroom in Ohio that was used for the training program was reserved as IQUIP space throughout the three-week program. Two projectors were used to provide both incoming and outgoing video feeds as well as a picture sheet containing still photos of all trainees and a place for graphic slides, video, or presentation material. This interaction technology helped to supplement the continued use of collaborative databases, e-mail, and instant messaging. The "video-spotlights" (five- to ten-minute segments to introduce a concept or technique) were a new element developed by the OUWB faculty and staff for the September 2001 program.

Specifically, these video-spotlights replaced the spotlights that were an important element of the face-to-face interaction between the faculty members and the trainees and coaches. In the face-to-face method these were rolled out as brief (5-10 minutes) lectures that introduced a concept or technique that was thought to be pertinent to the participants' progress at a given point in the project. There were normally no more than one or two of these provided each day and the actual time of delivery was flexible, based upon the actual movement of the trainees on the project deliverables. The video-spotlights developed for the September 2001 program were packaged and sent electronically to the coaches, so that they could be unveiled at appropriate times, typically in the morning hours of the trainees' work on the projects. They normally contained a video clip from a movie or other popular media source used to "hook" the trainees on the targeted content, slides that provided some key insights, and a video presentation of the faculty member. Often, the faculty members worked with the assistance of the technology manager for much of the afternoon to develop these important inputs. It became a way to pull together the prime elements of the content and move them into a message that was both compelling and engaging. It may even make sense to play these video-spotlights during future iterations of the face-to-face program.

5.   PROGRAM EVALUATION

5.1   Survey Data Results

Every one of the certificate programs is evaluated orally and in writing. For the purposes of this chapter, we will compare only the last three programs (i.e., IQUIP 5, 6, and 7), because they all share the same content. Remember that the program followed the MBA Without Boundaries format, which meant it was always in continuous improvement mode, with no two programs ever being exactly the same. But the content and learning outcomes remained the same for all programs under review in this chapter. By comparing the program that took place in September 2001 in Reeuwijk with the two prior programs (that took place in Athens, Ohio), we were able to draw more reliable conclusions. The next page contains the quantitative results from the surveys. In total, there are 45 evaluations: IQUIP 5 (n=15), IQUIP 6 (n=16), and IQUIP 7 (n=14).

The percentages are the sum of the number of answers in the specific cell divided by the total number of participants of that specific program. The score possibilities differ per question, but are always on a 4-point scale, that is, "very good, good, moderate, bad" or "strongly agree, agree, disagree, strongly disagree." In the data presented in Table 1 below all the scores are translated to "++, +, -, --."

Table 1. Program Evaluation Results

Program Total Score (in %)

	IQUIP 5				IQUIP 6				IQUIP 7			
	+ +	+	-	- -	+ +	+	-	--	+ +	+	-	- -
Total opinion	87	13	*	*	64	36	*	*	86	14	*	*
Quality of the Staff												
OUWB Faculty	56	44	*	*	61	34	5	*	50	45	5	*
IQUIP Coaches	25	38	37	*	82	18	*	*	52	38	10	*
Quality of the Projects												
Project 1	63	37	*	*	57	36	7	*	57	36	7	*
Project 2	31	69	*	*	22	78	*	*	43	57	*	*
Project 3	43	50	7	*	72	28	*	*	79	21	*	*
Meeting the Learning Outcomes												
Business Content	23	77	*	*	30	67	3	*	26	70	4	*
IT Content	28	53	17	2	39	46	5	*	18	64	18	*
Teamwork	45	52	3	*	73	26	1	*	42	51	7	*
Communication skills	38	59	3	*	50	46	4	*	26	65	9	*
Personal skills	23	77	*	*	60	39	1	*	36	60	4	*
Intensity and Experience												
Without the Ohio program the bond with the other trainees would be less strong	88	12	*	*	71	29	*	*	57	36	7	*
It was a pleasant experience	69	31	*	*	71	29	*	*	64	36	*	*
The work pressure was too high	6	25	56	13	7	7	64	22	*	20	67	13
Quality of Contact												
Contact with my manager	6	47	27	20	21	36	14	29	50	42	8	*
Ohio staff/ IQUIP coaches collaboration	19	75	6	*	43	57	*	*	29	64	7	*
Contact with other colleagues	12	44	44	*	14	79	7	*	21	79	*	*
Contact with OUWB faculty members	N/A.	N/A.	N/A.	N/A.	N/A.	N/A.	N/A.	N/A.	14	78	8	*

The opinions on "quality of the staff" are the aggregate scores of the Ohio University faculty members and IQUIP coaches and unit managers.

Typically these included three faculty members from Ohio University, one or two coaches from the IQUIP Academy, and a unit manager from IQUIP. The scores are also aggregated for each of the learning outcomes in the category "meeting the learning outcomes," with each heading comprising the four to six items within that outcome. The "total opinion" score reflects a single response to a request that the trainees provide an overall score on the learning experience.

The evaluation questionnaires also provided an area for additional remarks. A number of remarks concerned the technology (e.g., "faster computers") and the contact with the trainee's personal unit manager during the program. Some participants evaluated the overall experience as "fine" or offered a short explanation to a certain answer on the form. Below are a few of statements generated by the surveys from the September 2001 participants.

"I wouldn't know what other method of learning has a greater affect on the development of people. My compliments!"

"The work pressure was fairly high (well, that has probably been your strategy). But too high…it was all barely possible. In Ohio itself it certainly would have been different. Now I also had to travel to work and deal with a social life."

"Good job everybody, well done."

5.2   Conclusions from Survey Data

The statements sample the general belief that although there was a degree of disappointment that the trip to Ohio had been cancelled, there was still a spirit of completion and success generated during the three weeks. Evidence from the survey data supports that there is little significant difference in performance on learning outcomes between the face-to-face program executed in Athens, Ohio, where the trainees stayed for three weeks, and the distance delivery program that physically separated the faculty members and the participants. The actual grades provided by the faculty regarding the trainee work on the projects and the learning modules were of the same or higher caliber than during earlier programs.

In essence, what do these data suggest? Does a clear difference in learning exist between a program where direct human contact is possible, where teacher and student can utilize all senses in collaboration with each other, and a program where contact takes place via bits, bytes, cables, and screens? We think not.

The most important conclusion, therefore, is that based upon the survey results there is little difference between the actual outcomes of two learning methods. This conclusion by itself is a revelation that will not satisfy skeptics of e-learning. The second important conclusion is not based upon the difference of face-to-face versus distance learning but grounded in the similarities. A project-based action-learning model supported by the described e-learning architecture, leads to excellent results. Overall, as a learning experience, all seven programs have been evaluated as excellent by the participants. A great deal is still to be discovered regarding the value of e-learning. Nevertheless, the results of this implementation will have significant impact on the future of e-learning for IQUIP and OUWB.

We will conclude our reflections on the survey data with a few limitations. First, even though the cases can be well compared (distance delivery model in Reeuwijk versus on-site in Athens), the number of surveys (n=45) is too small to draw general conclusions based on statistically significant results. Second, and perhaps most important, there is the risk of losing ourselves in details. Because emotions tend to run high during personal growth experiences, it is possible that the results are somewhat skewed in the positive direction. Finally, we want to accept the obvious limitation of measuring the success of a company learning program via a self-evaluation questionnaire.

5.3   Other Measuring Points

At the end of the program, the results were evaluated in a round of discussions with the IQUIP trainees and coaches. The first discussion point was about the decision to do the program completely at a distance. As previously mentioned, most trainees had initially preferred flying to Athens. A significant number of trainees weighed the innovative training possibilities of IQUIP heavily when they considered applying for a position at the company. About one-third of the new hires said that the IQUIP trainee program with the international experience was an important factor in their decision to apply for a position at IQUIP. These trainees feared that not going to Athens would have a negative influence on the results of the program. On the other hand, the trainees did have a great deal of respect for the quality and effort of the Reeuwijk experience. As one of the trainees told us: "When I heard that we were not going I thought 'this is not going to be anything.' Many of us felt that way. But on the first morning, during the first video contact, we switched. We knew that everything was OK."

We had received the evaluation forms before we started the group discussions. We quickly scanned the results and immediately noticed that the results were close to those generated by participants of the earlier programs conducted in Athens. In the discussions we were looking for a confirmation of the data on the evaluation forms. Did it really not matter whether the trainees and coaches went to Ohio or stayed in the Netherlands?

At one point in the discussion, one of the coaches recalled that during the Reeuwijk experience there hadn't been any conflicts. After checking with the trainees, this appeared to be correct. During three weeks, no conflict had occurred, while each of the previous six classes had dealt with its share of personal conflicts. Nowhere in the program is it described that conflicts are something we seek. However, the direct human contact in the face-to-face program leads to more emotional interaction and, consequently, to more conflicts. Whether these conflicts and emotions lead to a better learning performance is clearly a question that still needs to be addressed. IQUIP management is tempted to say that conflicts during the training program are preferred. IQUIP management is looking for close ties among their professional staff, and emotions are important during the process of forming those ties.

One final evaluation discussion took place between the coaches in the Netherlands and the participating faculty members of the OUWB. This discussion made use of the same technology that was used in the distance delivery of the program. In this session as well, we looked for differences. The OUWB faculty members and the IQUIP coaches now had experience in both the face-to-face program and the distance delivery model.

A general feeling of satisfaction about the program could be sensed during the conversation. We had not expected that it would have gone so well. Nevertheless, the OUWB faculty members did bring out one important point. The touch and feel of a face-to-face program is only partly matched by technology. What was missing was the ability to see how somebody walks into the room; how someone's glance changes when he or she is asked an unexpected question; what body posture he or she takes when a faculty member suddenly joins a meeting. The OUWB faculty members said that they might just need one face-to-face meeting. Not being able to personally meet the trainees was considered a drawback, but it was not considered an unacceptable one. Together both the coaches (IQUIP) and faculty members (OUWB) concluded that this distance delivery model did work very well. At the same time, all agreed that even a small amount of face-to-face contact between the OUWB faculty members and the trainees and coaches would still improve the program.

One final noted impact of the Athens-based programs on the distance-mode program was that the "culture" of working till 6 PM has changed. In Athens, the teams regularly continued working until 10 PM. Personal work on individual learning assignments was also performed in a time structure that went well beyond the 40-hour workweek. In the IQUIP program based in Holland, trainees were accustomed to starting and stopping at fixed times. After work, or their day at the training facility in Reeuwijk, the trainees went home or to a nearby hotel, if they lived far away. After 6 PM no trainee would be found at the Reeuwijk training center.

When Program 7 was launched with no travel to the US, it was interesting to see what would happen to the workday schedule. Would the trainees continue until late at night as had been the norm in Athens, or would they pack up their stuff and leave at 5 PM or 6 PM as was the culture in Holland. The experience showed that the trainees in Program 7 displayed the same behavior as did the trainees in the earlier six programs in Athens. They just kept on going. More then once, the doorman at the Reeuwijk training center was asked to keep the facility open beyond the time he would normally lock the building into the evening.

6.   SUMMARY AND LESSONS LEARNED

At first, IQUIP started with an in-house trainee education program. Next, it took the steps to send newly hired employees to the US for a portion of their training experience. Here, e-learning was introduced. After the 11th of September 2001 it was decided to stay home and to rely more heavily on technology. This chapter provides an overview of the steps taken, the description of the original and modified programs, and the results of the program evaluation.

The question as to whether the distance delivery model delivers the same experiences and outcomes as the face-to-face model is very difficult to answer. The best answer we can give is that the models match each other very closely. And the actual outcomes of the learning are more similar than we had originally imagined. However, we will have to be very careful when translating the experiences of IQUIP and OUWB to general practice. As stated above, much of the technology terrain had already been explored before we started the distance delivery program. The trainees did not know the people in Ohio, but the coaches did. Moreover, we were familiar with the ins and outs of the program before we started, and from the beginning we had faith in each other's ability to make it work.

The tragic events of the 11th of September 2001 have in so many ways turned the world upside down. We will never know precisely what was their influence on the devotion and motivation levels of the trainees, and thus the results of the executed program. Yet, we still believe there is value in comparing two different delivery programs that share the exact same learning goals -- one executed in a face-to-face model and the other in a distance delivery model. As we move forward, we will continue to seek the best value from both face-to-face experiences and those interactions and collaboration that can take place at a distance.

REFERENCES

American Productivity and Quality Center. (2002). Consortium Learning Forum Best Practice Report. *Planning, Implementing, and Evaluating E-Learning Initiatives.* Houston: APQC International Benchmarking Clearinghouse.

Corporate University Xchange, Inc. (2002). *Corporate University Xchange's Pillars of e-Learning Success.* NY: CUX Publications.

Hambrecht, W. R. (1999). *Corporate E-Learning: Exploring a New Frontier.* San Francisco: W.R. Hambrecht & Co.

Littlejohn, M., & Lofink, C. (2001). Corporate learning: Blurring boundaries and breaking barriers. Somers, NY: IBM Global Services.

Milter, R. G. (2002). Innovation in learning methodologies for adult learners: Implications for theory and practice. *Virtual University Journal, 3 (6)*, 228-236.

Milter, R. G. (2001). Developing an MBA online degree program: Expanding knowledge and skills via technology-mediated learning communities.In P. Comeaux (Ed.), *Communication and Collaboration in the Online Classroom.* Bolton, MA: Anker Publishing.

Schank, R. (2001). *Designing World Class E-Learning.* NY: McGraw-Hill Professional Publishing.

Chapter 13

AN INNOVATIVE APPROACH TO ADDRESSING HETEROGENEITY OF LARGE CLASSES: RESULTS FROM TEACHING BUSINESS STATISTICS

Marc Humbert
Grenoble Ecole de Management, France

1.   INTRODUCTION

In many management programs at the undergraduate level, a certain number of courses are scheduled as large classes where students have heterogeneous knowledge, motivations, and learning styles. In Grenoble Ecole de Management, we have tried, like many others, to apply the various recommendations provided by Education Science specialists. We have also used Information and Communication Technology (ICT) to support our courses, hoping that it would increase flexibility and allow us to be more learner-centered. However, we were not entirely satisfied with our results. In the first part of this chapter, we describe this initial environment and the main issues we had to address.

In a second part, we present our new pedagogical model. For the last two years, we have experimented with an innovative two-phase organization of a Business Statistics course. The first phase allows to deliver the basic content to all the students and to divide our large classes into three clusters of students having more homogeneous motivations and knowledge. The second phase of the course is then personalized for each group. The whole process is supported by an efficient use of ICT.

After presentation of the promising results of this experiment, we are committed to the extensions, which are planned for the future.

R.G.Milter et al. (eds.), Educational Innovation in Economics and Business IX, 237–247.

2.   INITIAL ENVIRONMENT

2.1   A Large and Heterogeneous Class

In Grenoble Ecole de Management, like in many Universities and Business schools throughout the world, many undergraduate courses are taught to large classes (several hundred students).

In this chapter we are interested in the case of a Business Statistics course, which is a core course of our last year undergraduate program. In its traditional format, this course had a total duration of 36 hours, with 12 hours of lectures having 450 students in a large lecture hall and 24 hours of tutorials with small groups of 35 students. These small groups are formed randomly. Education Science specialists through guide books or Web sites (see, for example, MacGregor, Cooper, Smith, & Robinson, 2000) provide numerous recommendations on how to deal with issues raised by large classes. In relation to these environments, researchers have already studied the use of group work (De Vita, 2001), case methods (

Booth, Bowie, Jordan, & Rippin, 2000), or the role of ICT in enhancing collaborative learning (Renzi & Klobas, 2000).

Having taught this type of course for many years, we have tried to apply such recommendations, mainly related to how to turn passive students into active learners. In our case, however, the difficulties of scale are increased by the growing diversity of the audience regarding initial backgrounds, abilities, and motivation for the topic. The course was built for a "median" level and was not adapted to students who lacked background or to motivated students who would like to go further.

Two objectives for improving this course:

- First, to globally increase students' work outside the classroom. There is a strategic will of the school administration to decrease face-to-face courses in favor of more personal or group work of students outside the classroom.
- Second, to personalize learning for the different groups of students that we have in this large class. Since it is a core course in the program, we wanted to keep some common basic content for all students. However, we also wanted to give better support to students with difficulties, and to provide a deeper content to motivated students who are interested in learning more.

2.2   The First Attempt with ICT

Information and communication technologies have been used for two or three decades now to support teaching and learning. In the last decade, Web-based learning, or e-learning, has encountered much success. There is now an extensive academic literature covering e-learning issues, coming from various fields: Education Science, Target discipline (Management in our case), or Human-Computer interface. At first, this research was more focused on Web technological issues (Alavi, Yoo, & Vogel, 1997; Webster & Hackley, 1997) but it is now more open to pedagogical issues (Freeman & Capper, 2000; De Verneil & Berge, 2000). These technologies have been used either for distance courses or to support traditional courses. More research has been conducted in distance education but a large part of its outcomes can be used to support traditional education. Actually, the differences between these two applications are narrowing. There is a growing trend to mix different teaching and learning modes whenever possible: traditional "face-to-face classes" plus the addition of online teaching and learning. Mixed-mode or blended learning, which is becoming more and more popular (Mathew & Dohery-Poirier, 2000), supposes that "distance students" must sometimes attend face-to-face sessions and traditional students have some online work or lectures, even if they live on campus.

In Grenoble Ecole de Management, we have very little experience in distance education, but we have six years of experience in using online support resources for traditional classes, and the trend is to develop more emphasis on these resources. Our objective is to reduce "face-to-face" class interaction, to find ways of increasing work outside the classroom by providing students with an efficient VLE (Virtual Learning Environment), and to get a well-balanced blended learning.

Like many other faculty members, we have developed rather early (1996) a collaborative Web site, the first draft of a VLE, to support our Business Statistics course. Our idea was to give students access to a wide range of resources: course materials, cases, exercises, discussion lists, links to external resources on the Web, numerous very interesting sites (some with automatic correction), simulations, exchange forums, and links to other sites. We were expecting that by allowing each student to work at his or her own pace, VLE could help us to cope with the diversity of backgrounds and motivations. Not surprisingly, our findings parallel what is found in the literature on Web-based education (Gibson, Tesone & Blackwell, 2001; Hara & Kling 1999; Laurillard, 2000; Schrum & Hong, 2002).

Technology issues have not been an obstacle for us. One advantage of our environment is that our students are familiar with ICT. Our school has always emphasized computer usage: the infrastructure is excellent, and we have been requiring each student to own a laptop since 1988. Of course, at that time laptops were heavy and expensive, but they have been continuously improved during the last 15 years and now, when many universities come to that solution, we take advantage of having been pioneers in this approach.

Consequently, students and teaching staff do not have technological barriers with using IT.

Up to now, our VLEs at Grenoble Ecole de Management have been designed using Lotus Notes Domino or Lotus Quickplace. These general "groupware systems" do not have all the built-in features of large Learning Management Systems (LMS) but are quite sufficient for our present purposes, which are content management and facilitation of collaborative work among students. We totally agree with Schrum and Hong's recommendation (2002) to keep technology as simple as possible. With their laptops, students can easily access the servers with the Notes client or with a Web browser, either on campus through the local network or anywhere else through the Internet. In September 2001, wireless technology was set up on the campus, facilitating connection to an even greater degree. In fact, the barriers between activities inside and outside the classroom have been reduced because students can work with their classmates and instructors as well as access internal and external resources nearly in the same way whether they are inside or outside. At a distance, when their work does not require interaction, students can also work in a local mode thanks to the replication function of Notes Domino.

If technology was not a problem for us, this was not the case with functional effectiveness. Overall, this four-year experiment was interesting for students (better overall satisfaction, increased perception of learning), but its usage was too limited. In fact, with this VLE we did not measure an increased amount of students' work outside the classroom, as it was expected. Usage of external resources was as low online as traditionally with books and paper documents. And collaborative work and participation in online discussions remained at a disappointing level. In fact, if in a distance learning course the students (at least those who do not drop out) are generally strongly motivated to use the system because they have no choice, in a context where ICT is used as a support tool for traditional classes, less motivated students behave passively and do not use these resources enough.

To encourage ICT usage by these students, it is possible to add incentives by creating an evaluation connected to the activity or by dedicating a lot of time to livening up the site (making educational sites lively is often recognized as a key factor of success in e-learning). But the task of students' involvement and tutoring is made difficult by the size and the heterogeneity of the students. From students' interviews we had discovered that our VLE was considered too general, and many students did not need to make the effort to search for the resources adapted to their needs.

We have discovered yet another way to increase learning efficiency: by adapting to student diversity.

3. A NEW PEDAGOGICAL MODEL

3.1 Clustering the Student Cohort

Our discovery started from the simple assumption that students are much more motivated and active in courses or options which they chose. Before deciding on a radical solution of transforming this mandatory course into a totally "optional" course, we had an idea of an intermediary and flexible solution, aimed at designing a new environment that would reproduce the motivational environment in those situations where students are usually more active. Our solution was rather simple: to introduce a choice option within the core course, that is, to let students decide a part of their learning process. Recognizing the importance of curricular choices, we followed the same direction as Howorth (2001), but we stayed within the context of a core course and did not go into complete modularization.

In fact, we have found from our previous experience in teaching Business Statistics that in such large class core courses, students can be divided into three types. The first type includes students who are not very interested in the subject and just want to learn the "basic concepts" and pass the exam. The second type consists of students who are ready to perform the coursework but have real difficulties with the content. The third type comprises students who are motivated to learn, want to deepen the content, and who feel frustrated if the pace of the course is too slow. Our objective was to identify these types of students, place them into homogeneous groups, and to meet their needs by offering them a personalized solution. We had, of course, to satisfy the constraints set up by school administrators: to keep a "core content" for all students and to allocate no extra resources to this course. Our innovative approach to meeting the objective had three components: 1) a two-phase reorganization of the course, 2) an adapted assessment process, and 3) an adapted ICT support.

3.2 The New Organization of the Course and its Assessment

The course is divided into two phases. The first phase is common to all students. It has two objectives: to keep a core course, which is required by the program administration, and to identify the three types of students. It has reduced duration and content (2/3 of volume = 24 hours instead of 36 hours). Content has been limited to basic knowledge, which is supposed to be the only objective of our first group. Here comes our innovation in assessment:

Since the content is reduced, students cannot get the best grades with involvement in this first phase only. At the end of this period, an individual "pass-or-fail" exam is organized to check the basic knowledge acquisition. Then the division into three groups can happen: it is based both on assessment results and students' choices.

- Those who have passed the exam and have no motivation to go further can stop at this point but have a grade limited to 12/20 (C). These students constitute our "first group." During the first year of the experiment, this first group comprised 40 percent of the cohort, and it was reduced to 30 percent in the second year. With the previous traditional course, these students might have earned a better grade, but they have no grounds to complain because they know and accept the rule of limitation. Passing the basic exam only proves that they have the basic knowledge of the subject, and they do not deserve any better grade.
- Those who have failed have no choice: they are obliged to take a second step of a "support course" corresponding to 12 hours of face-to-face classes. At the end of this second step, another exam is organized. This exam is similar to the first one (designed to check the acquisition of basic knowledge), and the students' grade is also limited to 12/20. In the first year, this "second group" of students (students with difficulties) represented about 20 percent of the students, and 75 percent of them have passed the second exam. In the second year, these percentages were 15 and 80, respectively. With the previous traditional course, the percentage of students who had failed the exam was approximately the same, but they did not have a "second chance" so immediately after the first exam they had to wait for a new session.
- Those who have passed the exam and are motivated to deepen the content of the course have a "second step" corresponding to 12 hours. During that second step, their work and achievements can increase their grade above12/20 (Starting with a "C," they could get a "B" for a good achievement or an "A" for an excellent achievement). During the first year of the experiment, this third group represented about 40 percent of the students, but it was increased to 55 percent in the second year.

3.3   An Adapted Support of ICT

During the first phase, students could access the same VLE as in the previous years, a general collaborative Web site with internal and external resources to support the face-to-face courses; and as before, the usage of this "all purpose" site, designed for a large class was not very important. The second phase was really innovative because it allowed personalization according to the level of knowledge and motivation of the students.

In fact, two new VLEs have been created, enabling effective blended learning. The first one is designed for students of the second group. These students, having difficulties, do not need any extra content but additional explanations and assignments to be able to meet the basic requirements of this course. The 12 hours of additional "face-to-face" lectures allow us to reinforce the topics, which had caused them difficulties in the first phase. On the site, students can find adapted content and a large variety of interactive exercises and simulations, to acquire more know-how. The objective is to make students comfortable with the topics that frightened them in a "large class" environment. If necessary, they can get help from an online tutor in addition to face-to-face classes.

The second VLE is designed for students of the third group. These students have proved that they hold a basic knowledge in the subject because they have passed the exam and they have chosen to go further. For this group, the second step is also equivalent to 12 hours of traditional lectures, but, in fact, face-to-face lectures have been reduced to 6 hours and the remaining work is done online, using the VLE. It is built around projects that students must conduct in groups. The evaluation of these projects allows students to increase their grade. During the two years of the experiment, we have observed high motivation among the students of this group. The causes of motivation are diverse: interest in the subject, or expectation of a better grade, or both; but the fact that they have made a choice and that they are motivated to work, facilitates the adoption of a VLE. It has to be noted that the VLE allows for much flexibility in this case. Some students may prefer to go deeper into the theory, some students focus on practical applications of statistics in marketing, finance, or another domain. They all can get resources and conduct projects in their fields of interest.

3.4   Increasing Flexibility

With this two-phase process, it would have been difficult to plan many traditional face-to-face lectures in the second phase because the previous division into small groups for tutorials did not exist anymore. We would have met with many scheduling problems, if we had not blended the system by mixing a reduced number of traditional sessions with online sessions. A first (and necessary) consequence of our experience is an increased organizational flexibility.

From a pedagogical point of view, flexibility has also been increased. Our hypothesis was that we could improve the efficiency of VLEs by making students more responsible for their choices and by providing a learning environment that is more adapted to their wishes. To use a fashionable expression, our environment is now more "learner-centered."

4.   RESULTS OF THE EXPERIMENT

This experiment has now been conducted with two classes of students (between 400 and 450 students per class), and we have demonstrated interesting results.

4.1   Respect of Constraints

First point: we have respected our administrative constraints. With the first phase of the course, we have met the requirement of core content for all students. And our new organization is not more costly that the initial one. To summarize the process, let's state that the resources saved on the first group of students (with correct knowledge but low motivation) are used to serve the second group (students with difficulties) and the third group (motivated students).

4.2   Satisfaction of Students

To measure satisfaction, we have used our usual satisfaction questionnaire at the end of the course. As for other courses, this questionnaire contains 11 questions and has been administered to all students. We have just added the twelfth question to know whether the respondent had stopped after phase one. Table 1 below provides the results for the first question, that is, "Overall satisfaction with the course" (from 1= very unsatisfactory to 5= very satisfactory).

Table 1. Main Results of Satisfaction Questionnaire

	Average of 3 previous years	First year	Second year
N of students	406	425	429
N of respondents	369	388	371
Question 1	Average : 3,93	Average 4.11 3.98 for students who have stopped after phase one (first group) 4.21 for students who have followed the second phase.	Average: 4.08 3.96 for students who have stopped after phase one (first group) 4.18 for students who have followed the second phase.

We have received slightly (but not significantly: $p > 0.05$) higher results from students who have followed only the first phase of the course, compared to the previous years. Students, who have followed the second phase, have demonstrated a significant increase in satisfaction ($p < 0.01$). These results, though encouraging, must be interpreted cautiously because they are obtained with measures on the same course over a number of years.

4.3   Students' Work

As we were expecting, students' work outside the classroom has been improved through this two-phase process for those students who have followed both phases. In our questionnaire, students have identified a significant increase of workload compared to the previous years. In addition, we have a good traceability with ICT. The increase of VLE usage during the first phase was not significant because the conditions were very similar to those of the preceding years with an "all-purpose" VLE for all students. But students who have enrolled in the second phase have used three times more the VLEs, both for access to the resources and for online collaboration using the discussion groups.

4.4   Learning Efficiency

Learning efficiency is more difficult to assess. Since this experiment is very recent, we can only make assumptions based on exams results. For students of the first group, it is very unlikely that learning has been improved, since these students receive a "reduced" face-to-face lecture volume that is not compensated by an increased usage of VLE. Choosing a "light" version of the course, these students receive a basic learning level (and a basic grade) corresponding to these limited expectations.

For the students of the second group, we assume that learning was better because those students who had difficulties benefited from support lectures and VLEs specially adapted to their needs. If we trust the results of the exam, this assumption is confirmed because after the two phases, only 18 people failed, which represents only four percent of the 450 students of the class, and this percentage was even lower for the second year. With a similar level of requirements to pass the exam, the average failure rate for the preceding years with the traditional organization was around 10 percent. This decrease is highly significant ($p<0.01$).

For the students of the third group, we also believe that learning was enhanced. They should have benefited from additional lectures adapted to their higher motivation level, and from the adapted VLE. Assessment of the second phase for this group was not conducted via an exam but via group projects. With caution, due to this less quantitative evaluation process, we can say that instructors have judged these projects to be more interesting than in the previous years. From the students' point of view, perception of better learning outcomes has also increased.

Our main conclusion, which is consistent with e-learning literature, is that VLEs need to be adapted to students' diversity. In our opinion, in the context of a large undergraduate class, this adaptation is not automatic and must be supported by an effective organization and process of the course. Summative results of our evaluation of students' satisfaction are provided in Table 2 below.

Table 2. Summary of Main Experimentation Results

Category	Results
Satisfaction of students who have followed only phase one	Improved but not significantly (p>0.05)
Satisfaction of students after phase 2	Significantly improved (p<0,01)
VLE usage during phase 2	300% increase
Total failure rate for the course	Significantly decreased: from 10% to 4% (p<0.01)

5.   CONCLUSION AND FUTURE DEVELOPMENTS

We had two objectives for our experiment in this large class: first, to increase active learning outside the classroom and, second, to cope with students' diversity.

Our idea to organize this course in two phases that would allow us to break the cohort into three more homogeneous clusters, has proven rather successful after two years of experimentation. We have demonstrated significant improvement upon the previous learning environment. The restructuring of the course has allowed us to save time on a group of students with correct knowledge but low motivation and to devote more resources to the two other groups of students: a group of students with difficulties and a group of students with correct knowledge and high motivation. For these groups, we have obtained good results in terms of satisfaction, work motivation, and evaluation.

This innovation has been made feasible through a good usage of ICT. Obviously, a VLE can provide attractive flexibility, but it is not sufficient to have good software and to put good content online to transform students into active learners. We had experienced many years of rather unsatisfactory use of a general VLE. We have now demonstrated that adaptation of these learning environments to different groups of students can be effective.

In the future, we want to explore new adaptative learning environments. In addition to adapting to knowledge and motivation levels after conducting evaluations and taking into account the students' choices, we intend to conduct research on adaptation to different learning styles.

Finally, extension to other courses is also an important issue for Grenoble Ecole de Management. We are currently in the process of adapting this organization to three other courses.

REFERENCES

Alavi, M., Yoo, Y., & Vogel, D. R. (1997). Using information technology to add value to management education. *Academy of Management Journal, 40* (6), 1282-1309.

Booth, C., Bowie, S., Jordan, J., & Rippin, A. (2000). The use of the case method in large and diverse undergraduate business programmes: Problems and issues. *The International Journal of Management Education, 10* (10).

De Verneil, M. & Berge, Z. L. (2000). Going online: Guidelines for faculty in Higher Education. *International Journal of Educational Telecommunications, 6* (3), 227-242.

De Vita, G. (2001). The use of group work in large and diverse business management classes: Some critical issues. *The International Journal of Management Education, 1* (2), 27-35.

Freeman, M. A., & Capper, J. M., (2000). Obstacles and opportunities for technological innovation in business teaching and learning. *The International Journal of Management Education, 1*(1).

Gibson, J. W., Tesone, D. V., & Blackwell, C. W. (2001). The journey to cyberspace: Reflections from three online business professors. *S.A.M. Advanced Management Journal*, Winter 2001.

Hara, N., & Kling, R. (1999). Students' frustrations with a Web-based distance education course. *First Monday, 4* (12).

Howorth, C. (2001). An empirical examination of undergraduate students' module choices. *International Journal of Management Education, 2*, 19-30.

Laurillard, D. (2000). The e-university: what have we learned? *The International Journal of Management Education, 10* (1).

MacGregor, J., Cooper, J., Smith, K., & Robinson, P. (2000). *Strategies for Energizing Large Classes: From Small Groups to Learning Communities*. Number 81. Jossey-Bass Publishers.

Mathew, N., & Dohery-Poirier, M. (2000). Using the World Wide Web to enhance classroom instruction. *First Monday, 5* (3).

Renzi, S., & Klobas, J. (2000). Steps toward computer-supported collaborative learning for large classes. *Educational Technology and Society, 3* (3).

Schrum, L., & Hong, S. (2002). Dimensions and strategies for online success: voices from experienced educators. *Journal of Asynchronous Learning, 6 (1).*

Webster, J., & Hackley, P. (1997). Teaching effectiveness in technology-mediated distance learning. *Academy of Management Journal, 40* (6), 1282-1309.

Chapter 14

USING INFORMATION TECHNOLOGY IN TEAMWORK DURING COLLABORATIVE EXTRA-CLASS ACTIVITIES

Silvia Sánchez Vizcarra
ITESM Campus Mazatlán, Mexico

1.   INTRODUCTION

Extra class activities can use teamwork as an excellent strategy to help develop abilities required in most modern organizations. This research will present information about the use of Information Technology (IT) in the extra-class activities of undergraduate students from the Business Majors at ITESM Campus Mazatlán.

The use of IT in the teaching-learning process becomes a tool which helps students to develop the ability to analyze, synthesize, and interpret information. For example, the use of the Internet in extra-class teamwork activities can be valuable for both students and professors because it is simple to access and manipulate, and can provide the most up-to-date information available.

The use of IT in extra-class teamwork activities contributes to reaching certain learning goals. That is why it is suggested to focus education on implementing the use of IT as a tool to help in achieving these learning objectives, and to also consider an adequate use of technological resources.

R.G.Milter et al. (eds.), Educational Innovation in Economics and Business IX, 249–273.
©2004 *Springer. Printed in the Netherlands.*

2.   TEAMWORK AND INFORMATION TECHNOLOGY

2.1   Teamwork Used as a Teaching Strategy

Teamwork can be used as a learning strategy, where members are expected to develop coordination and leadership skills and a sense of responsibility, while initiating and conducting an activity. There will always be a member of the team who will coordinate and guide the team's activities; this person will be known as the leader. It is important for all the members of the team to have an opportunity to become the leader at some point; so that everyone can learn to coordinate activities and distribute responsibilities.

2.1.1   Team characteristics

An important issue for successful teamwork is the integration among members of the team. This integration is achieved through communication and acceptance by all members of the team.

We could say that this process of integration originates from the need of belonging to a certain team. Belonging is an important element of influencing all members to be proactive, in order to achieve all benchmarks and goals for the team. Integration helps to efficiently distribute roles among all members of the team avoiding redundant effort. It can also help in providing an opportunity to profile the activities of the team.

If the member of the team feels threatened or not confident with the rest of the team, he or she will be resistant to support and to work for the benefit of the team. This action creates tensions and conflicts among members of the team. The most effective way to solve this problem is to allow time for discussion and communication.

There are several rules established in the teams; some of them are formal and others informal. Formal rules can be written and verbal; informal rules include explicit and implicit ones. Explicit rules are known by the students, they are easy to understand. Additionally, there are rules that are performed in a subconscious manner, that is, implicit rules, such as those that control team attitudes. If the rules are broken, punishment can be established. The rules are broken when a member of the team does not finish a planned activity to the expectations of the other members.

When working in teams, there is always an outstanding student who frequently leads, coordinates, and guides the activities assigned to each member of the team; this person is considered to be the leader. The leader is responsible for creating good working conditions for a proper decision-making process. All the members of the team are responsible for accepting and implementing the solution, based upon previously assigned responsibilities.

2.1.2   Research

One of the main purposes for creating work teams is research. According to Moncayo (1997), to research means to seek, discover, and compile information that can help to find solutions to the problems. That is why research during teamwork is considered as a learning opportunity to develop habits, abilities, and social attitudes. During this process the professor will guide, supervise, and motivate students.

During the research phase the intention is to gather, select, and process information so that this knowledge can contribute to demonstrating the practical use of the information included in an activity. There are different types of research techniques such as observation, interview, and field-trips. In the field of education, in order to motivate students to research it is important to choose the topic that is appealing to the students. This appeal can occur when using electronic media because it is colorful and combines different elements (graphics, photographs, video, sound, text, and animation) that can hold students' attention and make it easier to learn. Campuzano (1992) states that according to experts, the more senses are involved in receiving information, the more possibilities exist for the receptor to grasp the meaning of the message.

2.2   Information Technology

Information Technology includes multiple technologies that have a vast area of application such as information processing and communication (Reyes, Gutiérrez, Salinas, Medrano, Caballero, Villaseñor & Hinojosa, 1997). Some examples of IT are television, video, databases, multimedia, Internet, digital library, and application software. According to Reyes et al. (1997), the use of a combination of different resources, such as satellite technology, multimedia, interactive television, information banks and so forth, and the possibility to connect to all of them through the World Wide Web of computers, constitutes the beginning of the information highway. Among the technological tools that facilitate research, the Internet is the most popular. It can allow you to search for information in different formats (www, gopher, etc.), organize group discussions (groupware), transfer files (FTP), and send messages through electronic mail (e-mail). For the users, the advantage is the great amount of available information with different focuses within the same topic, as well as easy access.

Another information technology that can be used in education is multimedia, which allows interactivity for all users. Certain multimedia CDs offer a variety of integrated support (photograph, video, animation, sound, text, etc.) that will guide students to the source of information. This facilitates objective and efficient evaluation of data, as well as provides access to the information at any given time. The ITESM as an educational institution possesses a great number of databases under the name of *Biblioteca Digital*, where students are able to get information on a vast variety of topics as long as they are connected to the school intranet.

2.3   Information Technology in Education

Modern IT is facing constant change, therefore the learning-teaching process is also being modified on a daily basis, since these changes motivate students and professors to use new learning-teaching processes made possible through IT upgrades. When using new models of education, it is important to consider the amount of information that the students are exposed to. If the amount of data is excessive, it can decrease the capacity of information assimilation. However, if the information is presented in visual and audio formats, the information is simultaneously processed through different senses. This makes concepts and ideas easier to understand and thus keeps the attention of the students more focused.

According to Campuzano (1992), the teachers are no longer information providers; instead they create conditions that help students identify the appropriate resources needed to construct valid knowledge. By using electronic means like the Internet, a professor orients and guides the students to the information and experiences that he or she wishes them to encounter. On the other hand, it can be disadvantageous if there is no control over technology. If the information is not well organized, students may become disoriented as they encounter different points of view on the same subject. Also, excessive data may be overwhelming.

The use of IT in education will cause a change in traditional forms of teaching. Due to the use of this new context of technology in the classroom, the teaching-learning methods have been influenced through the development of new educational models leaning towards self-learning or individual learning. These new models allow everyone to have access to a great amount of information that stimulates individual curiosity and imagination.

2.3.1 Information technology trends in education

In order to succeed in their future careers, students need to develop abilities that will provide the right background and skills required in the global IT environment.

Knowledge trends will require people to:

- Get trained in tools necessary to access information.
- Acquire necessary language skills to be able to communicate via the World Wide Web, since more countries are using this venue.
- Develop tolerance towards other cultures and corresponding values and beliefs of other team members.
- Learn to coordinate with other fields of knowledge to identify possible solutions.
- Gain access to continuing education programs through flexible educational systems that will allow independent learning processes.
- In relation to abilities, it will be necessary to:
- Adapt to constant changes that arise in the IT environment.
- Develop the ability to deal with large amounts of information.
- Learn to interact using new forms of social relations at work as well as in the field of education, sales, etc. An example of this is Virtual University, where people study using the technology to communicate and interact in different times and places.
- Use electronic tools that will allow companies to have horizontal development, in order to create virtual companies through the use of the Web, where employees and companies will be able to work in distant places. This will require coordination of team activities in both time and form.
- Use the appropriate technology channels for knowledge transfer.

3. METHODOLOGY

3.1 Methods

Method is a set of pre-established actions that are systematically executed in order to discover the reality (Perez, 1990). To accomplish this research, two methods were used: one is a quantitative approach, which provides a numerical value to our study, and the second is a qualitative approach, which provides us with the analysis of specific qualities that cannot be appropriately quantified. The text of the interview guide and a survey sample are provided in the Appendix at the end of the chapter.

3.1.1   Surveys

Surveys were used as tools for collecting the information. The issues under review included among others:
- Types of extra-class activities that involved the use of IT for research purposes.
- Students' utilization of IT as a resource for the research, and the frequency of its use.
- Use of special motivation for the use of IT for research purposes.
- Pros and cons of using IT for the research purposes.

Face-to-face interviews were conducted with professors of business in order to determine whether these professors were aware of IT, and whether they recommended the use of IT to their students. The outcomes of qualitative and quantitative studies were validated to complement each other since together they provide a broader perspective for the analysis.

The size of the sample for this research was limited to undergraduate Business Majors at ITESM Campus Mazatlán. Due to the use of different methodological tools for gathering the information related to the subject researched, we detailed each one separately. The following formula was used to determine the size of the sample in a finite universe for the survey:

$$ n = \frac{Z^2 * P (1-P) * N}{e^2 * (N-1) + Z^2 * P (1-P)} $$

Where:

n = 122 students (sample size)

Z = 95% = 1.96 (degree of freedom)

P = 0.07 (probability of success that all the people selected will have the characteristics required)

e = 5% (expected error)

N = 197 (universe of the undergraduate business major students, Spring semester 2002).

3.1.2   Interview

Given the size of the population (20 professors teaching undergraduate courses in the Business School at Campus Mazatlán), it was decided to conduct 12 interviews. This can be considered a representative sample, since it constitutes 60 percent of the entire population of professors. The professors who participated in this research belong to different disciplines and are involved in various teaching-learning methods in class. However, the information requested during the interview was focused on the form and purpose of extra-class activities, for example, identifying whether their students used IT, what were the benefits achieved, as well as how their roles as professors had changed with the use of IT.

4.   TEAMWORK IN EXTRA-CLASS ACTIVITIES

According to Moncayo (1997), the development of a country does not depend on the efforts and achievements of a single citizen, but rather on the accomplishment of the society as a team. Teamwork is part of a teaching-learning methodology that has been implemented at ITESM Campus Mazatlán as a teaching strategy to approach collaborative learning. Moncayo (1997) mentions that students should actively participate in the learning process by looking for information, processing it, and experimenting with their behavior. Moncayo also affirms that students must participate actively in learning tasks because nobody else can learn for them. Therefore, the participation of all the members of the team is important for the optimal learning development to occur.

4.1   The Use of Teamwork in Extra-Class Activities

In addition to being a learning technique, teamwork in extra-class activities seeks to teach students to approach collaborative work by avoiding individual attitudes. We can observe that teamwork constitutes 93 percent of extra-class activities at Campus Mazatlán. The main benefit received by students when participating in these activities is the opportunity to share their experiences and ideas, and to learn to work with other people. We found that the majority of the professors interviewed use extra-class team activities with their students as they consider them important strategies in developing certain abilities.

4.2   Frequency

Most of the students indicated that they have teamwork activities two to three times a week (Figure 1). It is important to mention that the regular workload per semester is seven courses.

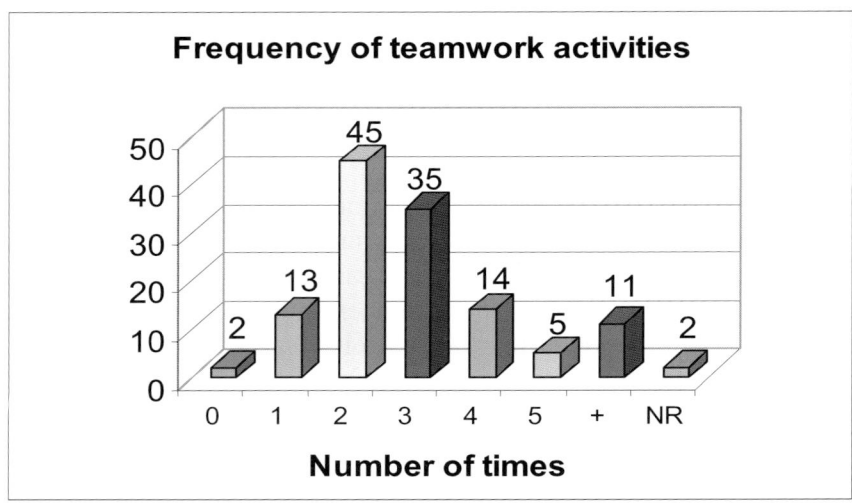

Figure 1. Frequency of Teamwork Activities per Week

Among the population of professors interviewed, we observed that professors apply extra-class activities at different moments along the course and with different frequency. For example, the professors apply the activities either once to three times each week or once every two weeks. This is based upon the fact that students work in teams throughout the semester.

4.3   Types of Activities for Teamwork

The survey questionnaire contained a listing of extra-class activities assigned for teamwork (Figure 2). School presentation was chosen as the most preferred option for the students. Team members must research, analyze, and synthesize the information before creating the presentation.

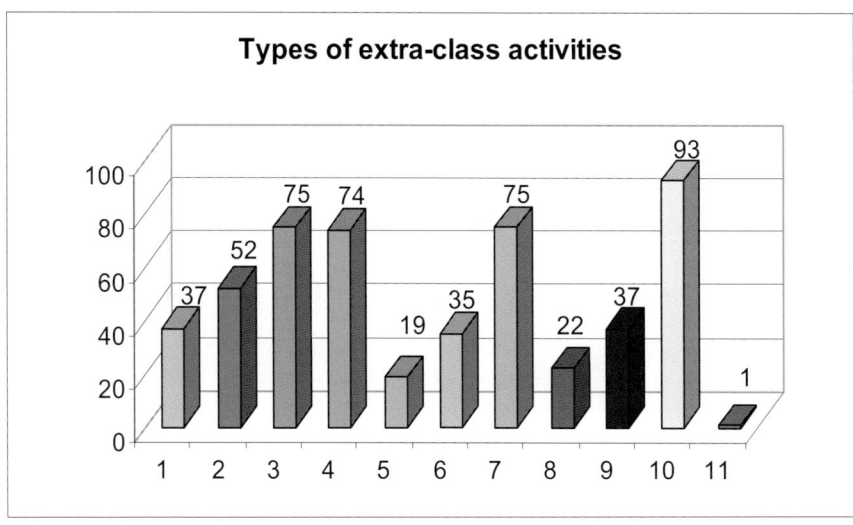

Figure 2. Types of Extra-Class Activities

Table 1 shows that students have to prepare presentations during different semesters. As the semesters continue, there is a tendency to apply activities to real situations that demand problem solving, as well as to share results with other teams in class.

Table 1. Types of Extra-Class Activities

	Type of extra-class activities	Semester (%)									
		1	**2**	**3**	**4**	**5**	**6**	**7**	**8**	**19**	**10**
1	Interviews, surveys	75	44	0	11	46	29	25	15	23	33
2	Look for concepts, topics	100	44	50	44	23	36	44	38	23	67
3	Prepare summaries, synthesis, essays, and analysis of texts.	75	81	75	44	69	43	44	62	46	33
4	Case solving	50	63	75	56	15	93	56	69	54	67
5	Market research	25	0	0	6	31	36	31	8	0	33
6	Problem solving	25	26	50	50	15	29	25	31	8	33
7	Projects	50	56	75	61	69	50	44	62	77	67
8	Community service activities	0	7	25	50	0	0	0	31	31	31
9	Company cases	0	15	0	17	46	14	44	38	69	33
10	Presentations	25	74	75	83	69	64	56	85	92	67
11	Other	0	4	0	0	0	0	0	0	0	0

One of the observations made by professors is that they prefer to assign investigation and problem solving throughout the semester, especially for upper-level courses.

4.4   Size of Teams for Extra-Class Activities

The size of the team is recommended to be between two and four members, but it may be larger depending on the assignment (Johnson, Johnson & Johnson 1995). It is suggested that teams consist of a small number of students to make planning, logistics, and decision making easier. In larger teams, the possibility of adaptation and acceptance among the members decreases. Since teamwork is the result of collective consensus, coordination may become complex in larger teams. In the survey, the majority of the work teams are comprised of four to five participants (see Figure 3).

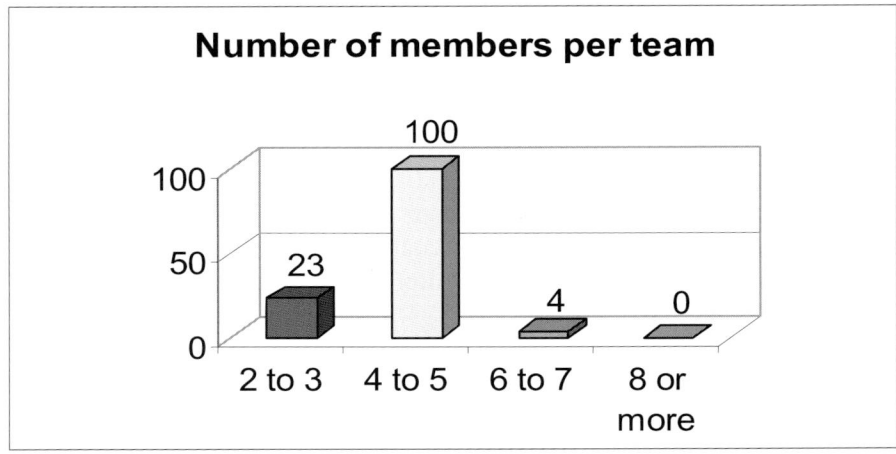

Figure 3. Number of Members per Team

Professors consider that the ideal number of participants for successful work is from three to five members. The smaller the team, the more opportunity does each member have to actively participate in teamwork.

4.5   Acceptance or Rejection of Extra-Class Teamwork

For some people teamwork is the most effective and rewarding form of work, but for others, teamwork is often just a waste of time, since some team members have to overwork for those who would not contribute their share (Moreno, 1997). In the following figure, we can point out that most of the students like to participate in teamwork, and this trend increases as the students advance in their degrees; few students dislike working in teams. In Figure 4, 1 equals to "I like it a lot", 5 equals to "I do not like it".

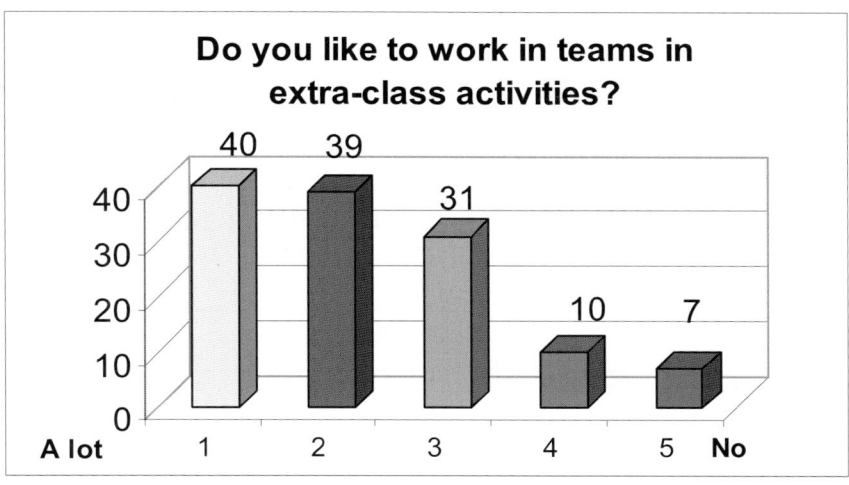

Figure 4. Appreciation of Working in Teams

Figure 5 reflects the outstanding results of teamwork where students:
1. Share ideas, learn to respect each other's ideas, and make collective decisions (answer #7).
2. Learn along with classmates, so they feel supported in areas they might have difficulty with and feel motivated to learn at the same time (answer #1).
3. Find it easier to research and/or complete team activities; it is fun and the workload is divided among several people (answer #5)

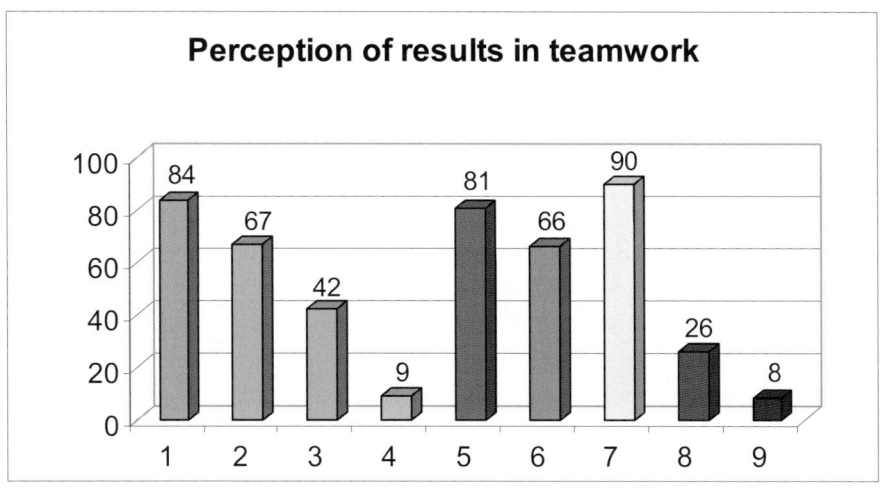

Figure 5. Perception of Results in Teamwork

From analyzing the information in Table 2 by semester, it is clear that during the first three semesters of the undergraduate program, students like working in teams because they feel supported in complex areas (answer #1). As the semesters progress, the students think it is important to learn to work with other people and respect other ideas and make decisions (answer #5 and #7). On the other hand, whatever may be considered negative or not applicable have got the lowest points (see #4 and #9 in Table 2).

Table 2. Perception of Results in Teamwork

Perception of results in teamwork	Semester (%)									
	1	2	3	4	5	6	7	8	9	10
1 I learn along with my classmates and I feel supported when some areas are complex; I am motivated to learn.	100	85	100	78	62	43	56	46	54	33
2 My assignments have much more quality.	75	44	50	61	62	43	44	69	62	33
3 The activity is designed so we have the same workload. We united our efforts to complete an activity faster.	50	26	50	28	46	36	44	31	15	33
4 I prefer to work individually, because I do not adapt to my classmates during the activity.	0	0	0	11	8	7	13	15	0	0
5 It is easy for me to research and/or complete activities in teams, it is fun, and work is divided among several people.	50	59	25	78	69	64	69	69	54	67
6 We have good communication among the members of the team; we learn to work with other people.	75	44	75	67	38	43	50	46	85	0
7 We share ideas, learn to respect others' ideas, and make decisions.	75	70	75	83	69	64	69	62	77	67
8 I lose my time, we talk too much and only a few work.	0	15	25	22	23	43	25	15	8	33
9 Other.	0	4	0	6	8	0	25	0	8	0

The fact that professors design extra-class teamwork activities on a constant basis might confirm the students' acceptance of the strategy, which is important to the student's learning process. In the survey, the professors stated their intention to teach students to work in teams, learn to organize their activities, complete activities effectively, and reach integration. Moreno (1997) indicates that when a person is not willing to work with others or when there is no interest in participating, it is very difficult for the person to integrate in a team. As a result, the person can create obstacles when completing an assignment or during team communication.

One of the reasons why students do not like to work in teams is because it is complicated for them to adapt to other classmates (even if it is in different subjects). As the degree of pressure increases, it is important to remember that teamwork requires certain degrees of adaptation, recognition, and acceptance. Additional teamwork is based upon agreement, which may vary from one team to another. With this variance, the degree of difficulty will more than likely increase.

Acceptance comes before integration in a team. The members of a team pursue their goals and personal needs related to the team's needs and goals. Every member has a different role that will be coordinated and organized by the rest of the team. The rules established will regulate the team's interests and will also determine the team's goal. When the members feel insecure or threatened, they will resist working in teams, which will cause a conflict. This type of potential conflict is the main reason why communication is required among the members of the team, namely to allow opinions and suggestions to be accepted.

In conclusion, the process of adaptation is slow. That is why students in the second semester are more resistant to teamwork. Second-semester students have individualistic attitudes, and they do not want to collaborate with other people. This will complicate the coordination of activities. As obstacles are overcome and integration becomes greater and greater, students begin to identify the advantages of working in teams, and therefore accept this learning strategy.

4.6   Forms of Team Organization in Extra-Class Activities

When students have team activities, they are organized differently, depending on the activity assigned. From the beginning of their planning, the professors must analyze what they wish their students to learn, since it is the professor who establishes the guidelines for the teams to work with.

In the survey we asked the students how they organize their work on extra-class assignments (see Figure 6).

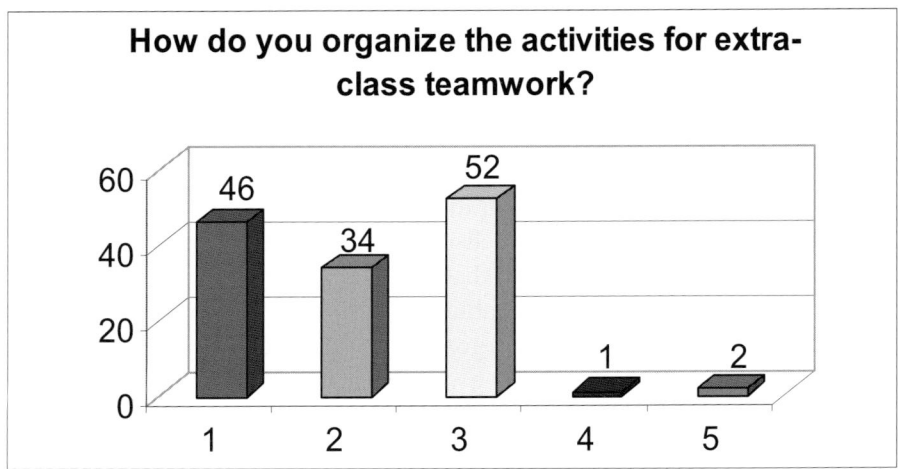

Figure 6. How Do You Organize the Activities for Extra-Class Teamwork?

Most commonly, the students divide the assignment among the team members; next, they communicate and exchange documents using the Internet; after that, one of the students collects all the information, which is then revised by the whole team.

The above-mentioned work distribution is performed through a process that changes from semester to semester. In Table 3 we can observe that first-semester students meet at a physical place. As for the fifth semester, the members have a tendency to divide the assignment and later integrate the information at one virtual place. As for the seventh-semester students, they divide the activity, use the Internet, exchange documents, and combine the information gathered so that they can revise the task as a team.

Table 3. How They Get Organized

How they get organized	Semester (%)									
	1	2	3	4	5	6	7	8	9	10
1 We held activities between all in a selected place (library, computer lab, home, etc.).	50	56	50	44	31	36	25	15	23	0
2 We divided the assignment among the members of the team and later we integrate everything, meeting at the same place.	25	22	0	28	46	36	19	23	23	67
3 We divide the assignment among the team members, we communicate using Internet, we exchange files. One person is responsible for collecting all the information, and we all revise it at the end as a team.	25	30	50	39	23	29	56	62	54	33
4 One of the members researches and the rest prepare the document.	0	0	0	6	0	0	0	0	0	0
5 Other.	0	0	0	0	0	7	0	8	0	0

As the students advance in their careers, they learn to work with other people, trust their classmates, and make collective decisions. With time, their activities become more complex, and they seek the help of technology to make their work easier. No matter where they meet to work on their extra-class assignments, good communication, feedback, and coordination will always be necessary to fulfill the task in an organized and participative manner.

Interviewed professors indicated that the most common places students meet at are: 1) a student's home, 2) the school library, or 3) the computer lab. The form of work organization, according to professors, varies depending on particular circumstances. When there is more time to spend on the assignment, the students tend to analyze the information in a team; they interact more actively, and as a result, the quality of the final product is much higher. On the other hand, when there is less time, the students divide the information, interact online or off-line, and then integrate the information (often by pasting the data). In these cases, the quality of their work will often be poorer. Therefore, the quality of the final product depends on proper cooperation, coordination, and exchange of ideas among teams members, whether online or off-line.

5.   USE OF INFORMATION TECHNOLOGY IN TEAMWORK

Reyes (1997) believes that Information Technology incorporates contributions from several fields and uses them for the processing and integration of information as well as communication. IT is also being used as an educational tool, mainly for information search and establishing communication with other people. During extra-class activities, students have the opportunity to use technological and other tools selected by the team to reach the set objectives. This chapter is focused on investigating the tendency towards the use of technology during extra-class activities.

5.1   Information Technology Used

Information Technology fortifies teamwork during the research phase, providing different alternatives to finding information, as well as the opportunity to research various points of view. The most common technological tools are Internet navigators such as search engines with user-friendly interface that give students easy access to a variety of information (Figure 7). The second most popular application is e-mail when used as a communication tool for sending and receiving data or homework papers. Electronic mail allows for file transfer and communication asynchronously.

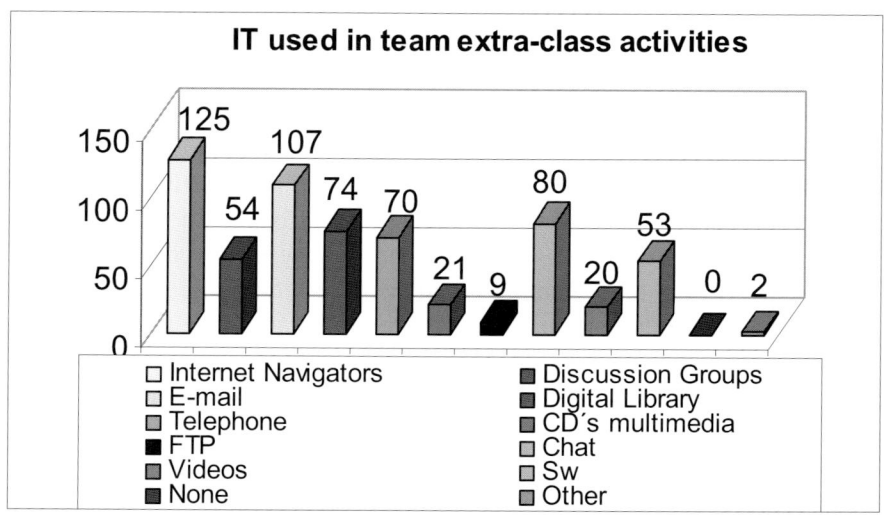

Figure 7. IT Used in Extra-Class Team Activities

The digital library, the Internet, and the electronic mail are the most professor-promoted information tools that help students with their learning process and the development of certain abilities. It is clear that these services provide information and communication opportunities to students during their extra-class work.

5.2   Use of IT in Teamwork

The answers for this survey were divided into three categories: communication, information, and learning. It is relevant to mention that most of the students expressed positive attitudes towards the use of IT in teamwork. Figure 8 presents the results of the information that concerns communication. Students indicate that the use of IT aids in communication and information exchange.

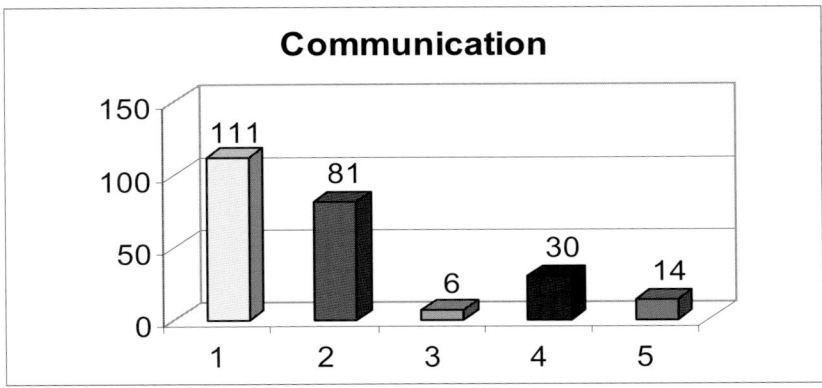

Figure 8. The Role of IT in Communication and Information Exchange

Under the category of Information, students indicated that they have gathered more specific and up-to-date information from different parts of the world as a result of IT use (see Figure 9).

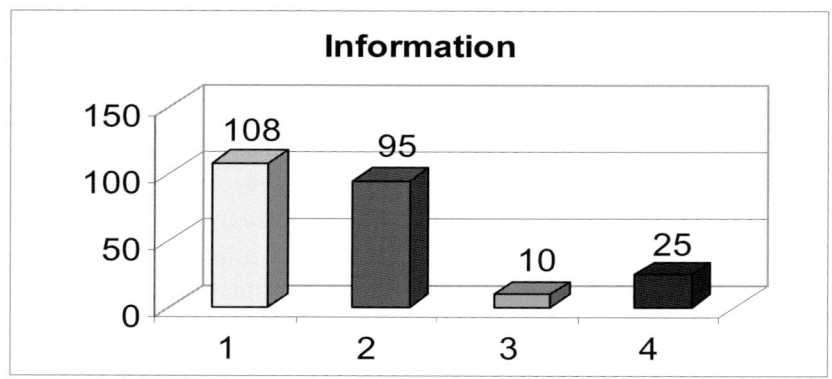

Figure 9. The Role of IT in Gathering Information

As far as the Learning category, the students' opinion was that due to IT: 1) their papers were neat and clean, 2) the capacity to learn on their own increased with their adaptation to new technologies (see Figure 10).

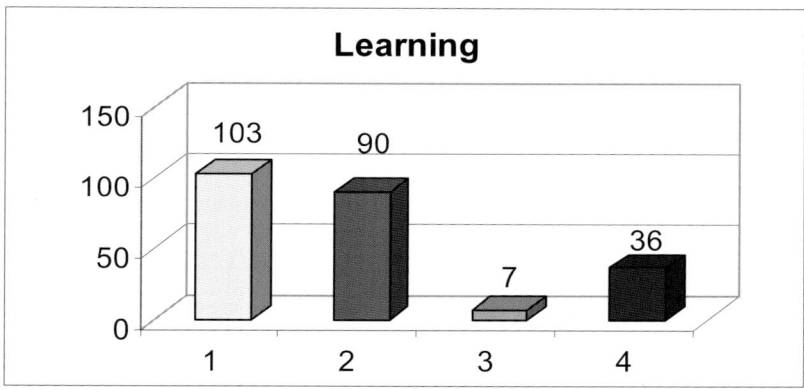

Figure 10. The Role of IT in Learning

With the goal toward helping students to use technology properly the students receive basic training in IT applications during their introductory courses. Of course only with actual application and practice in using these technologies will the students gain full benefits of the tools. Therefore, it is important that professors continually encourage the students to use IT methods in their teamwork.

Being in contact with IT, students obtain more information, are more participative, adapt easily to technological changes, are motivated to self-learning, and increase their capacity to interpret information, engage in critical thinking, and analyze. Most of the professors had the same opinion regarding the correct use of technological tools, and the quality of the students' assignments. Such quality is one of the benefits of using IT in extra-class activities.

One of the disadvantages identified is that some students do not have good reading habits, and have little or no skills in synthesis or analysis. When they have so many sources, they simply limit themselves to copying and pasting the information just as they find it, or else they do not know what to do with so much data. Not knowing how to eliminate irrelevant data overwhelms them, and some get completely lost. In this case, one has to consider that the professor, who is used to reading and analyzing the material, should guide the student.

Factors that were considered as advantageous for some students turned out to be disadvantageous for others. This happens when a student with no adequate technological skills finds tons of unorganized data. These disadvantages can be overcome with appropriate training and the promotion of different skills and abilities that are not only necessary for the use of technology, but for everyday work. Technology is available, and it only requires students to develop abilities that will allow them to access the correct information.

All of the professors agreed that the use of IT in extra-class team activities makes the search for information and communication agile due to search engines that help the students to manage time efficiently. As far as communication, professors have mentioned that when students cannot meet, chat is a good tool with which they can interact.

5.3   Motivation Towards the Use of Information Technology

According to the interviews, professors argue that they motivate their students to use IT by asking them:

- To use electronic tools for research.
- To document bibliographic or electronic sources in the bibliography section.
- To use the digital library, suggesting materials and showing them relevant information from this site.
- To participate in team discussions found on Learning Space (Lotus Notes).
- To use recommended links.
- To present innovations within the area of study.
- To use the World Wide Web as a resource.

- To use electronic means to search for information since they are user-friendly compared to a textbook.

5.4 Differences between Traditional Research and the Use of Information Technology

The interviewed professors stated that when students use IT during the course, it implies a different way of working, which also helps them to develop certain abilities, such as:

- Getting more in-depth information about a subject.
- Broadening their knowledge without the assistance of a textbook or a professor.
- Deciding what information is relevant for their learning process.
- Improving skills in analysis, synthesis, and interpretation of information interpretation skills.
- Developing more agile thinking.
- Collaborating with others on research activity.
- Maintaining an excellent growth of self-learning.
- Accessing current information.
- Completing work efficiently.

6.   CONCLUSIONS

Constant changes in technology and their applicability to daily life have increased the use of IT in education. This has caused a change in teaching-learning methods by leading the professor to be a guide who facilitates activities within the classroom and motivates students to discover their capacity towards self-learning and collaborative work.

One of the didactic strategies is to encourage teamwork during extra-class activities. This strategy is welcomed by the students, because they learn to work collaboratively to reach a common goal. To take a full advantage of IT, it is necessary for professors to receive training and integrate these technological innovations in their extra-class activities. This often provides a new view on the professor's role in the teaching-learning process.

The use of IT keeps students in contact with tons of information. The professor must guide the students and help them to focus on the type of information required. Students can then develop abilities to analyze and synthesize. This increases critical thinking ability, communication, organization, respect, and generally enriches their work quality. Actually, students adapt easily to technological changes because the graphic interface motivates them to learn, encourages them to be more participative, and allows them to express what they have seen and discovered.

Based on the results of the surveys and subsequent interviews, the following key conclusions were made:

1. When working in teams, the search for information is more agile when using IT, such as the Internet or multimedia. Results of the survey show that the most used IT among business undergraduate students are: a) Internet navigators, b) e-mail, c) chat, and d) digital library. Due to the vast, current, and complete information available, the students can use each media at the same time; however, they do not have to do that. It depends on the resources needed to finish their assignments. With the Internet services, it is easy and agile to search for information and communicate with the team. The results also reflected that students like to participate in research activities and teamwork using IT.

2. IT has a strong influence on the way teams coordinate their collaborative extra-class activities. The most common answers indicate that students feel that communication and information exchange in their extra-class activities are most practical through IT. Students divide their tasks and share files using the Internet; then have one of the members integrate the documents so that they can revise them as a team.

3. Professors design activities in such a way that students are motivated to use IT. The main use that students attribute to IT is searching for information. During the interviews, professors stated that they plan activities where they request information from the Internet or the Digital Library that includes electronic references. They also use interesting links during class periods, and plan their classes on technological platforms such as Learning Space or Blackboard.

Several additional observations regarding the undergraduate business students and professors at Campus Mazatlán can be made as a result of the study:

1. Students' acceptance of teamwork increases with each semester.

2. Electronic mail is a means of communication within the team.

3. Students adjust to all technological changes and become highly participative because they want to share the results gathered.

4. Professors must receive training in the use and integration of technological innovations for their academic activities.

5. The most important advantages of the use of IT are: they are easy to use and one can quickly find current information that includes photographs, and audio and video materials to be used in assignments (i.e., presentations).

The above results indicate the need to consider a reorientation of the traditional use of teamwork in extra-class activities. Use of IT can enhance information search and improve communication among team members and professors. Therefore, it appears evident that educators should continually develop ways to increase the use of IT tools as they seek to achieve learning goals.

APPENDIX

INTERVIEW GUIDE FOR PROFESSORS[1]

Name _____No._____
Courses _____ Gender _____ Age _____

1.   What are the teaching methods you normally use?
2.   During this semester, have you planned to assign extra-class activities for teamwork?
3.   What is the size of the teams?
4.   What is the intention of having students work in teams with extra-class activities?
5.   What kind of extra-class activities do you give students and how often?
6.   Where and how have your students worked on extra-class activities?
7.   What kind of technological tools have you observed that your students use with extra-class activities?
8.   What motivates your students to use technological tool while searching for information?
9.   What benefits do students receive through their learning process while using technology for their extra-class activities?
10. How does the Information Technology influence the abilities of the students?
11. When considering course activities where students can use IT, what roles or functions do you have to adapt in order to reach the learning goal?
12. Do you think that the use of IT makes search for information faster and communication among the members more efficient?
13. What instructions do you give your students when you ask them to work in teams?

STUDENT SURVEY

No._____

This survey has the objective of collecting information for a research paper with educational interests. We appreciate the objectivity of your answers.
Major: _____ Semester recently enrolled: _____
Age: _____   Gender : Female_____   Male____

---

[1] Documents presented in the Appendix present the translations of the original interview guides and questionnaires developed in Spanish.

1. - Have you participated in extra-class team activities this semester?
Yes_____   No_____
2. - How often do your professors organize team activities per week?

Sometimes	0	1	2	3	4	5	More
☐	☐	☐	☐	☐	☐	☐	

3. -What kind of extra-class activities do you have? Number the 4 most important.
____Interviews, surveys
____Look for concepts, topics
____Prepare summaries, synthesis, essays, analysis of texts
____Case solving
____Market research
____Problem solving
____Projects
____Community service activities
____Company cases
____Presentations
Other_____

4. -Do you like to work in teams?

A lot				No
1	2	3	4	5
☐	☐	☐	☐	☐

5. - What is the average number of students per team?
____2 to3   ____4 to 5   ____6 to 7   ____ more than 8

6. -What IT (Information Technology) do you use while working in teams on extra-class activities?

____Internet Navigators   ____CDs multimedia
____Team discussion   ____FTP
____E-mail   ____Chat (ICQ, yahoo, msn, etc).
____Digital Library   ____Videos
____Telephone   ____Programs and packages (software)
Other_____ ____None

7. - Form the following category; select the option that best describes your teamwork in extra-class activities.

☐ I learn along with my classmates and I feel supported when some areas are complex, I am motivated to learn.

☐ My assignments are of much better quality.

☐ The activity is designed so we have the same workload. We united our efforts to complete an activity faster.

☐ I prefer to work individually, because I do not adapt to may classmates during the activity.

☐ It is easy for me to research and/or complete activity in teams, it is fun, and work is divided among several people.

☐ We have good communication among the members of the team. We learn to work with other people.

☐ We share ideas, learn to respect others' ideas, and make decisions.

☐ I lose my time, we talk too much, and only a few work.

☐ OTHER:_____

8. - Select only 1 category that corresponds to the way your team regularly gets organized to work on extra-class activities.

☐ We all work at a selected place (library, computer lab, home, etc.).

☐ We divide the assignment among the members of the team and later we integrate everything, meeting at the same place.

☐ We divide the assignment among the team members, we communicate via Internet, we exchange files, one person is responsible for collecting all the information and we all revise it at the end as a team.

☐ One of the members conducts research and the rest prepare the document.

☐ Other.

9. - Select 2 elements of each team that you consider is the most important and that can summarize the use of IT in extra-class team activities.

Communication

☐ 1.- It is easy for me to communicate and exchange information, for example: E-mail.

☐   2.- To copy, send, receive, and print information is not a problem for me.

☐   3.- I do not have Internet access at home. It is expensive.

☐   4.- I depend on IT for finding the information.

☐   5.- I lose my time as the hardware and/or software is slow.

Information
☐   1.- I have more information available, specific, current and from any place in the world. The information is very complete.

☐   2.- It is easy for me to find information, reliable, and time saving.

☐   3.- I lose information due to a mistake or malfunction.

☐   4.- I cannot find the information I want, as it is sometimes not the right information, they are not reliable sources; it is not current and/or specific.

Learning
☐   1.- It allows me to perform assignments with better quality.

☐   2.- They help me to learn on my own and adapt to new technology.

☐   3.- I do not read the information, I copy and paste the information found directly to a word processor.

☐   4.- I forget to use book, I prefer to use the Internet

Other:_____

REFERENCES

Campuzano Ruiz, A. (1992). *Tecnologías Audiovisuales y Educación una visión desde la práctica*. España: Akal.

Johnson, D. W., Johnson R. T., & Johnson H. E. (1995). *Los nuevos círculos de aprendizaje: cooperación en el salón de clases y en la escuela.* Estados Unidos de América: Asociación para la supervisión y desarrollo de programas de estudio.

Moncayo, L. G. (1997). *Cómo trabajar en equipo.* México: Editorial Hexágono, S.A.

Moreno López, S. (1997). *Guía del aprendizaje participativo.* México: Editorial Trillas.

Perez Serrano, G. (1990). *Investigación - acción: aplicaciones al campo social y educativo.* México: Editorial Dykinson.

Reyes, M. E., Gutiérrez, A. E., Salinas, V., Medrano, G., Caballero, L., Villaseñor, G., & Hinojosa, T. (1997). *Escenarios del próximo siglo: perfil del ciudadano futuro.* Monterrey, N.L.: Centro de Apoyos a la Educación.

PART 5

PROGRAM-LEVEL INNOVATION STRATEGY

Chapter 15

CONTEXTUAL LEARNING IN HIGHER EDUCATION
Curriculum Development with Focus on Student Learning

Claus Nygaard & Ib Andersen[1]
CBS Learning Lab, Copenhagen Business School, Denmark

1. THE ROLE OF HIGHER EDUCATIONAL INSTITUTIONS

Curriculum development may at first be seen as an isolated process that goes on within Higher Educational (HE) institutions. Courses have to be developed, books have to be written, teachers have to be recruited, and so forth. This narrow view on the HE institution as an isolated learning space for selected students has long been refuted. Instead, we have witnessed an ever increasing body of literature on HE that has debated the role of HE institutions in national and international contexts inhabited by multiple stakeholders (Assiter, 1995; Harvey & Knight, 1996; Ramsden, 1998). Here it has been a great issue whether HE shall be research governed or market driven. In our view, none of the radical positions are fruitful for HE institutions or their students. We believe that HE institutions have to take the best from both worlds and implement research governed curricula that take into account current business practice. In our perspective, HE institutions have certain responsibilities for both students and the society at large in which they are located.

---

[1] Ib Andersen is associate professor and CEO of CBS (Copenhagen Business School) Learning Lab. Claus Nygaard is associate professor, Ph.D. and consultant at CBS Learning Lab. They have both worked for years as researchers and teachers at Department of Organization and Industrial Sociology at Copenhagen Business School.

R.G.Milter et al. (eds.), Educational Innovation in Economics and Business IX, 277–294.
©2004 *Springer. Printed in the Netherlands.*

HE institutions have to take into consideration that students are educated for flexible jobs in changing markets, and not for low-skilled routine work, as was the case during the time of mass-production. Tinkler, Lepani & Mitchell (1996) write the following about the knowledge economy, "Achieving productivity in this environment requires entirely different methods to those developed by Frederick Taylor for manual work in manufacturing. Key elements are team work, communication, continuous learning at both the organizational and the individual level, and the integration of business strategy with human resource development. This scenario presents a major challenge to the education industry…" (p. 69).

In a study of 61,885 university candidates' employment patterns in the region of Copenhagen in 1996, Maskell and Törnqvist (2001) show that only seven percent were employed in industrial firms, the remaining 93 percent found jobs outside industry. Maskell and Törnqvist (2001) define university candidates as persons on "ISCED level six+" including Ph.D.s. As institutions of Higher Education we need to take on the challenge of training and developing graduates that have the competencies necessary for working in a network and knowledge society. That means graduates with the ability to self-produce and self-develop. To get an active career in the job market today students need to possess higher-order thinking skills. This makes us define the following role of HE institutions.

1. HE institutions have to give students qualifications within a certain academic field. To do so they need to develop curricula that help students acquire knowledge *of* things and enable them to develop skills for using this knowledge in certain situations.

2. HE institutions have to give students competencies that can be used outside the learning context of HE institutions. To do so they need to develop study programs that enable students to develop higher-order thinking skills, which are transferable to contexts separate from the academic field studied.

Such responsibilities of HE institutions are not new to the field of teaching and learning, but have been discussed for quite some time. We believe that the competitive situation within the HE sector calls for a shift away from supply-driven HE programs that have a unilateral focus on academic reasoning. New kinds of competitors, such as corporate universities and vocational training centers with close ties to industry, have entered the market. If "traditional" HE institutions are to find their position among the leading business schools and universities of the world in the near future, they have to design a targeted strategy that will facilitate the development of students who are competent to participate as active learners in the relationship with industry and business.

In our view, we take a middle position in the debate, when we argue that students need to possess competencies within a certain academic field, but also need to possess higher-order thinking skills, which enable them to transfer their competencies to contexts outside HE institutions. Not all bachelor students become master students, and a marginal amount of master students become Ph.D. students. Therefore the role of HE institutions is to educate students for a career in the national and international society in which the HE institution is located. This role implies educating students to become active learners who are able to reflect on the means and ends of their own learning processes, persons who possess what have elsewhere been termed higher-order thinking skills. To fulfill this task, a new paradigm for curriculum development is needed, which explicitly focuses on the learning process of students as such.

The next section is devoted to a discussion of two broad streams within learning theory, and we shall argue that a shift from a conceptualization of decontextual learning to contextual learning helps us better understand the learning process of students.

2. FROM DECONTEXTUAL TO CONTEXTUAL LEARNING

The landscape of learning theories is breathtaking. Concepts and streams of thought dealing with aspects like cognition, psycho-dynamics, self, and society offer different roles in understanding the learning processes of people. It is hard to open a book about learning that does not go through the thoughts of Piaget, Vygotsky, Freud, Marx, Kolb, and Wenger, to name a few of the great ones. We shall refrain from repeating those theories here. Instead we take a broader and more conceptual approach as we discuss the aspects of decontextual and contextual learning.

2.1 Decontextual Learning

The decontextual conceptualization of learning sees learning as a psychological process that goes on within the individual. From years of experience in the Danish HE sector, we find that a very large part of traditional curriculum development is based on a decontextual conceptualization of learning. This is apparent when curriculum development processes center upon defining the syllabus itself, expressed by reading lists of scientific literature. The focus on literature demonstrates a particular view, where knowledge is seen as something absolute, something bound to the books. Finding a good book for a course is almost seen as the direct route to produce competent students. At the same time, in the decontextual conceptualization of learning, knowledge is seen as an object that can be transformed into learning across independent entities and contexts. Put simply, here a book is seen to represent knowledge, and all students are perceived as equal learners. Within this tradition, the only matters that affect learning are the students' own efforts to acquire the knowledge presented in books and by teachers. Key aspects of decontextual learning are shown in Table 1 below.

Table 1. Key Aspects of Decontextual Learning

Definition of learning	Definition of knowledge	Ways of acquiring knowledge	The relation between knowledge and competencies
To learn is to acquire knowledge.	Knowledge is an object; knowledge is propositional and is found in books and papers; knowledge is decontextual and can be transformed into learning across independent entities and contexts.	By reading books and papers, from teaching in classrooms.	To be competent is to possess knowledge about relevant rules and principles, competencies are universally transferable.

When curriculum development is based on a decontextual conceptualization of learning, it chiefly ignores the learning process of students. This is not to say that study developers do not recognize that students enter into HE to learn, and are undergoing a learning process during their period of study. Rather, decontextualists see learning as a process of acquiring prepositional knowledge found in books and papers, which can be transformed into learning across independent entities and contexts. In summary we can say that a competent student possesses knowledge about relevant rules and principles, and such competencies are universally transferable. It means that teachers can transfer knowledge (and thereby competencies) to students through verbal or written communication. These aspects of the decontextual conceptualization of learning have been criticized and are known in the literature as the problems of representation and transference of knowledge. We argue that it is necessary for curriculum developers to take another view on learning that requires that they explicitly focus on the learning processes of students.

2.2   Contextual Learning

The contextual conceptualization of learning offers an explicit focus on the learning process. Here knowledge is seen as an artificial object, which is situated and acquired during social activity, and learning is seen as an ongoing process. This is different from the view above. We subscribe to the concept of contextual learning, and we define learning as a process in which students gain qualifications and competencies. Hereby we distinguish qualifications from competencies. We view qualifications as knowledge and skills, whereas we define competencies as qualifications applied to solve problems in practice. Figure 1 below shows our definition of learning and the relationships between our terms.

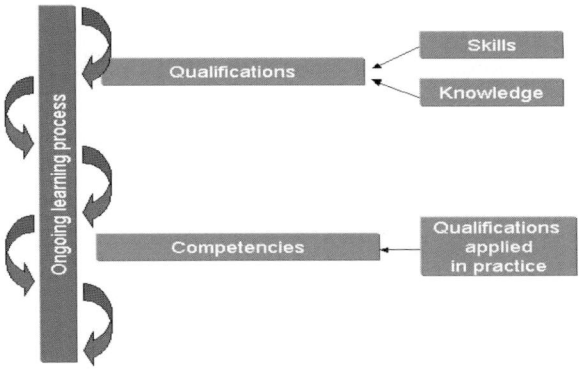

Figure 1: Elements of Learning.

As contextualists we argue that knowledge is of things, knowledge is something you know. Knowledge does not rest in things themselves! A book is not knowledge, but a container of information that facilitates knowledge production. In a book about macroeconomics presenting three different theories about the impact of exchange rates on interest rates and public spending, theories are not knowledge themselves. The theories are merely information which can help students construct knowledge of exchange rates, interest rates, and public spending in different markets or societies. It is, however, not an inevitable consequence that information will produce knowledge in given situations, because knowledge is a social product. Although it is the individual who learns, and knowledge might be said to be an individual product, knowledge production calls for a social process.

Knowledge production is an embedded process, which is affected by the person's position in ongoing systems of social relations. The argument for embeddedness has been defined as "the argument that the behaviour and institutions to be analysed are so constrained by ongoing social relations that to construe them as independent is a grievous misunderstanding... Actors do not behave or decide as atoms outside a social context, nor do they adhere slavishly to a script written for them by the particular intersection of social categories that they happen to occupy. Their attempts at purposive action are instead embedded in concrete, ongoing systems of social relations" (Granovetter, 1992, pp. 53-58).

Using Granovetter's concept of embeddedness, we argue that knowledge (or knowledge production) cannot be taken for granted. Knowledge production is personal, situational, and contextual (i.e, bound to a particular order of behavior that goes on in the particular class, group of students, and so on).

Skills are something you employ, such as the ability to analyze, compare, infer or evaluate, and are able to employ well. In this way we are able to reason within the frames of Quellmalz' (1985) taxonomy of learning and argue that knowledge equals the ability to recall information (something you know), whereas skills involve the higher-order thinking skills mentioned earlier. Due to the contextual aspect of learning, neither is an inevitable consequence that students will be able to convert knowledge into higher-order thinking skills.

Competencies are viewed as qualifications applied to solve problems in practice. Qualification expresses that students have achieved a certain level of knowledge or skills relative to the context of HE institutions. In the HE-sector qualifications are seen as degrees, such as B.S., M.S., or Ph.D. Competence expresses that students are able to apply their qualifications to solving problems in contexts outside the learning context of HE institutions.

We make this distinction between qualifications and competencies because we believe it shows the core constituents of learning. Furthermore, it gives us a terminology by which we can analyze the aspects of curriculum development in HE and discuss their contribution to student learning. Students learn when they obtain knowledge, transform that knowledge into skills, and are capable of solving a problem that appears in practice.

This learning process, however, could be random. Solutions to problems could be a coincidence, or not replicable in new situations or in different practices. We therefore require of students that they become active learners, which means that they are capable of reflecting on the means and ends of their own processes of producing both qualifications and competencies. This reflection on means and ends is a competence in itself, as it makes students capable of solving problems tied to their own learning processes. Students who are able to analyze their own learning processes apply higher-order thinking skills to their own methodologies and hence become active learners. In our view, learning is the acquiring of personal skills and knowledge which can be used when meeting new challenges and tasks in life. Skills and knowledge do not appear out of the blue, but are learned over time and transformed into competencies when applied in practice.

Table 2. Key Aspects of Contextual Learning

Definition of Learning	Definition of knowledge	Ways of acquiring knowledge	The relation between knowledge and competencies
Learning is an ongoing process that involves more than acquiring knowledge.	Knowledge is an artificial object; knowledge is not prepositional; knowledge cannot be expressed in books and papers; knowledge is situated and acquired during social activity.	By doing assignments or discussing information with others.	To be competent is "to be able to;" competencies are tied to situations as hand; competencies are not universally transferable.

McDermott (1999) writes about context that "…context is not so much something into which someone is put, but an order of behaviour of which one is a part" (p 15). This definition of context makes room for a particular focus on the process rather than the structure or architecture of the context. In student learning, the argument that systems are "ongoing" and context is an order of behavior, is the argument that relations between individual students and fellow students, teachers, administration, departments (and whatever key actors there are in and around HE institutions) are never stable, but constantly evolve into new formations over time. Hence the auditorium, the classroom, or the working group of students cannot be conceived as identical learning spaces over time. Each gathering of groups of students and teachers (and other key actors) constitutes an ongoing system of social relations. One could say that the learning context changes over time and thus is never identical.

This view on student learning has implications for the way in which we work as consultants within Copenhagen Business School (CBS), and for the role we define for CBS as a HE institution. "The contextualisation of learning is of major significance in enabling students to expand their learning competencies from the mastery of prepositional knowledge that has dominated the education industry, at least in non-explicitly vocational areas, to include experiential praxis, essential to the mastery of systems thinking and the ability to translate knowledge (about) into action (capacity to do)" (Tinkler et al., 1996, p. 87).

We reason within the frames of this concept because we believe that in practice it helps us focus on important aspects regarding student learning, hence it has positive implications for the ways in which we can educate students with qualifications and competencies suitable for the knowledge economy. In the coming section we turn to the case of CBS to show how our conceptualization of contextual learning has led to the implementation of a certain CBS pedagogy, which affects the way in which curricula are developed to enhance student learning. We believe that the distinction between conceptual and non-conceptual learning processes, and our efforts to advance the concept of contextual, learning-based teaching, can offer HE institutions in general a source for inspiration in the evaluation of their own curriculum development. Our experiences are therefore presented as suggestions or invitations to debate the best means in which to implement learning-based curriculum development.

3.   THE CASE OF THE CBS PEDAGOGY

Copenhagen Business School was built in 1917 by a private institution named The Danish Society for Advancement of Business Education. It was privately financed until 1965, when it was integrated into the national system of Higher Education. Today it is the largest business school in northern Europe. In October 2001 it had 13,899 students, 10,133 of whom were enrolled in one of the many full-time programs offered at the two faculties. The Faculty of Business Economics has nine bachelor programs and 17 master programs, while the Faculty of Modern Languages has two bachelor programs and three master programs. Overall, 3,492 students attended the open university programs spread over more than 10 four-year diploma courses in both faculties. In addition, 274 of the enrolled students attended five executive programs. Since October 2001, CBS has launched four new executive programs that start during 2002 or 2003. All study programs are grounded in research, and CBS has 11 departments within the Faculty of Business Economics and three departments within the Faculty of Modern Languages.

In order to coordinate and improve the quality of this large variety of study programs and strengthen the position of CBS in the national and international HE sector, in 1994 the Senate of CBS established the teaching and learning unit, CBS Learning Lab (the Senate being the supreme collegiate body of CBS). It consists of appointed external representatives of the business community, members elected from the academic as well as the administrative staff, and student representatives. The president of CBS is chairman of the Senate. CBS Learning Lab got its current name in 2001. From 1994 to 2001 it was named The Pedagogical Service Unit.

CBS Learning Lab is a professional pedagogic development and advisory unit that supports both faculties. Its overall task is to improve the quality of curriculum and teaching at CBS. To do so the employees first and foremost engage in research, particularly in order to develop new knowledge about the relationship between competence development, learning processes, and the role of new technology in HE. Furthermore, they engage in competence development of teachers, course coordinators, members of study boards, and administrative staff. They give advice about pedagogical and technological development in all study programs at CBS.

CBS Learning Lab also offers professional project management of larger development projects, such as development of new curricula or development of curricula based on e-learning concepts or virtual space learning. This is done by engaging in close dialogue with study boards, curriculum directors and course coordinators, in order to be able to service the needs of the study programs in the best possible way. Finally, they develop new products and technologies for teaching, such as ICT-based teaching and learning materials that can be applied across various curricula. They also produce more general materials on teaching and curricula, such as books and films on teaching, supervision, curriculum development, and ICT-based learning and pedagogy in Higher Education.

Since its establishment in 1994, CBS Learning Lab has worked with the formulation of a CBS pedagogy to frame all curricula. The first crucial step was a reform of the largest bachelor program in 1996, and it led to the Faculty Council for Business Economics' definition of "Principles for a CBS pedagogy" in 1998. Each fall the largest BS program at CBS starts with more than 550 full-time first-year students. During their three years of study, they follow 13 courses within the key areas of accounting, finance, organization, and marketing. They are organized in 14 parallel classes. The primary goal for all study programs at CBS is to enable the students to:

1. Take responsibility for and organize their own learning processes.
2. Apply theories analytically to issues and problems faced by companies.
3. Work methodically with the problems and issues contained in the subjects.
4. Reflect critically on the foundation and relevance of the theories.
5. Develop personal and interpersonal competencies.

The CBS pedagogy is based on the concept of contextual learning. The CBS pedagogy requires of study programs that they enable students to develop particular skills. The formulation of the CBS pedagogy presented above requires that students at CBS – in order to be regarded as skilled - have to be able to apply theories, work methodically, and reflect critically.

An example of the sort of approach which may be implemented is cited below from a book published by one of our teachers, demonstrating the teaching of monopoly theory.

If the students are to be able to relate themselves to the world around them with the aid of the theory, the teacher must necessarily define the surrounding world sufficiently concretely that the student can see the relevance and the connection, and the easiest way to do this is to make the perspective situational. In concrete terms this means that one shall construct an example that contains a situational problem which the students can identify with, and which demands a means of dealing with it that the students shall learn to apply.

EXAMPLE: If one is to teach about monopoly theory, the scenario could be that the students are employed in an EU-secretariat, where they shall advise the Commission on whether a given fusion between two businesses shall be permitted. In order to do this they must be able to analyze the consequences of a business' monopoly-like status on a market; and to make this determination, they must use theory (Herskin, 2001).

The above example demonstrates the implementation of our philosophy, stimulating the students to make a line of inquiry by specifying a context, a situation, and a problem to be solved, rather than the traditional passive learning and studying what others have experienced. As it appears, the primary goal requires high standards of students. It demands that they take responsibility for their own learning process (and its organization), and it calls for, as stated above, students who are able to apply theories analytically, work methodically, and reflect critically. The formulation of the CBS pedagogy also means that students are expected to take responsibility for and organize their own curriculum, and to develop personal and interpersonal competencies during their time of study at CBS. In our view, acquiring the skills demanded of the students at CBS requires a process of learning.

Quellmalz (1985) presents the following five thinking skills: 1) recall, 2) analyze, 3) compare, 4) infer, and 5) evaluate. Using these we can obtain a useful categorization that can help us work with curriculum development that benefits the learning process of students and fulfils the goals of the CBS pedagogy. In Figure 2 we relate Quellmalz' "taxonomy" to our definition of qualifications in Section 2.

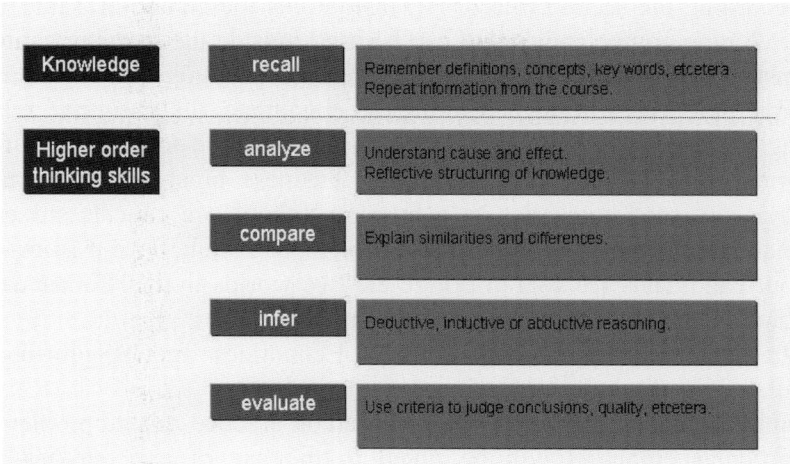

Figure 2: The Nature of Knowledge and Skills in the CBS Pedagogy.

In other words, we want our students to have knowledge of things (to be able to recall information) and to possess higher-order thinking skills to carry through analysis, comparison, inference, and evaluation. To facilitate this learning process of students, it has been decided that all study programs shall be grounded in ongoing research at CBS. It is our belief that the complex process of learning higher-order thinking skills needs to be rooted in more than textbook reading. Being a HE institution, in which the majority of the internal academic staff does empirical research themselves, we want to use this research as a way of training those skills.

In 1998 the Faculty Council for Business Economics at CBS decided that research-based curricula shall be reinforced by the following activities:
1. Application of up-to-date literature at a high academic level.
2. Application of cases, examples, and textbooks using CBS' own research as a springboard.
3. Incorporation of the latest research findings as well as researchers in teaching; and an increased integration of external lecturers in the research environments.

Together, the goals of the CBS pedagogy and the implementation of research governed curricula aims at facilitating the development of students' qualifications and fulfilling the first of the roles of HE as we mentioned in Table 1, that of giving students qualifications within a certain academic field. We believe that curricula developed due to the CBS pedagogy will help students to acquire knowledge of things and enable them to develop skills for using this knowledge in certain situations.

Regarding the second role of HE institutions mentioned in Table 1, that of developing competencies that can be used outside the learning context of HE institutions, this is done by basing the CBS pedagogy on an orientation towards practice. Although we highly encourage that original research among the academic staff at CBS is implemented in teaching, we find it important to take into account current business practices when making research governed curricula. As a business school, we educate students to face national or international business careers, and we believe it is important that our candidates are able to bridge the two worlds in their future careers. Otherwise, we do not find them to be competent.

The Faculty Council for Business Economics at CBS furthermore formulated these requirements for curricula in 1998:
1. Both teaching and projects will be based on practice-related problems.
2. Particular emphasis will be given to the use of case studies in all programs.
3. The subject's content and scope are given priority in accordance with their professional relevance. Representatives from the business community are continuously included in discussions concerning professional priorities, for example, in the form of advisory boards.

The basis for implementing both the CBS pedagogy and a unique profile of each individual study program originates with the study boards. Once a year the program directors report to the Faculty Council on the extent to which curriculum and academic development has developed in the direction of the CBS pedagogy and to what extent a unique profile of the individual program has been achieved.

To summarize the ways in which we believe our experiences at CBS might be valuable in designing contextual, learning-based programs at the HE institution in general, the below points may be noted:
1. All curricula are grounded in ongoing research.
2. Original research among academic staff is implemented in teaching.
3. Current business practices are taken into account when making research-governed curricula.
4. Responsibility for organizing the curriculum is on the students.
5. Students are able to apply theories, work methodically, reflect critically, and develop personal and interpersonal competencies.
6. Pedagogy is based on an orientation towards practice.

4.   NEW ROLES OF KEY STAKEHOLDERS

In its most simple form, the formulation of the CBS pedagogy in 1998 forced (or inspired) teachers, study boards, and so forth, to discuss aspects of student learning. After working as consultants on a variety of curriculum development projects, it has become clear to us at CBS Learning Lab that several questions spring to mind regarding the CBS pedagogy's implications for the roles of a) students, b) teachers, c) departments, and d) study boards. These questions are important to deal with explicitly, because they affect the new paradigm for curriculum development at CBS. In this section we will touch upon these implications. In implementing a new paradigm for curriculum development at the HE institution in general, we believe that we may offer valuable information from the experiences presented at CBS. The intention is to inspire institutions of learning to reflect on the usefulness of our experiences in the assessment of their own curriculum development.

5.   CONTEXTUAL LEARNING – NEW ROLE TO STUDENTS?

Although the curriculum will structure students' learning processes in particular ways, it is impossible to force students to learn. Therefore, it is at the core that students take responsibility for and organize their own curriculum. We believe that students learn more when they are actively engaged and explorative in problem solving. This is not to say that teachers have no role to play. Teachers have the overall responsibility for running the curriculum, and facilitating the courses. However, implemented with a contextual perspective of learning in mind, the CBS pedagogy does not rely on teachers spoon-feeding course readings to students – as we do not believe that students learn from this.

From our consultancy work at the bachelor level we can see that this shift from teaching to learning also implies a cultural shift within the groups of students from what they experienced in high schools to what we expect of them at the university level. It is a difficult task to make students active learners (in the ideal sense of the expression), but we argue that it is possible if we help them to become aware of their processes of learning, and offer them ways in which they can discuss these processes. That calls for new elements in the curriculum and it is such we wish to introduce in our new paradigm for curriculum development.

6.   CONTEXTUAL LEARNING - NEW ROLES FOR TEACHERS?

With regard to the responsibilities of teachers, it is important to stress that the CBS pedagogy leads to a shift in the role of the teacher from one who employs traditional didactic teaching to that of a process consultant. Teachers often ponder what kind of teaching they ought to deliver – instead of wondering what kind of learning processes the students need to experience. As contextualists we argue that teaching students is not in itself a guarantee that the students will learn. Students do not learn from being taught – that is, having the text gone over. Students do not learn until they engage in solving the problems that are relevant to them.

To give the students responsibility for developing and organizing their own curriculum does not imply non-classroom management. As process consultants, teachers will govern or guide the learning process with assignments, tests, and tasks to facilitate student learning.

The particular view on contextual knowledge affects teachers because it cannot be assumed that all students will acquire the same knowledge by reading the same book or attending the same class. In our development of a course, we therefore have to focus on possible ways in which the individual student can transform information in books into knowledge of things. This implies thorough discussions of which assignments to give to students, how group work has to be organized, which theoretical and empirical discussions to facilitate as a teacher, and so forth, all related to the time frame of the course. We do not intend to suggest that a course should use only one type of assignment, group work, or classroom activity. As Crawford (2001) states, the role of teachers is to engage students actively in the learning process, which implies students discussing with each other their strategies for problem solving. Students learn more from this explorative work with problems at hand than they do from being told the right solution to problems they have not experienced themselves.

The CBS pedagogy requires that teachers refrain from didactic teaching and take on the roles of facilitators and coaches. The teacher then needs a large repertoire of micro-pedagogical competencies in order to be able to organize learning situations where students collaborate with other students or with representatives of current business practice.

7. CONTEXTUAL LEARNING – NEW ROLES FOR DEPARTMENTS?

If we agree that the auditorium, the classroom, or the working group of students cannot be conceived as identical learning spaces over time, because student learning is an embedded process where relations unfold in new formations, departments have to approach staffing in a way that takes into account these situational aspects. Usually departments employ teachers (may it be part-time teachers or academic members of the department itself) based on their knowledge within a particular academic field, such as organization theory, financial theory, or accounting. Often economic considerations and aspects regarding the flexibility of the overall portfolio of teachers within the department determine which teacher is used for a particular course.

Contrary to this, we call for "intelligent staffing," where the department introduces alternative recruitment procedures that help them find the right person for the right course. To do this, departments need to recruit part-time teachers or full-time researchers based on the required type of input to the students' learning process. To state an example, it is thought-provoking to see that our course in Organization Theory and Methodology, which is the largest of the bachelor programs at CBS, has 14 teachers with quite different academic and practical profiles. Do we use members of staff in the best way (and do we facilitate students' learning processes in the best way) when we employ the same course with one assistant professor, five Ph.D. students, one external lecturer, and seven teaching assistants? We do not think so. We argue that it is important to base even first-year studies on ongoing research, because the sooner the students are confronted with learning processes that require higher-order thinking skills the better. Maybe "intelligent staffing" would be to employ active researchers, even professors, at the first-year level, and once the students have become familiar with the methodologies and processes following from the CBS pedagogy, confront them with teaching assistants. The question is thought provoking and our answer has great implications for the facilitation of students' learning processes.

8. CONTEXTUAL LEARNING - NEW ROLES FOR STUDY BOARDS?

At CBS, it is the study boards that approve curricula. Following the implementation of the CBS pedagogy and being at the verge of a new era governed by the credo of lifelong learning, study boards need to change their old approval mechanisms, whereby they simply ask responsible teachers for literature lists and approve courses based on this suggested literature. To approve selected literature for courses is a decontextual approach that does not take into account how HE institutions govern the education of students as active learners. With a curriculum that no longer has a unilateral focus on scientific literature, and with new roles to students, teachers, and departments, it is crucial for the implementation of the CBS pedagogy that study boards change their procedures for discussing, negotiating, approving, and evaluating curricula. We believe this has to be done from a contextual conception of learning.

Our goal is to introduce CBS' experiences as a frame of reference to other institutions who see the advantage in changing the approach towards curricula to a more learning-based and contextual one. Seen from our experiences, this demands the following adjustments in the perceptions and roles of the institutional bodies at the HE institution in general:

1. Students having responsibility for and given the task of organizing their own learning processes and parts of their curricula.
2. Students becoming active learners by becoming aware of their processes of learning.
3. The role of the teacher transforming to that of a process consultant.
4. The role of the teacher being to engage students actively in the curriculum.
5. Departments introducing "intelligent staffing": alternative recruitment procedures helping to find the right person for right course.
6. Departments recruiting part-time teachers, full-time researchers based on required type of input to students' learning process.
7. Departments basing even first-year studies on ongoing research.
8. Study boards no longer simply approving courses based on responsible teachers' suggested literature lists.
9. Study boards changing procedures for discussing, negotiating, approving, and evaluating study programs to accommodate a contextual conception of learning.

9.   CONCLUSION

At Copenhagen Business School's (CBS) Learning Lab, our conceptualization of contextual learning and learning-based teaching is implemented in a CBS pedagogy. We move from traditional syllabus-driven didactic teaching to establishing a new paradigm for study development based on students' learning processes. In the decontextual conceptualization of learning, learning is a psychological process within the individual, the important factor being students' own efforts to acquire knowledge presented in assignments, books, and by teachers. The contextual conceptualization of learning has its focus on the learning process. Knowledge production is seen as an embedded process, affected by the person's position in ongoing systems of social relations. With this paper we hope to inspire HE institutions to re-evaluate current methods of curriculum development. This may be done by 1) reconsidering the role of the HE institution in the context of a contemporary societal reality where more cooperation among the professional and educational spheres is beneficial; 2) reconsidering the learning processes of students by examining the students' role as passive vessel or active participant. Introducing the concepts of a decontextual conceptualization of learning, vs. a contextual conceptualization of learning in order to encourage the latter and improve the learning process of students and the relevance of the education to society as a whole; 3) discussing how new perspectives resulting from curriculum developments done with a new paradigm may be accommodated by the key stakeholders at the HE institution by changing some of the institutional practices and defining new roles for key stakeholders. We offer our own experiences at CBS as inspiration or a point of departure for an ongoing discussion of the development of HE curricula in the current societal frames.

Several implications have been defined, and overall we can say that the HE institution needs to focus the effort on creating a dynamic and positive interrelation between 1) industry, 2) ongoing research, and 3) the learning processes of students following the study programs. It is important that HE institutions leave behind the habit of communicating abstract theory without practical usefulness. As we see it, they must work constructively towards the creation of challenging learning situations that facilitate the solving of new kinds of business problems. By first defining this dual role of HE institutions, we can systematically discuss the requirements and new roles of key stakeholders needed in order to educate active learners who possess qualifications and competencies. We believe that curriculum development which takes into account the problems of transference and representation of knowledge leads us to an overall improvement of HE, when it comes down to producing knowledgeable students.

The work with curriculum development according to the CBS pedagogy continues, and it is our impression that we have made quite good progress, although there is still a long way to go. After all, HE institutions are complex political organizations to maneuver.

REFERENCES

Assiter, A. (1995). *Transferable skills in HigherEeducation*. London: Kogan Page.

Crawford, M. L. (2001). *Teaching contextually. Research, rationale, and techniques for improving student motivation and achievement in mathematics and science.* Waco, Texas: CCI Publishing, Inc.

Granovetter, M. (1992). Economic action and social structure. The problem of embeddedness. In M. Granovetter & R. Swedberg (Eds.), *The sociology of economic life.* Boulder: Westview Press.

Harvey, L., & Knight, P. T. (1996). *Transforming Higher Education.* Buckingham: Society for Research into Higher Education/ Open University Press.

Herskin, B. (2001). *Undervisningsteknik for universitetslærere - formidling og aktivering.* Copenhagen: Samfundslitteratur.

McDermott, R. P. (1999). On becoming labelled – the story of Adam. In P. Murphy (Ed.), *Learners, learning and assessment* (pp 1-21). London: Paul Champan Publishing, Ltd.

Maskell, P. & Törnqvist, G. (2001). Universiteternes rolle i den lærende region. In P. Maskell & H. Siggard Jensen (Eds.), *Universiteter for fremtiden. Universiteterne of videnssamfundet* (pp 91-107). Copenhagen: Rektorkollegiet.

Quellmalz, E. S. (1985). Developing reasoning skills. In J. B. Baron & R. J. Sternberg (Eds.), *Teaching thinking skills: theory and practice* (pp 86-105). New York: Freeman.

Ramsden, P. (1998). *Learning to lead in Higher Education.* London: Routledge.

Tinkler, D., Lepani, B. & Mitchell, J. (1996). Education and technology convergence. *A survey of technological infrastructure in education and the professional development and support of educators and trainers in information and communication technologies.* Commissioned Report No. 43, National Board of Employment Education and Training. Canberra: Employment and Skills Council, Australian Government Publishing Service.

Chapter 16

A MULTI-STEP PROCESS FOR ASSESSING STUDENT OUTCOMES IN THE BUSINESS CURRICULUM

Wendy L. Pirie, Michael K. McCuddy & Mary Y. Christ
College of Business Administration, Valparaiso University, Valparaiso, IN, USA

1. INTRODUCTION

Recent emphases on accountability and continuous improvement have caused many universities, colleges, and departments to develop and implement assessment plans with an emphasis on outcomes assessment. Some schools have been motivated by mandates from state legislatures (Herring & Izard, 1992; Kerby & Weber, 2000; Kottke & Shultz, 1997). Business schools are frequently motivated by AACSB standards (Kerby & Weber, 2000; Kimmell, Marquette & Olsen, 1998). Finally, competition as well as employer and other stakeholder comments have motivated business schools (and specific departments within those schools) to consider desired student outcomes and to assess whether those outcomes are being achieved.

Assessment involves the systematic generation and use of information regarding the educational environment, student characteristics, and desired learning outcomes. The intended result of assessment is to enhance student learning (Gainen & Locatelli, 1995). Outcomes assessment focuses explicitly on the outputs of the educational process rather than the inputs. An assessment program for a school of business includes many components. Typically, the focus of the assessment program concentrates on student performance in classes. However, many other sources of information are available to assess outcomes. Among these information sources are student surveys, alumni surveys, employer surveys, and measures from assessment

R.G.Milter et al. (eds.), Educational Innovation in Economics and Business IX, 295–315.
©2004 *Springer. Printed in the Netherlands.*

centers. Merely accumulating information does not make an assessment program or render it effective. Rather, assessment information should relate to the development of desired student competencies. A critical element of an effective assessment program is to tie the assessment activities to curricular activities, with the goal of continuously improving the educational program.

Broadly, and at the risk of over-simplification, our experience with assessment has led us to conclude that the assessment process should unfold as follows:

- Step 1: identifying skills and attributes that the educational program should develop in the students.
- Step 2: disseminating information with respect to desired goals and establishing where opportunities exist to develop desired skills and attributes.
- Step 3: developing appropriate measurement instruments for evaluating desired skills and attributes.
- Step 4: developing target goals or levels of achievement for desired skills and attributes.
- Step 5: assessing the students' acquisition of desired skills and attributes.
- Step 6: providing appropriate feedback to students for use in their personal development.
- Step 7: using the assessment information to evaluate current curriculum, plan future curricular changes, and make appropriate changes in resource allocations.
- Step 8: reinitiating the process.

This multi-step process should not occur in a vacuum, in isolation from other ongoing events and activities within the school and its relevant environments. Instead, we believe that this multi-step process should occur within the context of the school's mission and with recognition of the types of competencies required by prospective employers. In addition, multiple measures and/or multiple sources of measures of skills and attributes should be used. Moreover, this process can ¾ indeed, should ¾ be linked to the pursuit or maintenance of professional accreditation. An increasingly important challenge confronting colleges/schools of business is to gain or maintain professional accreditation as testimony to the quality and standards of the educational programs being offered.

This paper describes the assessment process that is used at Valparaiso University (VU) for linking the College of Business Administration (CBA) mission (see Appendix A for the original version of the mission statement and Appendix B for the revised version), outcomes assessment, and continuous improvement. Engaging in outcomes assessment and linking it to continuous improvement is of inherent value even without the pursuit of professional accreditation.

In the CBA, we have identified a variety of cognitive, behavioral, and affective outcomes that we seek to develop through our curriculum. These desired outcomes were developed using input from focus groups of executives in our constituent business community, an analysis of the literature on competencies required of business school graduates, the implications of our mission statement, and the requirements of our professional accrediting body (AACSB). We evaluate the desired cognitive, behavioral, and affective outcomes in a variety of ways, depending on the nature of the particular outcome and the available measures. Included among the various evaluation methods that we use are course work, evaluations done by internship employers, assessment center results, and the Educational Benchmarking Inc. (EBI) Undergraduate Student Satisfaction Survey[1] results. Relevant information from these sources is fed back to the students subsequent to the evaluation and is used by the CBA Assessment Committee and the CBA Curriculum Committee to pursue continuous improvement.

2. THE MULTI-STEP PROCESS

2.1 Step 1: Identifying Skills and Attributes That the Educational Program Should Develop in the Students

Initially, as stated above, the desired skills and attributes were identified using input from focus groups of executives in our constituent business community and an analysis of the literature on competencies required of business school graduates. The earlier version of the CBA's mission statement and the requirements of our professional accrediting body (AACSB) influenced our thinking as we developed the list of desired skills and attributes. With regard to the earlier CBA's mission statement, particular emphasis was placed on developing skills and attributes that emanate from and are consistent with the following elements: ethics, lifelong learning, embracing change, integrating liberal and professional studies, and social responsibility. The following list of general skills and attributes grew out of this process:

---

[1] This survey is endorsed by AACSB. This survey analyzed the responses of over 50,000 graduating undergraduate business students from over 250 business programs in order to identify perceived value-added curricular and co-curricular items.

Cognitive objectives:
- Solid knowledge base for business.
  Behavioral objectives:
- Communication skills.
- Information technology skills.
- Broad-based perspective on problem solving.
- Teamwork skills.
- Experience at interacting with the business community.
  Affective objectives:
- Ethics and service to the community.
- Self-management awareness and skills.
- Flexibility, tolerance for ambiguity, global thinking, ability to learn independently.

Each of these was then elaborated upon to develop detailed competencies encompassed within these general headings. For instance, with regard to the solid knowledge base for business, specific objectives were developed referencing each core course offered within the CBA.

As was done for the cognitive abilities within the context of courses, each of the behavioral and affective skills and attributes were elaborated upon. For instance, ethical behavior/values awareness had three components: sense of ethics — right and wrong, sense of service to the community, and a strong work ethic. Four key elements relating to self-management awareness and skills were: self-reliance, perseverance, self-motivation, and management of multiple responsibilities. It is clearly evident that proficiency in these skills and attributes is not well-identified in a typical testing format. However, unless there is agreement upon the necessity to develop these less easily measured skills and attributes, they are likely to be ignored.

The following are examples of objectives that were developed for two required junior-level courses: one that is more quantitative (Financial Management) and one that is more behavioral (Management and Organizational Behavior, MOB). It is important to recognize that the behavioral and affective objectives are an integral part of the more quantitatively oriented courses as well as the more behaviorally oriented courses. All too often those teaching more quantitatively oriented courses abrogate any responsibility for affective and behavioral outcomes. By using the approach we suggest, these desired outcomes become a concern for all faculty.

Looking at the major learning objectives for Financial Management and MOB, the concern in both courses for cognitive, behavioral, and affective objectives is evident, albeit with different emphases. The major learning objectives for these two courses are shown in Table 1.

Table 1. Comparison of Cognitive, Behavioral, and Affective Objectives for a Quantitatively Oriented Course and a Behaviorally Oriented Course

Objectives	Financial Management	Management and Organizational Behavior
Cognitive:	To develop a familiarity with the financial environment and basic terminology of finance, including international aspects.	To expose students to the terminology of management and organizational behavior.
	To introduce the financial concepts necessary to conduct business. Efficient markets. Time value of money and its application. Cost-volume-profit and leverage.	To promote conceptual understanding of organizations as functioning systems of interrelated structures, processes, and people.
	To provide a basis for further study in finance. Risk and return measurements.	To promote experiential understanding of how organizations function.
	To acquaint the students with tools useful in conducting their own finances. Financial statement analysis. Forecasting financial statements, including cash budgets. Valuation of financial instruments.	To promote understanding of the determinants and dynamics of individual behavior.
Behavioral:	To develop presentation skills and to practice working in teams.	To develop leadership and followership skills, teamwork skills, and the ability to work effectively in self-managing teams. Ability to work in teams. Ability to work without close, direct supervision. Ability to accept and be comfortable with peer-supervision. Ability to accept and be comfortable with peer evaluations. Ability to be flexible and

Objectives	Financial Management	Management and Organizational Behavior
		adaptable.
		Ability to solve problems and make decisions.
		Ability to communicate effectively.
		Ability to resolve conflicts constructively.
		Ability to tolerate ambiguity.
		Willingness to exercise initiative.
		To promote understanding of the determinants and dynamics of individual behavior.
Affective:	To discuss the ethical dimensions of finance.	To promote understanding of the ethical dimensions of leading people and managing organizations.
	To integrate current market events into the course in order to develop an appreciation of the necessity of lifelong learning.	

The achievement of some of the course objectives — primarily cognitive — is measured relatively easily with typical evaluation procedures, such as examinations and projects. Surveys, another typical evaluation procedure, solicit opinions and assess how individuals "feel," but the responses may not reflect actual competency. Both paper and pencil tests and surveys are indirect insofar as they do not involve the actual observation of behavior (Herring & Izard, 1992). Performance relative to objectives that are behavioral or affective in nature is not so easily evaluated and requires creative approaches. For example, proficiency regarding the ability to be flexible and adaptable is difficult for the professor to evaluate. An approach that is particularly well suited to evaluating the behavioral outcomes is the assessment center (McCuddy, Pirie, Christ, Mainstone, Schroeder, & Strasser, 2000).

2.2   Step 2: Disseminating Information with Respect to Desired Goals and Establishing Where Opportunities Exist to Develop Desired Skills and Attributes

In order to ensure that constituents are striving for a common goal, it is important that the information with respect to desired skills and attributes is disseminated. There were two primary methods that we used in the CBA to disseminate information to the faculty. The first was via the revised mission statement that implicitly encompasses much of the information regarding the desired competencies and attributes (see Appendix B). This information was and is available to all interested parties on the Valparaiso University CBA Web page. The second method was via a faculty retreat where each course was analyzed for its potential contribution toward the desired skills and attributes.

Appendix C shows the form that was used in analyzing each course. Also shown are the evaluative ratings for the two example courses — Financial Management and MOB. Completion of this form for all courses within the CBA identified areas of coverage and areas that lacked coverage. Where coverage was lacking there was discussion as to whether the skill or attribute could be developed within a course context or was more appropriately developed in some other fashion, such as with an internship. It should be noted that although a skill or attribute may be developed within a course, that may not be the appropriate context within which to evaluate its development.

Other constituents receive the information implicitly via the mission statement and in venues suited to them. Prospective students who visit campus, as well as admitted students, attend sessions where the desired skills and attributes are discussed and receive a handout listing these. Employers of student interns receive evaluation forms that contain the desired skills and attributes (see Appendix D). Assessors in VU's CBA Assessment Center receive a package of materials that includes the desired skills and attributes. Basically, at every opportunity the desired skills and attributes are reiterated. This encourages the reinforcement of the desired skills and attributes and ensures that appropriate emphasis is placed on evaluating them. It is critical that an appropriate method of measuring proficiency be developed in order to effectively ascertain objective attainment.

2.3   Step 3: Developing Appropriate Measurement Instruments for Evaluating Desired Skills and Attributes

In developing appropriate measurement instruments for assessment, it is necessary to consider the dual objectives of assessment: the development of desired student competencies on an individual basis — a micro-objective — and the continuous improvement of the overall curriculum and educational program — a macro-objective. Some of our measuring instruments focus primarily on one objective and others help achieve both objectives. Course work is more useful for monitoring individual student development, while overall class performance may be utilized by the instructor to improve the course. However, these are of less use for overall curricular purposes. Benchmarking surveys, such as the EBI Satisfaction Survey, on the other hand, are valuable in assessing the overall curriculum and educational program but are of little or no use in terms of development of competencies by individual students. An assessment center (Christ, Clark, McCuddy, Pirie, Schroeder, & Strasser, 1999; McCuddy et al., 2000) and internship evaluations by employers aid in the achievement of both objectives.[2]

In the CBA, the Assessment Committee listed the desired students outcomes and then considered what tools could be used to assess the achievement level of the students with respect to the desired skills and attributes. Appendix E shows the matrix developed by the Assessment Committee.[3]

2.4   Step 4: Developing Target Goals or Levels of Achievement for Desired Skills and Attributes

The Assessment Committee then developed measurement goals for the desired skills and attributes addressed by each of the instruments. For some

---

[2] Commonly used outcome measures include (1) performance measures such as job placement rates, graduate admission exam scores, college GPA, retention and graduation rates, and scores on major field exams and other publicly available standardized exams; and (2) survey data from students, alumni, and employers (Kimmell et al., 1998). The focus in the CBA on student competencies dictated our selection of measurement tools and some common measures such as GPA or job placement rates did not seem appropriate.

[3] Course work is listed under a variety of behavioral and affective outcomes but the emphasis on an objective and the measurement of its achievement differs dramatically from course to course. For instance, while teamwork may be used in a variety of courses, there may be little attempt to provide feedback to the student as to their performance as a team member (McCuddy & Pirie, 2004).

measuring instruments — primarily those used in course work — a goal was not stipulated because of the reluctance to impinge on professors' academic freedom. However, the general sense of the committee was that given the caliber of students in the CBA, 85 to 90 percent of the students should achieve a C or better. Those students who achieve less than C typically do so because of lack of effort — failure to attend classes, take tests, and so forth.

Appendix E indicates the goals for each of the assessment tools where possible. If development of desired individual student competencies — a micro-objective — is the focus of the measurement, then a specific level of proficiency is identified. If the continuous improvement of the overall curriculum and educational program — a macro-objective — is the desired outcome, then an emphasis on consistent improvement is appropriate.

2.5   Step 5: Assessing the Students' Acquisition of Desired Skills and Attributes

Our primary assessment tools are course work, the CBA Assessment Center, internship evaluations, and the EBI Student Satisfaction Survey. Each of these was chosen because it specifically addresses one or more of the desired outcomes.

As indicated in Appendix E, assessment of student proficiency in acquiring cognitive, behavioral, and affective outcomes through course work occurs according to the professor's prerogative. While enumerating all of the possibilities for assessment through course work is beyond the scope of this paper, we offer as illustration some of the more innovative approaches that have been used in the CBA. For instance, team learning is utilized and evaluated in numerous courses in accounting, finance, and management (Christ, Christ, Graham, McCuddy, & Pirie, 2004). The impact of team learning was not only considered in the context of teamwork skills but also with respect to cognitive skills. Another example is that every major in the CBA has a capstone course, in addition to the required business policy and strategy course, which uses projects and/or cases to further reinforce and assess most, if not all, of the desired cognitive, behavioral, and affective outcomes. In general, the use of active student involvement in various forms of problem-based learning is widespread within the CBA.

The CBA Assessment Center activities are conducted at the beginning of the sophomore year and again mid-way through the spring semester of the junior year. During each administration of the Assessment Center, students participate in a set of structured activities that enable them to display various behavioral and affective outcomes. Executives from our business stakeholders serve as assessors. They provide immediate verbal feedback to the students as well as more detailed written feedback on a variety of rating scales and checklists that are processed through the CBA Internship and Assessment Center Coordinator. Detailed information on the CBA Assessment Center may be found in McCuddy et al. (2000).

All CBA students are required to have an internship experience in their junior or senior year. At the end of the internship, the student's internship employer completes the evaluation form shown in Appendix D. The completed evaluation form is sent to the CBA Internship and Assessment Center Coordinator, who records the information for analytical purposes regarding the extent of goal attainment on the desired student outcomes. A copy of the employer's evaluation is also provided to the student.

The EBI Student Satisfaction Survey is administered on campus to graduating seniors in order to ensure a significant response rate. Many of the survey questions focus on assessing student satisfaction with outcomes that fall within the cognitive, behavioral, and affective domains. A particular advantage of the EBI Survey is the benchmarking that is available relative to other colleges and universities.

2.6   Step 6: Providing Appropriate Feedback to Students for Use in Their Personal Development

The primary sources of feedback to students are the grades and comments on course work, peer assessment of performance when teams are used in the classroom, the Employer Evaluation Form for internships, and the appraisals by assessors in the Assessment Center. Students are encouraged to use this constructive feedback to reinforce areas of strength and to ameliorate areas of weakness.

2.7   Step 7: Using the Assessment Information to Evaluate Current Curriculum, Plan Future Curricular Changes, and Make Appropriate Changes in Resource Allocations

The information from the EBI Satisfaction Survey and the aggregated feedback from employers of interns and assessors in the Assessment Center are the three primary sources of information used to evaluate the current curriculum. This information is used to identify areas of strength and weakness in students for potential curricular adjustment.

The collection of data has been phased in over a five-year period. It is critical to have longitudinal data because much of it is subjective in nature. In addition, because of the relatively small size of the CBA student body (approximately 400 undergraduates), a sufficient number of observations had to be accumulated over several academic years. The Assessment Committee is in the process of summarizing and evaluating all sources of data regarding the desired student outcomes. The Assessment Committee will use this information to formulate recommendations to the CBA Curriculum Committee and the faculty. The EBI Student Satisfaction Survey may also be particularly useful in identifying additional skills and attributes that are not currently identified as desired.

2.8   Step 8: Reinitiating the Process

Using the aggregate information, the CBA can evaluate both the achievement of the current desired outcomes and the completeness and appropriateness of the currently defined desired outcomes. It is critical that the desired outcomes and assessment tools be revisited given the dynamic nature of the business environment.

A potential trap is simply evaluating the achievement of previously defined goals without considering their ongoing relevance. The unwary would reinitiate the process at Step 5 rather than at Step 1. Continuous improvement requires ongoing completion of the entire cycle, not just the last four steps.

3.   CONCLUDING OBSERVATIONS

Based on our experience, we believe that whatever your mission and goals, a well thought out and executed assessment plan is a critical tool in accomplishing those goals and fulfilling the mission. Assessment should not simply be a response to external mandates but should be viewed as a useful tool in achieving your defined goals and mission. As noted in the introduction to this paper, engaging in outcomes assessment and linking it to continuous improvement is of inherent value even without external pressures.

The assessment process is clearly time-consuming and requires a great deal of effort, but is worthwhile from a cost/benefit perspective. Assessment is not a finite process with closure, but a continuous process that requires ongoing commitment. The CBA Assessment Committee continues to meet and evaluate the achievement of curricular objectives within the context of the CBA mission.

APPENDIX A: ORIGINAL CBA MISSION STATEMENT

Consistent with the Mission of Valparaiso University, the College of Business Administration (CBA) provides quality management education.

In fulfillment of its mission, the CBA fosters an environment for continuous improvement in pursuing its strategic objectives:

- CBA provides students with personal, ethics-based management education that leads them to value lifelong learning and to embrace change.
- CBA gives students a learning experience that integrates liberal and professional studies for attaining career goals.
- CBA supports faculty scholarship that results in intellectual contributions in the application of knowledge and instructional development.
- CBA enhances social responsibility among faculty and students by encouraging community and professional service.

APPENDIX B: REVISED CBA MISSION STATEMENT

To create an extraordinary learning environment for quality management education through a community that fosters mutual respect, engages in scholarly activities, values the University's Christian tradition, and is based on moral integrity.

Shared values:

- We strive to function in a learning-centered environment of mutual respect that is cooperative and team-oriented.
- We view students as whole persons and strive to prepare them for personal, as well as professional success.
- We strive for quality management education that provides integration of knowledge from all business disciplines through innovative curriculum development and delivery.
- We attempt to develop analytical, problem-solving, and critical thinking skills along with a curiosity for lifelong learning.
- Our community is a partnership of faculty, students, administration, staff, and business people.
- Our faculty is engaged in scholarly activities with a focus on intellectual contributions related to the application of knowledge and instructional development.
- We value the importance of ethics, integrity, and honesty.
- We value the Lutheran heritage of the University.
- We recognize the importance of giving to the community and stress enhanced social responsibility among faculty and students by encouraging community and professional service.

APPENDIX C: SKILLS DEVELOPMENT BY COURSE MATRIX

Cognitive Objectives (Declarative Knowledge)	Financial Management	Management and Organizational Behavior	... Other Courses
Business Perspectives — Context of Business			
Understand implications of ethical and faith issues in business	Introduction and Integrate 2	Build 2; Integrate 3	
Understand implications of global issues in business	Introduction 3	Review 1; Build 1; Integrate 2	
Understand implications of political issues in business	Introduction 0.5	Introduction 0.5	
Understand implications of social issues in business	Introduction 1	Build 1; Integrate 1	
Understand implications of legal and regulatory issues in business	Introduction 5	Review 0.5	
Understand implications of environmental issues in business	Introduction 0.5	Build 4	
Understand implications of technological issues in business	Introduction 2	Build 1; Integrate 1.5	
Understand implications of demographic diversity in business		Review 1; Integrate 2	

Legend: *Introduction*: First exposure, new information. *Build*: Move beyond introduction; application. *Review*: Revisit, nothing new. *Integrate*: With other subjects. Number equals hours per semester (1 Hour = 50 class minutes).

Behavioral Objectives (Human Activity — Skills and Abilities)	Financial Management	Management and Organizational Behavior	... Other Courses
Communication Skills			
Effective formal and informal communication	M	H	
Communicate with superiors, subordinates, and customers	M	H	
Ability to listen/active listening	M	H	
Articulate one's views in a logical, eloquent, and persuasive manner	M	H	
Write convincingly, logically, and concisely	M	H	
Use modern techniques of business writing (memos, letters and reports,	L	L	

Web pages)			
Grammatically correct, error-free writing	M	H	
Make effective oral presentations and arguments	L	H	
Telephone skills			
Information Technology Skills			
Effectively utilize the latest technology (*e.g.*, Web/Internet, ABI, library) to research and solve problems	H	M	
Computer skills			
Word processing	M	H	
Spreadsheets	L		
Presentations	L		
E-mail			
Applications			
File manipulation			

Behavioral Objectives (Human Activity — Skills and Abilities)	**Financial Management**	**Management and Organizational Behavior**	**… Other Courses**
Problem Solving/Critical Thinking/Creative Thinking Abilities			
Work with both structured and unstructured problems	M	H	
Identify central issues and assumptions in an argument	L	M	
Recognize important relationships and synthesize evidence	M	H	
Evaluate evidence or authority/ make correct inferences		M	
Deduce conclusions from information or data provided	M	L	
Interpret whether conclusions are warranted	L	L	
Brainstorm and generate alternatives		H	
Think cross-functionally and strategically	L	M	
Think globally	L	M	
Use multiple problem-solving techniques and divergent thinking	L	H	
Look beyond the obvious or existing approaches and policies	L	M	
Frame problems in ways that	L	H	

present new understandings and opportunities for improvement			
Teamwork/Leadership Abilities			
Ability to work with group members to accomplish goals	L	H	
Awareness of individual roles — leader, facilitator, and follower	L	H	
Awareness of group dynamics — group processes, group stress, hidden agendas, bases of power, and trust	L	H	
Conflict management — conflict management styles, intervention	L	M	
Tolerance of individual differences	L	M	
Identifying decision making styles	L	M	

Affective Objectives (Psychological Constructs)	Financial Management	Management and Organizational Behavior	… Other Courses
Ethical Behavior/Values Awareness			
Sense of ethics — right and wrong	M	M	
Sense of service to the community			
Strong work ethic	M	M	
Self-Concept/ Self-Awareness			
Self-reliance	M	H	
Perseverance	M	H	
Self-motivation	M	H	
Management of multiple responsibilities	M	M	
Attitudes (Feelings Toward Other People, Ideas, and Institutions)			
Ability to continue to learn	M	H	
Ability to deal with change	L	H	
Ability to tolerate ambiguity	M	H	
Understand that it is OK to be wrong, to fail	M	H	

Legend: *L*: Light Emphasis. *M*: Medium Emphasis. *H*: Heavy Emphasis.

APPENDIX D: EMPLOYER EVALUATION OF COLLEGE OF BUSINESS ADMINISTRATION INTERNSHIP STUDENT

Student's Name_____

Employer_____

Starting date _____**Ending date** _____**Hours worked** _____

Please rate the student on each of the attributes listed in the chart. The rating scale should be interpreted as follows:

  1 = Poor; 2 = Below Average; 3 = Average; 4 = Above Average; 5 = Outstanding.

Cognitive Skills	
Academic Knowledge	
Has good general business knowledge	1 2 3 4 5 NA
Quantitative analysis skills	1 2 3 4 5 NA
Understands business issues and problems from multiple perspectives	1 2 3 4 5 NA
Behavioral Skills	
Communication	
Writing skills	1 2 3 4 5 NA
Ability to listen	1 2 3 4 5 NA
Telephone skills	1 2 3 4 5 NA
Communicates well with superiors	1 2 3 4 5 NA
Communicates well with subordinates	1 2 3 4 5 NA
Communicates well with peers	1 2 3 4 5 NA
Communicates well with customers/clients	1 2 3 4 5 NA
Information Technology	
Computer literacy	1 2 3 4 5 NA
Competence in information research and technology	1 2 3 4 5 NA
Problem Solving	
Critical thinking	1 2 3 4 5 NA
Creativity	1 2 3 4 5 NA
Ability to solve unstructured problems	1 2 3 4 5 NA
Ability to develop cross-functional solutions for business problems	1 2 3 4 5 NA
Teamwork	
Ability to work in teams	1 2 3 4 5 NA
Ability to deal with conflicts	1 2 3 4 5 NA
Leadership	
Takes initiative; works independently	1 2 3 4 5 NA
Dependability	1 2 3 4 5 NA

Appendix D (cont'd)

Affective Skills	
Ethical Behavior	
Sense of integrity	1 2 3 4 5 NA
Sense of service to the community	1 2 3 4 5 NA
Self Concept/Self Awareness	
Self-reliant	1 2 3 4 5 NA
Manages multiple responsibilities	1 2 3 4 5 NA
Attitudes	
Learns work readily	1 2 3 4 5 NA
Exercises good judgment	1 2 3 4 5 NA
Shows interest in new ideas and skills	1 2 3 4 5 NA
Ability to deal with change	1 2 3 4 5 NA
Ability to deal with ambiguity	1 2 3 4 5 NA
Strong work ethic	1 2 3 4 5 NA

Briefly describe the student's work assignment.

List some of the contributions the student made during this work assignment.

List the personal characteristics that will help or hinder the student's professional development

Strengths: **Areas for Improvement:**
1_____   1_____
2_____   2_____
3_____   3_____

Would you recommend this student for future employment? _____Yes _____No
If no, please explain:_____

_____
_____
_____

Comments:

Evaluated by:_____ Title:_____
Date:_____
Has this report been shared with the student? _____Yes _____No
Student's Signature (optional):_____

Please return to: **Internship/Co-op Coordinator - Urschel 204**
                        College of Business Administration
                        Valparaiso University
                        Valparaiso IN 46383

Upon written request to the Internship/Co-op Coordinator, the student will be allowed to read and/or receive a copy of this evaluation in compliance with the Family Education Rights and Privacy Act of 1974.

APPENDIX E: CBA SKILLS ASSESSMENT MATRIX[4]

Desired Student Outcome	Assessment Tool	Assessment Timing	Measurement Scale	Goal
Cognitive Outcomes	Course Work	Professor's prerogative	Professor's prerogative	Professor's prerogative
Core Business Knowledge	Internship Evaluation	Junior/Senior Year	Scale of 1 to 5: 1 = Poor and 5 = Outstanding	85% ≥ 3 70% ≥ 4
	EBI Satisfaction Survey	Graduating Seniors	Scale of 1 to 7: 1 = Very Poor and 7 = Exceptional	Consistent improvement
Knowledge in Major	Course Work	Professor's prerogative	Professor's prerogative	Professor's prerogative
	EBI Satisfaction Survey	Graduating Seniors	Scale of 1 to 7: 1 = Very Poor and 7 = Exceptional	Consistent improvement
Understanding of Perspectives (Ethical, Global, Political, Social, Legal, and Regulatory, Environmental, Technological, Diversity)	Course Work	Professor's prerogative	Professor's prerogative	Professor's prerogative
	Internship Evaluation	Junior/Senior Year	Scale of 1 to 5: 1 = Poor and 5 = Outstanding	75% ≥ 3
	EBI Satisfaction Survey	Graduating Seniors	Scale of 1 to 7: 1 = Very Poor and 7 = Exceptional	Consistent improvement

[4] Appendix E contains only those parts of the CBA Skills Assessment Matrix that are relevant to the present discussion. The parts of the Matrix not included here are used to facilitate recording of results and recommended changes.

Appendix E (cont'd)

Desired Student Outcome	Assessment Tool	Assessment Timing	Measurement Scale	Goal
Behavioral Outcomes Communication	Course Work	Professor's prerogative	Professor's prerogative	Professor's prerogative
	Assessment Center	Fall of Sophomore Year	Various rating scales and checklists	Baseline
		Spring of Junior Year		Improvement from baseline
	Internship Evaluation	Junior/Senior Year	Scale of 1 to 5: 1 = Poor and 5 = Outstanding	Range of 75 % to 90% ≥3 depending upon skill
	EBI Satisfaction Survey	Graduating Seniors	Scale of 1 to 7: 1 = Very Poor and 7 = Exceptional	Consistent improvement
Information Technology	Course Work	Professor's prerogative	Professor's prerogative	Professor's prerogative
	Assessment Center	Fall of Sophomore Year	Various rating scales and checklists	Baseline
		Spring of Junior Year		Improvement from baseline
	Internship Evaluation	Junior/Senior Year	Scale of 1 to 5: 1 = Poor and 5 = Outstanding	Range of 75 % to 90% ≥3 depending upon skill
	EBI Satisfaction Survey	Graduating Seniors	Scale of 1 to 7: 1 = Very Poor and 7 = Exceptional	Consistent improvement
Problem Solving and Critical Thinking	Course Work	Professor's prerogative	Professor's prerogative	Professor's prerogative
	Assessment Center	Fall of Sophomore Year	Various rating scales and checklists	Baseline
		Spring of Junior Year		Improvement from baseline
	Internship Evaluation	Junior/Senior Year	Scale of 1 to 5: 1 = Poor and 5 = Outstanding	Range of 65 % to 85% ≥3 depending upon skill

Appendix E (cont'd)

Desired Student Outcome	Assessment Tool	Assessment Timing	Measurement Scale	Goal
Teamwork and Leadership	Course Work	Professor's prerogative	Professor's prerogative and peer evaluations	Professor's prerogative
	Assessment Center	Fall of Sophomore Year	Various rating scales and checklists	Baseline
		Spring of Junior Year		Improvement from baseline
	Internship Evaluation	Junior/Senior Year	Scale of 1 to 5: 1 = Poor and 5 = Outstanding	Range of 60 % to 95% ≥3 depending upon skill
	EBI Satisfaction Survey	Graduating Seniors	Scale of 1 to 7: 1 = Very Poor and 7 = Exceptional	Consistent improvement
Affective Outcomes Ethical Behavior and Values Awareness	Course Work	Professor's prerogative	Professor's prerogative	Professor's prerogative
	Assessment Center	Fall of Sophomore Year	Various rating scales and checklists	Baseline
		Spring of Junior Year		Improvement from baseline
	Internship Evaluation	Junior/Senior Year	Scale of 1 to 5: 1 = Poor and 5 = Outstanding	90% ≥ 4
	EBI Satisfaction Survey	Graduating Seniors	Scale of 1 to 7: 1 = Very Poor and 7 = Exceptional	Consistent improvement
Self Concept and Awareness	Course Work	Professor's prerogative	Professor's prerogative	Professor's prerogative
	Internship Evaluation	Junior/Senior Year	Scale of 1 to 5: 1 = Poor and 5 = Outstanding	Range of 70 % to 85% ≥3 depending upon skill
	EBI Satisfaction Survey	Graduating Seniors	Scale of 1 to 7: 1 = Very Poor and 7 = Exceptional	Consistent improvement
Attitudes	Course Work	Professor's prerogative	Professor's prerogative	Professor's prerogative
	Internship Evaluation	Junior/Senior Year	Scale of 1 to 5: 1 = Poor and 5 = Outstanding	70% ≥ 3

REFERENCES

Christ, L. F., Christ, M. Y., Graham, A. S., McCuddy, M. K., & Pirie, W. L. (2004). Using team learning in the classroom: Experiences and lessons. In R. Ottewill et al. (Eds.), *Educational Innovation in Economics and Business VIII: Technology, Pedagogy and Innovation* (pp.129-146). Dordrecht, The Netherlands: Kluwer Academic Publishers.

Christ, M., Clark, A., McCuddy, M., Pirie, W., Schroeder, D., & Strasser, S. (1999). But I am a "people person" or how to measure behavioral skills and foster professional development. In *Proceedings of The 5th International Conference of the Decision Sciences Institute "Integrating Technology and Human Decisions: Global Bridges Into the 21st Century"* (pp. 268-272). Athens, Greece.

Gainen, J., & Locatelli, P. (1995). *Assessment for the New Curriculum: A Guide for Professional Accounting Programs.* Sarasota, FL: AAA and AECC.

Herring, H. C., & Izard, C. D. (1992). Outcomes assessment of accounting majors. *Issues in Accounting Education*, 1-17.

Kerby, D., & Weber, S. (2000). Linking mission objectives to an assessment plan. *Journal of Education for Business*, 202-209.

Kimmell, S. L., Marquette, R. P., & Olsen, D. H. (1998). *Outcomes assessment programs: Historical perspective and state of the art. Issues in Accounting Education*, 851-868.

Kottke, J. L., & Shultz, K. S. (1997). Using an assessment center as a developmental tool for graduate students: A demonstration. *Journal of Social Behavior and Personality*, *12,* 5, 289-302.

McCuddy, M. K., Pirie, W. L., Christ, M. Y., Mainstone, L. E., Schroeder, D. L., & Strasser, S. E. (2000). The assessment center: Global issue and local responses. In L. Borghans et al. (Eds.), *Educational Innovation in Economics and Business V: Business Education for the Changing Workplace* (pp. 383-398). Dordrecht, The Netherlands: Kluwer Academic Publishers.

Chapter 17

STUDENT CHARACTERISTICS AND ACADEMIC SUCCESS:
An Econometric Study of the Performance of "Equity Groups"

Luke B. Connelly
Centre of National Research on Disability and Rehabilitation Medicine (CONROD), The University of Queensland, Australia

1. INTRODUCTION

Studies of the relationship between student characteristics and academic performance occupy considerable space in the education research literature. A focal point is the academic achievement of students from disadvantaged social, economic, cultural, and demographic groups, compared to that of their peers.[1] Research and policy interest in this issue show no signs of waning. Recently, for example, American civil rights leader Robert Moses argued that (math) literacy "...in urban and rural communities throughout [the USA] is an issue as urgent as the lack of Black voters in Mississippi was in 1961" (Moses, 2001, cited in Schoenfeld, 2002, p.13).

Studies of student characteristics and attainment represent an important source of information for educational institutions. By identifying student groups that systematically out- or under-perform their peers, these   present education providers (e.g., universities) and funders (e.g., governments, private firms, etc.) with a mechanism for assessing the adequacy of (i) their entry requirements and (ii) the services provided to students admitted to their programs. As Lewis (1994) has argued, these issues have both efficiency and equity dimensions.

---

[1] Hereinafter, such groups of students will be referred to as "equity groups."

R.G.Milter et al. (eds.), Educational Innovation in Economics and Business IX, 317–340.
©2004 *Springer. Printed in the Netherlands.*

The problem of efficient entry and student management processes, although complex in practice, is conceptually straightforward. If the probability of success of students with different characteristics, levels, and types of educational attainment can be ascertained, admission procedures and student support mechanisms can be fine-tuned so that the organization's goals are met at least cost. Of course, this efficiency concern is closely related to equity considerations. Institutions that are more efficient at identifying differentials in the performance of student sub-groups may also be more efficient providers of support services for those groups.

It is not the purpose of this chapter to critique the normative criteria upon which "equity" matters in education have been (or ought to be) discussed. This chapter is concerned with empirical analyses of a positive, analytical, kind. However, the research is motivated by, *inter alia*, a desire to inform an ongoing policy debate about equity issues in Higher Education. In this study, attention is directed to the relative success of students in equity groups and those in the general student population.

Two comments about the nature of this study are warranted. First, a limitation of the work is that it is concerned only with an analysis of outcomes, as measured by academic performance, in a particular course unit. Conclusions about the success, or otherwise, of programs that are designed to assist equity groups may be inferred from work such as this, but other methods can also be used. For example, the following measures are routinely used in the Australian Higher Education system:

- "Access": the proportion of commencing students in identified equity groups.
- "Participation": the proportion of an equity group's participation as a ratio of the expected representation in the relevant population.
- "Representation": the number of students who belong to an equity group, as a percentage of the student population.
- "Retention": the ratio of the Apparent Retention Rate (ARR) of the equity group to the ARR of other students. (The ARR is calculated as the ratio of students who re-enroll as a proportion of those who were enrolled the previous year, minus completions.)
- "Success": the ratio of the Student Progress Rate (SPR) of the equity group to the SPR of other students. The SPR is calculated as the ratio of "equivalent full-time student units" (EFTSU) passed, to EFTSU undertaken (Department of Education, Training and Youth Affairs, 2000).

Measures of "access," "participation," and "representation" are relevant to the admission procedures and policies of the university; while the measures of "retention" and "success" are pertinent to university policies that are designed to improve the rate at which students from equity groups remain in, and successfully complete, their courses.[2]

Higher Education institutions in Australia routinely collect data on the measures outlined above, for six equity groups (indigenous, non English-speaking background, rural and isolated background, low socio-economic background, and disability) that were identified, in 1990, by the (then) Commonwealth Department of Education, Employment, and Training Affairs (DEET) (Department of Education, Employment, and Training 1990). Summary data on equity groups and the measures listed above are published by the Commonwealth Department of Education, Science, and Training. See, in particular, Department of Education, Science, and Training (2002), for recent summary statistics for the sector. Also see Department of Education, Training, and Youth Affairs (1999) for descriptive, time series, data on equity groups in Higher Education. Batson, Sharp, Ramsay, and Mackinnon (2001) also provide a recent and quite detailed, descriptive study of the participation and access of equity groups in Higher Education at the bachelors (honors/pass) level.

If descriptive data on measures such as "success" (see above) are commonly available, why is it important to analyze student characteristics and performance? There are several reasons research of an analytical kind is important. First, aggregate measures of performance may disguise important detail and hide inefficiencies at the margin; this is a manifestation of the so-called "aggregation problem." A second, and related, point is that aggregating students as "equity groups" may disguise the true source(s) of inequality. This is, essentially, an argument that (i) the disadvantage to which members of equity groups may be subject is a latent (i.e., unobserved/unobservable) variable, and (ii) that grouping students on the basis of some grossly-specified characteristic, although simplifying, may sometimes be too simplistic. Additionally, the possibility that inequality may be compounded by the confluence of more than one disadvantageous characteristic (see, e.g., Essen & Wedge, 1982; Sammons, Kysel & Mortimore, 1983; Sammons, 1995) may be neglected when student data are aggregated.

Analyzing student characteristics and performance at a more disaggregate level may produce insights that are missed by aggregate, univariate analysis. Third, concentrating on groups of students that have been identified as targets of equity initiatives ignores the potential for unidentified inequalities to persist elsewhere in the student population.

---

[2] Chubin and Malcolm (1996) have proposed a taxonomy of intervention programs to improve the success of students in equity groups (Goodell, 1998).

Finally, inequality is not a static phenomenon: inequalities may widen, narrow, or disappear over time. Repeated research efforts in this field are worthwhile for that reason alone.

The work in this chapter is organized as follows. Section 2 provides a brief summary of some literature on predictors of academic performance, focusing on Australian studies. In Section 3, the data, methods, and results are presented, and Section 4 presents some conclusions.

2. PREDICTORS OF PERFORMANCE: AN OVERVIEW OF SOME EXISTING LITERATURE

This section presents a brief overview of the existing literature on predictors of student performance. The focus of the literature review is on multivariate studies on Higher Education in Australia. Of course, many of the equity groups identified in this study (e.g., indigenous people, people from non English-speaking backgrounds, and so on) are analogous to those identified in other parts of the literature. These similarities of kind, however, belie some of the important differences. Specifically, the confluence of a different set of social, cultural, economic, and institutional arrangements, for any given country, is likely to be at least as important as the themes that unify the international literature on equity groups in education. Thus, the emphasis of this review is on the results of empirical Australian studies. Furthermore, since performance, not participation is the focus of the empirical work presented here, this focus is also adopted for the literature review.

A useful starting point for this review is with Department of Education, Training, and Youth Affairs' (1999) recent summary of the performance of equity groups in Australian Higher Education. Its empirical study involved the production of descriptive statistics for cross-sectional state, and national Australian data, on equity group performance (access, participation, success, and retention) for 1997, as well as for participation rates over the period 1991-1997. The Department concluded that, while low participation rates for some groups (*viz.* low socioeconomic status; rural; and isolated, backgrounds) were of concern:

> the success and retention rates of members of equity groups are, in general (excluding the Indigenous and isolated groups), on a par with, or only slightly below, those for other (non-equity group) students. This indicates that once members of those equity groups are in the university system they can, with appropriate support, achieve outcomes little

different to those of the rest of the student body (Department of Education, Training, and Youth Affairs, 1999, p.61).

This conclusion, while based on detailed descriptive data, was univariate in nature.

The most recent, detailed, multivariate, Australian study of characteristics and tertiary education outcomes was undertaken by Professor Lewis (1994). He employed data derived from the student records of students who enrolled for study at the University of Wollongong in 1990, 1991, 1992, and 1993. In addition to simple correlation analyses, Lewis (1994) analyzed the relationships between student characteristics and (i) the mean aggregate mark (MAM) obtained (measured as the mean of the percentage result obtained by each student, in each course unit); and (ii) the probability of passing 75 percent or more of the credit points attempted. For the former variable, he employed ordinary least-squares (OLS) multiple regression analysis and, for the latter, a binomial logit model was used. Apart from age, the independent variables were mainly dichotomous, and were generated from measures of prior educational attainment/university entrance scores, school type (state/catholic/other private; and single sex/coeducational), country of birth, birthplace of mother, birthplace of father, language spoken at home, age, gender, disability, faculty of enrollment, address during semester, and whether or not the student identifies an Aborigine or Torres Strait Islander.

Lewis (1994) estimated both models on the results obtained in the first year of study, and for all years of study.[3] Briefly, the results suggest that, *ceteris paribus*:

- females substantially outperform males in the first year of study, and the gap between females and males widens further in subsequent years of study;[4]
- school leavers perform at a level almost identical to the entire student body;
- non school leavers perform at differing levels - non school leavers with a partially completed degree from another institution do particularly well;
- the results of students admitted through special entry (special consideration) and Aboriginal and Torres Strait Islander (ATSI) special entry, were consistently below the norm;

---

[3] For the 1993 cohort, data on only the first year of study were available.
[4] Furthermore, even in fields of study that are non-traditional for women, females outperformed males.

- students admitted via other modes of entry, including those from Tertiary and Further Education (TAFE) colleges perform at, or close to, the university average level;
- higher entrance scores are positively correlated with performance;
- students who speak English at home generally have an advantage over students from non English-speaking backgrounds (NESBs)[5];
- place of birth has no statistically significant impact on academic performance;
- the average marks of students with disabilities are equal to those of other students, but the likelihood of such students achieving the same pass rate is slightly lower;
- age has little effect on performance amongst school leavers but, amongst non school leavers, older students do better;
- students from government and coeducational schools outperform those from other schools (although it should be noted that Lewis describes the evidence on this matter as "weak"); and
- the results achieved by local students are typically better than those of non-local students.

The detailed work by Lewis also contains a comprehensive review of the state of the Australian literature on these issues as at the time of his study. Since a review of the literature revealed no advances on his work, interested readers are referred to Lewis (1994) for a discussion of the findings of earlier empirical studies and to the bibliography of the current paper for some of those sources. Our focus now shifts to the empirical analysis.

3.   DATA, METHODS, AND RESULTS

3.1   Data

This study employs unit record data on students and their performance (as measured by a final percentage mark) in a first-year, undergraduate course unit in economics, undertaken by students at a large, urban,

---

[5] Apparently, the *expression nouveau* for a person from "non English speaking-background (NESB)" is "culturally and linguistically diverse (CALD)." Whatever the etymology of this recent terminological innovation, we stick to NESB in this paper, to avoid confusion. (The acronym for the "censored least absolute deviations (CLAD)" estimator (see, e.g., Johnston & DiNardo, 1997), which is used some econometric work with qualitative dependent variables is, perhaps, a bit "too close for comfort.")

Australian university. The course unit involves two hours of lectures and one hour of tutorial time, per week, for 12 weeks. The total time input recommended to students enrolled in the unit is 120 hours. The unit is assessed using an invigilated final examination as well as several optional items of assessment.[6]

De-identified data on the population of students enrolled in the unit in Semester 1, 1999 and Semester 1, 2000 were obtained. Approximately 1000 students enrolled in each semester. In this paper, data from the 2000 cohort are analyzed. The total number of students who enrolled in, and completed, the assessment for this semester, was 972.[7] The quinquennial *Australian Census of Population and Housing* (Australian Bureau of Statistics, 1997) was also used to produce an income proxy. The income proxies were calculated by matching data on the student's postcode to mean and median income data from the *Census*. This is a crude approach to the approximation of student incomes. However, it is arguably the best approach currently available. (More will be said about these particular variables in the following section, on methodology.)

The variables described in Table 1 were generated using data from (i) student enrollment records; (ii) student academic records, and (iii) the 1996 *Census*. Three points of clarification are worthwhile regarding the data described in Table 1. First, all variables other than MARK and AGE are dichotomous. The prefix DV ("Dummy Variable") denotes all binary variables. The means for such variables are hence the population proportions. For example, the mean of DVPASS is 0.74, which indicates that 74 percent of students passed the unit in this semester. This proportion suggests a relatively high failure rate in the unit. This is somewhat misleading: DVPASS takes a value of unity for students who achieved a final percentage of 50, or greater. However, students with final marks of 47 percent, or greater, may also be considered to have "passed" the unit. In the university concerned, a 7-point grade scale is used, *viz.* 1 (Low Fail), 2 (Fail), 3 (Pass Conceded), 4 (Pass), 5 (Credit), 6 (Distinction), and 7 (High

---

[6] The optional items include an optional essay, for which there are several alternative topics and submission dates; and an optional invigilated mid-semester test. The summative role of these optional items (which also play a formative role), is contingent: results on optional items are only employed in to calculate the final grade if the percentages achieved exceed the percentage achieved on the final test. Thus, the ultimate weight of the final examination depends on student participation in, and performance on, the final examination. The minimum possible weight of the final examination in the semester of study was 60 percent, and the maximum possible weight was 100 percent.

[7] In this chapter, only the results of students who undertook the final examination for the unit are analyzed, i.e., students who enrolled in, but subsequently withdrew from, the unit are excluded from the analysis.

Distinction). The definition of success that will be emphasized in most of the
subsequent analyses is consistent with the attainment of a grade of 4, or
greater. The variable "DVPASSCON" invokes a less exclusive definition of
a "pass": it takes a value of unity for students who received a grade of 3, or
greater.[8]

Table 1. Variable Names, Descriptions and Descriptive Statistics

Variable	Description	Mean	Standard Deviation
MARK	The final mark in the course unit, expressed as a percentage.	57.69	16.85
DVPASS	The student obtained a mark of 50 percent, or greater.	0.74	0.43
DVPASSCON	The student obtained a mark of 47 percent, or greater.	0.80	0.40
AGE	Age, in years.	21.59	5.44
DVAES	Admitted via "alternative entry scheme."[(i)]	0.07	0.26
DVATSI	Aboriginal and/or Torres Strait Islander.	0.01	0.09
DVBUS	Enrolled in the business/commerce degree.[(ii)]	0.77	0.42
DVCOMPTAFE	Has a TAFE[(iii)] qualification.	0.03	0.18
DVCOMPTERT	Has a university qualification.	0.08	0.27
DVFEM	Is female.	0.63	0.48
DVFIRSTSEM	Is undertaking his/her first semester of university study.	0.61	0.49
DVINCOMPTAFE	Has an incomplete TAFE[(iii)] course attempt.	0.03	0.18
DVINCOMPTERT	Has an incomplete university course attempt.	0.19	0.39
DVNESB	Language spoken at home is not English.[(iv)]	0.08	0.27
DVORIGIN	Was born in a country other than Australia.	0.22	0.41
DVOTHER	Student was admitted upon successful completion a foundation program.[(v)]	0.01	0.08
DVPACIS	Citizen of a Pacific island.	0.02	0.14
DVLOWINCOME	Admitted via a program for low income candidates.[(vi)]	0.03	0.17
DVREPEAT	Is repeating the unit (due to a previous, failed, attempt).	0.09	0.29
DVSCHOOL	Is a school leaver.	0.51	0.50

[8] The Conceded Pass category allows students who achieve a score in a narrow band below
the pass level (typically 47-49 percent) to continue study without repeating the unit, and
credit for the unit is given. In Bachelor programs, this policy applies to a maximum of
three course units. For the fourth, and subsequent conceded passes, credit is withheld, so
the student must repeat the unit or, if the unit is not a compulsory component of the award,
successfully complete another one. In the semester concerned, 54 students (i.e.,
approximately 5.5 percent of the class) were awarded a Pass Conceded.

| MEANINC | Mean weekly income proxy (AUD1996) for the student's postcode of residence. | $335.44 | $67.52 |
| MEDIANINC | Median income proxy (AUD1996) for the student's postcode of residence. | $330.90 | $53.74 |

Source: Data on characteristics were derived from de-identified student university records for 2000. Income proxies were generated using these data, plus data from the *Australian Census of Population and Housing* (Australian Bureau of Statistics 1997).

Notes:

   i.   DVAES: the "alternative entry scheme" allows entry to some students who lack the usual educational prerequisites. Eligibility for entry is determined with reference to demonstrated ability, as manifested by, e.g., the employment history of a candidate.

   ii. DVBUS: a value of unity is assigned only to students who are enrolled in the single, undergraduate, business degree (e.g., double- degree candidates are assigned a value of zero, for this binary variable).

   iii. TAFE refers to "Technical and Further Education." (TAFE institutions are non-university providers of Higher Education.)

   iv. DVNESB: the student is deemed to be from a non English-speaking background (NESB), when the language spoken at home is not English.

   v.   DVOTHER: students was admitted directly from a foundation business program for students from non-English speaking backgrounds, upon successful completion of that program (and hence demonstration of sufficient English language skills to progress to the core program).

   vi. DVLOWINCOME: eligibility for special entry under this scheme involves an assessment of disadvantage on the grounds of low income and/or lower levels of access to financial assistance to undertake study at university.

The statistics in Table 1 provide useful information that can be used to construct a class profile. They allow, for example, a demographic profile of the class to be created: the average age of the class is approximately 22 years, 77 percent of the group is enrolled in a Business/Commerce degree, and 63 percent of the class is female.

A cultural profile of the class can also be constructed: 22 percent of the class was born abroad (DVORIGIN), and about eight percent speaks a language other than English, at home. Although not reported in this table, the data on students born abroad show that students of Asian origin comprise the largest group of international students (approximately 10 percent of the class). The proportions of students from other regions are typically relatively small. For example, the proportion of students from the proximate region (the Pacific Islands, including New Zealand) comprise a further four percent of the student body. The proportion of ATSI students in the class is quite small (0.01).

The educational profile of the class is as follows: 61 percent of students in this group were enrolled in their first semester of study at university. Relatively few students had a prior tertiary qualification (three percent had a TAFE qualification and eight percent had a university degree), but 19 percent had undertaken previous (incomplete) study at a university. Just over one-half of the class were school leavers, and nine percent of students enrolled were repeating the unit.

3.2   Methods

The empirical work in this paper involves the estimation of binomial logit models (see, e.g., Greene, 2000), in which the dependent variables are DVPASS and DVPASSCON. Another measure of the academic outcome, *viz.* the final mark (MARK), is also used ordinary least-squares (OLS), multiple regression analysis. With the exception of DVSCHOOL, the remaining variables in Table 1 constitute the independent variables for the general forms of each of the models.[9]

The analytical emphasis in this paper is on identifying systematic differences in the probability of academic success, as measured by the probability of the student passing the unit. Given the binary nature of the dependent variables DVPASS and DVPASSCON, simple linear regression on these variables is inappropriate for several reasons - not least of which are the production of negative variances and the possibility of generating predictions with nonsense probabilities (i.e., probabilities outside the 0-1 range) (Greene, 2000). Thus, linear probability model (LPM) results are not reported in this paper, even as a curiosity. Rather, a specification that handles the requirements of binary dependent variables is employed. The specification is explained below.

The probability of (say) passing can be modeled as follows:

$$\Pr(DVPASS = 1 | x_i \beta = 1 - F(-x'_i \beta) \tag{1}$$

(Lilien, Sueyoshi, Wilkins, Kawakatsu, Startz, Hall, Engle, Liang, Ellsworth & Noh, J. (2002) where F is any monotonically-increasing, continuous, function that maps from real numbers to the 0-1 interval (Davidson & MacKinnon, 1993).[10] There are, of course, numerous possibilities for the choice of F, but the common choices are the normal and the logistic distributions. The former choice results in the probit model and the latter, in the logit model. The relevant distributions for the error term are as follows:

---

[9] DVSCHOOL is not included explicitly in the models, because school leavers constitute the reference group for the purposes of examining the impact of alternative modes of entry. See Gujarati (1995), for example, for a discussion of the use of independent dummy variables and the "dummy variable trap."

[10]   It follows that the probability of not passing is: $\Pr(DVPASS = 0 | x_i \beta = F(-x'_i \beta)$.

Probit:
$$\Pr(DVPASS_i = 1 | x_i \beta) = 1 - e^{-x'\beta} / (1 + e^{-x'\beta}) = e^{x'\beta} / (1 + e^{x'\beta}) \qquad (2)$$

Logit:
$$\Pr(DVPASS_i = 1 | x_i \beta) = 1 - \Phi(-x'_i \beta) = \Phi(x'_i \beta) \qquad (3)$$

The choice between these models can sometimes result in different predictions from the same data set. However, the differences are typically trivial, in practice and, as Greene (2000, p.815) argues, "...it is difficult to justify the choice of one distribution or another on theoretical grounds." Empirical illustrations of the minor nature of differences generated by probit and logit applications are provided by, *inter alia*, Gujarati (2003), Johnston and DiNardo (1997), and Greene (2000). Moreover, the Monte Carlo work of Morimune (1979) shows that assuming the logistic form for F when the true distribution is normal, produces little difference in parameter estimates and their precision (Gourieroux, 2000). There is, of course, a scale factor: in a widely-reported study Amemiya (1981) found, by trial and error, that multiplying probit estimates by 1.6 provides a good approximation of the logit parameter estimates. This approximation tends to work best at the center of the distribution (i.e., where $F=0.5$) - when one moves further from the center of the distribution the ratio of logit, to probit, coefficients gets larger (Greene, 2000). Thus, in unbalanced samples (i.e., when the number of "1s" and "0s" in the sample is quite uneven), scale factors of 1.7 or 1.8 may provide more accurate approximations.

Given the virtual indifference, on theoretical grounds, between the probit and logit specifications, this paper employs the logit for mathematical convenience.[11] The maximum likelihood estimation (MLE) method (Davidson & MacKinnon, 1993) is employed. The first-order conditions of the resulting likelihood function are non-linear, so an iterative estimation algorithm is required. This study employs the Quadratic Hill Climbing approach, due to Goldfeld, Quandt, & Trotter (1966). (The advantages of this method are discussed briefly by Lilien et al. (2002), and Greene (2000) also provides a useful overview.)

Estimation of the models is undertaken by employing a general-to-specific, or "Hendry" (Pagan, 1995) approach to modeling. Specifically, the general form of the model is estimated first, and a more parsimonious model

---

[11] Indeed, Johnston, & DiNardo (1997, p.431) even go as far summarizing the problem of choosing between the LPM, logit and probit models by stating, "In sum, the key issue seems to be convenience."

is derived by subsequent omission of the redundant variables. The parsimonious model is then used to compute the marginal effects and estimate the probabilities of success for students with various characteristics.

A final point about the techniques employed here is relevant. The purpose of the paper is to test the equality, or otherwise, of the performance of students with different attributes. Thus, the empirical approach is "positive" (not normative) in nature. Although this focus on the equality/inequality of outcomes is not uncommon, it is nevertheless worth making explicit the following point: inequalities (e.g., unequal outcomes) constitute inequities (e.g., unfair outcomes) only for a specific conception of equity. Specifically, if one conceives of **equal** educational attainment, by all groups, as the only **fair** outcome, equality and equity become the same phenomenon. However, this conception may have quite different empirical implications to, for example, the (related) proposition that individuals be afforded equal opportunities to succeed.[12] With the exception of the conclusions, judgments of this kind are generally left to the reader in this study. Yet, it is worthwhile to bear the inherent reference to equality in mind, throughout. Now, attention is directed to the estimated results.

3.3   Results

The general form of the models estimated on DVPASS and DVPASSCON included all of the independent variables listed in Table 1. A single measure of income (MEDIANINC or MEANINC) was used for each model to test the sensitivity of the results to the choice of income proxy. Thus, four specifications of the logit model were estimated. In addition, cross products of both age (AGE) and income (MEANINC) with the dummies for four equity groups *viz.* DVATSI, DVFEM, DVNESB, and DVORIGIN were employed, to allow for interactions between these variables. Quadratic terms were also entered for age (AGE^2) and income ($MEANINC^2$, $MEDIANINC^2$).

3.3.1   Results from four general logit models

Estimates for the general specifications of the four different logit models are presented in Table 2. Columns (2) and (3) of Table 2 present the logit results for two models in which the dependent variable is DVPASS, while Columns (4) and (5) present the results from two models in which the

---

[12] For an introductory discussion of the various conceptions of equity and social justice see, e.g., Cullis and Jones (1992).

dependent variable is DVPASSCON. The independent variables have been grouped in Table 2, according to a loose taxonomy, *viz. Demographic Variables, Income Proxies, Social and Cultural Variables, Education Variables, Mode of Entry Variables,* and *Interactive Variables.* These categories are designed to facilitate a discussion of the coefficients estimated for each model. However, before the coefficients are discussed, it is worthwhile to provide an overview of the performance of these models.

Table 2. Results of Four General Binomial Logit Model Specifications

Independent Variables	Dependent Variable is DVPASS		Dependent Variable is DVPASSCON	
	Income Proxy is MEANINC	Income Proxy is MEDIANINC	Income Proxy is MEANINC	Income Proxy is MEDIANINC
(1)	(2)	(3)	(4)	(5)
Constant	-0.38	2.02	0.98	3.71
	(-0.14)	(0.62)	(0.33)	(0.98)
Demographic Variables				
AGE	-0.007	-0.10	-0.06	-0.19
	(-0.06)	(-0.68)	(-0.49)	(-1.10)
AGE^2	0.0002	0.0003	0.0003	0.006
	(0.14)	(0.26)	(0.19)	(0.39)
DVFEM	-2.57**	-3.47***	-2.64**	-3.71***
	(-2.26)	(-2.67)	(-2.14)	(-2.58)
Income Proxies[i]				
INCOME	0.01	0.005	0.01	0.004
	(1.19)	(0.39)	(0.96)	(0.31)
$INCOME^2$	-0.00001	-0.00002	-0.00002	-0.00002
	(-1.55)	(-1.00)	(-1.51)	(-1.25)
Social and Cultural Variables				
DVATSI	-0.05	-782.26	-0.36	-787.69
	(-0.01)	(-0.00)	(-0.05)	(-0.00)
DVNESB	-1.63	-0.03	-2.10	-0.68
	(-0.77)	(-0.01)	(-0.81)	(-0.23)
DVORIGIN	0.05	0.55	0.10	0.23
	(0.04)	(0.38)	(0.08)	(0.15)
Education Variables				
DVBUS	0.06	0.07	-0.11	-0.09
	(0.30)	(0.34)	(-0.50)	(-042)
DVCOMPTAFE	-0.05	-0.03	0.13	0.13
	(-0.11)	(-0.07)	(0.27)	(0.26)
DVCOMPTERT	-1.14***	-1.11***	-1.28***	-1.29***
	(-3.73)	(-3.71)	(-4.09)	(-4.19)

Table 2. (cont'd)

Independent Variables	Dependent Variable is DVPASS		Dependent Variable is DVPASSCON	
	Income Proxy is MEANINC	Income Proxy is MEDIANINC	Income Proxy is MEANINC	Income Proxy is MEDIANINC
(1)	(2)	(3)	(4)	(5)
Education Variables (cont'd)				
DVINCOMPTAFE	-1.18***	-1.17***	-1.18***	-1.18***
	(-2.91)	(-2.91)	(-2.81)	(-2.82)
DVINCOMPTERT	-0.51**	-0.49**	-0.31	-0.30
	(-2.40)	(-2.31)	(-1.31)	-1.27
DVREPEAT	-1.33***	-1.35***	-1.24***	-1.25***
	(-4.84)	(-4.95)	(-4.34)	(-4.39)
Mode of Entry Variables				
DVAES	-0.003	-0.02	-0.02	-0.04
	(-0.00)	(-0.04)	(-0.05)	(-0.09)
DVLOWINCOME	-1.00**	-1.22***	-0.89*	-1.07***
	(-2.14)	(-2.82)	(-1.86)	(-2.43)
DVOTHER	-0.002	-0.13	30.15	34.15
	(-0.00)	(-0.12)	(0.00)	(0.000)
Interactive Variables				
AGE*ATSI	0.0005	-45.45	-0.009	-46.09
	(0.02)	(-0.00)	(-0.04)	(-0.00)
AGE*DVFEM	0.05	0.05	0.07*	0.08**
	(1.39)	(1.61)	(1.83)	(2.08)
AGE*DVORIGIN	-0.004	0.0004	-0.01	-0.003
	(-0.12)	(0.01)	(-0.18)	(-0.06)
AGE*INCOME	-0.000005	0.0002	0.0001	0.0004
	(-0.02)	(0.72)	(0.45)	(1.17)
INCOME*DVATSI	-0.0004	5.61	0.0001	5.67
	(-0.03)	(0.00)	(0.01)	(0.00)
INCOME*DVNESB	0.002	0.03	0.0002	-0.01
	(0.46)	(0.35)	(0.05)	(-0.01)
INCOME*DVFEM	0.046	0.01**	0.004	0.01*
	(1.39)	(2.23)	(1.41)	1.85

Table 2. (cont'd)

Model Statistics				
Log likelihood	-501.26	-498.04	-442.60	-437.55
Restricted log likelihood	-553.08	-553.08	-487.22	-487.22
Log ratio index (LRI)	0.09	0.10	0.09	0.10
LR statistic (27 degrees of freedom)	103.64***	110.09***	89.24***	99.35***
Probability (LR statistic)	0.00	0.00	0.00	0.00
Akaike Information Criterion (AIC)	1.09	1.08	0.97	0.96
Schwartz Criterion (SC)	1.23	1.22	1.11	1.10
Hannan-Quinn Criterion (HQC)	1.15	1.14	1.02	1.01

Source: As for Table 1.
Notes:
   i.   Two income proxies were employed in the production of the coefficients reported for the *Income Variables* and *Interactive Variables* that involve an income measure (e.g., INCOME*AGE). The coefficients reported in Columns (2) and (4) employ the mean income proxy (MEANINC) and those that are reported in Columns (3) and (5) employ the median income proxy (MEDIANINC). See the definitions provided in Table 1. All other variables are as defined in Table 1.
   ii.   One, two and three asterisks denote statistical significance at the 10, five, and one percent levels, respectively.
   iii.   Data in parentheses are *Z*-statistics.

The "Model Statistics" that are reported in Table 2 provide some information about the overall performance of each model. Perhaps the most useful information, at this point, is provided by the likelihood ratio (LR)-statistic. The LR-statistic is the analog of the *F*-statistic for linear regression models: it tests the overall statistical significance of the model under the joint null hypothesis that all slope coefficients other than the constant, are zero (Lilien et al., 2002). This hypothesis is rejected at the one percent level for each of the four models.

The Likelihood Ratio Index (LRI) is also reported in Table 2. This statistic is calculated by taking the ratio of the maximized values of the log likelihood function and restricted log likelihood function from unity. The LRI takes values between 0 and 1. The LRI is sometimes referred to as the analog of the R^2 of linear regression models (indeed it is sometimes called the McFadden R^2; see, for example, Lilien , Sueyoshi, Ellsworth et al., 1997). However, notwithstanding such analogies, and suggestions that a unit value of the LRI implies a "perfect fit," Greene (2000, p.831-32) warns that "...[LRI] values between 0 and 1 have no natural interpretation." Furthermore, it is worthwhile remembering that the coefficients of the logit are not chosen to maximize, as they are in the linear regression model, a particular measure of fit (Greene, 2000). For subsequent estimations, additional measures of fit will also be employed, and the information criteria reported in Table 2 will also be considered in that context. However, it is first worthwhile to consider the estimated coefficients in more detail, with a view to deriving more parsimonious models of the relationships of interest.

An important focus, at this point, is on the results produced by different specifications of the relationship between learning outcomes and student characteristics. There are at least two meaningful ways of comparing the coefficients in Table 2. Comparing the coefficients in Columns (2) and (4) with those of Columns (3) and (5) constitutes an analysis of the sensitivity of the results to the definition of a "passing" grade. Comparing the coefficients in Columns (2) and (3) with those of Columns (4) and (5) constitutes an analysis of the sensitivity of the regression results to a change in the income proxy that is used.

The coefficients and Z-statistics on the *Demographic Variables* show that AGE and AGE^2 are statistically unimportant, but the coefficient on the gender variable, DVFEM, suggests that the probability of passing is lower for females. This result is statistically significant at the five or ten percent level and is consistently contrary to the findings produced by Lewis (1994) and other authors. Both the magnitudes and the statistical significance of the coefficient on DVFEM are greater for the models that employ a median income proxy (MEDIANINC), than those that employ a mean income proxy. It is noteworthy that the magnitudes and statistical significance of the coefficients on DVFEM (i.e., comparing Columns (2) and (4); and Columns (3) and (5)) are, however, quite insensitive to the specification of the dependent variable.

Regardless of the specification that is invoked, the coefficients on *Income Proxies* are both small in magnitude and statistically insignificant. However, the quadratic term ($INCOME^2$) on models that employ mean income (MEANINC) as the income proxy measure has a coefficient that is statistically significant at the 16 percent level (DVPASS model, Column (2)) and 16 percent (DVPASSCON model, Column (4)) levels.

Despite considerable numerical differences in the coefficients on *Social and Cultural Variables*, none of the coefficients (DVATSI, DVNESB, DVORIGIN) is statistically significant (even at the forty percent level). Note, in particular, that the numerically-large results on DVATSI reported in Columns (3) and (5) have Z-statistics of zero (and associated probabilities of approximately 1.00). These are interesting results: students from Aboriginal and Torres Strait Islander backgrounds, students from Non English-Speaking Backgrounds, and students born abroad, appear to have no worse chance of passing this first-year economics unit than do other students.

The coefficients derived for *Education Variables* repeat a similar theme: the different specifications do not result in any changes of sign; and the magnitudes of the coefficients are similar. The results suggest that students enrolled in a business/commerce degree (DVBUS) have no better, or worse, chance of passing than students enrolled in other courses. Students who have completed a TAFE qualification (DVCOMPTAFE) also appear to do no better or worse than school leavers. A surprising result is that students who have a tertiary qualification (DVCOMPTERT) also appear to have a lower probability of passing than do other students. Students who repeat the unit (DVREPEAT) have a statistically-significantly lower probability of passing, regardless of whether the criterion of DVPASS or DVPASSCON is employed.

The *Mode of Entry* variables suggest that students admitted via the Alternative Entry Scheme (DVAES) and the foundation scheme (DVOTHER) do no better or worse than school-leavers. However, students admitted via the scheme for low-income students (DVLOWINCOME) have a lower probability of passing, and the result is statistically significant, regardless of which definition of "pass" (DVPASS, DVPASSCON) is invoked.

Finally, few of the *Interactive Variables* have statistically significant coefficients. The exceptions are coefficients on two of the cross-products with the gender dummy, DVFEM. When DVPASSCON is the dependent variable, the coefficients on AGE*DVFEM (Columns (4) and (5)) are statistically significant at the 10 percent level, but are statistically insignificant for the more exclusive (DVPASS) definition of "pass." For the models that employ the median income as a proxy (MEDIANINC), but not for the mean income (MEANINC) models, the cross-product term INCOME*DVFEM also generates statistically significant results at the five and 10 percent levels. These results may suggest that the relationship between academic success and gender are not as simple as may sometimes be assumed.

3.3.2 Results from the estimation of four parsimonious logit models

The first estimation step for the specific forms of the models was to removing all variables, other than income, for which the estimated coefficients were statistically insignificant at the 15-percent level. See Table 2. Subsequently, the equations were re-estimated and variables (other than income) that were statistically insignificant at the ten percent level were excluded. The income proxies were retained in all specifications due to an expectation that measurement error and, in particular, the compression of the variance of the income measures (due to the use of means and medians, instead of unit-level incomes), might be expected to reduce its statistical significance, *ceteris paribus*. The sequential approach of exclusion for redundant variables was designed to account for the possible sensitivity of significance levels for individual coefficients that were statistically significant at the 15-percent level, to changes to the model specification. However, no substantial changes in statistical significance materialized and hence no additional variables were retained as a result of the sequential approach.

Table 3. Results of Four Parsimonious Binomial Logit Model Specifications

Independent Variables	Dependent Variable is DVPASS		Dependent Variable is DVPASSCON	
	Income Proxy is MEANINC	Income Proxy is MEDIANINC	Income Proxy is MEANINC	Income Proxy is MEDIANINC
(1)	(2)	(3)	(4)	(5)
Constant	0.01	0.84	-1.27	0.48
	(0.00)	(0.40)	(-0.79)	(0.21)
Demographic Variables				
DVFEM	-1.57**	-3.19***	-1.04**	-1.36**
	(-1.84)	(-2.82)	(-1.92)	(-5.14)
Income Proxies				
INCOME	0.01	0.01	0.02*	0.01
	(1.11)	(0.57)	(1.82)	(0.80)
$INCOME^2$	-0.00002	-0.00001	-0.00002*	-0.00002
	(-1.33)	(0.43)	(-1.69)	(-0.99)
Social and Cultural Variables				
Nil.	-	-	-	-
Education Variables				
DVCOMPTERT	-1.22***	-1.21***	-1.34***	-1.36***
	(-4.57)	(-4.54)	(-5.06)	(-5.14)
DVINCOMPTAFE				
	-1.09***	-1.08***	-1.06**	-1.07***
DVINCOMPTERT	(-2.84)	(-2.80)	(-2.68)	(-2.70)
DVREPEAT	-0.49***	-0.50**	-	-
	(-2.44)	(-2.52)		
	-1.59***	-1.53***	-1.43***	-1.51***
	(-6.61)	(-5.99)	(-5.99)	(-6.29)

Table 3. (cont'd)

Independent Variables	Dependent Variable is DVPASS		Dependent Variable is DVPASSCON	
	Income Proxy is MEANINC	Income Proxy is MEDIANINC	Income Proxy is MEANINC	Income Proxy is MEDIANINC
(1)	(2)	(3)	(4)	(5)
Mode of Entry Variables				
DVLOWINCOME	-1.15***	-1.28***	-0.93**	-1.18***
	(-2.70)	(-3.15)	(-2.15)	(-2.86)
Interactive Variables				
AGE*DVFEM	-	0.04**	0.05**	-
		(2.08)	(2.05)	
INCOME*DVFEM	0.005***	0.007**	-	0.005***
	(1.89)	(2.18)		(1.62)
Model Statistics				
Log likelihood	-509.02	-506.78	-118.68	-449.99
Restricted log likelihood	-553.08	-533.08	-487.22	-487.22
Log ratio index (LRI)	0.08	0.08	0.08	0.08
LR statistic (9 degrees of freedom)	88.12***	92.61***	77.08***	74.45***
Probability (LR statistic)	0.00	0.00	0.00	0.00
Akaike Information Criterion (AIC)	1.07	1.07	0.94	0.94
Schwartz Criterion (SC)	1.12	1.12	0.99	0.99
Hannan-Quinn Criterion (HQC)	1.09	1.09	0.96	0.96

Source: As for Table 1.
Notes: As for Table 1.

The estimation results for the four parsimonious logit models are reported in Table 3. The LR-statistic is statistically significant at the one percent level for all specifications, and the LRI is identical for all equations. The hypothesis that the slope coefficients are jointly zero is safely rejected.

The information criteria (AIC, SC, and HQC) provide no grounds for choosing one income specification (e.g., MEANINC, MEDIANINC) over the other. These criteria are, of course, strictly non-comparable as between models with different dependent variables, that is, for choosing between the DVPASS and DVPASSCON models. However, a comparison of the information criteria statistics in Tables 2 and 3 is useful. The statistics produced for the parsimonious models are lower than those for the general models. Thus, on the basis of the information criteria, the parsimonious models reported in Table 3 are superior to the general models reported in Table 2 (Lilien, Sueyoshi, Wilkins et al., 2002).

For each of the independent variables (excepting the slope), the estimated coefficient has the same sign, regardless of the specification employed. There are, however, some changes in the level of statistical significance and, for a few variables, there are notable changes in the magnitude of the coefficient.

The results show that, regardless of the specification, females have a lower chance of passing. The magnitude of the coefficient on gender (DVFEM) is somewhat sensitive both to the specification of the dependent variable and the income proxy that is invoked.

The estimated coefficients on INCOME and INCOME^2 are always positive and negative, respectively, but are statistically significant only in the specification that involves DVPASSCON as the dependent variable, and MEANINC as the income proxy (Column (4)). Nevertheless, the magnitudes of the coefficients are almost identical for each of the specifications. The magnitudes of the coefficients on income are really quite small. However, it is important to bear in mind that these values pertain to a measure of weekly income - if an annual equivalent were used, for example, one would expect the coefficient to be larger.

The four *Education Variables* that were retained in the model are clearly important: students with a prior degree (DVCOMPTERT), an incomplete TAFE qualification (DVINCOMPTAFE), or an incomplete tertiary qualification (DVINCOMPTERT), all appear to have statistically-significantly lower chances of passing. Students repeating the unit are also less likely to pass. While there are some variations in the level of statistical significance, there are only minor variations in the magnitudes of the coefficients produced by different specifications. Note, however, that the coefficient on DVINCOMPTERT was only statistically significant in the models with DVPASS as the dependent variable (and was deleted from the DVPASSCON specifications).

The *Mode of Entry* variable, DVLOWINCOME, was included in each specification. The reported coefficients are all negative and statistically significant at either the one, or five, percent levels. Thus, it appears that students admitted via this scheme also have a lower probability of passing this unit.

Finally, the interactive variables of importance comprise interactions of gender with age, and gender with income. The positive and statistically significant coefficients on these interactions are interesting, because they suggest that the apparently lower chance of females passing may be offset by age and by income. This appears to lend weight to the earlier argument that the relationship between gender and performance appears, for this population, to be rather complex.

4.   DISCUSSION

The results produced by this study are somewhat surprising in several respects. First, no statistically-significant differences between the performance of several important equity groups, *viz.* students from ATSI and NESB backgrounds, were found. Second, whereas the existing Australian literature suggests that females tend to outperform males in tertiary courses of all kinds (see Lewis, 1994), this study suggests that the converse is typically true in this undergraduate economics unit. Third, the result that students who hold tertiary or TAFE qualifications appear to have a lower probability of passing is somewhat perplexing. Are degree-holders generally more complacent about study than their peers? Or, are second degrees subject to a problem of "adverse selection" (e.g., are degree-qualified individuals with poorer levels of academic and/or employment attainment more likely to enroll in a subsequent undergraduate degree than higher-performance individuals)? Fourth, the result that those repeating the unit are more likely to fail is important. This result could be generated by any number of factors, so it would seem important to identify the root cause of repeated failed attempts at the unit.

Other important results are that students admitted via the "Alternative Entry Scheme," rather than on the basis of prior educational attainment (only), appear to have no worse chance of passing than other students. However, students admitted via a low-income university entry initiative appear to have a lower chance of passing than other students.

There are several limitations of this study. First, since disability data were not made available, the success of students with learning or physical disabilities could not be examined. This is an unfortunate omission. Second, the study was conducted on a single (albeit very large) cohort, for a specific course unit. The study is motivated by a concern with a discipline (i.e., economics)-specific performance of undergraduate students. Nevertheless, it would be useful to repeat this work on further cohorts of students enrolled in the same unit, at the same institution, to ensure that the results are not cohort-specific. It would be useful to repeat the work on a multinomial, rather than binary dependent variable, in order to test whether or not differences in the performance measure give rise to different results.

Additionally, studies of this nature, performed on a cross-section of institutions, might uncover different results, and these may be related to the entry policies and the student management programs of the different universities. The resulting quantitative evidence could prove useful for revisions of effective and efficient strategies for promoting the equity goals of those institutions.

5. CONCLUSION

Notwithstanding the limitations of this work, some practical implications may be drawn from it. Perhaps the most pertinent of these are that educators should be encouraged to (i) look for systematic differences in the performance levels of different groups of students within their own sphere of influence; and (ii) identify the reasons that such differences exist and/or persist. In this study, some surprising results were produced on the first of these matters – but the difficult causal issues associated with the latter are yet to be disentangled.

REFERENCES

Amemiya, T. (1981). Qualitative response models: A survey. *Journal of Economic Literature*, *19*, 481-536.

Australian Bureau of Statistics (1997) CDATA96. Canberra: Australian Bureau of Statistics.

Batson, C., Sharp, R., Ramsay, E., & Mackinnon, A. (2001). Combined courses of study: Equity group access and participation at the Bachelor (Honours/Pass) level. Canberra: Department of Education, Science and Training. Retrieved from http://www.detya.gov.au/highered/eippubs/eip01_11/.

Davidson, R., & MacKinnon, J. G. (1993). *Estimation and Inference in Econometrics*. Oxford: Oxford University Press.

Department of Education, Training and Youth Affairs. (2000). *2000-2002 Triennium Equity Plans*. Canberra: Department of Education, Training and Youth Affairs.

Essen, J., & Wedge, P. (1982). *Continuities in Childhood Disadvantages*. London: Heinemann.

Goldfeld, S., Quandt, R., & Trotter, H. (1966). Maximization by quadratic hill climbing. Reprinted in S. Goldfeld, R. Quandt, & H. Trotter, *The Collected Essays of Richard E. Quandt, Vol. 1*, pp. 299-309. Ashgate: Aldershot.

Gourieroux, C. (2000). *Econometrics of Qualitative Dependent Variables*. Cambridge: Cambridge University Press.

Greene, W. H. (2000). *Econometric Analysis*, 4th ed., Upper Saddle River: Prentice Hall.

Gujarati, D. N. (2003) Basic Econometrics. Boston: McGraw-Hill.

Johnston, J., & DiNardo, J. (1997). *Econometric Methods*. 4th ed., New York: McGraw-Hill.

Lewis, D. E. (1994). *The Performance at University of Equity Groups and Students Admitted Via Alternative Modes of Entry*. Canberra: Australian Government Publishing Service.

Lilien, D., Sueyoshi, G., Wilkins, C. Kawakatsu, H., Startz, R., Hall, R.E., Engle, R., Liang, G., Ellsworth, S., & Noh, J. (2002) EViews 4 User's Guide. Irvine: Quantitative Micro Software.

Morimune, K. (1979). Comparisons of normal and logistic models in the bivariate dichotomous analysis. *Econometrica, 47*, 957-75.

Pagan, A. (1995). Three Econometric Methodologies: A Critical Appraisal. In L. Oxley & C. J. Roberts (Eds.), Surveys in Econometrics. Oxford: Blackwell, 9-29.

Sammons, P. (1995). Gender, ethnic and socio-economic differences in attainment and progress: a longitudinal analysis of student achievement over 9 years. *British Educational Research Journal, 21*, 465-85.

Sammons, P., Kysel F., & Mortimore P. (1983). Educational priority indices: a new perspective. *British Educational Research Journal, 9*, 27-40.

Schoenfeld, A. H. (2002). Making mathematics work for all children: issues of standards, testing and equity. *Educational Researcher, 31*, 13-25.

Chapter 18

MAKING SPACE FOR TWENTY-FIRST CENTURY MANAGEMENT LEARNING

Clive Holtham & Martin Rich
Cass Business School, London, UK

1.   CONTEXT

This chapter evolved from four years of research and development, which has been dominated by the practicalities of designing and constructing one of the largest wholly new business school buildings in Europe. This is the Cass Business School, City of London, formerly known as the City University Business School. Its location on Bunhill Row was a former banknote factory, appropriate for a school serving the City as financial district. And it has local associations with creative icons such as Jonathan Swift, Daniel Defoe, and William Blake. The previous business school is spread over four buildings and its main building, Frobisher Crescent, was originally designed as apartments, so the transition to a single integrated building is itself of great significance.

At the very start of the $60m project, there was a decision to begin a study of how physical space can impact educational outcomes. From this initial point onwards, there has been an explicit and strong concern with the educational characteristics of the new physical space. Several criteria emerged for the client brief, which underpinned respectively the making of the business case for funding, the design brief to achieve planning permission, and the detailed architect's plans. The requirements emerging from consultation and discussion were:

- Flexibility
- Interactivity
- New types of augmented conversation

R.G.Milter et al. (eds.), Educational Innovation in Economics and Business IX, 341–362.
©2004 *Springer. Printed in the Netherlands.*

- Exploiting information richness
- Innovative pedagogy.

The Business School supported a program of academic research concurrent with the planning of the new building, which has resulted in a range of publications: Holtham & Tiwari, 1998; Ward & Holtham, 2000a; Ward & Holtham, 2000b; Holtham, Ward, & Rosander, 2001; Holtham, Ward, & Bohn, 2001. In addition there was a substantial level of visits and discussions by a design team that included representatives both of the architects and of the Business School, including most of the leading modern business schools in Europe and the USA, and to relevant non-university buildings. This chapter focuses on some of the influences that were studied during this process.

2.   THE SIGNIFICANCE OF SPACE IN THE PHYSICAL UNIVERSITY

One of the key features identified from our research has been the neglect of physical space as a fundamental pedagogic resource in Higher Education, and particularly in its role as a force for and against innovation in educational practice. In the UK for 1999/2000 (HESA, 2001), there were five broad areas of expenditure on universities:

1. Academic & Research   55%
2. Central & other services   19%
3. Premises   11%
4. Library & Computer   7%
5. Residences/Catering   7%

It can be seen that expenditure on physical premises (excluding those for residences) greatly exceeds that spent on library and computer combined. Yet Paechter, Edwards, Harrison & Twining (2001) correctly highlight that:

> Because learning has been seen traditionally as something that takes place only in the mind, the fact that learning is something that happens to embodied learners occupying particular spaces has been generally ignored or played down (p.2).

Edwards (2000) argues that "50-60 per-cent of a modern university is general teaching space," and that:

> universities have the almost unique challenge of relating the built fabric to academic discourse. Put another way, the university environment is part of the learning experience and buildings need to be silent

teachers…the principle of academic mission being expressed or explored through the estate of buildings is an important one (p. vii).

In considering why so little research has been carried out into the physical space of Higher Education, Paechter provided one explanation: because learning is in the mind, the nature of the space used is almost irrelevant. But we are also driven to consider that most front-line academics (and even heads of schools and departments) perceive themselves as having almost negligible control over the disposition of physical space. In Sweden, physical space is typically not even owned by the university itself, and elsewhere, the design and control of physical space is carried out by estates and facilities management experts. These are typically neither academics, nor part of the pedagogic culture of the university. One conclusion we reach from this is that in spite of such obstacles, it is perhaps all the more important for academics to become directly involved in the specification and design of physical space, so it better meets the pedagogic needs of students, faculty, and programs.

There are a few exceptions, for example, the efforts of OECD (2001) to stimulate innovation in educational building design. Many of the published documents on university buildings are purely functional, that is, concerned with students per square meter. In the worst cases, very few of the photos show any students in classes or on campus.

One notable contribution to the link between pedagogy and physical space is the work of Thomas Markus (1993), which though historic in nature and not specific to management education, serves as an excellent reminder of just how dominant medieval attitudes are toward learning spaces. This is true both at a micro level (of the individual course or learning experience) and at the macro level (institutional decisions on space, both physical and virtual).

3.   REQUIREMENTS TO PHYSICAL SPACE

3.1   Requirement 1: Flexibility

It was vital that an expensive physical building was not locked into particular models of either education or business because over its lifetime both of these are very likely to be subject to change. As part of the funding package, it was also necessary to ensure that the building could be converted to generic office use if necessary.

This was sought in several different dimensions:
a) Potential reconfiguration of the whole building away from academic use in the long term.
b) The ability to amend the broad configuration of the building in the light of changes in demand or changes in educational delivery in the medium term.
c) The ability to amend the detailed internal layouts periodically (Brand, 1993).
d) The ability for individual spaces to be used for multiple purposes in the short term.

3.2   Requirement 2: Interactivity

The rationale for a physical building was primarily seen as achieving rich human-to-human interactions. Given the very substantial choice of learning modes for MBA students globally and in the UK, the expectation of current and future students attracted to this school is primarily to be attending a physical school. But there is much to be done to make every aspect of the building become part of the learning space. The role of "third spaces" (Oldenburg, 1989) is of particular relevance to interactive management learning environments. The purpose of third spaces can be defined as follows:

- First space: Home
- Second space: Work
- Third space: Hangouts at the heart of a community

One key dimension is that third spaces lead to business innovation. An area studied in knowledge management is the role of "innovation laboratories." The lecture and case study based model of education typically envisions face-to-face learning as having a strong collective emphasis, whether in large or small groups. But there is also potential for reviewing other models of spaces for learning, which do not derive directly from those classically found in universities.

3.3   Requirement 3: Augmented Conversation

The combination of information richness and interactivity permits the human-to-human interaction to be effective both face-to-face and in virtual, extended, or augmented ways that integrate analogue and digital media. The historical origins of computer-supported collaboration can in particular be traced to the pioneering work of Douglas Englebart (1962). His research was concerned with the "augmentation of human intellect" and hence our own use of the adjective "augmented." We are interested here in the ways in which technology in the broadest sense can enhance conversation, since conversation lies at the heart of the knowledge creation process, and hence of the learning process.

One term that has had more common usage than "augmented" is "virtual," but we are increasingly dissatisfied with this term as it implies that the conversation is in some sense "not real." Our current preference is for the word "extended" conversation, as this actually implies some benefit from the use of technology to support the conversation. Our intention is to include face-to-face same-time same-place augmentation, such as with group decision support systems (Dennis, George, Jessup Nunamaker & Vogel (1988). Of course, we also wish to include both same-time different-place conversations, such as video-conferencing, as well as different-time approaches such as computer conferencing. It is also worth bearing in mind the relatively unusual same-place different-time approaches, such as the use of notice boards.

3.4   Requirement 4: Exploiting Information Richness

A physical building also has a role to play in permitting and stimulating access to information in a variety of media, both analogue and digital. One of the purposes of physical space is to provide a convenient location for the assembly of information resources that underpin and indeed fuel the process of knowledge creation. Historically, this has meant the creation of a physical library of books and journals. But electronic media is steadily replacing the physical library, especially in relation to academic journals and, to a lesser extent, books. A physical library will, however, still be needed for access to librarians, for access to specialist resources and for the availability of several forms of study space.

There is also the question of access to the Internet. Despite the growth of remote wired access and even several methods of wireless access, the laws of physics suggest that university wired access (increasingly via fiber optic) will always have a significant speed advantage over domestic services transmitted via copper wire or wireless. In addition to essentially text-based information resources, high-speed non-domestic network access will also allow for the possible use of, for example, advanced audio- and video-conferencing.

3.5   Requirement 5: Innovative Pedagogy

It was vital that the new building was not specifically designed to achieve the best of twentieth-century learning methods, but in effect the building does contribute to the development of innovation in twenty-first century management learning. Of key importance are the types of pedagogic models envisioned. The first century and a half of formal management education has been dominated by face-to-face education. The models that have dominated have typically evolved from the more traditional professions of medicine (lectures) and law (case studies) (Hall, 1966; Kaplan & Kaplan, 1982).

Didactic teaching is very closely linked to the lecture theater. It is important to see the origins of the tiered lecture room in the need for medical students to be able to see the body being operated on. The closest analogy, when lecture theaters first came into use, was with a place of entertainment or the tiered theater, which brought about the term lecture "theater." But the lecture theater need not necessarily equate to didactic teaching. The formal lecture theater of the Royal Institution in London was an interactive place for leading scientists to present to and discuss with their peers. From 1826 onwards, Michael Faraday introduced a series of lectures which were seen as interactive fora, where scientists could debate ideas with their audience. The title "Friday Evening Discourse" introduced by Faraday and still in use today, reflects the importance of interaction in these events. The Royal Institution lecture theater is geared to student-to-student interaction similar to the modern case study classroom.

These face-to-face models are under significant challenge from the advocates of open and distance learning, as well as from newer paradigms of learning, such as Problem Based Learning. This is most visible in the growth of business courses that are reliant on some form of open learning, and in the UK the number of people enrolled in MBA programs at the Open University is evidence of this. However, it is tempting to assume that open learning be incorporated into a course simply because of the availability of the technology. It is essential to reiterate that consideration of pedagogy should precede design of tools, but tool innovation may enable pedagogic innovation, and on a wide scale.

In the study of knowledge management in general, there has been a growing interest in the capabilities of physical space to enhance the creation and sharing of knowledge. These studies have tended to emphasize the potential of informal, rather than formal, spaces (Steinbeck, 1999). We review below the theoretical potential for further innovative models of learning which challenge the status quo, but still involve physical space in face-to-face education (Evans, 1995). Subsequently, we discuss the lessons of experiments with these innovative models as part of the process of developing a specification for the pedagogy underpinning the move to a new business school building. Four possible models are discussed: Primary School; Museum/Gallery (Falk & Balling, 1982; Hein, 1998); Architecture Studio/ Medieval Craft Workshop (Boyer & Mitgang, 1966); and Club (Duffy, 1997).

4.   NEED FOR PHYSICAL UNIVERSITY

The new building was opened towards the end of 2002. Yet this new physical building was conceived and constructed during the very time when there were the fierce criticisms of the physical university itself. It is essential, therefore, to review these criticisms that derive from a wide variety of sources, which we group into two: technology critics and non-technology critics. The non-technology critics tend to concentrate on the elitism of the traditional physical university (Illich, 1971). As with the open university movement, they criticize its inflexibility and economics (Daniel, 1996), and in some cases they criticize both (Drucker, 1997).

The technology critics argue that the physical university is an outdated concept that can now be partially or wholly replaced by technology, which is more convenient and flexible for the learner (Noam, 1995). This has been a long-standing promise from the early experiments in the '50s and '60s with "teaching machines." The "no significant difference" movement (Russell, 1999) reviews a range of studies of (increasingly technology-supported) distance learning and argues that, in general, research has not yielded any (quantifiable) differences.

In practice, the e-universities have done no more to supersede conventional universities than did the first computer-based learning systems of the 1970s. Most of the e-universities either failed after the dot.com boom ended in early 2000, or have modified their scope to become providers of content or tools. The most successful universities providing distance learning, such as the (UK) Open University and the University of Phoenix, are much longer-established institutions which were set up to provide instruction to students to whom traditional universities did not cater.

An essential part of the business plan for the new building was to evaluate these criticisms, and to assess whether there was in fact a viable case for a new city-center physical building being contemplated. The outcome of this evaluation was a mapping of the relative contributions of electronic and face-to-face learning (Figure 1). Our own work has involved virtual learning environment use since 1993 and subsequent use of the most advanced digital library facilities. We have been active in research and development into the next generation of academic video-conferencing (Holtham & Knudsen, 2001). Yet the more we used virtual space, the more significant we actually saw the role of physical space in our particular version of the learning experience. Due to our geographical location and market positioning, this is primarily face-to-face interaction. However, as in our new face-to-face MBA for the Bank of China, we actively utilize electronic media when the UK- based faculty members are not present in China.

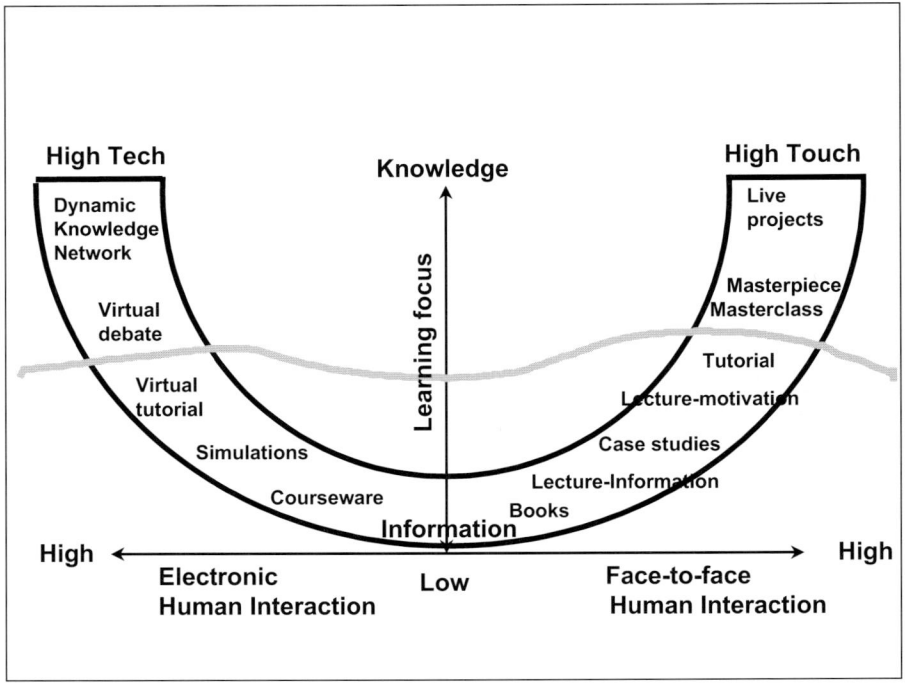

Figure 1. Learning Environment: Focuses

It is rarely the case that electronic communication replaces face-to-face interaction. The conclusion reached from this evaluation was that the school would need to aim for a combination of "high touch," that is face-to-face, and "high tech" tools that would support face-to-face learning. The school envisioned face-to-face as its principal delivery method, not least in the light of being in such an exceptional physical location serving the City of London, and being itself part of central London and a leading center of world trade and business.

5.   SEARCH FOR A METAPHOR FOR MANAGEMENT LEARNING SPACE

A central message from the preliminary research was that to maximize thought and knowledge creation, it is necessary to create as diverse a range of knowledge spaces as possible. Where standard types of space are necessary, such as spaces essential for enclosed academic offices, they should still be potentially reconfigurable at a micro level.

One of the next areas of research attention was the search for a metaphor. Jilk and Copa (2001) emphasized the importance of the symbol or metaphor in focusing strategic direction in building design. The City University Business School search was for institutions that had a primary focus on the creation and extension of knowledge, combined with hosting a variety of transients and location independent workers. The most powerful metaphor we found during the initial design phase related to medieval monasteries. When Stoddard (1966) elegantly describes life in French monasteries, he starts to raise ideas relevant to a new business school, notably those of "corporate worship" and a set of interconnected spaces.

Stoddard talks of multi-functional space, such as Fontenay's monk's hall, which is a meeting place available for both reading and discussion at prescribed times. And at the Benedictine cloister of Saint-Trophime at Arles, Stoddard enthuses over its sculpted piers and capitals depicting scenes from both old and new Testaments.

> The Christian story enfolded in stone as monks strolled, read and went about their daily schedule along these lighted walks... It is in these Normanesque cloisters, perhaps more than any other part of the monastery, that the sense of reflective peace and calm is most acutely felt (p. 25).

Barren modern office headquarters and the Aircraft Hanger university learning resource centers have absolutely no "sense of reflective peace and calm." Spence (1984) also reminds us in his terminology how some of our building terms are influenced by monastic life:

- Office = Monastic Church Service
- Carrel = Seating recess in cloister wall, used by monks for study.

Three particular features of the monastery are worth considering. The first is the library. Monasteries were often places of learning and education. At San Marco, the great Dominican monastery in Florence, Scudieri (1995) notes the parallel between the library and a temple. Today the role of paper-based books and writings is diminishing, but there is undoubtedly still a need for at least one physical space that provides intensive support to the creation of knowledge. To achieve a "temple" of knowledge might be too great an ambition for Cass. But the San Marco example shows that it is possible to rise well above the ordinary, so we aimed to follow some of its lessons and create our own parallel to San Marco's, describing it as an ideal place for study, as a remarkable "City of God" set within the chaotic "city of men."

Second, there is the chapter house, named because (Wright, 1998) each morning "the monks assembled there for a sort of business meeting, which began with a reading that always included a chapter from St Benedict's Rules" (p. 34). The Chapter House is a superb example of a highly specialized meeting space, optimized for a particular function, and perhaps only used for a very small portion of the day.

A third relevant feature of the monastery is the concept of the cloister:

> Cloisters served many purposes. Primarily they were galleries of communication between the various domestic buildings themselves, and between them and the church. The cloister alley next to the church wall was the recognised place for meditation, and the monks would spend their allotted periods of prayer, reading, study and meditation in that alley. Some cloisters had stone benches along the church wall for the monks to sit on. The outer wall of this alley was divided into carrels, each carrel occupying the space of half a window (Wright, 1998, pp.31-32).

6.   UPDATING THE METAPHOR

The Oxbridge physical cloister or quadrangle is inappropriate to most modern urban behavior patterns, and it was not feasible in the City of London to allow for any external quadrangle, even on the roof. So the real question is not copying the medieval cloister; it is essentially about trying to recreate some of the spirit and functionality of the cloister within a totally modern urban environment.

We visualized a space that is dedicated to a multi-functional approach to study, reflection, and discussion. The cloister allowed for accidental contact, for the conversion of private study into small group discussion, and back again. This should be a key objective of the modern equivalent of the cloister. The cloister was not the same as Fontenay's hall - which was more like a library reading room. It was much more geared to reflection and knowledge development and creation.

For a modern block, the modern cloister might physically look like a set of connected wide corridors. But if it does look like this, then it is essential that the corridor is not a through-traffic route, or a busy communication channel, but in fact a dedicated space. The study carrel is a space that is personalized as long as someone is using it, but is very definitely multi-user. Some carrels in monasteries were almost private, and maybe there should in the modern cloister be different grades of carrel, with increasing indications of privacy. For the less private carrels, the potential of interruption should be recognized.

Some space needs to be for informal small group discussion. This might involve coffee, but this area is quite different in intention from a cafe area. It is definitely aimed at academic discussion and dispute. We would not envision whiteboards in a cafe - they would be essential in the modern cloister. It would deliberately be only semi-private in that it is important to encourage people to overhear the talking of others. This must have been a feature of the cloister since the words of the monks in discussion must have been audible to those working individually in their carrels.

7. SPACES FOR KNOWLEDGE WORK

Figure 2 is based on a review of a wide variety of metaphors or styles of knowledge work. Two types of spaces are identified – individual and open, each subdivided into their own spectrum. In carrying out an assessment of suitability for knowledge work, it can be seen that open plan is generally unsuitable for private knowledge work because of the impossibility of avoiding any interruptions, and possibly because of the need for space which staff could identify as "individual."

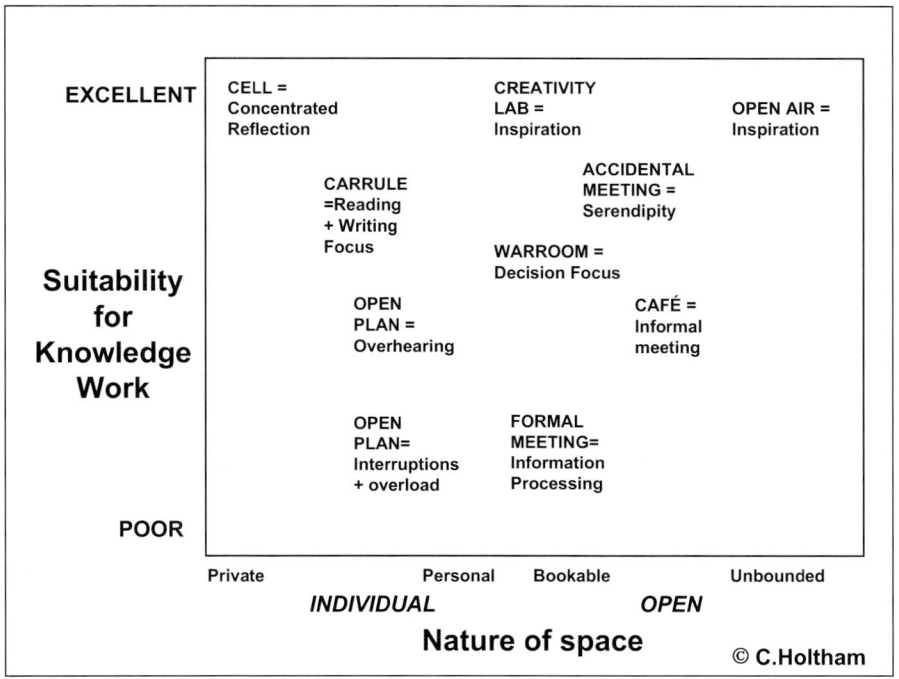

Figure 2. Spaces for Knowledge Work

There are, however, a minority of conventional office staff who are able to undertake knowledge work in open plan. The basic cause of this seems to be a delight in being interrupted, and the ability to overhear (legitimately) the work of others, and to interact with them. Within an open-plan area, individual space can be observed to be arranged in many different ways. For example, staff who are very dependent on team-working often work well in clusters of desks in an open area.

As already mentioned, the no-significant-difference movement is skeptical about the value of lectures. However, for many universities with a face-to-face policy, there is a question of building on any economical ways to remain physically in contact with students. The lecture may not be very effective, but it is quite economical. The "right sort" of lecture can be highly stimulating to students. It needs to be seen more as a motivational or inspirational device, rather than just as a vehicle for transmitting information or knowledge.

Spectators pay good money to attend theaters or stadiums where they are "only" passive recipients. But we can find a play or match exciting and fun, and we can feel part of it even with minimal interaction. So a role can be envisioned for an equivalent type of lecture. The issue is not implementing "entertainment-style" lectures. It is rather evolving towards a lecture that is a genuinely collective human experience. In relation to physical space, it is important to see that a dominance of any one form of learning method is probably a bad thing, because both our students and we have such a diverse range of learning styles.

A variety of space needs to be provided for non-lecture based study, which can include:
- Small independent group work
- Electronic group work
- Facilitated group work
- Library supported independent study
- Web supported independent
- Course book packs with paper and/or electronic self-assessment
- CD-ROM's of learning resources
- Specially made or off-the-shelf videos (but **not**, in general, videos of lectures)
- Business Games.

8.   INNOVATIVE MODELS OF PHYSICAL SPACE

8.1   School as Model

It is a minor irony that as a result of progressive educational theory since World War II, secondary and especially primary schools have been redesigned to involve much more group work, and much more learning by doing. The modern UK secondary school is much more learner-centered than the modern UK University, with a great emphasis on individualized worksheets, and on detailed and continuous measures of achievement. A modern secondary school has much less emphasis on lecturing than it did three decades ago, and in part, this creates a generation of young UK undergraduates who literally have to adapt to a more traditional system. Our experience of working with an international student body suggests that some European and Asian countries still do retain a more didactic style, and students from these countries have fewer problems in adapting.

For older MBA and executive learning students there may be more expertise in sitting passively in a lecture, but attention spans of younger students are shorter for a different reason. Younger students want to learn fast and they want relevance, plus skills and insights that are immediately applicable in the workplace. Older learners may also have participated in executive education classes, which were likely to be based around small group and experiential learning.

Probably the nearest metaphor is that of the nursery school or pre-school - rooms that are much less formal even than primary school. A typical nursery school also includes a number of separate spaces with different purposes (music, playing with water, and so on) between which children can move. The nursery school encourages learning by playing and learning by doing. We need physical locations that can help unfreeze thinking. But we also need places to plan for or even achieve action. We need a toolset so that knowledge-rich products can be created or simulated then and there. We have always been attracted to the war room as a place for collecting information, analyzing it, and taking decisions.

Stafford Beer's 1972 Operations Room designed for President Allende of Chile and destroyed after his assassination in the military coup, probably remains the peak of radical modern thinking about executive meetings. Eight relaxed swiveling chairs, no paper, and a wide variety of wall displays controlled from on-chair keypads all added up to a unique environment for executive work (Beer, 1981).

Somehow subsequent computer-based electronic boardrooms have never quite recaptured the holistic dimension of Beer's work, perhaps because they have over-concentrated on the digital media at the expense of analogue. They have also tended to be over-dependent on a facilitator-centered style of meeting. An action-orientated environment needs to avoid being based on a single information processing style - it must embrace both analogue and digital approaches. It needs to avoid being based on a single leadership style. A rigorous mathematical basis for intensive teamworking has been proposed by Stafford Beer (1994). This envisions groups of 30 organized in ever rotating teams of six. Team syntegrity is based on the icosahedron for the size of the group, and the size of breakout teams literally derives from Beer's observation of relationships between geometrical designs and effective business meetings.

8.2   Medieval Craft Studio

Schön's (1983) "Reflective Practitioner" has stimulated a whole vein of thinking about management learning. Schön partly envisioned a return to the learning style of the medieval apprentice. He envisioned learning spaces for adults that were not based on didactic traditions, but rather on a medieval craft studio. As part of our planning for the new building we developed a brief for a "business" craft studio. The description that follows reflects the brief used at this planning stage.

> There may well be a whole range of possible management learning studios, but we can envisage some repeating themes. The first is that learners should feel physically comfortable in them.

> The next feature should be the encouragement of varied interaction. This can be at a whole variety of levels. A group of 20 might want to form a single large circle. They might want 5 sub groups. They might want a lecturette.

> They will certainly need flexible methods for brainstorming and recording their ideas and progress. Some learning environments do not make this easy. The best we have seen have made walls, which are flip chart, blue tack and sticky tape friendly. Walls covered in whiteboard material offer the possibility of being able to write on the wall itself.

> The modern management learning studio should be information rich. In the middle ages the library would have been in a separate physical location, not least for reasons of security. Today we would expect all

learners to have immediate access in team rooms to a wide range of information resources, email, internet discussions etc, and perhaps also audio- and video-conferencing.

The learning studio should facilitate analytical work. Almost all of this will today be carried out by a variety of computer software, and hence there needs to be a range of high quality software readily available so that most analytical tasks can be readily handled.

The studio is also a place to display and present the masterpiece. This could be in one of the traditional analogue formats - flip chart, OHP, typewritten report, or even physical model or pastiche. Equally it could be displayed and presented in computer-based format.

Wake Forest University in North Carolina created an executive learning center called an "Executive Sandpit," and this was influential in helping us design the West London TEC's "Executive Studio." There are two other contemporary examples that have influenced our thinking on the above. The first is the Hoechst-Celanese Innovation Lab in Charlotte, North Carolina. We were fortunate to have visited this center at the invitation of Tom Woczyck shortly before it closed as a result of a merger. The high-tech/high-touch ambience of this center influenced us greatly. In the UK, the Post Office's Innovative Center near Rugby has similar aims.

8.3   Museum/Art Gallery

There is great potential for examining the contribution of the museum, exhibition, and display in management learning environments (Ward & Holtham, 2000c). One particular collaboration was between Sparknow Consultancy and City University Business School who decided to jointly use the format of an art exhibition to communicate key concepts in knowledge management to a group of executives from many sectors, including several Chief Knowledge Officers. It reflected a conscious decision to experiment with a different type of learning space. The event was titled Spark 005, as it was the 5th event in a series related to knowledge management, but adopted an artistic or performance-oriented approach. One influence was Bacon's four-part prescription for a repository of knowledge (Markus, 1993):
1. A library
2. A zoological and botanical garden
3. An experimental laboratory and
4. A goodly huge cabinet, wherein whatsoever the hand of man by exquisite art or engine has made rare in stuff, form or motion; whatsoever singularity, chance, and the shuffle of things hath produced;

whatsoever Nature has wrought in things that want life, and may be kept; shall be sorted and included (p.190).

The zoological and botanical aspects support an organic metaphor for evolutionary project processes, and there is an even closer relationship between the library, laboratory, and "goodly huge cabinet" and our methodology for knowledge management. Markus (1993) also usefully contrasts the active learning of a museum with the passive learning of the lecture hall:

> Because a museum is a classifying device, by moving through its space the visitor recovers the entire system. In the auditorium the visitor is stationary and recovers a fragment of the system (p. 170).

Many museums provide visitors with an opportunity to move between different spaces with different purposes. The Great Court at the British Museum and the turbine hall at the Tate Modern Gallery are examples in London of major new public spaces that have been created in museums.

An early decision was made to create some unspecified type of artifacts that could be first used at an evening event and then re-used at the Design and Learning exhibition. Several investigations and much brainstorming had failed to yield a satisfactory concept. At a very late stage in the project planning, theater designer, writer, and poet Angie Dove suggested that the artifacts should be a garden shed. Reading a book on Dr. James A. H. Murray, the first editor of the Oxford English Dictionary, had stimulated her imagination. He created the dictionary from thousands of small slips of paper sent in by volunteer readers. These grew too voluminous for his house, so he was banished to work in a metal shed in his garden, filled with pigeonholes, which he called his "scriptorium." (The OED defines this as "a writing-room; specifically the room in a religious house set apart for the copying of manuscripts.")

The central artifact developed was a standard 8' x 6' wooden garden shed purchased from a garden superstore. Inside, specially made wooden pigeonholes were added to mimic those of Murray, but more specifically to represent tangibly the logical classification system developed and evolved by Sparknow. Inside the shed were many additional items that hung from the wall and roof in the manner of tools in a garden shed, except these were documents and photographs relating to knowledge management. Advanced publicity described this as the "Scriptorium."

The format of an art exhibition, with the garden shed as the central exhibit, led to a quite exceptional level of response and stimulation, with particular stimulation achieved by the Shed exhibit. However, other exhibits, even those planned to be "interactive," attracted less interest.

With the benefit of experience, it can be seen that the shed and its contents proved to be a powerful and tangible metaphor for key aspects of knowledge management. It created a self-evident climate of warmth and intimacy, quite different from exhibits in open space just a meter or two away. The sharing of experiences via the "seed packets" was very candid. So the shed worked at three levels:

1. In literally making the intangible into a tangible form, for example, with the physical analogue classification system.
2. At a metaphorical level, containing a wealth of symbolism relating to key processes in knowledge management. It reinforced the idea of knowledge as "organic" rather than "mechanistic."
3. Its sheer unexpectedness acted as a stimulus to ideas about knowledge management and essentially as a source of creativity. It appeared to act as an "unfreezing" device and there is little doubt that the shed played the role of a transitional object.

8.4   Club

The idea of the office as Club derives from the work of Frank Duffy (1997). The type of club he refers to is what might be called the London Club. These are members-only institutions used for a combination of social, but more particularly business networking purposes, whether politics (the Carlton Club) or show business (the Garrick Club). They perform multiple roles and have diverse spaces to reflect those roles. For example, a club will have a library and/or very comfortable reading room, but it might also have a more utilitarian "writing room." The club is a classic third space. There is a heavy emphasis on meeting the needs of peripatetic visitors, and there is a special emphasis on stimulating serendipity.

The office as a Club has most particularly been implemented in management consultancies, such as Accenture's London office. In this case there are a wide range of spaces geared to the nomadic consultant. The club can also be found in a particular type of corporate headquarters, such as BA's HQ at Waterside near Heathrow airport. Here, the whole metaphor of the building is of the English country village with a high street through which walking is channeled, and geared to serendipitous contact. There is even a village stream. The dominant club theme is seen in the centrally located cafe. This is not simply a place for refreshment; it is more particularly a place for informal meetings. The Relationship Marketing Department of BA has fully deployed the club metaphor for its whole space.

Figure 3. The Front Atrium of the Cass Business School

In a large modern business school the club metaphor is potentially of great significance. The typical academic may be fairly peripatetic, and so will have a particular need for informal and serendipitous space. In the case of Cass, a key decision was taken in 2001 to brand the new school as welcoming to outsiders (a key monastic strength) with the new strap line to the logo: "the intellectual hub of the City."

The Cass architects have fully grasped the significance of the club metaphor and have sought out a wide range of opportunities for informal spaces in particular. Most of these are in areas used jointly by staff and students. There are also informal spaces created in the staff/research office area. One of the single most impressive academic club environments we have seen is the combined student center and library at George Mason University, Virginia. Unusually, this treats the whole building as "library" space, so books can be read in the refectory. Equally, almost the whole building is a social space, so there are drink and food machines amongst the book-stacks. Within the formal library area, there is a huge range of different styles of study space.

9. CONCLUSION

One of the most striking conclusions from our study has been the relative lack of attention devoted to the implications of physical space in higher education in general, and in management education in particular. The physical space of a business school typically represents a far greater proportion of the operating expenses of a school than does the virtual space. So we need to recognize the importance of developing physical spaces that are better geared to twenty-first century learning.

We then need our institutional and national funders of universities also to grasp that educational effectiveness depends on more varied, more flexible, and more extensive learning spaces. Physical space is as important an educational tool as are the tools of information technology and library content.

Physical space is a "Cinderella" of Higher Education pedagogy, yet it is a costly "Cinderella." We need to reconfigure at least parts of our physical space away from extremely traditional didactic spaces. Although financial resources are a key dimension of achieving this, probably an even more serious constraint is the serious mindset gap that often exists between university strategists and pedagogic experts. A similar gap also exists between many academic faculty and pedagogic innovators.

Over the four-year period, we have been able to carry out experimental work on spaces for learning and also reviews of relevant theory and leading-edge practice internationally. This is a particularly difficult period to review the lessons learned, as the ultimate test lies in the effective use of the actual building (Brand, 1997). However, in Figure 4 we have set out an initial indication of the lessons from our particular experience, relative to the five initial criteria set for physical space. This grid could be extended by adding other approaches, including the classic lecture and case study.

	Primary school	Museum	Work-shop	Club
Flexibility	HIGH	MED	HIGH	MED
Interactivity	HIGH	LOW	HIGH	MED
Exploiting information richness	LOW	MED	HIGH	MED
Augmented conversation	MED	HIGH	HIGH	HIGH
Innovative Pedagogy	MED	HIGH	MED	MED

Figure 4. Preliminary Assessment of the Impacts of the Four Methods

Our findings perhaps inevitably point to the need for a great deal more research at the intersection of learning, physical space, and virtual space. We offer the following as tentative hypotheses for further study:

1. The physical university will continue, but not necessarily only as we have known it.
2. In business education in particular, there will be pressures to move to a high-tech plus high-touch physical and virtual environment.
3. There will be increasing realization of the importance of physical university space to stimulate the move from information to knowledge.
4. Part of the key to understanding both physical and virtual space will be a third dimension, which for shorthand can be called "emotional space."
5. Innovative pedagogy is essential, but the problem of exploiting physical space is not a new one, so we need not to be afraid to take well-established ideas from other areas.

The massive investment in university buildings has often been carried out in a highly instrumental way to ensure that there are enough student spaces available under conventional learning methods, particularly lecturing. Learning innovations often have to fit into physical spaces designed conventionally, and as a result, they are less than ideal for implementing the innovation. The nature of university decision making is often that decisions on physical space are taken on a technical or financial base rather than a pedagogic base. Of course, the same is often true of information technology decisions.

One piece of good fortune caused by a wholly new building for a single school with a clear vision is that it was more feasible to synchronize technical, financial, and pedagogic dimensions. Of crucial significance was acceptance by the dean and other senior staff of the link between pedagogy and the priorities for the physical design of the new building. Such acceptance is not inevitable in either academic or business life. But it is a precondition of making spaces fit for twenty-first century management learning.

REFERENCES

Beer, S. (1981). *Brain of the Firm. (2nd ed.).* Chichester: Wiley.

Beer, S. (1994). *Beyond Dispute: The Invention of Team Syntegrity.* Chichester: Wiley.

Boyer, E. L., & Mitgang, L. D. (1966). *Building Community: A New Future for Architecture Education and Practice.* Carnegie Foundation for the Advancement of Teaching.

Brand, S. (1993). *How Buildings Learn.* New York: Viking Penguin.

Daniel, J. (1996). *Mega-universities and knowledge media.* London: Kogan Page

Dennis, A. R., George, J. F. Jessup. L. M., Nunamaker, J. F., & Vogel, D. R. (1988). Information technology to support electronic meetings. *MIS Quarterly, 12 (4)*, 591-624.

Drucker, P. (1997). Interview in *Forbes.* 10 March 1997.

Duffy, F. (1997). *The New Office.* London: Conran Octopus Limited.

Edwards, B. (2000). *University Architecture.* London: Spon Press.

Englebart, D. C. (1962). *Augmenting Human Intellect: A Conceptual Framework.* Summary Report, Stanford Research Institute, on Contract AF 49(63-8)-1024, October.

Evans, G W. (1995). Learning and the Physical Environment. In J. Falk, & L. Dierking, (Eds.), *Public Institutions for Personal Learning: Establishing a Research Agenda,* p.p.119-126. American Association of Museums, Washington.

Falk, J., & Balling, J. (1982). The field trip milieu: Learning and behavior as a function of contextual events. *Journal of Educational Research, 76* (1), 22-28.

Hall, E. R. (1966). *The hidden dimension.* New York: Doubleday.

Hein, G. (1998). *Learning in the museum.* New York: Routledge.

HESA. (2001). *Higher Education Statistics for the United Kingdom 1999/2000.* Higher Education Statistics Agency, Cheltenham.

Holtham, C. & Tiwari, A. (1998). *Adapting the physical office of the twenty first century to capitalize on emerging information system opportunities for managerial productivity and creativity.* Proceedings of Business Information Technology 98 Conference, Manchester.

Holtham, C., Ward, V., & Rosander, C. (2001, April). *Designing spaces for knowledge work: can the use of fiction help construct new realities?* Knowledge Management Conference, Leicester University.

Holtham, C., & Knudsen, C. (2001, July). *In-office Videoconferencing: New Opportunities, New Skills.* DIVERSE First Conference on Video and Videoconferencing in Higher Education, Derby.

Holtham, C., Ward, V., & Bohn, M. (2001, April). *Slow knowledge: the importance of tempo in debriefing and in individual learning.* Proceedings of Organisational Knowledge, Learning and Competencies Conference: Athens 5-6th April 2002.

Illich, I. (1971). *Deschooling Society.* London: Calder and Boyers.

Jilk, B., & Copa, G. (2001, June). *Knowledge Reintegration: Emerging paradigm, designs for learning, and supporting environment.* 8th International EDINEB Conference, Nice, 20-22nd June 2001.

Kaplan, S., & Kaplan, R. (1982). *Cognition and environment.* New York: Praeger.

Markus, T. (1993). *Buildings and power -- Freedom and control in the origin of modern building types.* London: Routledge.

Noam, E. (1995, October 13). Electronics and the Dim Future of the University. *Science*, p.p. 247-49.

OECD. (2001). *Designs for Learning.* Paris: Organisation for Economic Co-operation and Development.

Oldenburg, R. (1989). *The Great Good Place: Cafés, coffee shops, community centers, beauty parlors, general stores, bars, hangouts and how they got you through the day.* New York: Paragon House.

Paechter, C., Edwards, R., Harrison, R., & Twining, P. (2001). *Learning, Space, and Identity.* London: Paul Chapman in association with Open University.

Russell, T. L. (1999). *No significant difference phenomenon.* Raleigh, NC: North Carolina State University.

Schön, D.A. (1983). *The Reflective Practitioner: how professionals think in action.* London: Temple Smith.

Scudieri, M. (1995). *San Marco: Complete Guide to the Museum and Church.* Florence: Scala Becocci.

Spence, K. (1984). *Cathedrals and Abbeys of England and Wales.* London: Ernest Benn Ltd.

Steinbeck, R. (1999, June). Breaking the Mold: *Beyond Traditional Learning Spaces - Distributed Learning at Stanford University.* ED-MEDIA 1999 Conference.

Stoddard, W. S. (1966). *Monastery and Cathedral in France.* Middletown, CT: Wesleyan University Press.

Ward, V., & Holtham, C. (2000a). The Role of Psychological and Physical Spaces in Knowledge Management. In Proceedings of ESRC Conference on "Knowledge Management: Concepts and Controversies," 10 – 11 February 2000: University of Warwick.

Ward, V., & Holtham, C. (2000b). *Accelerated Executive Learning – the significance of physical and virtual space in knowledge for strategy.* In Annual Conference "Building Tomorrow Today: Community, Design and Technology," Jonkoping 14th September 2000.

Ward, V., & Holtham, C. (2000c). *Experimenting with Learning About Knowledge: The Art Exhibition and The Garden Shed.* PKADD Conference. Lyon, September 2000.

Wright, G. N. (1998). *Discovering Abbeys and Priories.* (3rd ed). Princes Risborough: Shire Publications Ltd.

Chapter 19

THE VALUE OF MULTIDISCIPLINARY INTEGRATION: EVIDENCE FROM TWO ENGINEERING COURSES

Willem van Woerden[†] & Waling Bandsma
School of Business, Public Administration & Technology; University of Twente, the Netherlands

1. INTRODUCTION

The students of our industrial engineering program have the opportunity to choose, under special conditions, between two types of courses, which are equally focused on integrating their knowledge, insights, and skills in engineering and management. In one course – the Management of Technology (MT) - they cooperate in homogeneous groups, consisting of industrial engineering students with different technology backgrounds. In the other course – the Multidisciplinary Design (MD) – they cooperate in heterogeneous groups, comprising students from different engineering disciplines. In both courses the students study complex problems and must design solutions for those problems. Both courses are focused on learning to integrate knowledge and skills.

Our research questions in this paper are related to the concept of integration: what do we understand about integration? Which kind of educational settings foster integration of knowledge and skills? Which instructional conditions are required to achieve the intended integration objective? Some results of the evaluation studies conducted after the MT-course and MD-course will be reported.

R.G.Milter et al. (eds.), Educational Innovation in Economics and Business IX, 363–381.

2.   THEORY

In our industrial engineering program students become familiar with two kinds of knowledge domains: the domain of technology and the domain of management; students are separately taught in both domains. Half of the time they follow courses in technology, like mechanical engineering or computer science, and half of the time they follow courses in management subjects. Until a few years ago, students had to integrate knowledge and skills gained in different disciplines by themselves during their final graduation assignment.

To assist them, we introduced an integration course in the curriculum.

1. What do we mean by "integration"?

   a) According to the taxonomy of Bloom (1956), the level of **cognitive** integration comes after the stages of acquiring knowledge, utilization of facts, concepts, and skills, and the analysis of problems. Integration takes place after one passes through the previous stages. Nowadays, the concept of "competence" (Barnett, 1994) is emerging, that is, pretending that students learn from the beginning to combine knowledge, insights, and skills when solving problems. One builds up "transferable skills" when working on projects, utilizing all kinds of knowledges, methods, and techniques to solve problems. But hard empirical evidence for these pretentions is still not there (Assiter, 1995).

   b) When we speak of multidisciplinary or interdisciplinary work, we mean also integration on the **discipline** level. In higher education it is rather common to work in multidisciplinary teams on all kinds of design problems, because, in practice, problems are always multidisciplinary. But experience shows that students of different disciplines have developed different design styles. In practice, it takes students a lot of time to make explicit to each other how, for instance, a mechanical engineering design approach differs from an industrial engineering one. In multidisciplinary teams, it takes time to understand each other's approach to tackling a problem and to design a common solution. Recently, Schmithals (1997, p. 96) stated, "There is a strong demand for new courses at university level, which are genuinely transdisciplinary and cannot been managed within the framework of traditional disciplinary education."

2. Which kind of educational settings foster integration of knowledge, concepts, and skills? In his model, Romiszowsky (1986) distinguished four instructional set-ups that are "worth studying reality": case studies, role-plays, simulations, and games (see Figure 1). In our view, projects

also belong to this collection of didactical methods which are suitable for tackling real-life problems. All these methods are useful to achieve integration objectives. Particularly in the domain of economics and business, these instructional set-ups are utilized to bring about an integration of economic and managerial problems.

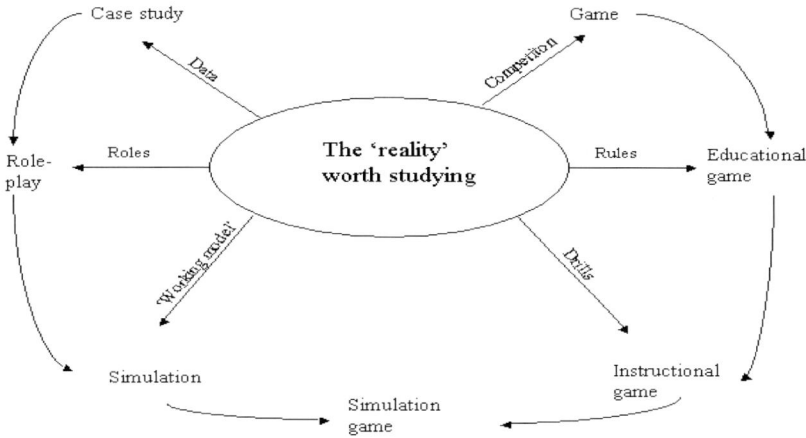

Figure 1. Model of Romiszowsky

3.   Which instructional conditions are required to achieve the objectives of integration? Basically, the above-mentioned didactical methods are adequate to contribute to the integration objective, provided certain conditions are met. Van Woerden (1991) showed that for the project method at least five variables are at stake. How the problem is formulated influences to what extent the integration will be achieved. The composition of the group (e.g., homogeneous or heterogeneous) is relevant for the outcome of the project. The same goes for the role of a tutor in coaching the group to achieve the objective of integration. Also the availability of materials, information, and sufficient study time is an important factor. Finally, the method of assessment, including the way in which students are asked to reflect on the process and product of their efforts, has a great impact on the success or failure of achieving the goal of integration.

3.   PRACTICE

We now will present two courses in our industrial engineering curriculum focused on integrating knowledge, concepts, and skills gained within the management program. These two courses are positioned in the domains of "management" and "technology." One course is called "Management of Technology" (MT) and the other course - "Multidisciplinary Design" (MD). We will describe both courses to compare lessons learned from them, considering the objective of integration.

3.1   The Management of Technology Course

The objectives of the course are:
a) To be able to utilize managerial principles in a technological context.
b) To analyze relationships between technological and organizational aspects of management and use these as a basis for formulating a relevant problem.
c) To design potential problem solutions that would be methodically well founded and would consider a successful implementation of the proposed solution in a technological organizational context.

To achieve these objectives, the following *educational set-up* has been made (see Figure 2).

The course runs during a trimester (of 14 weeks), taking half of the students' study time. In the first (general) part of the course, the students learn to understand the characteristics of a technological innovation process, illustrated by some cases. In the second (technology) part, the students study a specific innovation in the technology domain that they choose for the non-management half of their studies, for example, mechanical engineering or logistics.

Students have to apply the conceptual frameworks learned in the first part of the course to studying a technological innovation process in the second part.

THEORY				PRACTICE	
Management of Technology Model				Study of Implementation of a Technological Innovation	
			Phases		
Technology assessment	Adoption	Implemen-tation	Planning	Casework	Report
R & D	Design process	Design method			Presentation

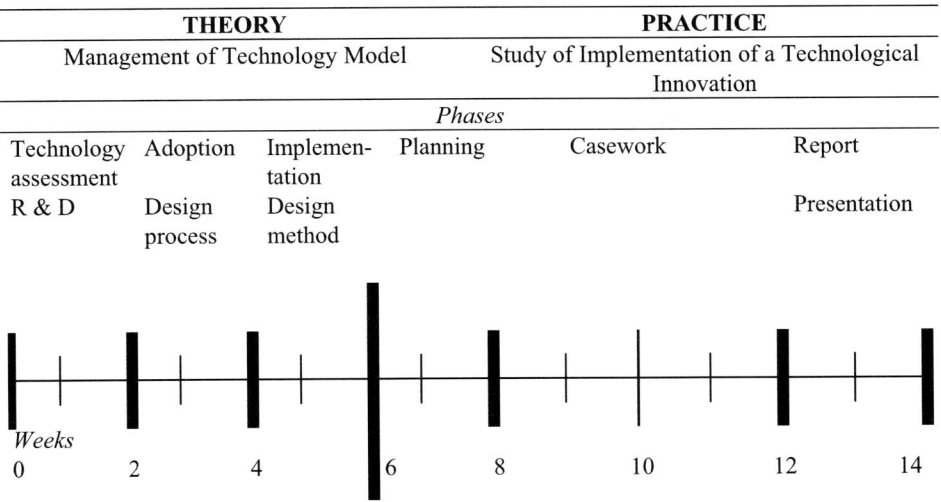

Figure 2. Timetable and Work Schedule of the Management of Technology Course

Originally, the general, first part of the course had a high-pace approach: one area of technology management concepts per week, lectures, briefing, and submission of assignments included. Through this continuous involvement, students should be better prepared for the specific second part of the course, with a technology specific setting.

In this second, technology part of the course, the provider of the innovation problem in a certain technology field developed the course design and the assessment procedure, including a short report as proof of achievement. The fields are: Computer Science, Logistics, Civil Engineering, Mechanical Engineering, Process Technology, and Medical Technology.

The students work together in small groups. In the first part of the course, they cooperate in heterogeneous groups (with different technology background); in the second part, the groups are homogeneous in composition (same technology background). The results of the groupwork are regularly discussed with the tutor(s) and presented and defended afterwards in a plenary session with other groups and tutors at the end of the course.

The MT-course runs at the end of the third year of the five-year program. One should realize that the course was planned to fit in between an internship and a graduation assignment. It was considered important for students to experience differences in the vision on technology and management as apparent in literature, explicated in several lectures, and demonstrated in a number of cases.

The content of the course consists of the following. Starting-point for the design of the MT-course content was a situation where one or more organizations were confronted with a breakthrough technology change (incremental innovation, important as it is, is covered in other courses in the curriculum). A breakthrough new technology would cause organizations to acquire and use insights about assessment, adoption, and diffusion of the technology, about the amount of research and development involved and the management, as well as about the implementation of that technology, including the design of the implementation processes. This led to six areas of technology management concepts, described in the course material. These areas were organized in a model for the "general" part of this course (see Figure 3).

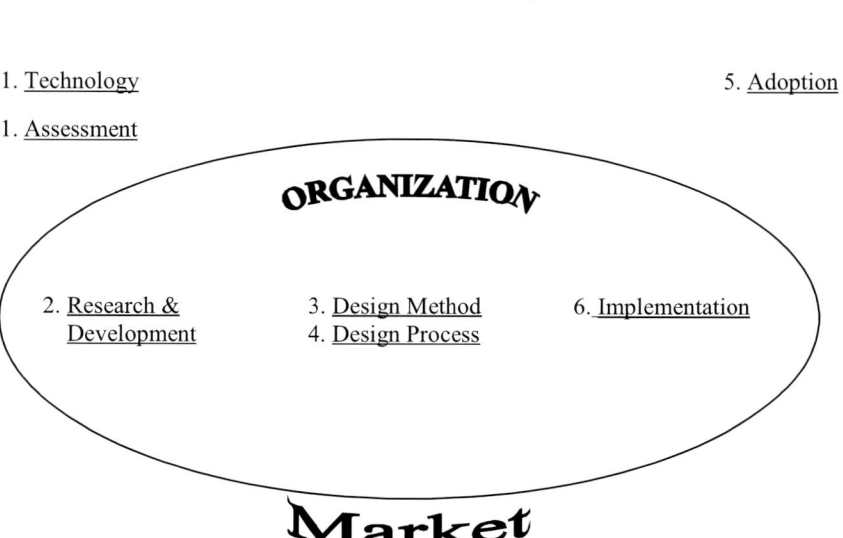

Figure 3. Model of Technological Innovation Process (MT)

The *general* part of the course was dedicated to assignments, based on additional or new theories on these subjects, and would also call for reconsideration of related subjects from preceding courses. As the aim of the course is to integrate the domains of management and technology, present in the curriculum as a whole, the above left us with the need to bring in the "technology;" this was done by the use of a textbook to clarify the concepts in this field (Tidd, Bessant & Pavitt, 2001).

After the theoretical (re)incubation period, students should be able to apply the new (and existing) insights and, as every student had already specialized in a technological field, the obvious thing to do was to create a second part in the course for that application.

In this *technology (domain specific)* part, the students were confronted with a technology management problem from the technological subdomains the students had chosen to specialize in from the second year of their studies.

3.2 The Multidisciplinary Design Course

The objectives of the course are:
a) To cooperate with students of other disciplines in designing and realizing a solution for a complex realistic problem.
b) To reflect on multidisciplinary cooperation and utilize knowledge of your own discipline within a multidisciplinary team.
c) To communicate effectively internally (within the project group) and externally (with a customer, the supplier of the problem).

The MD-course has the following *educational set-up:*
The course runs during a trimester (of 14 weeks), taking half of the students' study time (identical with the MT-course). See Figure 4.

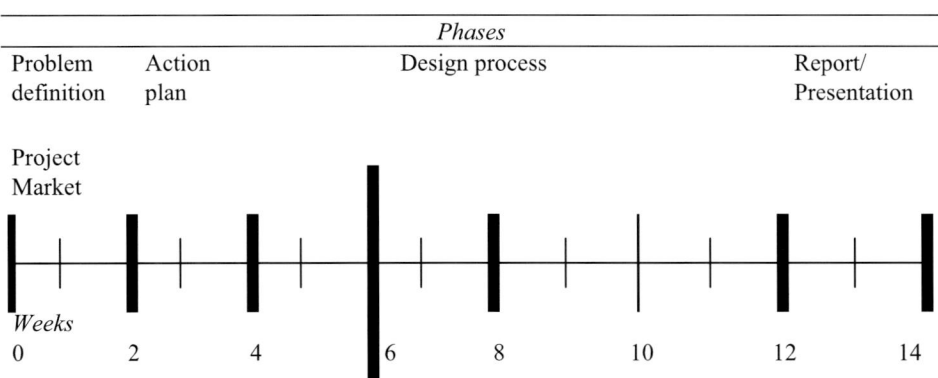

Figure 4. Timetable and Work Schedule of the Multidisciplinary Design Course

The problems, put on the market by "customers" (from industry or university), need input of at least three different disciplines to make sure that a multidisciplinary cooperation will occur. Groups of 6-10 students are formed, preferably with two students per discipline covered. After about three weeks the students have to submit a plan of action, in which the problem approach, the division of tasks, and the planning of the project are described. After approval, students cooperate during the following eight weeks on their design project, both on a disciplinary as well as a multidisciplinary level. They are coached by a tutor and experts in their respective disciplinary fields and can also consult with the customer. In the last three weeks, the group makes a final report, including the design of a problem solution for the customer. Also, they must write a short paper in which the group reflects on the common design process and the multidisciplinary cooperation process. The report is presented to a forum, comprised of the tutors, customers, and fellow students from other groups.

The content of the course covers two different areas:

a) Making an integrative design as solution for the complex, multidisciplinary problem. Every discipline has its own contribution, but this is only part of the total problem. Therefore, discussion is needed to tune this disciplinary aspect to the contributions of the other participating disciplines.

b) The students are also asked to reflect as a group on the whole process of designing in a multidisciplinary group. This is an essential part of the course, which can contribute to a better understanding of the cooperation in a multidisciplinary team (applying the concept of the "reflective practitioner," Schön, 1987). Figure 5 does illustrate the subsequent phases in the design process.

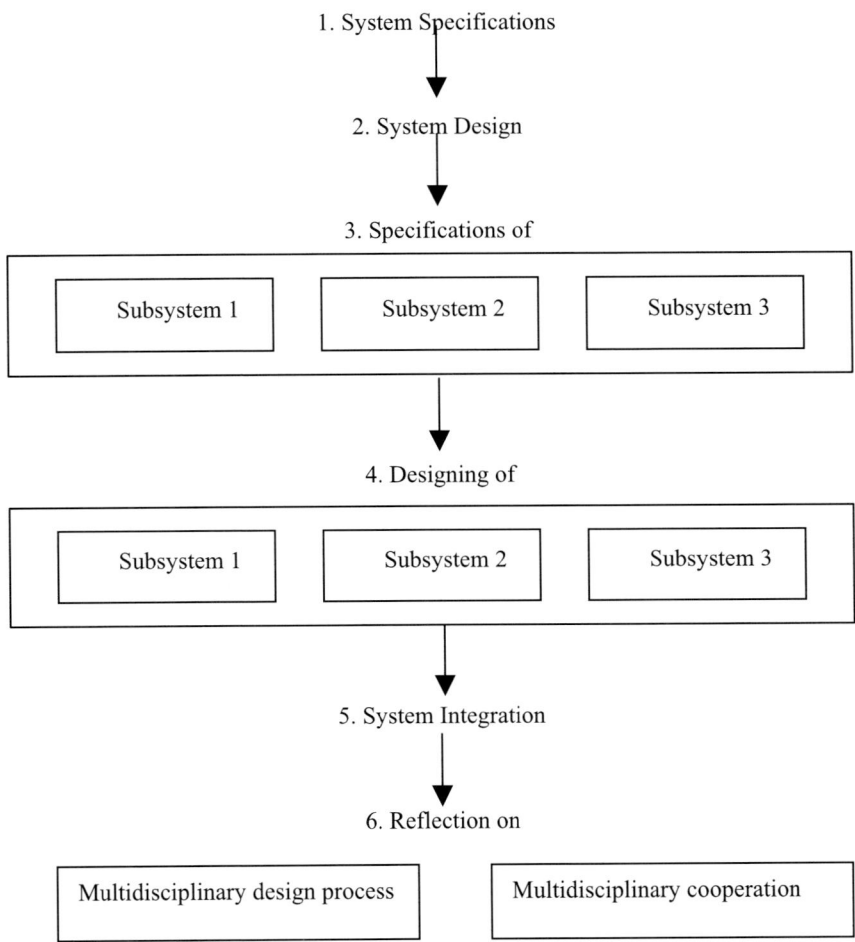

Figure 5. Model of the Multidisciplinary Design Process

4.   RESULTS

4.1   The Management of Technology Course

4.1.1   Evaluation method

The MT-course has been evaluated by means of questionnaires sent to all the participants, one after the first "general" part of the course and the second after the "technology specific" part of the course.

The questions of the first questionnaire were distributed over five categories, namely, opinions about (1) the course as a whole, (2) the organization, (3) the content, (4) the cohesion, and (5) the specific subjects of the course (the aspects of the technological innovation process). Half of the participants (N=78) responded to the questionnaire. Afterwards, some of them were invited to discuss the results with the coordinator and the involved tutors, under the supervision of the course evaluator.

The second questionnaire had the same structure as the first one, but the questions were now related to the experiences acquired by students in the respective technology domains they had worked on in their project. About 40 percent of the students filled in the questionnaire. The discussions about the outcome of the questionnaire, between students, tutors, the course coordinator, and an evaluator, were held separately for each technology domain.

4.1.2   Evaluation results

The general opinion of the students is that the MT-course meets their expectations. On the scale of 1 to 10, they rate the general part of the course on the average with a mark 6 (sufficient level) and the specific part with a mark 7 (amply sufficient level); see Table 1. Generally spoken, the students are more satisfied with the specific technology part of the course, except for those in the field of mechanical engineering. Here it turned out that the subject of the technological innovation studied did not sufficiently match the competences of these students.

Table 1. Overall Assessment of the MT Course (by students)

| | Part I | TECHNOLOGY | | | | | |
| | | Part II | | | | | |
		Computer science	Logistics	Civil Enginee-ring	Mechanical Enginee-ring	Process Techn.	Medical Techn.
Content	6.5	7.0	7.3	7.2	6.1	8.0	7.7
Format	6.0	7.8	7.0	7.2	4.9	7.0	7.3

First, we will look in more detail at the opinions about the *general part of the course.*

Unfortunately, some materials to be studied were not available on time, creating time pressure for the students; though generally spoken, the students had enough information at their disposal to work on the cases. The students regularly consulted Teletop, a special facility of computerized support that consists of information and feedback by the coordinator. The project groups functioned very well. The cases were adequate to work on, given their knowledge, insights, and skills in the field of management.

The students criticized the lack of cohesion between several parts of the course, with respect to different subjects as well as the participating tutors. Because of this drawback of the course, we may conclude that the objective of integration was hard to achieve.

Now we will focus on the *specific part of the course.*

Generally, students' opinions were more positive when they were working in their own professional field, studying a technological innovation from a managerial point of view. As previously stated, the tutors were free to choose the technological innovation problem and to make an educational set-up suitable to achieve the stated objective. One teacher chose the workshop format to discuss the issue with a relevant textbook; another teacher preferred to study cases -related to the presented theory; a third teacher let the students study the implementation of a managerial innovation in a realistic technological context, and so on.

But all teachers were focused in their assignments on achieving the same objective of the course: a better understanding of the management-of-technology concept.

Table 2. Assessment of Achieving the Objectives of the MT Course (by students)

		TECHNOLOGY					
Objectives	**Part I**	**Part II**					
		Comp. Science	*Logistics*	*Civil Enginee-ring*	*Mech. Enginee-ring*	*Process Techn.*	*Medical Techn.*
Understanding of MT-concept	±	+	±	+	-	+	±
Deepening relationship M~T	±	+	±	±	-	+	±

We now focus on the MT-course in more detail, following the six technological areas (Table 2).

a) The Computer Science group cooperated in the format of a workshop. The students found it very stimulating to work on the issues related to the consequences of implementing information technology in organizations. However, they reported that the workshop mainly trained already existing skills and didn't give them a better understanding of the management-of-technology concept.

b) The Logistics group said that the cases studied were relevant and helped to deepen their insight into the effects of logistic measures on organizations. However, the students would have liked to have plenary group discussions under the supervision of the tutor in order to become familiar with appropriate critical thinking when managing technology.

c) The Civil Engineering group concluded that they learned the most from applying their theoretical notions about "external quality assurance" to some civil engineering projects in practice. Matching theory with reality made them better understand the relationship between technology and management.

d) The Mechanical Engineering group had to study a rather original technological innovation, related to "research and development in the field of Sport and Leisure engineering." However, this subject was so new that the students spent most of the time searching for relevant literature. Besides, they were disappointed by the fact that they could not utilize their mechanical engineering competences.

e) The Process Technology group studied the implementation of a new technological concept in a chemical process. The students were very motivated, utilizing their specific technological knowledge and skills. They were coached by two chemical engineers and by the coordinator of the course (who has a chemical engineering background). They reported positive learning experiences on all points.

f) The Medical Technology group – consisting of only five group members – studied the subject of "assessment of the implementation of digital X-ray sensors in dental surgery." For that purpose they visited a dental clinic and interviewed some dentists and technicians. Unfortunately, they lacked the background technological knowledge needed to properly assess the implementation process. As a result, they have hardly deepened their insight into the concept of technology management.

4.2   The Multidisciplinary Design Course

4.2.1   The evaluation method

The course has been evaluated by the Educational Center of the University. That center developed a questionnaire to be filled in by the participating students and tutors. At that time the course was in its second offering, so the coordinators and the tutors involved had already some experience with these multidisciplinary projects. The tutors were prepared for their coaching role, as nobody had prior experience in tutoring a multidisciplinary project. This training was particularly focused on coaching multidisciplinary designing and on supporting a group of students with very different engineering backgrounds.

The evaluation study targeted such topics as the suitability of the problems for multidisciplinary design work, the way students try to integrate different design styles, and the skills required from the students to work in a multidisciplinary team.

The evaluators of the Educational Center attended the final sessions of the project groups, in which the students presented their findings to a forum of customers (the suppliers of the problems), to the tutors and fellow students. Also, the evaluators analyzed some reports of the multidisciplinary projects.

4.2.2   The evaluation results

We will report here the main findings of the evaluation study, according to the objectives of the course. In this second experimental year, 45 students participated in the MD-course, working in nine project groups. Four of the multidisciplinary problems were presented by external customers. The remaining problems came from departments of the university.

Table 3. Assessment of the Objectives of the MD Course (by students)

Objectives	Assessment	
	+	-
Cooperative design	Cooperation	Different design styles
Reflection on co-operation	Group process	Design process
Utilizing knowledge	Contribution	Integration
Communicating with a customer	Motivation	Consulting skills

We discuss now the various objectives of the MD-course (see Table 3). Learning to cooperate with students from different disciplines in making a design for a multidisciplinary problem was an objective that challenged the students. It brought about vehement discussions in some groups, but the design process was more successful in more homogeneous groups, consisting of students all with an engineering background. In more heterogeneous groups, comprised of students with different backgrounds, some trained in engineering and others trained in social sciences, students had difficulties in achieving a common approach for designing a satisfying solution to the problem.

Some project groups reported that they could not sufficiently utilize the knowledge and skills of their own discipline. It turned out that the problems these groups were studying, were not well chosen and did not cover all the disciplines presented in the group.

Learning to communicate with fellow students from different disciplines has been reported as the most striking learning experience of working in a multidisciplinary group. The students have been learning from the various ways their fellow students were tackling an engineering problem, based on different personal design styles and diverse technical backgrounds. On the other hand, communicating with a customer, as the supplier of the problem, was not easy to do. The students said they missed "consulting skills" necessary to put their theoretical knowledge into practice.

It was concluded from the evaluation study that the set-up of the MD-course was satisfactory. This course brings about some of the expected learning outcomes while also improving the students' communication skills in a multidisciplinary team environment. Learning to integrate knowledge and skills into one multidisciplinary design is an objective still to achieve.

Still, some improvements are needed to the course, namely, selecting problems that would be more suitable for multidisciplinary work and for utilizing the gained knowledge and skills. Preferably, the problems should be brought up by customers from respective industries, giving students an opportunity to exercise their consulting skills.

5.   DISCUSSION

Now we will discuss the outcome of the evaluation of both courses. Although MT and MD courses differ in didactical set-ups, they share the common objective of integrating the knowledge, insights, and skills gained from different disciplines by solving complex problems in the field of management and technology. By comparing these two multidisciplinary courses, we hope to better understand which educational effects are produced by each of the didactical set-ups.

5.1   Multidisciplinary Cooperation

Of course, it makes a difference whether to cooperate in a rather homogeneous group of industrial engineering students (MT-course) or to cooperate in a heterogeneous group of students coming from different disciplines (MD-course). In the MT case, students learn to integrate concepts about management and technology "in their heads" during discussions concerning the impact of a new technology on the organization with their fellow students. In the MD case, each student has to integrate his or her discipline perspective on the solution with the inputs from other group members who represent other disciplines. Apparently, two different approaches to the concept of cognitive integration can be observed.

Nevertheless, both courses focus on the impact of different disciplines on solving technological problems. To that end, the MD course has a built-in phase of reflection on the multidisciplinary co-operation process. Based on the experiential learning cycle of Kolb (1984), this phase is an essential part of the learning process, particularly in cases where a higher level of abstraction is to be achieved (see Figure 6).

PROCESS OF EXPERIENTAL LEARNING

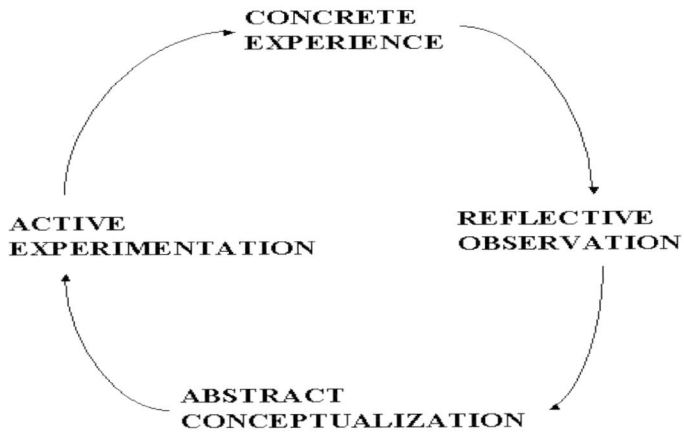

Figure 6. The Model of Kolb

The students in the MD-course must reflect on their multidisciplinary co-operation process by means of group discussions and by making a so-called reflection report. This procedure seems to be a prerequisite for better understanding of the concept of multidisciplinary thinking and acting (designing); however, it is not yet a part of the MT-course.

5.2   Division of Tasks and Cooperation

In groupwork, students are willing to divide the tasks and to work individually or in couples on subproblems. Often, this is a consequence of the time pressure they must work under. Besides, particularly in certain engineering disciplines such as computer science, physics, and electrical engineering, students tend to work individually. Only when there is a need to cooperate, for instance, in the formulation of the assignments or preparing a group product, are students willing to cooperate and to seek consensus in the group. Also, much depends on the tutor's role in the group in encouraging discussions on multidisciplinary issues and making the students aware of underlying discrepancies between different design styles (MD-course).

5.3   Team Teaching

Experience with the MT-course shows that, generally speaking, some tutors appeared to be unable to coach students in two disciplines, technology as well as management. This is because they are not used to working in two disciplines. There is a discrepancy between the policy of the faculty to aim at multidisciplinary objectives in the program and the interests of tutors in spending time coaching multidisciplinary projects.

When tutors have no time or interest in this double role, team teaching can be a solution. In a single group session in the MT-course, we had a nice experience with team teaching. That session was remembered well by the students when answering the questionnaire about their best experience in integrating their knowledge and skills in "Technology and Management."

5.4   Transferable Skills

The students involved in both courses are trained in monodisciplinary programs and only get familiar with multidisciplinary projects near the end of their study. Consequently, their attitudes, knowledge, and skills in solving engineering problems are developed rather unidirectionally. This is particularly true in the field of designing, where they develop a personal design style, as was observed in the MD-course. It seemed difficult for students to go beyond their discipline-bound methods. Even the students in the MT-course, studying in the same industrial engineering program, were not yet able to utilize some design tools, acquired in the first part of the course, in the second technological part of the course.

These experiences argue in favor of training students in multidisciplinary cooperation at an earlier stage of the curriculum. Nowadays, more and more engineering curricula become multidisciplinary in set-up and offer the opportunity to build up so-called "transferable skills." Exposing students to multidisciplinary tasks only at the end of the study seems to hinder the achievement of the integration objective.

5.5   Integrating Technology and Management

In the MD-course as well as in the MT-course, students become familiar with the skills of designing, particularly related to the implementation of technological innovations in organizations. For our industrial engineering students, this is the "core of their business." However, the evaluation studies show that the students do not yet succeed in achieving the ultimate objective of the curriculum: to integrate technology and management.

Our students are not sufficiently trained in designing processes, at least the organizational processes (but to some extent the technological ones as well). Recently, we have concluded from an internal assessment study that our curriculum lacks a subject, such as "the philosophy and methodology of design." In such a subject students learn to deal with various styles of designing, as taught in different engineering programs. This seems to be a prerequisite for exposing our students to design tasks, particularly when they are facing such a complex task as the implementation of a technological innovation in an industrial organization.

6.   CONCLUSIONS

1. In traditional discipline-based curricula, it is difficult to achieve objectives like multidisciplinary design and management of technology. The evaluation of both courses researched shows that students are very willing to cooperate in multidisciplinary teams, but they often lack the skills needed to integrate the knowledge and concepts acquired from different disciplines in order to solve complex technological problems.

2. Experiences with the above two courses demonstrate that some measures are helpful in bridging the gap between the monodisciplinary theoretical knowledge of the students and the real-life multidisciplinary problems.
   - The availability of realistic problems, which enable interaction between students and an external client as a supplier of the problem.
   - The heterogeneous composition of groups, which enables discussions between students from different disciplines about a common approach to the problem.
   - Training of tutors in coaching multidisciplinary groups and the presence of two tutors in one group, respectively competent in the domains of technology and management, to pursue a kind of team teaching.

3. From the MD-course we have learned that reflecting on the cooperation process in solving a multidisciplinary problem is an essential part of the project. Not only at the end of the project, but also during the problem-solving process, "reflection-in-action" (Schön, 1987) is needed to make students aware of the different design styles applied in different disciplines as a prerequisite for multidisciplinary problem solving.

REFERENCES

Assiter, A. (1995). *Transferable Skills in Higher Education*. London: Kogan Page.

Barnett, R. (1994). *The Limits of Competence*. Milton Keynes: The Open University.

Bloom, B. S. (1956). Taxonomy of Objectives, Handbook I: the Cognitive Domain. New York: Mc Kay.

Kolb, D. A. (1984). *Experiential Learning*. Englewood Cliffs: Prentice Hall.

Romiszowsky, A. J. (1986). *Developing Auto-instructional Materials*. London: Kogan Page.

Schmithals, F. (1997). *A Challenge for Transdisciplinary Studies in German Higher Education*. Roskilde: Roskilde University, Proceedings of the International Conference on Projectwork in University Studies, 14-17 September 1997, Volume III, 93-96.

Schön, D. (1987). *Educating the Reflective Practitioner*. San Francisco: Jossey-Bass Publishers.

Tidd, J., Bessant, J., & Pavitt, K. (2001). *Managing Innovation. Integrating technological, market and organizational change*. New York: John Wiley & Sons, Ltd.

Woerden, W. M. van (1991). *Het projectonderwijs onderzocht* (Research on the Project Method of Teaching). Enschede: University of Twente (Thesis).

Chapter 20

A SURVEY OF DISTANCE EDUCATION PROGRAMS

Morgan M. Shepherd, Ben Martz, Jeff Ferguson & Gary Klein
University of Colorado at Colorado Springs, Colorado Springs, CO, USA

1.   INTRODUCTION

1.1   Defining "Distance Education"

According to Martin and Samels (Martin & Samels, 1995), distance education is one of the least understood areas of technological change in higher education today. The constant improvement in technology, the rapidly changing student demographics, the constant demand for better educated students, the need for more Information Technology (IT) professionals, and the lack of more universally accepted definitions and learning models have all created a wealth of opportunities in this field. One of the challenges for researchers in this field is finding an accepted definition for "distance education." For some (Keegan, 1986; Verduin & Clark, 1991), distance education takes place whenever the instructor and student are physically distant from each other. Others (Baird & Monson, 1992) require that distance education (as opposed to distance learning) should also include the influence of an educational organization and the use of educational media, such as print and two-way communication between the students and teacher(s). Many simply use the phrase distance education as an umbrella to describe a methodology for providing a means of transferring a known skill or knowledge deficiency between separated (geographically or in time)

R.G.Milter et al. (eds.), Educational Innovation in Economics and Business IX, 383–398.
©2004 *Springer. Printed in the Netherlands.*

students and instructors (Moller & Draper, 1996; Wagner, 1992; Willis, 1993).

So that we did not limit our population, we integrated portions of all of the above in our definition of distance education programs. They all sufficiently entailed providing education to a distributed population. However, we did not include computer-based training institutions, nor did we include correspondence schools. It is important to point out that while our definition of distance education was very inclusive, the more detailed definitions will have strategic implications for those starting or implementing new distance education programs.

1.2 "Scoping" the Implementation

When deciding how to develop a distance education program, many look at what their options are in terms of available technology first, and then define the mission and the scope of the program. While technology is certainly an important component, other factors to consider include funding, the potential student population, the class size(s), the geographical area covered, the availability of instructors and support staff, the availability of course developers, the mission of the university or institution, whether synchronous or asynchronous communication will be used, the courses to be taught, the scope of the program, and various accrediting agencies under which the university or institution operates (Shepherd & Amoroso, 1998). There are also secondary issues, concerning such things as student support and access to libraries. These issues are relevant in setting the scope of the implementation project. As the scope of the implementation increases, typically more components are involved. Additional components have a tendency to increase the complexity of the implementation.

1.3 Viability of Distance Education Programs

Researchers in the field of education and technology are providing more and more information about the different learning styles of students. They are finding that the traditional Socratic method of teaching is inadequate. Many instructors are turning to technology to help supplement their teaching. Here, technology can be simply PowerPoint or a chat-enabling program. However, as the demographics of the typical college student population change, we are looking at different ways of providing education for them. Here, the supporting technology is far more complex.

Twigg (1994) states that we are redefining what students are learning and how they are learning. She also points out that as working adults, students will be far more discriminating "consumers of education services." They will not settle for what is available from the faculty at the local university or college. In addition, these students are much more computer literate, and have had a broader exposure to the capabilities of all modes of communication. These students have learning habits that are different from those of the traditional on-campus students. Twigg goes on to point out that as learning is not confined to the classroom, the distance education concept fits in well with what is happening in the real world. Learning occurs at work, at home, and during travel, and the education process needs to provide adequate support to leverage this.

Approximately one-fourth of the higher education institutions in the U.S. are part of the United States Distance Learning Association, an organization comprised of over 1500 organizations (Martin & Samels, 1995). Many universities and organizations have already developed distance education programs, or are presently considering such programs. Distance learning has been used in higher education to provide business courses since the early 1970s. However, concerns about educational and training costs, access to educational opportunities for site-bound students, and the rapid development of video conferencing technology have greatly spurred the development of distance learning for both business and higher education (Magiera, 1994/95). In summary, there seems to be a viable demand for distance education MBA programs.

1.4   Target Audience

Military personnel and students working for high tech firms are strong potential consumers of distance education. Both of these student groups are typically transferred every few years, and are constantly losing course credits every time they transfer to the local college/university wherever they end up. Twenty-four percent of the enrollment at U.S. colleges and universities is comprised of part-time students (LaFollette, Hoban, & Benkato, 1996). Of this group, the successful distance learning student is over 26 years of age, highly motivated, goal oriented, and unable to attend the traditional classroom setting (Magiera, 1994/95). Distance education programs allow these student groups to continue their education from anywhere in the world, and do not penalize them when they are transferred.

2. PURPOSE OF THIS RESEARCH

This survey tried to ascertain the current practices among organizations and institutions that provide distance education offerings. Specifically, we tried to address some of the issues identified in Section 1.2 above:

- What was the reason for getting into distance education?
- How successful are those organizations/institutions that are delivering distance education?
- How is "success" in distance education measured?
- What are the current technologies that are being used?
- Which technologies are being targeted for the future?
- How much funding is required to start a distance education program?
- How well are distance education programs being managed?
- While this is certainly not a comprehensive list, it did serve as an excellent starting point for this research.

2.1 Sample Model Used for this Research

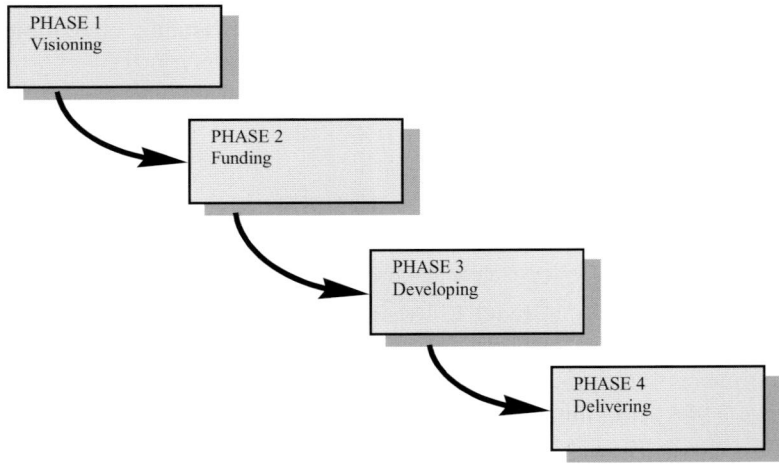

Figure 1. Program Activities

The model shown in Figure 1 is used to illustrate distance learning program activities. This model is loosely structured around the phases in the technology acceptance model such as the "Organization and Information Technology Design Model" by Cash and McLeod (1996). We will discuss each of the phases below.

2.1.1   Phase 1: Visioning

We anticipated that publicly funded institutions would only get into distance education when it was deemed necessary to serve their missions. This is in contrast to those institutions that embark on distance education for the potential return on investment. It was also anticipated that the quality of the product would not be allowed to suffer. The following paragraphs provide some insight into issues concerning program quality.

Gary Miller, one-time assistant vice president for continuing and distance education at Pennsylvania State University, cautions institutions against letting the available technology define the distance education policy. He urges institutions to keep their core values and mission statement at the heart of any distance education program, and to let the mission statement determine the type of technology used in the distance education program (Martin & Samels, 1995).

Johnson and Silvernail (1994) present a model of course effectiveness as evaluated by distance learning students. The dependent variable in their model was the end-of-course evaluation which was filled out by the students.

Steven Crow (1994/95) suggests the following list of "good practices" that should be adopted by institutions with distance education programs:

1. The institution's distance delivery programs have a clearly defined purpose congruent with the institutional mission and purposes.
2. The institution admits to its distance delivery programs students who meet the institutional admission requirements but who also have the capability to succeed in the distance delivery environment.
3. The institution's financial documents (e.g., audits and budgets) show sufficient financial capacity and commitment to support the distance delivery programs. That support includes appropriate administration for the program as well as development programs for faculty and others providing support services.
4. The faculty provide appropriate oversight for all distance delivery of education, assuring both the rigor of the curriculum and the quality of instruction.
5. The institution provides access to the learning and support services necessary for the distant-learning student to succeed.
6. The institution evaluates its distance delivery programs on a regular and systematic basis and makes the changes necessary to improve their quality.
7. The institution assures that its distance delivery programs facilitate appropriate student-faculty and student-student interaction.

8. The program delivered through distance delivery has a coherence and comprehensiveness comparable to the program offered on the home campus.
9. The expected learning outcomes for courses and programs offered through distance delivery are the same as those used for compatible courses and programs on the home campus.
10. The institution's system of distance delivery includes appropriate back-up systems to compensate for short-run technological difficulties.

Thach and Murphy (1995) discuss hiring the appropriate staff personnel in order to build core competencies. They state that the core competencies of any high quality distance learning program must involve communication-type skills and organization-type skills. This is important when considering issues such as accreditation, and meeting certain requirements imposed by the accrediting bodies.

These all serve to underline the different aspects of providing a quality program. A clear vision statement, an understanding of the program measurements, qualified personnel, and an education policy-driven technology plan are some of the indicators of a well thought out program.

We wanted to answer the questions of why the institutions got into distance education, how successful they were, how they defined success, were there written goals, were they meeting those goals, and whether or not accreditation issues affected the program.

2.1.2   Phase 2: Funding

We were interested to see how much start-up funding was obtained from outside sources. Funding is a major hurdle for many educational institutions. Finding a benefactor is one of the most difficult phases of the developing program. Funding can come from the government sector, although there are few research grants that are large enough. The major benefit of using grant money is that the educational institution can retain the full tuition for each course in the program.

An alternate source of funding is the private sector. However, there are a few challenges to be worked out with a private sector partner. One challenge is that providers may have to share the student tuition. Another challenge is to make sure that provider and funding source agree on who is in charge of the program. Institutions of higher learning are in the business of producing quality students, and do this by providing a quality program. This usually means limiting the number of students in each course or section. However, a private sector partner is in the business of producing a profit. This means enrolling as many students into each section as possible. Since this is a distance program, the physical constraint of available chairs goes away, and it is possible to put hundreds or thousands of students in each course or section.

AACSB imposes some barriers on admitting students, such as requiring prerequisites and making sure certain faculty/student ratios are met. However the private sector partner may not recognize these constraints for what they are (attempts to ensure quality) and may want every student who applies to be admitted. It is suggested that in time, the educational institution plan on weaning itself from a benefactor, and becoming self-sufficient. This can require a five- or ten-year plan but should reduce potential arguments over quantity of students versus quality of program.

2.1.3   Phase 3: Developing

The third phase involves developing the curriculum. This will depend in part upon the vision developed in phase one, the available instructors, the available support staff for course development, and the available technologies. It is important to ensure that all faculty have sufficient input into the curriculum, even those faculty who are not likely to participate in the program. If the full faculty is not involved, there is a risk of rift between faculty and many may not participate in the program. This could be a problem later on, should there be a need for additional faculty resources as the program grows.

Projects that reach this stage often need a great degree of change in terms of their scope and desired deliverables. For distance learning programs, tied predominantly to technologies, specific technologies need to be decided upon, learned, and invested in. The initial distance learning curriculum is agreed upon by the faculty in conjunction with decisions about the technologies to be used after agreeing upon a clear vision. In this phase, the project has progressed significantly to where structure is in place, roles and skills required of each person for development of courses have been outlined, and the results will be more predictable. The development of the distance program is not a one-time static project. As with traditional curricula, courses change and constantly need to be upgraded. The curricula should be developed with resources in mind to upgrade courses as necessary.

We wanted to answer the questions of whether the program was developed one course at a time or all courses at once, and how much buy-in there was from the faculty.

2.1.4   Phase 4: Delivering

In this phase, the courses have been developed, budgets have been spent, and developed courses are placed online. The distance-learning program is (hopefully) embraced throughout the institutions involved, and the focus is on delivering and teaching the developed courses. As time passes, new technologies continue to emerge that offer the university the opportunity to either move into new application areas or to redevelop old courses.

The method(s) of course delivery are fairly dependent on the technology, but as previously stated, should drive the choice of technology. Institutions are concerned with keeping costs down, without sacrificing quality. In general, the "richer" technologies (two-way full motion video, one-way video, phone conferencing) will be more expensive to utilize than the simpler technologies (e-mail, listserver, Internet, or fax). Part of the additional expense comes from the fact that new infrastructures may need to be installed in institutions to support them, whereas most institutions already have an installed base to support e-mail, phone, and Internet communication. The cost to add one additional remote site to a listserver is small (possibly free), while the cost to transmit a synchronous video session to that same remote site could run between one to several dollars per minute. Granted, the video session is probably going to provide a much richer interchange, but it will be more expensive.

It is also important to provide a similar feel to each of the courses. While the fit between courses and media richness will vary (i.e., an accounting course vs. a management course), the same general platform should be used throughout the program. This issue is more easily handled if there is a single person overseeing the entire program (Shepherd & Amoroso, 1998).

We wanted to answer the questions of which current technologies are being used, which technologies are being targeted for future use, and whether or not there was a single person in charge of the program.

2.2   Research Methodology

A pilot survey was sent to ten institutions. Follow-up phone calls (30 minutes in duration) were used to verify a subset of the answers, and to determine if there were any problems with any of the questions. The ten pilot surveys were returned with no reported problems and apparent validity.

The survey was then sent to 500 institutions that provided distance education courses. The institutions were randomly selected from information garnered from the Internet, Barron's Guide to Distance Learning, Kaplan's Guide to Distance Learning, Peterson's Guide to Distance Learning, the AACSB, and cold calls to colleges and universities. Two hundred and sixty-four surveys were returned for a response rate of 53 percent. Respondents were given two weeks from the initial mailing to return their surveys. Follow-up e-mails and a second round of surveys were sent out three weeks from the initial mailing. The last surveys were returned within six weeks of the initial mailing. As the response rate was very good, we did not send out a third round of surveys.

The survey consisted of 45 Likert-scale (1-10) and open-ended questions. The survey was sent to the person in charge of the institutions' distance education program. The survey took approximately 20 minutes to complete.

The questions were used to determine which institutions were successful, and what they had done to achieve that success. Questions were asked about the degree programs (if any), accreditation issues, number of course offerings per term, number of students per course, and issues relating to visioning, funding, program and course development, and program and course delivery.

In summary, using the Cash and McLeod model in Figure 1 as a starting point (see detailed explanation of the model in Sections 2.1.1 – 2.1.4 above) we researched the following issues in distance education:

1. Measures of success in a distance program
2. Reasons distance programs were initiated
3. Current technologies used in distance programs
4. Technologies planned for use in distance programs
5. Funding issues
6. Program development issues
7. Management of distance education programs.

3. RESULTS AND DISCUSSION

An analysis shows that only some of the questions were significantly correlated to the distance program success as we detailed above. Table 1 identifies these questions, which are discussed in more detail in the remainder of this section. The full questions are provided here for ease of readability.

Table 1. Factors Significant to Success

Questions	Significance
Q8. Do you have a vision statement?	.001
Q9. Do you have specific written goals?	.002
Q12. How much buy-in is there from faculty?	.000
Q14. Start-up funding	.039
Q16 Is this program now self-supporting?	.001
Q19. Was program developed all at once?	.047
Q36. How successful is the program?	.004
Q38. How closely are you meeting your vision statement goals?	.001
Q41. Do you have a marketing plan?	.000

3.1   Indicators of Distance Program Success

We created a research construct called "distance program success" to represent the objective success of the programs in the study. We used three of the objective measures provided by Q1, Q2, and Q3 (length of time the institution has been offering distance education courses, number of students in the distance education program, and the number of courses being offered each term, respectively). To create this construct from continuous responses we used the statistical package, SPSS, to place each case in one of five "Ntiles." The Ntile values were then combined to produce a value for the construct.

For example, the 53 programs that had been offering their distance program the longest (Q1), were assigned an Ntile value of 1, the next 53 programs were assigned a 2, and so on. A similar process was performed for number of students (Q2) and for number of courses (Q3). The Ntile values were summed to provide a measure of program success with lower numbers implying greater success because that program rated higher across the three questions (Q1, Q2, Q3).

Two subjective questions were included in the survey to help validate our construct. One question simply asked, "How successful is your distance education program?" and the other "How closely are you meeting the goals stated in your vision statement?" These questions were significantly correlated ($p<.004$ and $p<.001$, respectively) to our more objective measure of distance program success described above. These correlations support our use of the objective measure of success as we move forward in the analysis.

3.2   How Success is Measured

We asked each respondent to provide the measures of success that they used to evaluate their program. Respondents were asked to mark all that applied to their program, which can provide response totals above 264 for some items. The following are the frequencies of the different measures of success reported by the respondents:

Table 2. Measures of Success

Measure of Success	Frequency
FTE or increase in enrollments	225
Increase revenue	133
Improve learning	130
Increase student placement	43
Other	91

The dominant measure reported was to increase enrollments in the program, followed by the tangible measure "increase revenue," and the more intangible "improve learning." The dominant measure provides additional support for our development of the distance education program success construct used in our analysis.

3.3   Reasons for Getting into Distance Education

We asked respondents to list their primary drivers for getting into distance education. The following are the frequencies of the reasons for providing distance education:

Table 3. Drivers for Providing Distance Education

Drivers	Frequency
Reach additional markets	161
Instructed by governing body	26
Income generation	31
Faculty interest	28
Technology is available	37
Funds were available	22
To be involved in Distance Education	29
To affiliate with other schools	13
Public relations	1

The dominant driver provided by the respondents, "reach additional markets," is again consistent with our measure of distance education program success. It also ties back into the dominant reason provided for how success is measured, "increase in enrollments." The third ranked driver, "income generation," also provides an excellent tie with the measures of success, where "increase revenue" was the second ranked driver. As increased revenue can be tied to increased enrollments, this secondarily provides support for our construct of distance education program success.

3.4   Current Technologies Being Used in Distance Education

We asked each respondent to provide a listing of the technologies currently being used in their distance education program. The following are the frequencies of the different technologies being used:

Table 4. Technologies Used in Distance Education

Technology	Frequency
Internet	213
Live video with no interaction	178
Live video with interaction	52
Pre-recorded video	199
Phone	193
E-mail	225
Facsimile	202

3.5   Sources of Funding

We asked each respondent to provide the sources for start-up funding and sources for operating funding. The sources of start-up funding came primarily from private grants/endowments, industry grants, institution grants, federal/state grants, and other. The breakdown is given below:

Table 5. Sources of Start-up Funding

Funding Source	Frequency
Private Grants/Endowments	97
Private Industry	24
Home Institution	197
Federal/State Grant	81
Other	25

The sources of operating funding came primarily from private grants/endowments, industry grants, the home institution (not including tuition), federal/state grants, tuition, and other. The breakdown is shown in Table 6.

As might be expected, distance programs look first to their home institution and to their distance course tuition to provide funding for both the start-up (76 percent) and ongoing operations (75 percent) of their distance education program. In addition, federal and state grants helped 37 percent of the distance education programs with start-up funding; and 26 percent of the distance education programs with operating funds. Private industry was less helpful with support, as 9 percent of respondents reported receiving funds from this source for start-up and 8 percent of respondents reported receiving funds for ongoing operations.

Table 6. Sources of Operating Funds

Funding Source	Frequency
Private Grants/Endowments	57
Private Industry	20
Home Institution	201
Federal/State Grants	85
Distance Course Tuition	162
Other	17

3.6 How Well Distance Education Programs are Being Managed

Several questions were asked to try to get some insight into this. In addition, some oddities were observed when we were attempting to find out who the contact people were within each of the institutions that were researched. For example, Barron's Guide listed institution X as providing distance education, but upon calling institution X we found out that they did not realize they had a distance education program. It is not uncommon for different departments in large institutions to be unaware of what is happening in other departments. However in this case, we called the number listed in Barron's, as well as the institution's continuing education department, the outreach education department, and the on-campus counterpart to the distance education program (i.e., if the distance education program was in Russian Studies, we called the on-campus Russian Studies department). It took several calls before we were finally able to reach the appropriate person. This was an indication to us that the program was not as cohesive as it could have been.

In addition, approximately 12 percent of the respondents did not know if their program was financially self-supporting at this point in time. This is another indication concerning the level of program management at these institutions.

We used the following questions as indicators of a well managed program: having a vision statement (Q8), having specific written goals (Q9), having a 5-year plan (Q10), having buy-in from the faculty (Q12), having a program that is self-supporting (Q16), having a single individual in charge of the program (Q31), and having a marketing plan (Q41). Table 7 shows the breakdown of the responses to each. For Table 7, "Response" is a frequency/percentage of those answering "yes" in a binary question OR the mean value of a 10-point question.

Table 7. Program Management Indicators

Question	Response	Correlation w/ Success
Q8	132 (57%)	.001
Q9	150 (58%)	.002
Q10	125 (50%)	.190
Q12	6.5	.000
Q16	110 (42%)	.001
Q31	209 (80%)	.138
Q41	101 (41%)	.000

Question 12 (having buy-in from the faculty) used a 10-point scale, with 1 = no buy-in and 10 = complete buy-in. The mean value was 6.5.

4.   IMPLICATIONS

It is interesting to see how closely the success factors follow current practices in project planning and implementation. Having a plan, lining up funding, getting buy-in from participants, marketing the product, having a single focus for responsibility, and so forth, prove to be indicators of success for distance education programs. In addition, the "big bang" implementation strategy (Q19) used in industry also correlates with successful distance programs. In a distance program, when prospective students see that an entire program is available, they may be more likely to enroll in courses. The perception of quality may also be higher for courses that are part of a program, as opposed to stand-alone courses.

It should be noted that having vision statements, along with written goals was strongly correlated with program success. This finding seems logical, as the two serve to provide the guidance necessary to get the program started with fewer surprises. This also parallels current project management practices and thinking in that time spent up front usually saves time throughout the rest of the project.

Meeting the goals (Q38) was also strongly correlated with program success. Again, this finding seems logical. Programs that are meeting their goals are probably meeting their measures of success (Table 2) and fulfilling their reasons for stating their program (Table 3).

Table 7 may suggest how well the program is managed (Section 3.6). Only Q10 (having a 5-year plan) and Q31 (having a single individual in charge of the program) were not significantly correlated with success.

In some ways, accreditation equals quality, although accreditation issues were not correlated to program success (Q6). This may be due to the fact that some accrediting agencies (i.e., AACSB) are looking to reward institutions for developing alternative instructional methods and are more lenient towards institutions that are developing programs such as distance education.

5.   SUMMARY AND FUTURE RESEARCH

In this chapter, we report on a survey of distance education programs. We reported on and looked at some of the issues associated with distance education programs. We reported on 1) measures of success, 2) reasons distance programs were initiated, 3) current technologies used and planned for future use, 4) a management profile of successful distance education programs, and 5) funding and program development issues. We were able to create a measure of program success based on objective measures, which tied in well with self-reported, subjective measures in the questionnaire. We were able to identify several key characteristics in successful programs such as management practices, implementation strategy, and funding.

The results of this research study point to many areas for future research. The first area would be the long-term success of distance education programs, specifically the enablers and inhibitors to success. Do the characteristics found in this study hold up when viewed over longer periods of time?

In addition to success, future research in distance education programs should address the issue of quality in distance education programs. For example, quality comparisons between distance programs and online programs could prove useful.

Further research should examine differences between distance programs at two and four year institutions. The target audience of each is different, and there may well be differences in the quality, visioning, funding, development, and delivery of the programs.

REFERENCES

Baird, M. A., & Monson, M. K. (1992). Distance education: Meeting diverse learners' needs in a changing world. *New Directions for Teaching and Learning*, *51*, 65-76. Jossey-Bass.

Cash, J. I., & McLeod, P. L. (1996). *Corporate information systems management*. In L. Applegate, W. McFarlan, & J. McKenney (Eds.), (pp. 377-379). Chicago: Irwin.

Crow, S. D. (1994/1995). Distance learning: Challenges for institutional accreditation. *NCA Quarterly*, 69, 354-358.

Johnson, J., & Silvernail, D. (1994). Impact of interactive television and distance education on student evaluation of courses: A causal model. *Community College Journal of Research and Practice*, *18*, 431-440.

Keegan, D. (1986). *The foundations of distance education.* London, England: Croom Helm.

LaFollette, W. R., Hoban, J. P. Jr., & Benkato, O. M. (1996). Teaching finance by television. *Journal of Financial Education, 22,* 74-79.

Magiera, F. (1994/1995). Teaching personal investments via long-distance. *Journal of Educational Technology Systems, 23*(4), 295-307.

Martin, J., & Samels, J. E. (1995). The near and far of distance learning. *ACB Trusteeship,* 26-31.

Moller, L., & Draper, D. (1996). Examining the viability of distance education as an instructional approach. *Journal of Continuing Higher Education, 44,* (1), 12-19.

Shepherd, M., & Amoroso, D. (1998). Designing a distance education program. The University of Colorado at Colorado Springs, Proceedings of the Thirty-first Annual Hawaii Conference on Systems Sciences, Vol. 3, pp. 315-328.

Thach, L., & Murphy, L. (1995). Instructional design and adaptation issues in distance learning via satellite. *International Journal of Instructional Media, 22,* 93-110.

Twigg, C. (1994, July/August). The changing definition of learning. *Educom Review, 29,* (4), 23-25.

Verduin, J. R. Jr., & Clark, T. A. (1991). *Distance education: The foundations of effective practice.* San Francisco: Jossey-Bass.

Wagner, E. (1992). In Stolovich, & Keeps (Eds.), *Distance education systems: Handbook of human performance technology.* San Francisco: Jossey Bass.

Willis, B. (1993). *Distance education: A practical guide.* New Jersey: Educational Technology Publications.

Index

Adam, M., 53, 74
Aitken, J., 52, 63, 74
Akerson, V. L., 76, 89
Alavi, M., 239, 247
Alexander, S., 112, 113
Althaus, S., 52, 63, 65, 72
Alvarez, A., 119, 135, 136
Amelsvoort, M. van, 218
Amemiya, T., 327, 339
American Productivity and Quality
    Center, 223, 236
Amoroso, D., 384, 390, 398
Andersen, I., xvii, 8, 277
Anderson, J. A., 74
Anderson, P., 59, 72
Anderson, T., 199, 218
Andreu, R., 108, 114
Applegate, L., 397
Argyris, C., 142, 155, 184, 190, 193
Arts, J. A. R., 144, 155
Assiter, A., 277, 293, 364, 381
Atsumi, T., 59, 72
Australian Bureau of Statistics, 323, 325,
    339

Backley, P., 197, 198, 218
Bahgat, A., 52, 74
Baird, M. A., 383, 397
Baker, M., 218
Bales, R. F., 13, 19, 20, 31
Balling, J., 346, 361

Bandalos, D. L., 22, 31
Bandsma, W., xvii, 9, 363
Bargh, J. A., 184, 193
Barnett, R., 364, 381
Baron, J. B., 47, 294
Barsoux, J., 53, 54, 57, 74
Bates, A. W., 143, 155
Batson, C., 319, 339
Beaty, L., 100, 102, 113
Beckman, M., 4, 9
Beer, S., 353, 354, 361
Bellanca, J., 76, 89
Belynne, K., 192, 193
Benkato, O. M., 385, 398
Bennebroek Gravenhorst, K. M., 142,
    155
Benson-Amer, R., 51, 52, 57, 72
Berge, Z., 198, 218
Berge, Z. L., 239, 247
Bessant, J., 368, 381
Bhagat, R. S., 53, 72
Biggs, J., 95, 96, 98, 113
Bikson, T., 51, 74
Birks, E., 99, 114
Black, R. L., 33, 34, 36, 47
Blackwell, C. W., 239, 247
Bloom, B. S., 36, 37, 47, 364, 381
Bohn, M., 342, 362
Bollen, K. A., 22, 31
Boonstra, J. J., 142, 155
Booth, C., 238, 247

Borgatta, E. F., 31
Borghans, L., 315
Bosworth, K., 4, 9, 14, 31
Boud, D., 112, 113
Boudreau, S., 124, 129, 136
Bourner, T., 100, 113
Bowie, S., 238, 247
Boyer, E. L., 346, 361
Brand, S., 344, 359, 361
Brogden, J., 62, 72
Brown, A. L., 184, 194
Brown, S., 96, 113, 114
Brusilovsky, P., 193
Bull, J., 96, 113
Burleson, B. R., 218
Butler, D., 60, 65, 66, 72
Byrne, B. M., 22, 23, 31

Caballero, L., 251, 273
Campuzano Ruiz, A., 251, 252, 273
Capper, J. M., 239, 247
Caprio, M. W., 76, 89
Carlson, H., 63, 73
Cash, J. I., 386, 391, 397
Chaiklin, S., 121, 135
Christ, L. F., 303, 315
Christ, M. Y., xix, 8, 295, 300, 302, 303,
    315
Christensen, C. R., 163, 177
Christensen, G., 163, 164, 177
Christensen, R., 76, 77, 89
Ciborra, C. U., 108, 114
Clark, A., 302, 315
Clark, T. A., 383, 398
Close, A., 161, 177
Cochrane, C., 99, 114
Cohen, S., 51, 74
Cole, M., 119, 120, 135
Cole, P., 158, 163, 177
Comeaux, P., 236
Connelly, L. B., xviii, 9, 317
Cooper, C. L., 72
Cooper, J., 238, 247
Cooper, J. L., 31
Cooper, P. J., 191, 194
Copa, G., 349, 362
Cornillon, J., xviii, xx, xxix, 7, 195
Corporate University Xchange, 222, 236
Cottell, P. G., 33, 47
Crawford, M. L., 290, 294

Crawford, S. E., 53, 72
Crow, S. D., 387, 397

Daniel, J., 347, 361
Davidson, 89
Davidson, R., 326, 327, 339
De Alemeida, M., 66, 74
De Marie, A., 51, 74
De Verneil, M., 239, 247
De Vita, G., 238, 247
Del Rio, P., 119, 135, 136
Dennis, A. R., 345, 361
Department of Education, Training and
    Youth Affairs, 318, 339
DETYA, 161, 177
Dewey, J., 98, 114
DeZure, D., 47
Dierking, L., 361
Digman, J. M., 18, 31
Dikareva, S., 193
Dillenbourg, P., 199, 218
DiNardo, J., 327, 339
Dohery-Poirier, M., 239, 247
Dolmans, D. H. J. M., 13, 14, 20, 30, 31
Donnellon, A., 49, 72
Doorn, M. van, xix, 7, 221
Draper, D., 384, 398
Driskill, J. E., 15, 31
Drucker, P., 184, 193, 347, 361
Duarte, D., 52, 64, 72
Duffy, F., 346, 357, 361
Duffy, T., 156
Duymedjian, R., xx, 7, 181

Editors, 54, 72
Edwards, B., 342, 361
Edwards, R., 342, 362
Eiglier, P., 189, 193
Ellsworth, S., 326, 332, 339
Engeström, Y., 119, 120, 134, 135
Engle, R., 326, 339
Englebart, D. C., 344, 361
Entwistle, N., 53, 72, 94, 103, 114
Eringa, K., 144, 155
Essen, J., 319, 339
Evans, G. W., 346, 361

Falk, D., 63, 73
Falk, J., 346, 361

Felder, R. M., 76, 89
Ferguson, J. M., xx, 9, 383
Fineman, S., 125, 135
Fink, L. D., 33, 34, 37, 47
Flinders University, 161, 177
Fogarty, R., 76, 89
Fontaine, G., 67, 73
Fowler, S., 59, 73
Francisco, G., 54, 73
Frank, H., 100, 114
Freeman, H., 95, 114
Freeman, M. A., 239, 247
Frost, P., 100, 113
Fry, H., 111, 115

Gainen, J., 295, 315
Garton, L., 199, 218
Garvin, D., 76, 89
George, J. F., 345, 361
Gibson, J. W., 239, 247
Gijselaers, W. H., xv, 144, 155
Glenn, E., 53, 73
Goldberg, L. R., 16, 31
Goldfeld, S., 327, 339
Goodfellow, R., 54, 65, 73
Gourieroux, C., 327, 339
Graham, A. S., 303, 315
Granovetter, M., 282, 294
Greene, W. H., 326, 327, 332, 333, 339
Greer, J., 193
Gujarati, D. N., 327, 339
Gundykunst, W. B., 53, 73
Guo, Y., 66, 74
Gupta, I., 50, 73
Gutiérrez, A. E., 251, 273

Haaken, S., 163, 164, 177
Hackley, P., 239, 247
Hall, E., 53, 54, 57, 62, 73
Hall, E. R., 346, 361
Hall, M., 53, 54, 57, 62, 73
Hall, R. E., 326, 339
Hambrecht, W. R., 222, 236
Hamilton, H., 193
Hamilton, S., 9
Hamilton, S. J., 14, 31
Hanks, W. F., 121, 135
Hansen, A., 163, 177
Hara, N., 239, 247

Harasim, L., 52, 63, 73
Hare, A. P., 31
Harrison, R., 342, 362
Harvey, L., 277, 294
Hattie, J., 95, 114
Hearn, G., 161, 177
Hedge, N., 97, 114
Hein, G., 346, 361
Hendrichson, A., 51, 74
Hendrick, C., 31
Herring, H. C., 295, 300, 315
Herskin, B., 286, 294
Hertz-Lazarowitz, R., 76, 89
HESA, 342, 361
Heywood, M., 51, 52, 73
Hill, C. W., 49, 50, 61, 73
Hiltz, S. R., 52, 63, 73, 74
Hinojosa, T., 251, 273
Hirsch, L., xviii, xx, xxi, xxix, 7, 195
Hoban, J. P. Jr., 385, 398
Hofstede, G., 53, 73
Hogan, R., 15, 31
Holtham, C., xxi, 9, 341, 342, 347, 355, 361, 362
Honey, P., 105, 114
Hong, S., 239, 240, 247
Houldsworth, C., 14, 15, 31
Houston, W. R., 135
Howorth, C., 241, 247
Hsieh, T., 51, 52, 57, 72
Huling-Austin, L., 118, 135
Humbert, M., xxi, 8, 237

Illich, I., 347, 362
Inglis, A., 95, 114
Itzkan, S. J., 144, 155
Izard, C. D., 295, 300, 315

Jacobs, N., 50, 73
Jehng, J-C., 158, 177
Jensen, M. C., 34, 47
Jessup, L. M., 345, 361
Jilk, B., 349, 362
Johannessen, T. A., 155
Johnson, C., 99, 114
Johnson, D. W., 4, 10, 77, 78, 89, 184, 193, 258, 273
Johnson, F., 78, 89
Johnson, H. E., 258, 273

Johnson, J., 387, 397
Johnson, R., 77, 78, 89, 184, 193
Johnson, R. T., 4, 10, 258, 273
Johnston, J., 327, 339
Joosten, V., 95, 114
Jordan, J., 238, 247

Kanuka, H., 199, 218
Kaplan, M. R., 53, 72
Kaplan, R., 346, 362
Kaplan, S., 346, 362
Karpin, D., 161, 177
Katzenbach, J., 51, 73
Kawakatsu, H., 326, 339
Kedia, B. L., 53, 72
Keegan, D., 383, 398
Keeps, 398
Kerby, D., 295, 315
Kimmell, S. L., 295, 315
King, G. A., xxii, 5, 33
Kipnis, D., 59, 72
Kirkus, V., 76, 89
Klein, G., xxii, 9, 383
Kling, R., 239, 247
Klobas, J., 238, 247
Knight, A. B., 34, 37, 47
Knight, P. T., 277, 294
Knowles, M., 111, 114
Knudsen, C., 347, 361
Kolb, D. A., 111, 114, 279, 377, 378, 381
Korac-Kakabadse, A., 53, 73
Korac-Kakabadse, N., 53, 62, 73
Koritz, H., 76, 89
Kottke, J. L., 295, 315
Kouzmin, A., 53, 73
Kumar, 41, 47
Kysel, F., 319, 340

LaFollette, W. R., 385, 398
Lahire, B., 187, 194
Langeard, E., 189, 193
Larreche, J. C., 59, 73
Laurel, B., 192, 193
Laurillard, D., 239, 247
Laurinen, L., 198, 214, 218
Lave, J., 98, 111, 114, 119, 121, 135, 136
Lawton, L., 59, 72
Le Maistre, C., xxiii, xxvii, 6, 117, 124,
   129, 136

Lea, M., 54, 73
Leelawong, K., 192, 193
Leike, M. S., 66, 74
Leont'ev, A. N., 119, 136
Lepani, B., 278, 294
Levine, J. M., 136
Lewin, K., 77, 89
Lewis, D. E., 317, 321, 322, 333, 338,
   339
Liang, G., 326, 339
Lilien, D., 326, 327, 332, 337, 339
Linde, C., 190, 193
Linden, J. van der, 156
Ling, P., 95, 114
Lipnack, J., 50, 51, 73
Litosseliti, L., xxiii, 7, 195
Littlejohn, M., 222, 236
Livingstone, D. W., 138, 155
Locatelli, P., 295, 315
Lofink, C., 222, 236

MacGregor, J., 14, 31, 238, 247
Mackinnon, A., 319, 339
MacKinnon, J. G., 326, 327, 339
Maes, R., 138, 155
Magiera, F., 385, 398
Mainstone, L. E., 300, 315
Makepeace, E., 53, 73
Mankin, D., 51, 74
Markus, T., 343, 355, 356, 362
Marquette, R. P., 295, 315
Marsh, H. W., 95, 114
Martens, R. L., 137, 155
Martin, J., 383, 385, 387, 398
Marton, F., 94, 96, 101, 103, 114
Marttunen, M., 198, 214, 218
Martz, B., xxiii, 9, 383
Maskell, P., 278, 294
Mason, R., 54, 73
Masoner, M., 160, 161, 177
Matheson, M. P., 198, 218
Mathew, N., 239, 247
Mathews, B. P., 14, 15, 31
Maulini, O., 190, 193
Maxwell, G., 53, 65, 74
McCowan, C., 161, 177
McCuddy, M. K., xxiv, 8, 295, 300, 302,
   303, 304, 315
McCune, V., 94, 114

McDermott, R. P., 283, 294
McFarlan, W., 397
McInnes, J., 95, 114
McIntosh, W., 76, 89
McKenney, J., 397
McLain, R., 142, 155
McLaughlin, C., 163, 177
McLeod, P. L., 386, 391, 397
McNaught, C., 95, 114
Medina, V., 76, 89
Medrano, G., 251, 273
Meeuwsen, H. J., xxiv, 5, 33
Merrieënboer, J. J. G., 137, 155
Michaelsen, L. K., 5, 6, 33, 34, 35, 36,
    37, 41, 47
Miller, G., 387
Miller, N., 76, 89
Millichap, N., 4, 10
Millis, B. J., 33, 47
Milter, R. G., xxv, 3, 7, 221, 223, 226,
    236
Minami, H., 59, 72
Misumi, J., 59, 72
Mitchell, J., 278, 294
Mitgang, L. D., 346, 361
Moller, L., 384, 398
Moncayo, L. G., 251, 255, 273
Monson, M. K., 383, 397
Moore, P. J., 113
Moreno López, S., 258, 260, 273
Morimune, K., 327, 340
Morse, K. O., xxv, 6, 49, 50, 52, 54, 55,
    62, 74
Mortimore, P., 319, 340
Munneke, L., 218
Murphy, L., 388, 398
Murphy, P., 294

National Curriculum online, 196, 218
Neuendorf, K., 58, 74
Newman, D. R., 99, 114
Nichols, D., 182, 193
Nix, D., 177
Noam, E., 347, 362
Noh, J., 326, 339
Nunamaker, J. F., 345, 361
Nygaard, C., xxvi, 8, 277

OECD, 73, 343, 362

Oetzel, J. G., 15, 31
Olaniran, B. A., 199, 218
Oldenburg, R., 344, 362
Oliver, R., 163, 177
Olsen, D. H., 295, 315
Orr, J., 190, 194
Osland, G. E., 53, 74
Ottewill, R., 315
Otting, H., 144, 155
Owen, M., 99, 114
Owens, T., xxvi, 6, 93, 105, 114
Oxley, L., 340

Paechter, C., 342, 343, 362
Pagan, A., 327, 340
Palincsar, A. S., 184, 194
Paré, A., xxvii, 6, 117, 124, 129, 136
Parhizgar, K. D., 52, 62, 74
Parker-Jones, C. H., 198, 218
Parry, S. B., 137, 155
Patel, D., 95, 114
Pavitt, K., 368, 381
Peat, M., 95, 114
Pedersen, A., 155
Perez Serrano, G., 253, 273
Perkins, D., 45, 47
Perotti, V., xxvii
Peter, B., 59, 72
Petersen, K., 155
Peterson, M. F., 59, 72
Petrushin, V., 193
Pilkington, R. M., 198, 218
Pirie, W. L., xxviii, 8, 295, 300, 302, 303,
    315
Polanyi, M., 135, 136
Pooran, J., 53, 74
Porter, M. E., 138, 155
Prosser, M., 96, 114
Putman, R., 142, 155

Quandt, R., 327, 339
Quellmalz, E. S., 282, 286, 294

Race, P., 95, 96, 113, 114
Radbourne, J., xxviii, 7, 157, 159, 160,
    165
Ramirez Uresti, J. A., 192, 194
Ramsay, E., 319, 339
Ramsden, P., 96, 103, 104, 114, 277, 294

Rana, A., 52, 74
Ravenscroft, A., 198, 218
Reiman, A. J., 130, 136
Renzi, S., 238, 247
Resnick, L. B., 136
Reyes, 160
Reyes, M. E., 251, 264, 273
Rich, M., xxix, 9, 341
Richards, L., 58, 74
Richardson, A., 161, 177
Richlin, L., 47
Rippin, A., 238, 247
Rives, C., 191, 194
Roberts, C. J., 340
Robertson, T., 72
Robinson, P., 31, 238, 247
Rodríguez, M., xxix, 6, 75
Rogoff, B., 121, 136
Ronen, S., 54, 57, 74
Rosander, C., 342, 361
Rosen, L., 61, 62, 63, 74
Rowland, S., 95, 114
Rugarcia, A., 76, 89
Russell, T. L., 347, 362
Rust, C., 114
Ryan, S., 95, 114
Ryu, T., 66, 74

Saeedi, M., xviii, xx, xxix, 7, 195
Salas, E., 15, 31
Salinas, V., 251, 273
Säljö, R., 94, 96, 103, 114
Salomon, G., 120, 135, 136
Samels, J. E., 383, 385, 387, 398
Sammons, P., 319, 340
Sánchez Vizcarra, S., xxx, 8, 249
Savery, L., 53, 73
Saxton, M., 197, 218
SCALE project, xxix, 200, 202, 203, 204, 205, 207, 213, 218, 219
Schank, R., 223, 236
Schermerhorn, R. H., 144, 156
Schiffrin, D., 193
Schmithals, F., 364, 381
Schneider, S., 53, 54, 57, 74
Schoenfeld, A. H., 317, 340
Schön, D., 99, 106, 114, 142, 155, 158, 177, 184, 190, 193, 354, 362, 370, 380, 381

Schroeder, D., 300, 302, 315
Schrum, L., 239, 240, 247
Schul, Y., 184, 193
Schwartz, D., 192, 193
Scott, B., 53, 74, 95, 114
Scudieri, M., 349, 362
Segers, M. S. R., xxx, 144, 155
Sellbom, M., 60, 65, 66, 72
Servaes, J., 53, 74
Shapiro, C., 51, 52, 57, 74
Sharp, R., 319, 339
Sharp, W., 41, 47
Shedletsky, L., 52, 63, 74
Shenkar, O., 54, 57, 74
Shepherd, M. M., xxxi, 9, 383, 384, 390, 398
Shultz, K. S., 295, 315
Siggard Jensen, H., 294
Sillince, J. A. A., 197, 218
Silvernail, D., 387, 397
Simons, R. J., 156
Skinner, J. D., 181, 182, 194
Slavin, R. E., 13, 14, 31
Smith, B., 114, 161, 177
Smith, D., 51, 73, 142, 155
Smith, K., 77, 78, 89, 184, 193, 238, 247
Smith, K. A., 4, 10, 31
Smith, P., 59, 72
Snyder, N., 52, 64, 72
Southey, G., 161, 177
Spence, K., 349, 362
Spiro, R. J., 158, 177
Stamps, J., 50, 51, 73
Startz, R., 326, 339
Steinbeck, R., 346, 362
Sternberg, R. J., 47, 294
Stewart, T., 185, 194
Stice, J. E., 76, 89
Stoddard, W. S., 349, 362
Stolovich, 398
Stoof, A., 137, 155
Strasser, S., 300, 302, 315
Sueyoshi, G., 326, 332, 337, 339
Swedberg, R., 294
Sweet, A., 76, 89

Tait, H., 94, 114
Tannen, D., 193
Tanzer, N., 59, 72

Tayeb, M., 59, 72
Teasley, S. D., 136
Tempelaar, D., xxxi, 5, 13
Tesone, D. V., 239, 247
Thach, L., 388, 398
Thies-Sprinthall, L., 130, 136
Thijssen, T. J. P., xxxi, xxxii, 6, 137, 138, 144, 155, 156
Thin, D., 187, 194
Tidd, J., 368, 381
Ting-Toomey, S., 53, 73
Tinkler, D., 278, 283, 294
Tiwari, A., 342, 361
Törnqvist, G., 278, 294
Townsend, A., 51, 52, 74
Treacy, M., 148, 155
Trigwell, K., 96, 114
Trotter, H., 327, 339
Tuckman, B. W., 34, 41, 47
Turoff, M., 52, 63, 74
Twigg, C., 384, 385, 398
Twining, P., 342, 362

Varian, H., 51, 52, 57, 74
Veenman, S., 135, 136
Verduin, J. R. Jr., 383, 398
Vermunt, J. D., 16, 17, 32, 144, 145, 156
Vernooij, A. T. J., xxxii, 6, 137, 138, 144, 152, 155, 156
Verschaffel, L., 144, 145, 156
Villaseñor, G., 251, 273
Vincent, G., 187, 194
Vleuten, C. P. M. van der, 13, 31
Vogel, D. R., 239, 247, 345, 361
Vygotsky, L. S., 119, 121, 123, 136, 279

Wagner, E., 384, 398
Wang, N., 76, 89
Wang, Z., 66, 74
Ward, V., 342, 355, 361, 362
Watson, W. E., 41, 47
Webb, B., 99, 114
Webb, N. M., 183, 194
Weber, R., 43, 48
Weber, S., 295, 315
Webster, J., 239, 247
Wedge, P., 319, 339
Wellman, B., 52, 73, 199, 218
Wenger, E., 98, 111, 114, 120, 121, 135, 136, 185, 194, 279
Werkman, R. A., 142, 155
Wertsch, J. V., 119, 135, 136
Wiel, M. van de, 61, 62, 63, 74
Wiersema, F., 148, 155
Wilkins, C., 326, 337, 339
Williams, C., 62, 72
Williams, G., 111, 115
Willis, B., 384, 398
Wilson, B., 158, 163, 177
Woerden, W. M. van, xv, xxxiii, 9, 363, 365, 381
Wolfhagen, I. H. A. P., 13, 31
Woolnough, B., 66, 74
Worsham, 89
Wright, G. N., 349, 350, 362
Wurman, R. S., 185, 194

Yamaguchi, S., 59, 72
Yoo, Y., 239, 247
Young, D., 66, 74

Zwaal, W., 144, 155

Educational Innovation in Economics and Business

1. W.H. Gijselaers, D.T. Tempelaar, P.K. Keizer, J.M. Blommaert, E.M. Bernard and H. Kasper (eds.): *Educational Innovation in Economics and Business Administration. The Case of Problem Based Learning.* 1995   ISBN 0-7923-3272-5

2. D.T. Tempelaar, F. Wiedersheim-Paul and E. Gunnarsson (eds.): *Educational Innovation in Economics and Business II.* In Search of Quality. 1998
     ISBN 0-7923-4901-6

3. R.G. Milter, J.E. Stinson and W.H. Gijselaers (eds.): *Educational Innovation in Economics and Business III.* Innovative Practices in Business Education. 1998
     ISBN 0-7923-5001-4

4. J. Hommes, P.K. Keizer, M. Pettigrew and J. Troy (eds.): *Educational Innovation in Economics and Business IV.* Learning in a Changing Environment. 1999
     ISBN 0-7923-5855-4

5. L. Borghans, W.H. Gijselaers, R.G. Milter and J.E. Stinson (eds.): *Educational Innovation in Economics and Business V.* Business Education for the Changing Workplace. 2000   ISBN 0-7923-6550-X

6. T.A. Johannessen, A. Pedersen and K. Petersen (eds): *Educational Innovation in Economics and Business VI.* Teaching Today the Knowledge of Tomorrow. 2002
     ISBN 1-4020-0478-8

7. A. Bentzen-Bilkvist, W.H. Gijselaers and R.G. Milter (eds.): *Educational Innovation in Economics and Business VII.* Educating Knowledge Workers for Corporate Leadership: Learning into the Future. 2002   ISBN 1-4020-1064-8

8. R. Ottewill, L. Borredon, L. Falque, B. Macfarlane and A. Wall (eds.): *Educational Innovation in Economics and Business VIII.* Pedagogy, Technology and Innovation. 2003   ISBN 1-4020-1787-1

9. R.G. Milter, V.S. Perotti and M.S.R. Segers (eds.): *Educational Innovation in Economics and Business IX.* Breaking Boundaries for Global Learning. 2004
     ISBN 1-4020-3170-X